Save yourself the time and trouble of manual file entry ...

Order the *UNIX Programming on the 80286/80386, 2nd Edition,* disk today!!

The UNIX disk includes source code for all the examples and Shell scripts featured in this book. You'll also find C source code that documents both system functions and device drivers, such as the Graphics device driver and Multi-port serial communicator, for both Microport V/AT and SCO XENIX. Enjoy your UNIX book to the fullest — order your disk today!

To order, return this postage-paid self-mailer with your payment of $20, plus sales tax if you are a California resident; to: **M&T Books**, 501 Galveston Drive, Redwood City, CA 94063. Or, call toll-free 800-533-4372 (In CA 800-356-2002). Ask for **Item #061-3**.

YES! Please send me the UNIX 5-1/4" disk for $20 _____
California residents add applicable sales tax _____% _____
TOTAL _____

_____ Check enclosed. Make payable to **M&T Books**.

Charge my _____ VISA _____ MasterCard _____ American Express

Card # _____ Exp. date _____

Name _____

Address _____

City _____ State _____ Zip _____

4028

BUSINESS REPLY MAIL
FIRST CLASS PERMIT 871 REDWOOD CITY, CA

POSTAGE WILL BE PAID BY ADDRESSEE

M&T BOOKS
501 Galveston Drive
Redwood City, CA 94063

NO POSTAGE
NECESSARY
IF MAILED
IN THE
UNITED STATES

— PLEASE FOLD ALONG LINE AND STAPLE OR TAPE CLOSED —

UNIX Programming on the 80286/80386

Second Edition

M&T Publishing, Inc.
Redwood City, California

UNIX Programming on the 80286/80386

Second Edition

Alan Deikman

M&T Publishing, Inc.
Redwood City, California

M&T Books
A Division of M&T Publishing, Inc.
501 Galveston Drive
Redwood City, CA 94063

M&T Books
General Manager, Ellen Ablow
Editorial Project Manager, Michelle Hudun
Technical Editor, John Sancho
Project Editor, David Rosenthal
Editorial Assistant, Kurt Rosenthal
Cover Art Director, Michael Hollister
Cover Designer, Kate Paddock
Illustrator, Lynn Sanford

© 1988, 1989 by M&T Publishing, Inc.

Printed in the United States of America
First Edition published 1988. Second Edition 1989

All rights reserved. No part of this book may be reproduced or transmitted in any form or by any means, electronic or mechanical, including photocopying, recording, or by any information storage and retrieval system, without prior written permission from the Publisher. Contact the Publisher for information on foreign rights.

Library of Congress Cataloging in Publication Data

Deikman, Alan.
    UNIX programming on the 80286/80386.

    Includes index.
    1. UNIX (computer operating system) 2. Intel 80286 (Microprocessor)—Programming. 3. Intel 80386 (Microprocessor)—Programming. I. Title.
QA76.76.063D45   1989   005.4'2   89-8207

ISBN 1-55851-060-5 $24.95 (book)
ISBN 1-55851-062-1 $39.95 (book and disk)
ISBN 1-55851-061-3 $20.00 (disk)

93 92 91 90 89   4 3 2

UNIX is a trademark of AT&T.
Intel is a trademark of Intel Corporation.
IBM, IBM PC, and IBM AT are trademarks of International Business Machines.
DEC, VAX, VMS, RSX, and PDP are trademarks of Digital Equipment Corporation.
Microsoft, XENIX, DOS, and MS-DOS are trademarks of Microsoft Corporation.
CP/M is a trademark of Digital Research.
All other trademarks are acknowledged in the book.

How to Order the Accompanying Disk

The UNIX disk includes source code for all the examples and Shell scripts featured in this book. You'll also find C source code that documents both system functions and device drivers, such as the Graphics device driver and Multi-port serial communicator, for both Microport V/AT and SCO XENIX. Enjoy your UNIX book to the fullest—order your disk today!

The disk price is $20.00. California residents must add the appropriate sales tax. Order by sending a check or credit card number (VISA, MasterCard, or American Express) and expiration date, to:

UNIX, Second Edition Disk
M&T Books
501 Galveston Drive
Redwood City, CA 94063

Or, you may order by calling our toll-free number between 8 A.M. and 5:00 P.M., Monday through Friday, Pacific Standard Time: 800/533-4372 (800/356-2002 in California). Ask for **Item #061-3.**

Limits of Liability and Disclaimer of Warranty

The Author and Publisher of this book have used their best efforts in preparing the book and the programs contained in it. These efforts include the development, research, and testing of the theories and programs to determine their effectiveness.

The Author and Publisher make no warranty of any kind, expressed or implied, with regard to these programs or the documentation contained in this book. The Author and Publisher shall not be liable in any event for incidental or consequential damages in connection with, or arising out of, the furnishing, performance, or use of these programs.

Contents

Acknowledgments 9

Foreword 11

  1 UNIX Overview 13

  2 UNIX Program Environment 23

  3 UNIX File System 57

  4 The UNIX Bourne Shell 93

  5 The UNIX C Shell 129

  6 Shell Programming Example 147

  7 Basic UNIX Utilities 163

  8 awk 177

  9 Spooler 201

10 C Programming Under UNIX 215

11 Named Pipes 233

12 Shared Memory 247

13 Mass Storage Programs 259

14 DOS Support 271

15 Basics of 80286 Architecture 277

16 Basics of 80386 Architecture 293

17 Floating Point 299

18 Segment Register Programming 303

19 Programming Terminals 317

20 UNIX System Administration 341

21 Device Drivers 355

22 Kernel Support Routines for Device Drivers 377

23 Sample Device Driver 381

Appendix A   UNIX Documentation 395

Appendix B   Shell Script Examples 401

Appendix C   List of Curses Functions 415

Appendix D   Programming Style Notes 419

Appendix E   Directory of Software Companion Disk 435

Bibliography 439

About the Author 441

Index 443

Acknowledgments

No book of this nature is accomplished without the help of many people, both directly and indirectly. I would like to thank my editors, Ellen Ablow and Michelle Hudun of M&T Books, for making this book possible; John Sancho for his technical editing and comments; Lynn Sanford for her technical illustrations; Dwight Leu of Microport for his input and assistance; and finally, Laird Foshay and my fiancée Connie Austin, for their continued support and for getting the whole thing started in the first place.

Foreword

All computer professionals sooner or later have to face making a migration from one computer system to another. The reasons for this happening are as inescapable as the law of gravity, with the lead weight of raw economics at the bottom of it all. It could be that old, unmaintainable hardware has to be retired. Maybe the company needs new software. Or perhaps you are just changing jobs.

Somehow, if you picked up this book, you are facing the possibility or the reality of using UNIX or XENIX on the Intel 286/386 microcomputers. If you have used UNIX before, on mainframes, minicomputers, or another type of microcomputer, you are in for an easy time. The products available for the Intel 286/386 are good, full-featured implementations of AT&T standard UNIX. There are a few things different, most notably the memory models in the C and assembler languages, and this book can help you make the transition.

However, if you have not used UNIX before, this book is a must. There are very few people in the world who know "everything" about UNIX, and if this is your goal you have more than 20,000 (minimum) pages of dense reading to do. Most UNIX gurus have not done this, at least not all at once, but have attained what they know over a period of time by osmosis, by trial and error, and by just playing with the system. Often this happens in a university environment, where the bills have already been paid.

It is theoretically possible to gain a working knowledge of UNIX by reading the AT&T UNIX manuals cover to cover. Unfortunately, this is not the best way to start developing software on UNIX. For one thing, the documentation is huge. If you have the SCO XENIX system with the Software Development System option, you are facing seven thick binders. To their credit, both Microport and Santa Cruz Operation (SCO) have added their own tutorials and reference chapters to the standard AT&T documentation. All the writing they have done is excellent, but there are many quirks and pitfalls to UNIX and they cannot document them all.

To make matters worse, UNIX, originally developed as an academic experiment rather than a commercial product, has its documentation organized as if it were a series of papers at a symposium. Unless you have plenty of time for trial-and-error, you will lose the forest for the trees by reading this documentation as reprinted by the manufacturer. If you work in private industry, it is not likely you have the luxury of time in getting to know UNIX. That is what this volume is about. Our purpose here is to get you programming on UNIX as fast as possible. We do not attempt to document everything in UNIX to the finest detail, but we will give you the basic tools needed to do the job at hand. As for the rest, we will lead you straight to the correct and best reference materials. This is a practical "how-to" and "where-is-it" book with pertinent examples.

Throughout this text we will use indented boldface type such as this to make citations to one of several references, including the Microport and SCO XENIX manuals. See the reference section at the back for a list of all the materials referenced.

As of this writing there are quite a few vendors for UNIX on the 286/386 available today. Unfortunately, there has not been time to make a detailed study of them all. Also, there is a lot that is so similar that 95% of what is contained herein applies to any UNIX system on the 80286/80386. For those reasons, we will focus on two of the most significant vendors of UNIX for the Intel 80286: Santa Cruz Operation, which provides SCO XENIX System V, and Microport, which vends Microport System V/AT. Both of these vendors also have versions of their products for the 80386. These systems are also considered in this work, so we have four different products to consider. Fortunately, the 80386 systems were wisely designed to be upwards compatible.

The occupation of computer software writing has had such an appeal because it is such a wide open medium for our artistic expressions. To add to the fun, the commercial sector is more willing to pay for a well written program than it is for any other piece of creative work of similar size. If the path to creative and economic satisfaction is generally seen to be a rocky road, UNIX can be viewed as a super-highway. If this book gets you on that road sooner, and thereby reduces the development time of your project by any measurable fraction, I think it has done its job.

It is well known among authors that no book is ever finished, it is merely abandoned sooner or later by its hapless creator. Once committed to print, any such work is cast out to the wide world, to succeed or fail on its own merits. So it was with this volume, and on the happy occasion that a book succeeds, we occasionally are asked to take it up again. I believe that this edition is even more accurate and complete than the first.

1
UNIX Overview

All the pieces of UNIX taken together, packaged at a low cost for the 286/386 market, comprise the most versatile and usable software product in the market. Each copy of UNIX contains literally hundreds of individual programs that can be connected together like an ether-space tinkertoy set. There are so many of them that some will lie unused, solely for lack of visibility. This cornucopia of software is not without its trade-offs or problems, however, and that is one of the main purposes of this book. Not everybody likes UNIX. Most notably, mainframe COBOL and RPG programmers often seem to have difficulty with many of the same things that UNIX proponents love so dearly. Note that this is not an issue of "user-friendliness," a term that has been widely discredited. It is no more difficult to formulate or understand a UNIX command line than it is a command in, say, VAX/VMS, GUARDIAN,[1] or IBM S/36 OCL.

Personal prejudices come into play, which are difficult to overcome, added to the fact that there are differences in concept to deal with. For example, nowhere in UNIX has the concept of a "fixed record size" come into play. COBOL/RPG programmers have a foundation kicked out from under them. Those who do not like UNIX (other than those who have a vested interest in some other Operating System vein in the industry) are becoming less visible every day. The rising educational level of the computing community, coupled with the new low prices of a UNIX system have made this a software phenomenon that is here to stay.

On the other hand, it should be understood that UNIX is not the Ultimate Operating System for All Purposes, as some crusaders would have us believe. It comes close, particularly when you consider the enhancements and the layered products available. Still, there is always room for improvement, and modifications will show up in future versions of UNIX and competing products. For now, we will have our hands full working our way through what is currently available. Later in this section we will discuss some of the

---

[1] VAX/VMS is a DEC proprietary operating system for VAX machines, and GUARDIAN is Tandem's proprietary operating system.

limitations of UNIX.

The History of UNIX

UNIX originally began on an unused PDP-7 computer, and was programmed in assembly language. Its creators, Ken Thompson and Dennis Ritchie, won the 1983 Turing Award of the Association of Computing Machinery for their efforts. That version of UNIX had very little in common with what we have today, but a couple of very basic precepts carried through:

1. Any program, once written, should not be written again for a different purpose by a different programmer. Build on the work of others. Make things easy for programmers.

2. The internal operating system (the part which is the central core of UNIX, called the kernel) should be as small as possible, and any function or facility that can be implemented outside the kernel should be implemented that way.

3. The operating system is separate from the computer. When the C language was developed, UNIX was recoded mostly in C, which made it relatively easy to transport from one computer to another.

These edicts were very popular for programmers but not with marketing departments of corporations that built minicomputer, who wanted "user friendly" operating systems that they could control completely. As a result, two trends which shaped the future of UNIX occurred:

1. Major computer corporations ignored UNIX for the first five to ten years of its life, preferring to support their own operating systems such as RSTS/E, VAX/VMS (DEC), and AOS (Data General). Smaller companies that could not afford to develop their own operating systems did start using UNIX.

2. Several key Universities, notably the University of California at Berkeley, started using UNIX for their own work and research, not only in computer science fields, but also as "end users."

Under the anti-trust laws at that time, AT&T was not supposed to sell software, but that was one of the terms that changed in the negotiated "breakup" of AT&T. By that time, UNIX was accepted as the operating system of choice by almost every major university or college.

This transfer of technology was not all one way. UC Berkeley had a made project out of UNIX and had developed some notable enhancements to the product, both internal to the kernel and as layered "user mode" products. Some, if not all, of these modifications found their way back to Bell Labs and were incorporated into later releases of the product.

When the students attending these universities graduated and started working in the private sector, it was only natural that they would want to take UNIX with them wherever possible. In fact, many started new companies solely for the purpose of vending, teaching, or writing software for UNIX. In 1977, a license to resell UNIX was awarded to Interactive Systems, and that year marked the start of an explosion of UNIX offerings on incredibly diverse hardware platforms.

One popular microprocessor platform for UNIX was the Motorola 68000 series products. Companies that used this processor included Sun Microsystems, Integrated Solutions, Dual, Wicat, Apple (only after market demand), and others too numerous to list. It was only inevitable that Motorola's arch-rival in the microprocessor business, Intel, would eventually sponsor a port to its own series of processors.

This was done by Interactive Systems, and the ported UNIX operating system was made available to other companies, such as Microport, SCO, and others, to package as their own. This history is detailed in Figure 1.1.

As the figure shows, the UNIX we get out of the box has pieces from different development houses all over the country. In addition to that, the vendors who packaged UNIX have added some of their own features, most notably in the areas of system management and documentation. These make the product even better. For now, we can simply call our product UNIX System V.

Features of UNIX

There are two types of features we will enumerate in this section:

1. *Base features*, those that are rooted in the Operating System kernel, or the Bourne and C Shell.

2. *45*, those that have been added on top of the primitives.

Figure 1.1

UNIX Family Tree

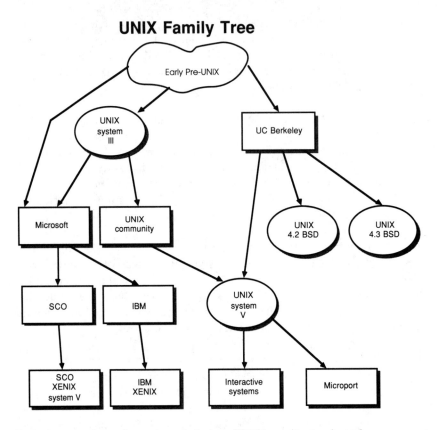

It is important to keep in mind that UNIX as it stands today was never "designed" for the market in which it is being used. Individual software components and subsystems within UNIX were designed, but many of the components were added on later as the need for them arose. Those that were successful eventually were added into the distributed product.

For example, the mail system (the "mail" command) is a separate program that could be completely removed from UNIX by deleting a handful of files, and a substitute written in its place. This can be done without access to any of the UNIX internal routines. The most noteworthy base features are:

- *Single-thread multiple-processes environment.* The limit of the number of processes that can be active at any one time is defined at the system compilation/load time.

- *Tree structure file system.* This is the single most imitated feature of UNIX. File names are organized in a hierarchy in which any file in the system can be specified by a single consistent name format.

- *Device nodes within the file system.* Peripheral devices, such as terminals, tape drives, printers, and disk drives outside the file system are represented by files that are used in the same fashion as regular disk files. A unique capability of UNIX is to create these special files while the system is running.

- *Pipes.* The output of one process can be routed into the input of another process. Small programs can be implemented as "filters" which can be connected easily. Pipes can be either private or public, which make them also useful for setting up "server processes" in multi-user applications.

- *Shared Memory.* Two or more processes can have a segment of their environment mapped into the same physical memory space.

- *Message queues.* Message packets can be sent to and from processes efficiently.

- *Shell processes.* The interactive command line interpreter is implemented as a user program that runs in user "unprivileged" mode. This allows flexibility for the system designer that can provide substitutes for the shell as needed.

- *Modularized device handlers.* Special software to provide new device types can be added without access to the UNIX system source code.

On this foundation, there are many other parts that appear to us as part of "UNIX" when in actuality they are "user" programs distributed with the product. Indeed, UNIX would not be very useful without these other programs:

- *Bourne Shell.* This is the basic interactive command interpreter that is delivered with UNIX.

- *C Shell.* A more "advanced" shell that originally came from UC Berkeley.

- *C programming language.* UNIX, although not the first operating system to be developed in a high level language, is the first to have its own compiled language designed for it. C has gained tremendous acceptance as a programming language outside of UNIX. The C language and its library of program development software is available as a separate product from Microport and SCO.

- *Login processor.* A special program that controls access to the UNIX system.

- *Spoolers.* Line printers and other devices can be shared without interaction on the part of the user.

- *Text Processing.* The *nroff* and *troff* text processing software is what was used to write the original documentation for UNIX. These are available as separate products from Microport and SCO.
- *Mail.* Electronic mailboxes, from user to user.

- *Editors.* From the simplistic line editor *ed,* which is what UNIX started out with, to the highly versatile ex/vi editors.

- *uucp.* This highly useful set of programs allows any user to connect his terminal to any other system, UNIX or non-UNIX DOS support facilities.

All of these features and sub-systems are covered in other parts of this volume.

Relationship to DOS

The original DOS 1.0 systems from Microsoft (MS-DOS) and IBM (PC-DOS) had nothing in common with the versions of UNIX that were around at that time. DOS was a product originally conceived to uproot Digital Research's CP/M from the marketplace, and succeeded in doing just that.

However, certain popular features of UNIX must have strongly influenced the design of DOS 2.0, because suddenly DOS had

1. tree structured file systems[3]
2. a crude pipe and I/O redirect facility
3. a somewhat programmable shell (command interpreter)

Additionally, it wasn't long before a number of independent vendors, such as Lattice, Whitesmiths, and a long list of others, developed C compilers for the Intel processors which were using DOS. In order to help make programs portable between UNIX and DOS, these manufacturers included subroutine libraries that were so similar to their UNIX counterparts that many programs were able to work without modification.

SCO XENIX V provides facilities by which it is possible to write programs that run in the DOS environment. The same C compiler is used, although with different libraries and link-loading procedures. Both SCO XENIX and Microport have utilities that read and write DOS media from UNIX. It is not likely that UNIX will ever displace DOS completely. For one thing, the number of applications and support programs written for DOS preclude such an event.

Another aspect is that the industry has been taking turns that many did not anticipate, in making systems that can run both DOS and UNIX simultaneously. The Interactive Systems VP/IX and Locus DOS/MERGE have already succeeded in this.

UNIX Limitations and Weaknesses

UNIX has few weaknesses as a commercial product. This is ironic in view of the fact that it was not originally designed to be a commercial product. However, there are shortcomings which, for the time being, users have to live with. The major sections of these problems are:

1. *Documentation.* This volume addresses this problem somewhat, and both Microport and SCO have added their own layers of text. AT&T's newest editions of the Programmer's guide and the Programmer's Reference Manual published through Prentice Hall

---

[3] The pathname syntax of DOS uses the back-slash (\) to separate pathname elements, where UNIX uses the forward slash (/). The reason for this is that CP/M allowed the use of the slash as part of a file name, and DOS 1.0 was designed to be closely compatible to CP/M. Therefore DOS 2.0, in order to be upwardly compatible with DOS 1.0, had to use a character other than slash to separate pathname elements.

are also very good. The reason that this has not been a crippling problem is that once a user attains a certain level of understanding, many things become clear.

2. *Obscure terminology.* Computer science students have no trouble with understanding the bizarre, albeit succinct, command names UNIX uses, such as *pwd, cat, cp,* and so on. They have the time to study them, and for the most part do not have to train anyone but themselves.

   To make matters worse, the syntax of some complicated commands involving pipes and I/O redirection cause conniptions in the "average" end user. It is a testament to the viability of UNIX as a product that this problem gets worked around as much as it does.

3. *Real-time processes.* Standard UNIX does not have operating system calls and extension designed for real time applications. This does not deter many developers, however, because with a link kit a "user" can implement code that runs as a privileged task. Properly done, real-time devices and process can be supported. There are also versions of "real-time" UNIX that are appearing on the market, although many of these reportedly have compatibility problems.

4. *Security.* Every Operating System has holes through which data can get lost or compromised, accidentally or maliciously. UNIX has its share of these, although it is not as vulnerable as some others. A dedicated hacker can usually break down UNIX security. This should not be too much of a problem if the usual UNIX security mechanisms are applied, but UNIX security requires a high level of attention from the system manager. See Chapter 20 for details.

5. *Bulkiness.* For buyers of minicomputer and mainframe Operating Systems, the UNIX requirement of 2 to 20 megabytes of overhead does not seem like much. To an upgrading DOS user, the size of the system is intimidating. It was not until 30-40 megabyte disk drives became inexpensive that UNIX for the 286/386 became a viable market alternative. There are several hundred files distributed with UNIX, many optional, and it will take time to get to know them all.

None of these problem areas is difficult to overcome, particularly because the largest segment of buyers of computer hardware are interested in applications rather than Operating Systems. This dumps the task of making the whole thing workable in the lap of the applications programmers. If they did it for DOS, why not UNIX?

UNIX vs. OS/2 and Others

There are alternatives to UNIX. The careful system buyer will want to study them all, and weigh the trade-offs before making a financial commitment. Some of the possible alternatives are:

1. Any one of a number of LAN systems with multiple workstations
2. QNX, a proprietary, real-time operating system
3. Concurrent DOS from Digital Research
4. PC-MOS, from The Software Link
5. Microsoft OS/2

It would take more space than is available here to give a fair treatment to all the features of all these products. Instead, we will discuss the one that is likely to have the largest user base other than DOS and UNIX over the next several years. This is Microsoft's OS/2, which is set up to be the operating system of the Intel 286 processors.

Advantages of UNIX: UNIX has been around a lot longer than most people realize, and has been the system of choice among most major universities domestic and international. This has created a large community of users (and not just from the Computer Science/Electrical Engineering departments) who understand and are familiar with UNIX. If you are hiring for a new project that is not tied to the IBM mini/mainframe sub-industry, your best bet is to advertise for a UNIX programmer.

More and more vendors for software products on UNIX are showing up every day. For the most part when new products do appear they are immediately available on both XENIX and UNIX at the same time, as their developers are familiar with the buyer's dilemma.

Advantages of OS/2: OS/2 was designed specifically for what the business community seemed to be demanding over the years prior to its introduction: 1) DOS compatibility for the existing software base, 2) interactive graphics, 3) a windows/workstation environment, and 4) the ability to connect to other systems. There will be a huge segment of the market, as always, that will buy it simply because IBM put their label and seal of approval on it.

The philosophy of one-user-one-CPU is carried through in OS/2. There is a lot to be said for this approach, particularly considering the price trends of hardware we once thought was science fiction. Thanks to work originally done at Xerox PARC and later implemented by Apple Computers, the window/graphics workstation concept has a mass market appeal.

Disadvantages of UNIX: We have already discussed some of the problems that UNIX has as a commercial product. All of these concerns apply, but the system implementer will mostly be concerned with how easy it is for the end-user to use the system. Most computers are used by persons trained only in a specific use. A general purpose tool such as UNIX may seem bewilderingly complex.

Disadvantages of OS/2: There are alternatives to OS/2 because of its late arrival. Microsoft's own Windows/386 and Desqview are only two. This will cause some contention among users as to which is the better product, and some will buy one, some the other. This presents the applications programmer with the problem of which environment to support. The major applications blockade has to do with multi-user applications. Since OS/2 by itself will not establish a standard way of doing such things, multi-user applications will be difficult to market, if not to implement.

In conclusion, the buyers of systems will be grouped into two categories: those who want to run existing software, and those who want to develop new software. For those who want to run existing software, the choice of operating systems will boil down to which one best supports the product being run. As far as new software developers are concerned, they must be sensitive to the type of equipment their market is likely to either have or be willing to buy. That, in turn, will be controlled by what other applications are available for that same environment.

UNIX, either Interactive Systems, SCO XENIX or Microport, has been shown to be a good choice in many cases. I am sorry to say that the problems associated with choosing between them can only get more difficult, as both companies are fighting for market share against a growing field of competition.

2
UNIX Program Environment

UNIX was originally developed on hardware the likes of which the vast majority of computer buyers and users today will never see. Ask any old hand who was around when the PDP-8 was just fading into the shadow of its successor, the PDP-11,[1] and core memory (used where we use RAM today) cost $1 a byte and had a full cycle time of 1.6 microseconds. Today, 120 nanosecond (0.120 microsecond) DRAM costs about $0.00008 per byte. The value of computers has changed and, as a result, how they are programmed.

The design of UNIX was largely molded by the constraints of those computers. For one thing, there was no way to support a program that would require more than 128K bytes (64K for instructions, 64K for data, and earlier PDP-11s had one 64K segment for both) to load and execute. One potential solution to the problem of running larger programs is the extensive support of overlays. The path UNIX took, however, was to make it possible to use larger numbers of smaller programs concurrently, each one doing a part of an overall task. Figure 2-1 illustrates this contrast.

The reason this is so important is that it can make program development much easier than ever before. Suppose that, in the bottom of Figure 2-1, the programs in Process A and Process C were already in the system library of programs. That would leave the programmer with the task of programming only Process B. You can do this with a well-organized and extensive subroutine library, but the restrictions are: 1) the program has to be compiled in a compatible language to the subroutine library, and 2) the

---

[1] The PDP-8 (Programmed Data Processor) was the first commercial mini-computer, developed and manufactured by Digital Equipment Corporation. It had a 12-bit word, eight basic instructions, and 4096 words of core memory. With 8192 words of memory, you could run the FORTRAN compiler and a time-sharing system. The first 16-bit PDP-11 was introduced in 1970, and a later version of the PDP-11 was to host the development of the earliest UNIX systems.

subroutines are difficult to run by themselves, so the inputs and outputs are hard to examine. We will see how this works in shell programming in later chapters.

There are other aspects of processes that are "UNIXish" that we will discover along the way. In this chapter we will look at the UNIX Operating System from the processes' point of view. As is typical with UNIX, it can be difficult to separate out what is ordained by the operating system's design, and what is merely conventional. This is because certain conventions are so unilaterally followed by all the programs that run under UNIX, they might as well be considered part of the design. Take for example the concept of "standard input" and "standard output," described later. There is nothing in the UNIX kernel saying that a process need to have such things, but the shell programs (see Chapter 4) which start up other programs for the user set up I/O that way. By no coincidence, the C subroutine library just happens to support I/O with the "standard input/output" convention firmly in place. The mechanism is so effortless that "standard I/O" is, in effect, a UNIX feature.

The phenomenon of conventions becoming features also occurs with the way dynamic memory, through the *malloc* subroutines, are implemented. There is also the shell environment. All of these are not "UNIX" per se, but the design of the programs that run under the control of UNIX. The issue can be confused, because a great many programs are delivered with UNIX as part of the "Operating System package," which we buy from Interactive Systems, Santa Cruz Operation, or Microport.

We could plow through discussions of C programs and how they work without being too concerned with these distinctions. For programming in many applications an empirical knowledge is sufficient. You do not need to know how the internals of the system library work any more than you need to know how a DRAM or a DMA controller works to use a computer. However, there is a good reason for peeling away at these onion layers. If you know how the whole interlocking structure of UNIX is fit together, you can more quickly visualize the pieces that must be there but that you have not yet been told about. And when you do get to the documentation on that piece, you can integrate it into your understanding more quickly.

Rapid integration would be a good thing, because there is a lot to cover. We will be able to provide only the barest discussion of some of the more commonly used functions, and will only mention others. As for the rest, you will need to refer to the articles in the UNIX documentation. The material which follows should give you adequate background for making the greatest use of them.

Figure 2-1

Overlay vs. Multi-process

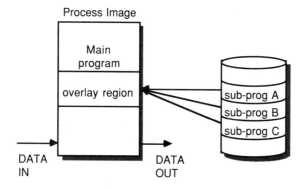

In an overlay scheme, large programs are built with subroutines on disk. These subroutines share the same region in the process' RAM image.

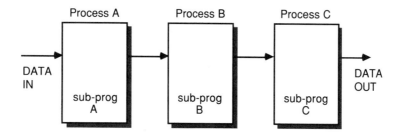

In a multi-process environment, multiple processes are part of the same "program" that pass data in a stream. This is the type of software design encouraged by the design of UNIX.

Functional Organization of a Process

From the lowest level perspective of a running program, the UNIX system does not look substantially different from most operating systems. The program runs as a "process" when it is given CPU time, and can perform three categories of operations:

1. Make computations, which means changing its memory image in some way. It can keep this up for any length of time, although the operating system will occasionally interrupt it to reschedule the CPU, or an external event can prematurely terminate it.

2. Call the operating system to do something.

3. Commit a hardware error, such as divide by zero, or reference unallocated memory, to cause the operating system to terminate it.

The latter category of operations should happen only by accident, rather than by design of the program.

Whenever a process calls the operating system to perform some service, it enters UNIX "kernel mode" and starts executing privileged instructions that are part of the UNIX kernel. These routines are encoded in such a way that they will voluntarily give up control of the CPU to the scheduler when no further action can be taken, until an external, asynchronous event occurs. Before entering the scheduler in this case, the current status and registers of the process are saved. When the external event occurs (for example, input data is available from a terminal) the scheduler will give the CPU to the process as soon as conditions permit.

Processes of the highest priority are executed first, and those of equal priority share the CPU on a time-shared basis. If a process appears to be using large segments of CPU time, its priority will automatically be lowered. This helps keep computation intensive programs from degrading the performance of interactive applications. A process will only run when there are no processes of higher priority able to execute.

To understand the universe of potentials for a UNIX process, there are two concepts to examine: the process model and the operating system calls that the process can make.

The basic process model is diagrammed in Figure 2-2, which will serve as a generic model for the purposes in this chapter. On the Intel 286 processors, there is more than one model the programmer can choose, and the issues arising from this are discussed in Chapter 13.

The Process Table

The UNIX kernel maintains a fixed size table called the "process table," which contains pertinent information on each currently active process. If the process table is full, and some process attempts to create a new process (see the description of the *fork()* system call later in this chapter), the attempt will fail and the error message:

    NO MORE PROCESSES

will appear on the system console. New processes can only then be created when some entry in the process table becomes free through the termination of some process in the system.

The primary purpose of the process table is for the kernel's management of processes. The table can be examined by the user with the *ps* command, which yields many useful facts regarding all the processes running.[2]

The most frequent use of the *ps* command is to simply obtain a list of all the processes running and what programs they are executing. Some of the additional information available includes:

- UID   The user ID number (or name) of the process owner. This is a number that is given meaning by the special file */etc/passwd*, which is described in Chapter 20.

- PID   The process ID (see the description of the *getpid()* call later in this chapter). This number can be used in a subsequent *kill* command to terminate the process.

- SZ   The size of the process, in memory blocks. Each block is 1024K bytes, and can change dynamically. On the 386 versions of UNIX and XENIX, it is possible for this number to be larger than the total amount of physical RAM memory available.

---

[2] See articles PS(C) (XENIX VRM), PS(1) (Microport RSM), PS(1) (AT&T VRM)

Figure 2-2

UNIX Process Model

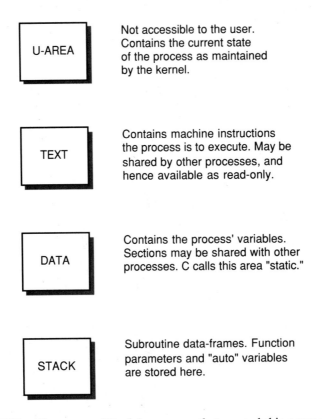

PPID   The process ID of the process that created this process.

TTY   Which "terminal" this process belongs to. Note that this might be a virtual terminal, and might be a ? if there is no controlling terminal.

TIME   The amount of execution time consumed by this process.

COMMAND   The command being executed (if available).

Chapter 2   UNIX Program Environment

There will always be a certain number of processes in the the process table that were not created by any user. These processes, depending on which system you are using include:

- *init*   Always process number 1 in the system, the one that controls the execution of the login tasks and other system housekeeping activities.

- *sched*   System scheduler.

- *vhand*   Virtual screen handler.

- *update* A special process that makes sure critical disk housekeeping information gets written out to the disk drives routinely.

- *cron*   A process started at the system manager's option that controls the startup and execution of time-delayed tasks.

Other non-user processes may be present in your system. They can be examined with the *-e* option to *ps*.

Operating System Calls

To the programmer, UNIX operating system calls appear as C functions that are loaded with the program. These functions are found in the directory */lib* with the basic system calls being in the file */lib/libc.a*. By default, the cc^3 command automatically calls the loader with this (and potentially other) libraries specified for searching.

UNIX goes one step further in its high level language support of operating system calls. The documentation does not even bother to say exactly how the calls are made in assembly language. Instead, all of the calls are supported as C functions. The implication is that you do not need to know how to call a routine in assembly language. If you must program in assembly language you can follow the C function calling protocol and do so by using the support routines in *libc.a*.

This path is not advised. Aside from issues of portability and cross-version

---

[3] See articles cc(cp) (XENIX PRM), cc(1) (Microport RSM), cc(1) (AT&T PRM)

support (i.e. from 286 to 386), there is precious little support or sympathy for assembly language diehards. The documentation in the Interactive Systems and Microport manuals for the assembler is nonexistent, and the SCO XENIX documentation is skimpy at best. Also, the operating system calls in assembly language are not documented. Unless you are trying to take advantage of some specific feature of the 80286 or the 80386 instruction set, you are much better off programming in C or some other high-level language. For the purposes of this Chapter we will continue the tradition, and demonstrate the operating system calls in C.

It is important to recognize the distinctions between operating system calls and system library routines, particularly if you are expecting to transport a C program written in UNIX to another operating system. Many of the operating system calls are not supportable in non-UNIX environments, although most C compilers for other systems come with libraries that emulate as many UNIX calls as possible.[4]

The functions that are operating system calls directly invoke the UNIX kernel, leaving protected mode to do so. In the Microport and standard AT&T UNIX documentation, these functions are documented in Chapter 2 of the documentation set. SCO, however, chose to integrate all the operating system calls and library routines into the single "S" (for System) chapter of the *Programmer's Reference Manual*.

In the first part of this chapter, we will concentrate on the actual operating system calls supported by the UNIX kernel for Interactive Systems, SCO, and Microport. In later sections, we will examine some of the higher level routines.

Error Conditions

A program can determine the success of any operating-system call by examining the value returned by the C function that invokes the call. For most calls, a return value of -1 indicates an abnormal condition of some sort, and a 0 or higher value indicates success.

---

[4] Up to the limits of the Operating System involved. MS-DOS, for example, cannot emulate many of the features native to UNIX such as most of the *signal()* and *chmod()* features, and the *fork()* system call.

If an error occurred, the nature of the condition can be set by interrogating the value in the external integer *errno*.[5] The possible values for the *errno* variable vary depending on which call was made, but each specific value has a consistent meaning across all calls. For example, the value ETOOMANY (as defined in the file */usr/include/errno.h* described below) is associated with "Too many open files," regardless of which call caused the condition.

To aid in coding, an *include* file is provided which gives names to all the values *errno* can take. An example of this is:

```
#include <errno.h>

extern int errno;

{
    if ((fd = open("datafile", O_RDONLY)) < 0) {
        /* an error condition occurred */
        if (errno == EACCES) {
            /* an illegal access was attempted */
        }
    }
```

For the sake of simplicity in the examples that follow, error checking will be largely ignored.

Low-Level I/O

The easiest way to begin a discussion on low-level operating system calls is with the low-level I/O calls. The C language has no primitive verbs or operators for I/O at all, so these functions, supported by the *libc.a* library, are considered de-facto extensions of the C language standard.[6] To the extent

---

[5] See articles INTRO(5) (XENIX PRM), INTRO(2) (Microport 505 Vol. 2), INTRO(2) (AT&T PRM).

[6] At the time of this writing, the committee for ANSI Standard C has not completed the entire C specification. However, those issues that have been decided have in fact named and documented most of the UNIX C library functions, particularly the Operating System calls, as part of the proposed C standard. It is likely that any implementation of the C compiler, whether on UNIX or not, will include a library that includes these routines.

which this is possible, most of the formats of the I/O function calls appear in non-UNIX C implementations.

All disk, terminal, pipe, and other device I/O is accomplished with the following routines:

open()	Open a file, possibly creating it
dup()	Duplicate a file descriptor
close()	Close an open file
pipe()	Create a pipe
lseek()	Move an open file's file pointer
read()	Read from an open file or pipe
write()	Write to an open file or pipe
ioctl()	Perform certain device control operations

In addition to the above, we also have routines that are used to manipulate the file system.

creat()	Create a file and a directory link
mknod()	Make a node or directory
link()	Create a directory link
unlink()	Remove a directory link
fcntl()	File control
stat()	Get file status
fstat()	Get file status for an open file
chmod()	Change the mode of a file
umask()	Change the default file creation mode bits

File Descriptors, Standard Input, and Standard Output

Before we get started with examples of how these routines are used, there are some basic concepts to establish. The first is the concept of a "file descriptor."

A file descriptor is an integer in the range of 0 to 19 that identifies an open channel which the process can use in making I/O requests of the operating system. No process can have over twenty active file descriptors. This is a constant which holds true for most UNIX implementations.[7] When a

---

[7] The symbol -NFILE, defined by stdio.h is almost always set to 20.

process makes an I/O request, the UNIX kernel uses the file descriptor to index a fixed-sized table that it keeps for the process.

At any given time a file descriptor is "open" or "closed." When open, I/O requests may be processed by the UNIX file system. An attempt to make use of a closed file descriptor always results in an error.

The process obtains file descriptors from one of two sources:

1. The process' parent (the process that created this one) may set up file descriptors for the process to use.

2. From a successful *open()*, *creat()*, *dup()*, *fcntl()*, or *pipe()* system call.

The UNIX shell programs, which are commonly used to create and execute processes, follow a convention that allows us to generally assume that when a process starts it has three open file descriptors:

File Descriptor	Use
0	Standard Input
1	Standard Output
2	Standard Error

Most programs can make the assumption that these file descriptors are available, but cannot assume they are directed to any particular device. For example, if we have a program named *speak* that writes a message "Hello There" to standard output, we could type at the shell:

```
speak
```

and the response would be

```
Hello There
$
```

(the $ is the shell prompt, telling us that it is waiting for the next command). On the other hand, if we type

```
speak > msg
```

the message "Hello There" would not be sent to the terminal, but would be placed in a file named *msg* instead. Even though the program *speak* did not change in any way, we could do this because speak assumed that the standard output would be opened for it. These concepts are discussed in greater detail in Chapter 4, the UNIX shell, and we will discover the tools that are used to make this happen in the following discussions.

The concept of standard input and standard output implies "stream mode" I/O. That is, the data is presented sequentially, and is never rewound or read more than once. Consider the following program, which takes all the data on standard input, strips out any vowels, and writes the result to standard output.

```
/* dtv.c - death to vowels */

char bufr[1025];

main() {
    register int count;
    register char *p;
    char *strpbrk();

    /* loop until EOF */

    while ((count = read(0, bufr, 1024)) > 0) {

      /* terminate input with a null, and compress out all vowels.
         update count if characters are eliminated. */

      bufr[count] = 0;
      p = bufr;
      while ((p = strpbrk(bufr, "aeiouyAEIOUY")) != (char *) 0) {
         strcpy(p, p + 1);
         count -= 1; }

      /* if there is anything left, output it */

      if (count) write(1, bufr, count); }

    /* done */

    exit(0); }
```

This is a simple program that illustrates several issues that arise when programming on UNIX:

Chapter 2 UNIX Program Environment

1. Because there were no explicit *open()* or *creat()* calls, we are assuming that file descriptors 0 and 1 are open. Normally, the shell program will set up this program according to the command line typed by the user.

2. The *read()* function call returns the number of bytes to be read. If the number returned is zero or less, we assume that an end-of-file (EOF) condition has occurred. Actually, a different error, such as a hardware fault, could have occurred, but we have coded this loop such that any error would terminate it.

3. We have avoided any zero byte *write()* calls with the use of the *if* statement.

4. The EOF need not be written to the output, as it is not a special character. When the program exits, the EOF will be assumed to be after the last byte actually written.

File Pointers

Along with each of the file descriptors in use by each process, the UNIX file system keeps track of a byte position within the file that is being accessed by the file descriptors. A file can be opened any number of times, even more than once by a single process.

The UNIX file model, illustrated in Figure 2-3, is simply a contiguous stream of bytes, whose first byte is addressed as 0. Any *read()* or *write()* call will affect the data currently addressed by the file pointer.

The file pointer changes after most low level I/O operations in a manner consistent with usual file I/O. If a specific file position is desired by the process, an *lseek()* call can be performed. In each of the descriptions of I/O calls that follow, it is important to note how the status of the file pointer is changed.

Figure 2-3

UNIX File model

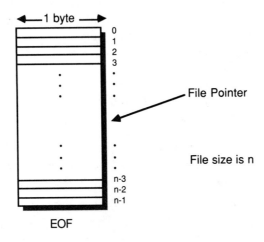

open() call

The *open()* call, if successful, returns a file descriptor number that can be used to access the file in following I/O calls. All the low level system calls that perform I/O use file descriptors as one of the parameters.

open() can be invoked with two or three parameters. For example:

```
open("data", O_RDONLY);

open("ledger.t", O_RDWR);
```

or

```
open("/tmp/scratch", O_RDWR | O_CREAT | O_TRUNC, 0600);
```

In order to make coding of the *open()* call easier, the include file *fcntl.h* is provided, which defines the numeric constants that specify the options the programmer wishes. When more than one constant is desired for a call, the bits are ORed together as in the second example above.

An example program that makes use of a file descriptor from an *open()* call is:

```
#include <fcntl.h>

int fd;
char b[4];

main() {

    fd = open("source/termi.c", O_RDONLY);
    if (fd < 0) exit(2);

    read(fd, b, 2);
    if (b[0] != '/' || b[1] != '*')
        printf("termi.c does not start with a comment!\n");

    close(fd);
    exit(0); }
```

The file *source/termi.c* is opened for reading. If the *open()* call fails, the file descriptor returned will be the constant -1, and *exit()* is called, terminating the program. Otherwise, the file pointer is assumed to point to byte 0 of the file. The first two bytes are read and checked to see if they are "/*". If not, an advisory message is generated. In any case, the file is closed and the program terminates.

Note that the symbol *O_RDONLY* was defined within the *fcntl.h* file that was accessed by the *#include <fcntl.h>* statement. The second parameter can contain one of the following values:

O_RDONLY	Reading only
O_WRONLY	Writing only
O_RDWR	Both reading and writing

The file system checks to see if the targeted file is accessible to the user according to certain security checks. The checks performed by the security mechanism are described in Chapter 20.

The *O_WRONLY* setting bears some explanation. Why couldn't we simply use *O_RDWR*, when a program intends to write a file without ever reading it? One of the few answers I have found is in some inter-process communications situations, where a *FIFO* (named pipe)[8] is used. It is

---

[8] Named pipes are special files in file system that do not store data on the disk drive, but serve as a special name that un-related processes can *open()* to create a pipe between them. See Chapter

possible for a program, using the *O_NDELAY* bits described below, to sense whether any other process has the named pipe open for reading without committing itself to a write operation. Another possibility is that a process can have write access to a file without read access, causing a *O_WRONLY* to succeed where *O_RDWR* would fail. I once implemented a subroutine that allows the maintenance of a log file in a standard format, which makes use of the open call:

```
fd = open("/usr/syslog/logfile", O_WRONLY | O_APPEND);
```

which causes all subsequent writes to write at the end of the file. The use of *O_WRONLY* and *O_APPEND* (described below) allows a non-privileged process to append to the file without potentially damaging an earlier part of it.[9]

Only one of the above constants can appear in the second parameter. However, they may be modified with other bits that change the interpretation of the basic operation. These are:

O_NDELAY	Used for "no-wait" I/O.
O_APPEND	All writes happen at EOF
O_CREAT	Create the file if it does not exist, i.e. perform a *creat()* call.
O_TRUNC	If the file exists, throw away all the file's contents without changing the owner, group, or file permissions associated with the file.
O_EXCL	Causes *open()* to fail when O_CREAT is specified and the file already exists.

When the file is being created, the third parameter of the *open()* call must be specified. This parameter sets the file permission bits that control who can access the file. Most often, these are coded in C as an octal constant because it is easier to visualize them that way. See Chapter 3 for a map of these bits.

---

4 and Chapter 11.

[9] Note that this scheme does not guarantee the inviolability of the log file, because a malicious process could still open the file without the O_APPEND bit set, and write over any part of the file. A 100% secure scheme could make use of named pipes and a "log server" process, which we show in Chapter 11.

Chapter 2   UNIX Program Environment

Use of *O_EXCL* is warranted when a scratch file is being created. Scratch files are usually named something unique, and it would be considered an error if some other process already had a file by that name. In this case, we want *open()* to return with an error should the file exist. For example:

```
char fnam[16];      /* unique file name */
int  tfd;           /* temporary file descriptor */


    {
        char *mktemp();

        strcpy(fnam, "/tmp/junkXXXXXX");
        tfd = open(mktemp(fnam), O_RDWR, O_CREAT | O_EXCL, 0600);
        if (tfd < 0) {
            fprintf(stderr, "ERROR: temporary file collision\n");
            exit(2); }
    }
```

The segment of code will fail if the temporary file[10] already existed before the *open()* call.

O_NDELAY is useful for polling the status of named pipes, as described earlier, or of communications lines. Without *O_NDELAY,* a process attempting to open a pipe with an *O_RDONLY* or *O_WRONLY* set will wait until another process has made an *open()* call that complements the process that was being held. For communications lines (special files that are associated with terminals, modems, or printers) the process will be held if there is no "carrier"[11] detected.

In either case, specifying *O_NDELAY* will cause *open()* to return with a -1 instead of holding the process. If *open()* does return a valid file descriptor, it can be assumed that the communications link has been completed.

dup()   call

---

[10] See article MKTEMP(S) (XENIX PRM), MKTEMP(3C) (Microport SDS Vol. 2), MKTEMP(3C) (AT&T PRM).

[11] The term "carrier" refers to the Carrier Detect (CD) signal that is defined by the RS-232 communication standard. Typically, if the carrier signal is not there, it is taken to mean that a modem does not have a communication link established. For devices such as terminals and printers that are not communicating through a modem, this signal is often simulated whenever the equipment is switched on.

The primary use of the *dup()* system call is for creating pipes between processes, as done by the shell. Examples of this usage will be seen in the later discussion of the *pipe()* call. If *fd* is an open file descriptor of any file type, the C statement

```
newfd = dup(fd);
```

will set *newfd* to the lowest numbered, available file descriptor. *newfd* can now be used interchangeably with *fd* to reference the same file with the same file pointer.

Although *dup()* is essential to support the standard I/O concept, it is also inelegant, because the only control the user process has over the value returned is by which file descriptors are already open. For example, if we had a file that was open, referred to by file descriptor *fd,* and we wanted to associate that file with standard output, we would write:

```
close(1);      /* close standard output */
dup(fd);       /* duplicate */
```

Now the code following could write to standard output. The inelegance of this is that we are assuming the *dup()* call will return file descriptor 1, because file descriptor 0 is presumably in use as standard input. We also have to assume that the O/S will assign file descriptors lowest number first. SCO XENIX has a system call, *dup2()*, which allows the user to specify which file descriptor to use. The Microport documentation does not feature this, but it can be easily replaced as follows:

```
int dup2(old, new)
int  old;         /* existing file descriptor */
int  new;         /* desired file descriptor */
{
    int fd;
    close(new);   /* close any file currently open on new file
                        descriptor */
    if ((fd = dup(old)) != new) {
        dup2(old, new);    /* try again */
        close fd; }        /* clean up litter */
    return new; }          /* return new file descriptor */
```

This is crude, but effective.

The new file descriptor shares a file pointer with the old one as long as neither one is closed. All other operations on either file descriptor are functionally equivalent. Again, the primary purpose of the *dup()* call is to allow a program to "set up" the file descriptors for another process or section of code that is written to use "standardized I/O."

close() call

The *close()* call is very predictable. The only failure that can occur is if the file descriptor passed to close is not an open file descriptor. Although an *exit()* call will close all the open file descriptors on a process, it is often desirable to close a file descriptor before the program is ready to exit, most notably in cases where many files need to be accessed. The SCO XENIX and Microport V/AT implementations of UNIX will not allow a process to have more than 20 open file descriptors at any one time.

If the file descriptor passed to *close()* was referencing a pipe open for writing, an EOF signal will be sent to the receiving process if there are no other processes that have an open to that pipe. On a pipe open for reading, *close()* will cause the sending process to incur an error condition (*errno* set to *EPIPE*) if there are no other processes with an open file descriptor for reading on that pipe.

pipe() call

Pipes are communication paths, used as if they were files, between two processes. There are two types of pipes in UNIX: "named" pipes, that are opened with the *open()* call, and "un-named" pipes that are opened with the *pipe()* call. Un-named pipes require no interaction with the file system and can only be used between closely related processes.

In fact, when *pipe()* is called, it actually sets up a communication path that starts and ends with itself. Taken only that far, it would seem to be a useless thing to do. However, the process that called *pipe()* can now create other processes with the *fork()* system call—described later in this chapter—that uses the pipe.

The following skeleton program, supported by the discussion on the *fork()* system call illustrates this use.

```
int   pfd[2];            /* file descriptors of pipe */
char bufr[64];           /* receive buffer */
```

```
char msg[] = "This message is sent"

main() {

    pipe(pfd);          /* create pipe (assume no error) */

    if (fork()) {       /* create new process */
        write(pfd[1], msg, sizeof(msg));
        exit(0);    }

    read(pfd[0], bufr, sizeof(bufr));       /* receive message */
    exit(0); }
```

The *pipe()* call creates two file descriptors into the array *pfd*. The first, *pfd[0]* is open for reading, and the second, *pfd[1]*, is open for writing. After the *fork()* call is made, there are two processes, each with all the same file descriptors, including the two just created in *pfd*. The "parent" process executes the *write()* call and exits, and the "child" process executes the *read()* call and exits.

There is nothing to stop the parent process from spawning more children that use the pipe created with the *pipe()* call. The shell, when given with the command

```
        ls | wc
```

will perform three steps, once the command is passed:

1. Execute a *pipe()* system call.

2. Create a new process with *fork()*, which then uses *dup()* to associate the "write" file descriptor with standard output. The new process then calls *exec()* to execute the *ls* file.

3. Create another new process with the *fork()*, which then uses *dup()* to associate the "read" file descriptor with the standard input. The new process then calls *exec()* to execute the *wc* file.

The shell will then wait for both children to terminate. The syntax covering pipes, as used by the shell, is covered in Chapter 4.

read() call

All data transferred from the file system and the device handlers to a process is accomplished with the *read()* call. The syntax of the *read()* call in C is as follows:

```
int n;
n = read(fd, buf, nch);
```

where *fd* is the file descriptor of an open file, *buf* is a character pointer to a region in the process's address space that will receive the data, and is at least *nch* characters long.

The calling process may be suspended for the length of time that the actual data transfer needs to take place, unless the file's status was set with the *O_NDELAY* bit on when the file was opened. If the file descriptor being read from is associated with a pipe or a terminal device, and no data is available in the system buffers to accommodate the read request, the process will be suspended until data becomes available.

If the read was from a pipe, and the *O_NDELAY* bit was set with the *open()* call that opened the pipe, the call will always return without suspending the process, even if zero bytes were read.

The actual number of characters read is returned as the function's value. Fewer than *nch* characters will be read if an EOF is encountered on a disk file or the terminal, or the pipe is closed at the other end.

For disk files, the file pointer is moved by the actual number of characters read, so that a subsequent *read()* call will read the next byte after the last byte read.

On an error, the return value is -1 and the global *errno* is set to a value indicating the nature of the error. In practical programming, any error is most often processed as an EOF condition, as in our example *dtv.c* program earlier in the chapter.

write() call

For transferring data from the process's virtual environment to the outside world, the *write()* system call is used. The syntax is very similar to the *read()* call:

```
int n;
n = write(fd, buf, nch);
```

except that *n* is set to the actual number of characters written, or -1 if an error condition occurred. In cases where the device being written has run out of room, it is possible for *n* to be set to a value less than *nch*.

The parameters *fd* and *buf* are used the same as the *read()* call, except that *buf* refers to an area which has the data to be written.

The file pointer is set to the byte position after the last byte written. If the write was made at the end of file, the file's actual EOF is changed accordingly.

If the *O_APPEND* bit was set on the *open()* call, the file pointer is always set to the EOF before each write, regardless of its previous value. A *write()* call will suspend the calling process for as long as it takes to transfer the data from the calling process' environment. If the write was to a pipe, and the write would cause more than 5120 bytes of data to be left un-read in the pipe, the calling process is suspended until some process empties the data from the pipe.

As with the *read()* call, the process can avoid being suspended by setting the *O_NDELAY* bit with the *open()* call. If a -1 was returned, the error condition has occurred as described by the value of the *errno* global value.

lseek() call

Many applications require random access to a file. The *lseek()* call can be used to alter the file pointer prior to a *write()* or *read()* call to allow this activity. *lseek()* returns a long integer and takes three parameters:

```
long newpos, lseek(), pos;
newpos = lseek(fd, pos, whence);
```

There are three possible values for the parameter *whence*:

    0   means that the file pointer will be the value *pos* .

    1   means that the current file pointer will be *added* to the value of *pos* to obtain the new file pointer. *pos* can be either positive or negative.

    2   means that the file pointer will be set to the size of the file plus the value of *pos*.

Two common forms of *lseek()* involve a rewind operation, and a skip to the EOF. These can be coded as:

```
lseek(fd, 0L, 0);            /* rewind file */
np = lseek(fd, 0L, 2);       /* skip to EOF */
```

The value returned by *lseek()* is the value of the new file pointer. Therefore, the size of the file associated with *fd* is placed in the variable *np* in the second example above.

It is possible to create subroutines for reading and writing fixed size records in a data file. For example, a random-access-record read routine for 256 byte records might look like this:

```
int recread(fd, buf, rec)
int   fd;            /* file descriptor */
char *buf;           /* buffer to receive record */
int   rec;           /* record number to read */
{
     long pos = ((long) rec) << 8;

     if (lseek(fd, pos, 0) != pos)
         return -1;    /* record not in file */
     return read(fd, buf, 256); }
```

It is assumed that the records are numbered starting from zero. A similar routine can be used for writing.

ioctl() *call*

So far, all of the low level I/O calls were, for the most part, device independent. For non file-system devices, such as terminals and tape drives, we need a call that can perform actions specific to that device. The *ioctl()* call provides that mechanism.

The basic syntax of the *ioctl()* call[12] is as follows:

---

[12] See articles in section (m) of the XENIX manuals and section 7 of the Microport and AT&T manuals for descriptions of how the *ioctl()* call affects certain devices.

```
ioctl(fd, cmd, arg);
```

where *fd* is a valid, open file descriptor, and *cmd* and *arg* are specific to the device being accessed. The actual commands that can be used are covered in the articles documenting those particular devices.

Process Management

By now we have some familiarity with the I/O functions that a process can perform. The other major category of operations includes those that change the processes themselves. In order to implement programs of the form described in Figure 2-1, a process needs to be able to create and manage other processes. UNIX provides a series of operating system calls for these functions, some of which we have already seen by necessity in previous examples. Those we will demonstrate are:

brk()	Set memory break value (adjust the amount of memory allocated to the process's data space.
getpid()	Get the process's ID number.
getuid()	Get the process's user ID.
exec()	Execute another program as this process.
exit()	Exit this process.
fork()	Create a new process.
kill()	Send a signal to a process.

These are some of the most commonly used "process control" operating system calls. In other chapters of this volume, we will encounter others as they are needed.

brk()

This operating system call is the primary departure the UNIX implementations (for the 286 and 386) make from the "standard" UNIX, and is one of the few real differences between XENIX and UNIX for the 286. The 386 XENIX is more closely aligned with UNIX. The reason this series of operating system calls is different, has to do with the segment address architecture of the Intel 286. The issues that arise from this are discussed in detail in Chapter 18.

When a program is first loaded for execution by one of the *exec()* calls (described later), a data space will be allocated as part of the environment of the process, as shown earlier in Figure 2-2. Associated with each process is a variable called the "break value," which is the the highest valid address of the data area that is currently allocated. The break value will initially be set to a value appropriate to hold all the global variables and data areas declared by data structures, as computed and output by the *ld* program. Once the program is running as a process, it can allocate and deallocate new areas of memory with the *brk(), sbrk()* and *brkctl()* operating system calls.

Both *sbrk()* and *brk()* perform the same function, but are coded with different techniques. *sbrk()* is passed an integer that is taken to be the amount of memory to allocate, which may be negative if memory is to be de-allocated. The return value from *sbrk()* is a character pointer that points to the start of the newly allocated memory. The *brk()* routine, however, takes a character pointer that is intended to be used as the new break value, and returns a 0 for success and -1 for failure.

SCO XENIX has added the *brkctl()* function to allow the programmer to have greater control over the memory allocations within specific segments. This subject is covered in greater detail in Chapter 18.[13]

getpid()

Each process in UNIX is given a unique number to identify it when it is created. The number of the next process to be created starts at zero, and is incremented by one for each new process up to a limit of 32,000, after which it is reset to zero. If a new process number is to be assigned which is already in use by an active process, it is skipped.

The *getpid()* function returns the process number of the currently running process. This number can be used for a variety of purposes, although some of the most likely applications are for the generation of unique file names

---

[13] See articles BRKCTL(5) (XENIX PRM), SBRK(5) (XENIX PRM), BRK(2) (Microport SDS Vol. 2), BRK(2) (AT&T PRM)

and for messages that are written from multi-process, non-interactive programs. In other words, a series of programs might keep a log file, with entries identified by their Process I.D. numbers.

getuid()

Each process is associated with the "real" user and group I.D. number, and the "effective" user and group I.D. number. The effective user and group I.D. numbers are used to check file permissions whenever a file is opened. (Chapter 15 discusses the nature of the UNIX security systems.) The following routines return short integers that correspond to the values currently associated with the running process:

getuid()	Get user I.D.
geteuid()	Get effective user I.D.
getgid()	Get group I.D.
getegid()	Get effective group I.D.

The user and group I.D. numbers can be interpreted by reading the specially formatted files */etc/passwd* and */etc/groups*, respectively.

exec()

This section actually refers to a series of routines, which are all documented in the same article and all perform the same function. The only variance is the coding technique and syntax actually used to invoke the *exec()* operating system call.

The purpose of the *exec* series of operating system calls is to start the execution of a new program, loaded from a specific file in the file system. The named file must be an executable file of the proper format, written by the *ld* or equivalent program.[14]

In UNIX, main programs can be written as subroutines, and are often treated as such by shell scripts and other programs. Programs written in C have a function declaration for the main program as follows:

---

[14] The *ld* program is usually not directly invoked by the user when compiling programs. Most compiler commands, notably the *cc* command which compiles C programs, automatically invoke the *ld* program when needed.

Chapter 2 UNIX Program Environment

```
main(argc, argv)
int   argc;           /* number of arguments */
char **argv;          /* array of pointers to arguments */
{

      (program)

}
```

The values of *argc* and *argv* are compiled for the program by the shell, which issues a *fork()* call to make a clone of itself, and then the clone overwrites itself with one of the *exec()* calls. The parameters passed to the *exec()* call are put into a proper form and place, then passed again to the main program through the *argc* and *argv* variables. The main program has in effect become a subroutine.

Programs other than the shell can perform this same process by using the *exec* calls. To make things simpler for the programmer, a variety of *exec()* calls are provided that take differing parameter formats and protocols. The programmer can choose the form that is most convenient.

Because there is no standard way for a C function to detect the number of parameters with which it was called, the variable list of arguments passed to the *exec()* calls rely on the calling routine terminating a list with a *(char *)* 0 constant. The syntax of the calls is:

```
execl(path, arglist)

execv(path, argv)

execle(path, arglist, envp)

execve(path, argv, envp)

execlp(file, arglist)

execvp(file, argv)
```

The only possible return from this function is when an error occurs, and the return value will always be -1, with *errno* set to the error value. In the above prototypes the symbols are interpreted as follows:

path A character pointer to the pathname of the file to execute.

file The name of a file (not a pathname) which will be sought in each directory in the current PATH variable in the environment.

arglist A series of character pointers pointing to the argument values to be passed to the newly executed program. Note that the first of these should usually be the name of the program itself, following a convention used by the shell. The argument list is of the form:

```
arg1, arg2, ..., argn, (char *) 0
```

and can be of any length.

argv A pointer to an array of pointers that are the arguments to be passed to the newly executed program. The last element of the array must be a *(char *)* 0 constant.

envp A pointer to an array of pointers that are to become the new environment. As with the *argv* parameter, this is a pointer to an array of pointers whose last element is set to the value *(char*)* 0.

For those calls that include the *envp* parameter, the environment for the new program is changed. The environment is a small in-RAM data base of variables that are used as global parameters to all programs running for a particular user. Chapter 4, on the shell, provides a discussion of the program environment.[15]

exit()

This call terminates a process, and optionally passes a value back to the process which created it. The C compiler and library automatically generates

---

[15] See article ENVIRON(M) (XENIX PRM).

[16] A possible exception might be an interpreted language processor, in which a user might enter an expression that results in a divide by zero. This could be handled with the SIGFPE (floating point exception) signal. Also, the use of "programming error" signals can sometimes help trap obscure bugs by setting up the program to dump critical variables when the problem occurs.

an *exit()* call by default when the main program of a process executes a *return* statement.

The parent process must use the *wait()* call to obtain the Process I.D. and the *exit()* value. For example:

```
int status, pid;

pid = wait(&status);
```

The calling process will block until one of its children terminates, or another signal is received. If the wait finished because of the child process terminating, the variable *pid* will be set to the process I.D. of the terminated process, and the variable *status* will have the value passed by that process to the *exit()* call.

For asynchronous execution, the calling process can also use the *signal()* call to set up a signal task that will be asynchronously executed whenever the process receives the "death of child" signal (*SIGCLD*). See the section describing signals later in this chapter.

The *wait()* call performs another important function. When a child process terminates it becomes inactive, but remains in the system until its parent acknowledges the event with a *wait()* call. If the parent process never does this, the child process hangs about in the system as a "zombie" process. Since the number of processes that can be active at any one time is limited, this is a housekeeping problem that will eventually inhibit the creation of new processes if it is ignored.

If a process is orphaned, i.e., its parent terminates before it does, the system automatically assigns the process's parent process I.D. number to 1. Process 1 is always the *init* program which (among its other tasks) will automatically acknowledge any termination signals.

fork()

The *fork()* call is the only way new processes are created in the UNIX system. The call itself is very elegant, but difficult to visualize until you get used to it.

Upon completion of the *fork()* call there will be two processes in existence, so the call actually returns twice. For the parent process, *fork()* returns either a -1 for an error condition (in the case where the *fork()* did not actually occur) or the Process I.D. of the newly created file process. The child process commences execution at the same point, except that its *fork()* call returns a zero.

The interesting thing is that after *fork()* we have two processes that are the same, except for the value returned by the *fork()* call and a few other resources, such as file locks. The duplication includes all the text, stack, and data space of the process, and the open file descriptors. A skeleton example of how a *fork()* almost always appears is as follows:

```
int cpid;

if (cpid = fork()) {
    /* the "parent" process executes here, with cpid set to
       the process I.D. of the new process */

}
else {

    /* the "child" process executes here */

}
```

Most often, the child process will execute an *exec()* system call to bring in a new program, and the parent process will call *wait()* to wait for the new program to terminate. This is not necessarily so. Both the parent and the child process are free to go on to do other things, including creating other processes.

In cases where both parent and child continue execution, care must be taken to avoid conflicts with I/O to common file descriptors. I/O requests to a file, the terminal screen, or keyboard will be handled on a first-come-first-serve basis, with unpredictable results. Most often this is avoided by redirecting I/O to other, non-shared devices, files, or pipes, as in our earlier example with the *pipe()* system call.

Signals

One important part of the process environment is signals. Signals are designed to allow a process to accommodate irregular, asynchronous events.

Chapter 2   UNIX Program Environment

When the event, called a "signal," occurs, an action specified by the program, the process is running can be taken. The names of some of the more useful signals, taken from the system file */usr/include/signal.h* are:

SIGHUP   Hangup. The terminal connection has been broken.

SIGKILL Kill. Some other process has sent this signal.

SIGPIPE Write to closed pipe. The process has made a *write()* call to a pipe when no process is open to read from it on the other end.

SIGALARM Alarm clock. The process has made an *alarm()* system call, which instructs the system to generate this signal in a specified number of seconds. This is useful for timeout conditions.

SIGUSR1 User defined. May be sent by another process via the *kill()* system call.

SIGUSR2 User defined. May be sent by another process via the *kill()* system call.

SIGCLD   Death of a child. A process created by a *fork()* call made by this process has terminated.

There are other signals that can occur, which generally refer to hardware and programming errors. These are not often used by applications programs, because most programs are designed in such a way as to not invoke illegal instructions or accommodate failures in the hardware on which the system is running.[16]

When a signal occurs to a process, a default action is taken unless the program has made a *system()* system call to set up some other action to be taken. The default action is usually to terminate the process. In addition, a file named *core* which contains an image of the contents of the process's environment might be written if the signal appeared to be caused by a programming error.

The three possible actions that can be set up for each signal by the *signal()*[17] system call are:

1. Terminate the process. (The default action may be specified explicitly.)

2. Ignore the signal. (Cannot be done with *SIGKILL.*)

3. Execute a special function within the process's environment. (Cannot be done with *SIGKILL.*)

This last option bears further explanation. The *signal()* call can name a function. This is treated very much like an interrupt routine in the kernel. When the associated signal occurs, the process stops what it is doing, then enters the "signal catching" function. The signal catching function can take whatever action the programmer desires, then must execute a *return* statement, which will cause the process to resume at the point it was interrupted.

The method to set and catch the *SIGALRM* signal in is as follows:

```
#include <signal.h>

main()
{
    int sigcatch();

    signal(SIGALRM, sigcatch);

    ...

}

sigcatch(sig)
int sig;
{
    if (sig == SIGALRM) {

        /* ALARM WENT OFF */

        signal(SIGALRM, sigcatch);

        }
```

---

[17] See articles SIGNAL(5) (XENIX PRM), SIGNAL(2) (Microport SDS Vol. 2), SIGNAL(2) (AT&T PRM).

```
        return;
}
```

The parameter sent to the signal catching function is the number of the signal received. With this facility more than one type of signal can be handled by the same routine.

It is important for the signal catching function to execute a return, rather than attempting to directly re-enter the code that was interrupted. If this is not done, the process's stack area will be filled at the state it was prior to the signal, and will bear the added burden of the re-entered code. Subsequent signals handled this way can cause the process' stack to overflow. The signal, once received, must also be set again with another *signal( )* call if the process is to handle another signal in this way.

It is important to note that, with the exception of *SIGCLD*, signals are not queued. For example, if *SIGUSR1* is being used to activate a server process in a multi-process environment, and more than one process is generating signals to the server process, more signals might be sent than received by the process. For this reason signals are not normally used as a communications device.

3
UNIX File System

One of the greatest contributions made by UNIX to the community of computers today is its file system. So strong was the appeal of its tree-structured file system that Microsoft incorporated it into its DOS product[1] starting with DOS Version 2.0, and there are other commercial operating systems that are being re-written to provide it. Once users, both novice and expert, understand it they never want to use anything else. It is difficult to imagine a more practical approach to organizing large amounts of data files, even though there are some weaknesses that are not obvious at first.

In this chapter we will view the UNIX file system from two perspectives. First is how the user perceives the file system, and second, how the file system is actually implemented. The structure of a file system on the 286/386 UNIX systems is the same as other UNIX implementations, except for the concept of disk partitioning, which has its own section in this chapter.

Any reference book on UNIX will show a typical tree-structured file system in a manner similar to that shown in Figure 3-1. The structure is so named because it resembles a tree, except with the root at the top. Every branch and every leaf is given its own name.

In the figure, squares represent "directories" (branches) and circles represent "files" (leaves). Notice that all directories and files except for the root directory are subordinate to another directory. On the lower left side of the tree, for example, the file *report* appears within the directory *ellen*. Sometimes in naming this relationship it is said that *report* is the "child" of *ellen*, and that *ellen* is the "parent" of *report*.[2]

---

[1] The DOS adaptation to tree-structured file systems caused that implementation to differ in two important ways: 1) the backslash character is used to separate parts of the pathname instead of the forward slash, and 2) DOS directories are not readable as files by a program.

[2] I prefer not to use this naming convention for the hierarchical relationship, because its application is more appropriate when discussing "parent" and "child" processes, as described in

Tutorial guides to the UNIX file system from the user's perspective are in Chapter C-6 of the Microport Runtime System Manual, and in Chapter 3 of the SCO XENIX Run Time Environment Manual, and the AT&T Programmer's Guide.

A file is a data structure that may contain any information. A directory may only have the names of other files. The UNIX user, provided he has security access to access a file, may modify the file in any way.[3] Only the UNIX File System within the kernel can change information within a directory, although it only does so at the request of some processes.

Most files are located on one of the disk drives installed on the system. There is another type of file, called a "device file," which refers to data on a device other than the disk drives. In the discussion which follows, we will ignore device files until we get to the section "Device Files."

Notice that in Figure 3-1 there are two files named *letter1*. It is fairly easy to see that they are different because one is within the directory *connie* and the other is in the directory *ellen*. But how does the user specify one and not the other? The answer is the usage of "pathnames." The full for the first file is:

    /usr/connie/letter1

This is the UNIX way of saying: "the file to be accessed is *letter1*, which is in the directory *connie*, which is in the directory *usr*, which is in the root directory." Naturally, the other *letter1* file would have a pathname of:

    /usr/ellen/letter1

The derivation of the term "pathname" is fairly obvious. Starting at the root, the path to a file is defined by a series of names, separated by slash (/) characters. The rule is that you can only travel along the lines from one level to the next, and any name you pass (or arrive at) in the process is a pathname element.

You can go upwards as well as downwards in a pathname. The special

---

Chapter 2. It is usually more precise to say that the file *report* appears in directory *ellen*.

[3] With one exception. UNIX files may never be "shrunk" to a smaller size. They can be erased, then re-written.

pathname element of .. (two periods) represents the parent directory of the preceding directory. In our example, the pathname:

```
/usr/connie/letter1
```

is equivalent to:

```
/usr/lib/../connie/letter1
```

The file pointer changes after most low level I/O operations in a manner consistent with usual file I/O. If a specific file position is desired by the process, an lseek() call can be performed. In each of the descriptions of I/O calls that follow, it is important to note how the status of the file pointer is changed.

How is this useful? So far we have been dealing only with "absolute" pathnames, those that start with a slash ("/"). An absolute pathname is 100% unambiguous in that there is only one file in an entire UNIX system that can be referenced with that given pathname. The double-period ("..") is generally not useful for this type of pathname. Most often we use "relative" pathnames. The most common relative pathname we use in UNIX is simply a file name that is relative to the "present working directory." The present working directory is simply a default pathname that is prepended to any pathname that does not begin with a slash. Relative pathnames have two advantages:

1. They are shorter, making them easier to type.
2. A program using relative pathnames can be used any number of different places within the file system using the same file names, but in different directories.

For example, say we are logged on to the UNIX file system in Figure 3-1 as the user *ellen*, and our present working directory is */usr/ellen*. (We can find out what our present working directory is by typing the *pwd* command.) If we type the command:

```
more letter1
```

to the shell (see Chapter 4) the *more* program will be loaded into a new process, and it will be provided with the pathname "letter1." The *more* program will in turn pass an open request to the UNIX kernel with that same pathname, and proceed to read the file and display it on the screen.

Note that we did not have to type:

```
more /usr/ellen/letter1
```

which would have yielded the same result. Because the present working directory /usr/ellen/ was assumed, the *more* program did not have to be given the full pathname. Now suppose that user *ellen* wanted to access user *connie*'s recipe file. She could type:

```
more /usr/connie/recipe
```

which would override the default present working directory. However, it would be the same thing to type:

```
more ../connie/recipe
```

which would end up being (as far as the kernel was concerned):

```
more /usr/ellen/../connie/recipe
```

Figure 3-1

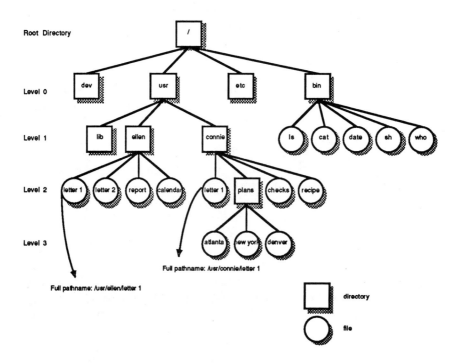

Obviously, using the double-dot convention is more useful where longer pathnames are concerned. Also, application programs that manipulate complex directory structures rely on the double period convention.

The pathname approach to organizing data is not exactly new, and certainly not original to UNIX. An outline for a term paper is really a similar hierarchy. For example, the paragraphs in the outline:

```
II. Media effect on Politics
    A.  "Free Press" nations
        1. United States
        2. France
        3. Great Britain
    B.  "Non-Free Press" nations
        1. USSR
        2. People's Republic of China
```

could be put into a pathname nomenclature as follows:

```
MediaEffect/Free/UnitedStates
MediaEffect/Free/France
MediaEffect/Free/GreatBritain
MediaEffect/NonFree/USSR
MediaEffect/NonFree/PRC
```

(Note that there is not a preceding slash ("/") in front of the pathnames. This is because the directory *MediaEffect* appears inside some other directory which is not named here.) UNIX applies a simple syntax for pathnames, stated as follows:

UNIX RULES FOR PATHNAMES

1. A pathname is made up of elements separated, and optionally preceded, by slash characters ("/"). Each element is a string of characters that names either a file or a directory.

2. Any pathname element appearing to the left of a slash character must be the name of a directory.

3. Any characters other than the slash ("/") are legal for pathname elements. However, some characters are best avoided, because they have special meanings to the shells (see Chapter 4). These characters include:

```
@  #  $  ^  &  *  (  )  `  [  ]  {  }  \
|  ;  "  '  <  >
```

Also permissible are the space character and non-graphic characters (such as the TAB key). From inside a program, all these characters can be used freely, because they are not interpreted in system calls.

4. Upper and lower case are distinct. The name "Fred" is different from "FRED" which is different from "fred". Standard UNIX programs tend to use lower case almost exclusively to avoid confusion.

5. Each pathname element may consist of up to 14 characters.

6. A pathname that starts with a slash is an absolute pathname, and is located by a path starting at the root.

7. A pathname that does not start with a slash is a relative pathname, and will be located either relative to the present working directory or according to the rules set up by the program to which that pathname is given.

8. A pathname element of two periods ("..") means "the parent directory." For example, the full pathname "/usr/spool/../lib/terminfo" is the same as "/usr/lib/terminfo."

9. The pathname element of one period (".") means "this directory." For example "filea" is the same as "./filea". This form is often used to signify that the file desired is only in the current directory.

Other than the file names for "current directory" (one period: ".") and "parent directory" (two periods: "..") the UNIX operating system kernel does not enforce any conventions regarding the format or significance of file names. However, there are many programs that are delivered with UNIX that do enforce conventions, starting with the UNIX shells. As far as the UNIX shells are concerned, the only general convention they promote is that file names starting with a period "." are normally considered "hidden files."

These files are not included when the shell is directed to search for files in the general case. See Chapter 4, which describes how the shells work for further explanation.

There are many file naming conventions that are used by the utilities and subsystems that run as user programs under UNIX. Most of these conventions specify a certain character string, usually a period and one letter, to follow the user supplied file name. For example, if "interest" is the name of your program, the C compiler won't compile it unless the actual source code is in a file named *interest.c*. By default, it will place the object output in a file named *interest.o*, and the executable output in *a.out*.

The following table shows a few of the standard conventions so you can get a feel for them, but the best source for learning what conventions to use is the documentation on the particular program.

File Name Ends with	Meaning	Programs
.c	A C source code file	C compiler (cc)
.f	A FORTRAN77 source code file	The f77 compiler
.h	A C source "include" file	C compiler (cc)
.o	An object file	C compiler (cc), The relocatable loader (ld), and others.
.s	An assembly language source	The assembler (as)
.y	A YACC source file	The yacc compiler
.z	A packed file	pack program

As a rule, the file naming conventions are very loosely enforced in UNIX. Compilers use naming conventions so that object files they produce can be associated easily with the source files they were compiled from. Most programs allow you to override defaults with an arbitrary file name.

Scanning Directory Entries a C Program

A C program can readily peruse the hierarchy of a directory structure, provided it has read permission to all of the various directory files. Such a C program is given in the following example:

```
  1 0: /* dirlist.c - directory listing program
  2 0*
  3 0*    alan deikman 3/89
  4 0*
  5 0*    This program will use the DIRECTORY(3X) programs to produce
  6 0*    an indented listing of directories and the number of files
  7 0*    in each.
  8 0*
  9 0*    Synopsis:
 10 0*
 11 0*         dirlist [<path> ..]
 12 0*
 13 0*    where <path> is the pathname to a directory, assumed to be the
 14 0*    root directory if not specified.
 15 0*
 16 0*    */
 17 0:
 18 0: #include <stdio.h>
 19 0: #include <sys/types.h>
 20 0: #include <dirent.h>
 21 0:
 22 0: short   depth;          /* depth of directory */
 23 0:
 24 0: main(ac, av)
 25 0: int      ac;
 26 0: char     **av;
 27 0: {
 28 1:
 29 1:   if (ac <= 1)       { depth = 0;  dirlist("/"); }
 30 1:   else while (--ac)  { depth = 0;  dirlist(*++av); }
 31 1:   exit(0); }
 32 0:
 33 0:
 34 0: dirlist(d)
 35 0: char    *d;     /* directory to search */
 36 0: {
 37 1:   DIR    *dir;           /* current directory stream */
 38 1:   struct dirent *p;      /* current entry */
 39 1:   char   bufr[128];      /* pathname buffer */
 40 1:   short  i;
 41 1:
 42 1:   if ((dir = opendir(d)) == NULL) return;
 43 1:
 44 1:   depth += 1;
 45 1:   for (i = 0; i < depth; i++) printf("  ");
 46 1:   printf("%s\n", d);
 47 1:
 48 1:   while ((p = readdir(dir)) != NULL) {
 49 2:     if (!strcmp(p->d_name, ".") || !strcmp(p->d_name, "..")) continue;
 50 2:     strcpy(bufr, d);
 51 2:     strcat(bufr, "/");
 52 2:     strcat(bufr, p->d_name);
 53 2:     dirlist(bufr); }
 54 1:
 55 1:   depth -= 1;
 56 1:   closedir(dir); }
```

The recursively accessed function *dirlist()* attempts to open a directory with *opendir()*, and simply returns if *opendir()* fails, assuming that the parameter was not a directory. If the open succeeds, it then prints out the directory name and scans all files within the directory using *readdir()*, calling itself each time.

Conventional Directories

The UNIX kernel does not enforce any directory naming conventions or place any significance on any directory name. However, there are directories that you will see on every UNIX system, and they are used for the same purpose on all of them. The programs and files distributed with UNIX will be found in these directories:

Directory	Conventional Usage
/dev	The directory where all the device files are kept.
/	The "root" directory, where all other directories originate.
/bin	The most commonly used programs in executable format (at one time called "binaries").
/dev	The standard directory of device files, or device nodes.
/dev/dsk	The directory of "lock" hard disk and floppy disk devices.
/dev/rdsk	The directory of "raw" hard disk and floppy disk devices.
/dev/rmt	The directory of "raw" magnetic tape devices.
/etc	Special system-operator programs and files, intended to be used only by super-user programs. The list of users and groups, plus a description of each terminal, is in this directory.
/etc/atconf	The "configure" directory, which contains all the pieces to build a new system kernel.
/etc/atconf/in	Programs used in system kernel building.
/etc/atconf/kernels	The ready-to-run system kernels left by the system-building process.

Path	Description
/etc/atconf/modules	The object modules and source code necessary for building a new kernel.
/etc/atconf/systems	The source files that specify the parameters for various system kernels.
/etc/rc?.d	Run commands (*rc*) for state *?* of the system. See the discussion on *init* states in the chapter on system administration.
/install	A work directory for the */etc/install* program, which installs prepackaged programs.
/li	The most commonly accessed object libraries, object files, and bits, and pieces of compilers.
/lost+found	A special directory where lost files are stored. Lost files are caused by system crashes and detected by the *fsck* program. In some cases the file contents can be recovered, but not any of its original links.
/mnt	An empty directory that is used as a mount point.
/shlib	A directory of commonly used "shared memory" libraries.
/tmp	A general purpose directory for temporary file storage that anybody can use. The *ex/vi* editors use this directory.
/usr	The "sub-root" directory for all "user" files on the system disk drive. For large system hard disk drives this is often the a separate file system on the first disk drive.
/usr/adm	Process accounting files are stored here.
/usr/admin	Administrator programs.
/usr/games	A popular directory for entertainment programs.

/usr/guest	This directory is often seen on systems that have a "guest" account.
/usr/include	A directory of C-source include files that are used in conjunction with the standard C/UNIX library.
/usr/include/sys	A directory of C-source include files that define constants and structures within the UNIX system itself. The use of these include files should provide programs with a high degree of portability between different UNIX implementations.
/usr/lib	Libraries, object files, programs and other data files that have been installed on top of the basic core of UNIX.
/usr/lib/acct	Programs related to process accounting.
/usr/lib/cron	Directory used by the *cron* accounting program
/usr/lib/ctrace	Contains a source file used by the *ctrace* utility.
/usr/lib/terminfo	This directory contains a data base which describes the programming details for a variety of different terminal devices. See the chapter on programming terminals.
/usr/lib/uucp	The library routines and data files for the *uucp* subsystem.
/usr/lost+found	Same as /lost+found except for the /usr file system.
/usr/mail	The directory where mail between users is stored, as accessed by the *mail* command.
/usr/news	A directory containing news for users.
/usr/options	A directory containing files which name all the

optional programs installed.

/usr/spool
The working directories for the spooling subsystems have their roots here.

/usr/spool/cron
The root for the *cron* spooler.

/usr/spool/cron/atjobs
When an *at* command is executed, scheduling a program to be executed at a later time, the shell script to be executed is placed in this directory.

/usr/spool/cron/crontabs
In this directory are files that authorized users can place instructions to run various programs at specified intervals.

/usr/spool/lp
The root for the *l* spooler.

/usr/spool/uucp
The working directory for the *uucp* subsystem.

/usr/spool/uucppublic
A directory where users from other systems can place files temporarily.

/usr/tmp
The same as */tmp* except it is allocated out of the */usr* file system.

/u
In systems that contain an additional file system past the */usr* file system (usually when there is more than one physical hard disk drive). This directory serves as the "mount" point. All files which start with this as a path name will be on that file system.

In addition to the above table, users and other software packages can establish other directories. If a sensible convention is established and adhered to, substantial time and effort can be saved in busy systems.

Normally, the directory which is "home" to any user can be found in the */usr* directory, with the same name as the user's login I.D.

Links

A surprisingly useful feature of the UNIX file system is the concept of "links." A link,[4] created by the *link* system call or the *ln* command,[5] creates a new directory entry that is the exact equivalent of another file in the file system in every respect except the full pathname. Note that this is not a copy of the file, it is the same file, and any change to either will be seen through both pathnames.

Referring back to our previous example, where the user *ellen* wished to use *connie*'s recipes, it is possible that *ellen* could type the command:

```
ln ../connie/recipe pies
```

which is a command that says "link the file in *recipe* in *connie*'s directory to the file *pies* in the present working directory." There will now two pathnames that can be used to access this same file:

```
/usr/connie/recipe
/usr/ellen/pies
```

So any time user *connie* edits the file *recipe*, the file that appears in *ellen*'s directory will also be changed. Notice that having two links to a file does not use up any more disk space, except for a nominal 16 byte directory entry, than would a file with one link.

Note that if we were to perform an *rm* command on the file "/usr/connie/recipe" the file would not cease to exist. Why? Because the directory entry corresponding to the pathname "/usr/ellen/pies" is still "linked" to the file. The file only disappears (and its disk space is returned to the file system as free blocks) when the last link is removed.[6] Any

---

[4] Programmers are cautioned on the use of the term "link." In many operating systems, this term refers to the process of link-loading a relocatable program to make an absolute image. In UNIX, that process is performed by the *ld* program, which is described in the UNIX manuals as "a link editor." In this context the term "link" has nothing to do with "link loading."

[5] See articles CP(1) (Microport RSM), CP(1) (AT&T VRM), LN(C) (XENIX VRM)

[6] The *rm* command makes the system call *unlink*. There is no explicit "delete file" system call as there is in most Operating Systems. In order to learn this, I once spent four hours looking for the "remove file from system" system call in UNIX, which does not exist.

practical number of links can be made to a file. The actual limit would be $2^{15}-1$, which would never be reached in a sane file system.

Links are automatically created for directories by the file system. The special pathname elements "." and ".." are actually directory links that are created in each and every new directory, and refer to the "current directory," and the "parent directory" respectively.

The concept of links becomes more clear once the structure of the file system is understood. Later in this chapter there is a program that will discover all the links for a given file.

Device Files

As mentioned earlier, a file named in a directory might be what is called a "device file". Device files (sometimes called "nodes") are created with the operating system call *mknod* (make node),[7] which is most often accessed by the user with a program provided by UNIX of the same name.

This approach is a distinct departure from the methods of providing I/O services used by most other operating systems. Although it is common to perform I/O to special file names within the system (for example, "LPT1" in DOS refers to the first parallel printer) it is rare to have a file system that can create and remove such "device handles" on demand while the system is running. Chapter 16 is devoted to the programming of the actual system code to which these device files relate.

A device file appears within the file system and is accessed by programs generally in the same way that regular files are accessed. The major difference is that instead of data going to and from the disk drive, it goes to and from some device attached to the computer. The installation defaults UNIX device files, and their usual pathnames are shown in the following table.

This table shows some of the more common device names that are used in UNIX System V.3. Earlier versions of UNIX, nonstandard devices, or

---

[7] See articles MKNOD(1M) (Microport RSM), MKNOD(C) (XENIX VRM), MKNOD(1) (AT&T SARM)

devices added by third-party manufacturers will have other names.

Device	Device Name
This system console (the display and keyboard)	/dev/console
Serial interfaces (RS-232 terminals and other devices)	/dev/tty??
Parallel printer ports	/dev/lp?
The kernel-RAM memory	/dev/kmem
The system-RAM memory	/dev/mem
The system real-time clock	/dev/rtc
A phantom device (always reads as End-of-File, data written is thrown away)	/dev/null
The user's generic terminal (This device is always the terminal associated with the requesting process)	/dev/tty
The first hard disk (entire disk)	/dev/rdsk/0s0 (raw form) /dev/dsk/0s0 (block form)
The root partition	/dev/root
The swap device	/dev/swap
The second hard disk (entire disk)	/dev/rdsk/1s0 (raw form) /dev/dsk/1s0 (block form)
The first floppy disk drive	/dev/rdsk/f0
The second floppy disk drive	/dev/rdsk/f1
Virtual consoles	/dev/vt??
Mouse device (no serial mouse)	/dev/mouse

Because devices are more complex than the simple file model that is associated with regular UNIX files, it is usual to have more than one way of accessing a particular device. For example, a high density 5-1/4" inch floppy disk drive is typically able to read 1.2MB or 360KB floppy disks. Different modes of the same disk drive can be accessed by accessing different file names:

/dev/rdsk/f0q15dt   For "quad" density 15-sector format, which is for 1.2MB disks

/dev/rdsk/f0d9dt   For double density, 9-sector formatting, for 360KB disks

/dev/rdsk/f0d8dt   For double density, 8-sector formatting, for 320KB disks

The hard disk drive also has multiple paths of access. We will discuss hard disk drive devices later in this chapter.

Named Pipes

We saw in Chapter 2 how pipes could be created with the *pipe* system call to send data from one process to another in a stream. However, this technique only works for processes that are closely related, i.e. where one is created from another with the *fork* system call. How can we set up a pipe between two processes that are more distantly related?

The *mknod* command and system call can create a special file in the system that is a "named pipe." Named pipes can be used the same way we use unnamed pipes. The only difference is that the two processes each open the same special file with the regular *open* calls, and one will write into the file while the other reads.

After the *open* call, named pipes behave differently in the following ways. (These rules assume that the processes have not set the *O_NDELAY* bit by the *open* system call that was used to open the pipe.)

1. Bytes enter and leave the pipe on a First-In-First-Out (FIFO) basis.

2. A process reading the named pipe will be suspended until data becomes available, if necessary, to satisfy the *read* request. If there

is no process that has the pipe open for writing, (or if a process that did have the pipe open closed it) the process reading the pipe will receive an "end-of-file" condition.

3. A process writing to the named pipe will be suspended if the *write* request would cause more than a certain number of bytes to accumulate in the pipe.

An example of how to use names pipes is given in Chapter 11.

Disk Partitions

So far, we have concentrated on the user's perspective of how UNIX file systems are put together. From this point on, we will examine the actual data structures used to accomplish the foregoing effect. For the most part, a programmer or user does not need to know how the file system accomplishes what it does, although there are some programming projects where this knowledge is needed.

The original UNIX systems did not have to share their disk drives with other operating systems. With a PDP-11, if we want to alternately use UNIX and RSX-11,[8] we would have to switch disk packs on a removable media drive. When UNIX was ported to the IBM compatible market, things were different.

It was IBM's own conception of the IBM PC that made this possible. When IBM was working on the first hard disk drive for the PC (which by inclusion of a hard disk was named the XT) the possibility of multiple operating systems on one computer was considered. This was because at the time the CP/M and MP/M operating systems (by Digital Research) were still strong contenders in the market, and others such as the UCSD (University of California at San Diego) Pascal system were showing promise.

As a result of this, the concept of hard disk partitioning was implemented on the IBM XT, and IBM made its PC-DOS operating system use the hard disk within the constraints of its own hard disk partition. DOS, when re-implemented later on the IBM AT, and all the subsequent 286 and 386 systems which followed, carried with it the disk partition structure.

---

[8] RSX-11 is one of Digital Equipment Corporation's (DEC) proprietary operating systems.

The disk partition concept simply calls for the dividing of the hard disk into the maximum of four contiguous regions, each with independent file systems formatted by different operating systems. A table of the location and size of the partitions is kept on the first sector of the disk. Most DOS users who have no need for another operating system set up their drives so that there is one partition that uses the entire disk for DOS.

A UNIX or DOS operating system that is bootstrapped on a computer is supposed to immediately read the partition tables from all the hard disks attached to the system. From this it finds out what offset and what limit it will place on every hard disk request it generates.

UNIX provides utilities[9] that implement file transfers between the operating systems. DOS does not.

To edit the partition table, UNIX provides the *fdisk* program, named after its DOS counterpart. With *fdisk*, you can

1. Create a partition
2. Delete a partition
3. Make a partition "Active"

(The Microport version of *fdisk* also can scan for bad blocks and create the bad block table.)

Partitions cannot be "changed." If you need to move, shrink, or increase the size of a partition, you need to delete the original, then re-create it. This process destroys any data inside the partition.

At any time one of the partitions on the disk may be made "active." The operating system in the active partition is the one that will be loaded by the bootstrap program when the computer is reset.

---

[9] Both Microport, Interactive Solutions, and XENIX provide routines that allow a UNIX user to read and write DOS floppy disks, and any DOS partition that may be on the hard disk. These programs run as user mode programs.

UNIX Partition Divisions

Once UNIX has been assigned a partition, it is further divided up by the UNIX system, as shown by example in Figure 3-2. In the illustration, the second partition has been assigned to UNIX, which further divides it up as follows:

Figure 3-2

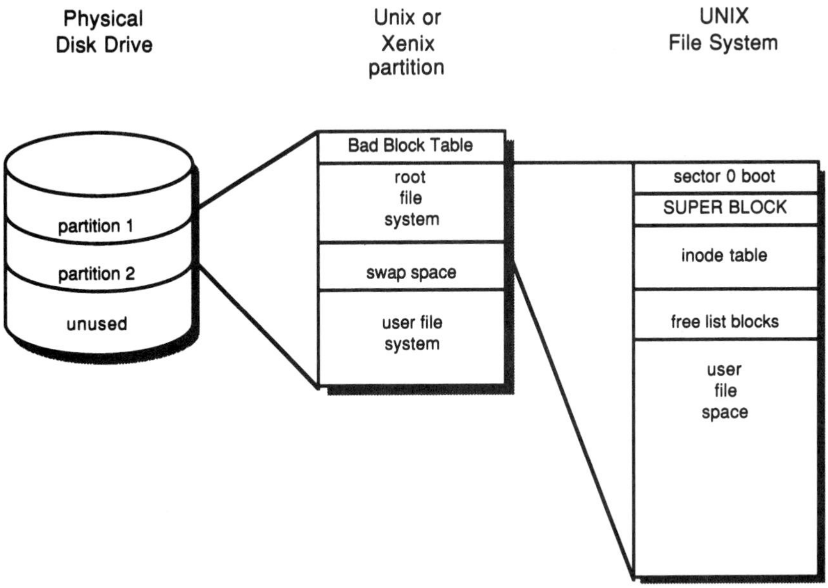

Physical Disk Drive	Unix or Xenix partition	UNIX File System
partition 1	Bad Block Table	sector 0 boot
partition 2	root file system	SUPER BLOCK
unused	swap space	inode table
	user file system	free list blocks
		user file space

1. **Bad block table.** This table shows the known bad blocks on the hard disk within the UNIX partition. The UNIX file system automatically works around these blocks. In Microport UNIX, the bad block table is created by the *fdisk* program. In SCO XENIX, the *badtrk* program is used.[10]

2. **Root file system.** This is the "system" file system which is available to running programs as soon as UNIX is bootstrapped. It contains at least the root directory, and the /bin, /etc, /dev, and /tmp directories.

---

[10] See article BADTRK(M) (XENIX VRM).

3. **The swap area.** This section does not contain a file system. It is an area where the UNIX kernel can write temporarily inactive processes to supplement RAM memory.

4. **User file system.** Normally this file system is mounted onto the system as the */usr* directory in Microport UNIX, and as the */u* directory in SCO XENIX.

Other than practical minimums and maximums, the user can control the size of each of the partitions and sections at installation time. On earlier versions of XENIX and UNIX, the *divvy* program is used to do this. UNIX system V.3 provides the *mkpart* program, which also handles bad track remapping.

If your system uses *mkpart*, the division of the UNIX partition can be seen by examining the file */etc/partitions*. An example of this file is:

```
disk0:
     heads = 6, cyls = 809, sectors = 26, bpsec = 512,
     vtocsec = 26, altsec = 27, boot = "/etc/boot",
     device = "/dev/rdsk/0s0"

rootus:
     partition = 1, start = 182, size = 26494,
     tag = ROOT, perm = VALID

swap:
     partition = 2, start = 26676, size = 14976,
     tag = SWAP, perm = NOMOUNT, perm = VALID

usr:
     partition = 3, start = 41652, size = 84396,
     tag = USR, perm = VALID

reserved:
     partition = 6, start = 0, size = 52,
     tag = BOOT, perm = NOMOUNT, perm = VALID

alts:
     partition = 7, start = 52, size = 62,
     tag = ALTS, perm = NOMOUNT, perm = VALID
```

As the labels implies, there are to be seven partitions within the UNIX partition, each specified with its own starting address and size. The other parameters specify whether the partition is "mountable." Mountable partitions are expected to have file systems within them, which we discuss in the following section.

Normally, a programmer or system installer need not be overly concerned with the determination of the numbers given in the tables above. The automatic installation procedures with each UNIX product give very acceptable values.

Mountable File Systems

When the UNIX system is booted, only one file system, the "root" file system, is available to the processes running under UNIX. This "root" file system usually has common directories in it, such as */bin*, */etc*, and so forth. File systems on other disk parcels (as allocated by the *divvy* program) or on other hard and floppy disk drives, cannot be accessed until they are "mounted." Mounting a file system is the act of associating a directory in an already mounted file system with the root directory of another, previously unmounted file system. From the user's standpoint, it simply looks as if the root file system just got bigger.

The most common example is the automatic mounting of the "user" file system to the */usr* directory in the *rc* startup file. The command:

```
/etc/mount /dev/rdsk/0s2 /usr
```

is executed. Before executing this command, the */usr* directory would appear as if it had no files in it. Indeed, it doesn't have any. After the command has executed, the */usr* directory now appears to have all of the files in the file system on the device */usr/rdsk/0s2*, with the entire subordinate directory structure intact.

Another common mounting example is:

```
/etc/mount /dev/rdsk/fd0 floppy
```

This will mount the file system on the first floppy disk drive as the directory *floppy* in the current working directory. Mountable file systems can be un-mounted as long as there are no active i-nodes within them. For example:

```
/etc/umount /dev/rdsk/fd0
```

To see what file systems are currently mounted, any user can run the *df* command, which will list the amount of disk space free on every mounted file system. A sample output is:

```
/       (/dev/dsk/0s1   ):     11208 blocks    2668 i-nodes
/usr    (/dev/dsk/0s3   ):     32358 blocks    8602 i-nodes
```

This shows two file systems mounted, one on the device /dev/dsk/0s1, as the root, and /dev/dsk/0s2 as the /usr file system.

File Systems

A file system for UNIX holds all of overhead and control information necessary to make the tree-structured directory scheme work. This data base has the following elements, as illustrated in Figure 3-3.

The parcel of disk space allocated to a file system is divided up into physical sectors of 512 bytes. Most older UNIX installations use the 512 byte sector as a block, but both UNIX and SCO XENIX use 1024 byte blocks, which are more efficient. The first sectors of the file system are allocated as follows:

1. A *Boot Block* at sector 0.

2. The *Super Block* at sector 1. The *Super Block* has within it a flag that indicates whether this file system uses 512 byte or 1024 byte blocks.

3. The *i-node* table starting at sector 2.

4. The user directory space starting immediately after the i-node table and continuing for the rest of the disk.

A file system can reside on a hard disk, within a UNIX partition as allocated by the *mkpart* or *divvy* program, or on a floppy disk. The initial data structure is written by a program called *mkfs* (make file system) which can be run at any time, but usually at system installation time. When *mkfs* is run it creates the root directory for the file system, an otherwise blank i-node table, and a free list that encompasses every free block within the file system.

Super Block

The entire file system structure is centered upon the *Super Block*, which is accessed each and every time a real disk access occurs. Because it is accessed so frequently, the UNIX kernel does not bother to write it out to the disk

Chapter 3 UNIX File System

drive. To do so would require the disk heads to seek to track 0 each and every time the file system is changed by any program. This would have a catastrophic effect on the effective throughput of the system.

Figure 3-3

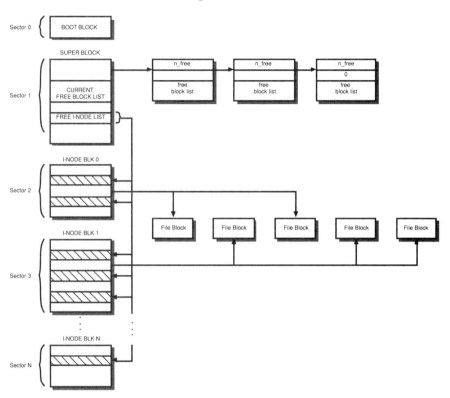

Instead, the *Super Block* is kept in RAM memory, and is only written out to the disk drive when any process in the system makes a *sync* operating system call. There is one process normally started up in UNIX (by the *rc* shell script that is executed when the system is booted) called *update*, whose sole function is to make a *sync* operating system call every 30 seconds.[11] A hypothetical C source code for *update* is as follows:

```
main() {                /* the update program */
    while (1) {         /* repeat forever */
```

---

[11] See article FS(4) (Microport SDS Vol. 2), FILESYSTEM (F) (XENIX VRM).

```
            sync();          /* write out all super-blocks */
            sleep(30); } }   /* wait for 30 seconds */
```

The *sync* system call also writes out any in-RAM copies of the i-nodes, described later.

Following is an element-by-element description of the *Super Block,* based on the structure found in the file */usr/include/sys/filsys.h.*

Data objects in the Super Block

NICFREE is the size of the Super Block Free Block List.

NICINODE is the size of the Super Block Free i-node List.

s_isize The size of the i-node table in blocks. A legal disk reference to a file in the file system will never be less than this number.

s_fsize The size of the entire file system. A legal disk reference will never be greater than or equal to this number.

s_nfree The number of free blocks in the *s_free* array, which follows.

s_free This is an array of up to *NICFREE* blocks available in the file system.

s_ninode The number of free i-nodes in the *s_inode* array which follows.

s_inode An array of up to *NICINOD* free i-node numbers.

s_flock A lock flag for free list manipulation.

s_ilock A lock flag for i-node table manipulation.

s_fmod	A flag indicating that the Super Block has been modified.
s_ronly	A flag that indicates that the file system is read-only.
s_time	The last time the Super Block was updated.
s_dinfo	Device information.
s_tfree	Total free blocks.
s_tinode	Total free i-nodes.
s_fname	A six character file system name.
s_fpack	A six character pack-ID.
s_fill	Filler to make the size of the Super Block 512 bytes.
s_magic	A number which must tells the file system what version of the file system this is.
s_stype	Set to 1 for a 512 byte block system, 2 for a 1024 byte block.

A user program can read the super block. This is what the *fsck* and *df* programs, among others, do to report on the status of the file system. The following is a program that will read and dump the contents of the super block.

```
1  0: /* dumpsb.c - Dump super-block of file system
2  0*
3  0*     alan deikman 3/89
4  0*
5  0*     This program will read and print out the current contents of
6  0*     the system super-block.
7  0*
8  0*     Synopsis
9  0*
10 0*         dumpsb [<fs> ..]
11 0*
12 0*     where <fs> is the raw device name of a file system.  If <fs>
13 0*     is not given the file /etc/mnttab is read to see all mounted
14 0*     file systems.
15 0*
16 0*  */
17 0:
18 0: #include <stdio.h>
```

UNIX Programming for the 80286/80386, Second Edition

```
19 0:    #include <fcntl.h>
20 0:    #include <sys/types.h>
21 0:    #include <mnttab.h>
22 0:    #include <sys/fs/s5param.h>
23 0:    #include <sys/fs/s5filsys.h>
24 0:
25 0:    struct filsys   SB;             /* super block structure */
26 0:    struct mnttab   M;              /* mount table structure */
27 0:
28 0:    main(ac, av)
29 0:    int      ac;
30 0:    char     **av;
31 0:    {
32 1:       int f;
33 1:
34 1:       /* scan mount table if user did not specify options */
35 1:
36 1:       if (ac <= 1) {
37 2:          if ((f = open("/etc/mnttab", O_RDONLY)) < 0) {
38 3:             fprintf(stderr, "dumpsb: can't access /etc/mnttab\n");
39 3:             exit(2); }
40 2:          while (read(f, &M, sizeof(M)) == sizeof(M)) dumpsb(M.mt_dev);
41 2:          close(f); }
42 1:
43 1:       /* dump specified file systems */
44 1:
45 1:       else while (--ac) dumpsb(*++av);
46 1:       exit(0); }
47 0:
48 0:
49 0:    dumpsb(df)
50 0:    char     *df;                   /* device file to read */
51 0:    {
52 1:       int f, i;
53 1:
54 1:       printf("\n*** File system: %s\n", df);
55 1:       if ((f = open(df, O_RDONLY)) < 0) {
56 2:          fprintf(stderr, "dumpsb: can't open %s\n", df);
57 2:          return; }
58 1:
59 1:       /* skip the first sector and read the super block */
60 1:
61 1:       sync();
62 1:       lseek(f, 512L, 0);
63 1:       if (read(f, &SB, sizeof(SB)) != sizeof(SB)) {
64 2:          fprintf(stderr, "dumpsb: read failed\n");
65 2:          return; }
66 1:       if (SB.s_magic != FsMAGIC) {
67 2:          fprintf(stderr, "ERROR: could not find super block\n");
68 2:          return; }
69 1:
70 1:       /* print block out */
71 1:
72 1:       printf("      Super block found at: %8X\n",    i * sizeof(SB));
73 1:       printf("              i-list size: %8d\n",     SB.s_isize);
74 1:       printf("     volume size in blocks: %8d\n",    SB.s_fsize);
75 1:       printf("    number avail in s_free: %8d\n",    SB.s_nfree);
76 1:       printf("      free blocks (first 4): ");
77 1:       for (i = 0; i < 4; i++)     printf("%8d",      SB.s_free[i]);
78 1:       printf("\n");
79 1:       printf("   number avail in s_inode: %8d\n",    SB.s_ninode);
80 1:       printf("          inodes (first 4): ", SB.s_inode[NICINOD]);
81 1:       for (i = 0; i < 4; i++)     printf("%8d",      SB.s_inode[i]);
82 1:       printf("\n");
83 1:       printf("            free list lock: %8d\n",    SB.s_flock);
84 1:       printf("           inode list lock: %8d\n",    SB.s_ilock);
85 1:       printf("       block modified flag: %8d\n",    SB.s_fmod);
86 1:       printf("            read only flag: %8d\n",    SB.s_ronly);
87 1:       printf("          last update time: %8X\n",    SB.s_time);
88 1:       printf("        device information: ");
89 1:       for (i = 0; i < 4; i++)     printf("%8d",      SB.s_dinfo[i]);
90 1:       printf("\n");
91 1:       printf("          total free blocks: %8d\n",   SB.s_tfree);
```

Chapter 3 UNIX File System

```
 92 1:    printf("          total free inodes: %8d\n",     SB.s_tinode);
 93 1:    printf("          file system name:  %6.6s\n",   SB.s_fname);
 94 1:    printf("     file system pack name:  %6.6s\n",   SB.s_fpack);
 95 1:    printf("     file system state flag: %8X\n",     SB.s_state);
 96 1:    printf("             magic number:   %8X\n",     SB.s_magic);
 97 1:    printf("          file system type:  %8d\n",     SB.s_type);
 98 1:
 99 1:    /* done */
100 1:
101 1:    close(f);
102 1:    return; }
```

Note the use of the *sync()* system call just before the *read()* call. If this was not done it is likely that the super-blockread could be up to 30 seconds out of date.

Since the *Super Block* is only 512 bytes long, it is obvious that a list of all the available blocks and i-nodes cannot reside within it. The techniques for accessing free blocks and the i-node table are described in the following sections.

i-node Table

The i-node table is a fixed size array of 64 byte data structures. For each file, device file, and directory there is one and only one i-node entry. From the i-node structure, you can directly determine everything about a file except the pathname(s) by which it can be referenced.

Each i-node in the file system is identified by its address in the i-node table, which is called the i-node number. In directories within the file system, each pathname element that appears in a directory has an i-node number associated with it. In this relationship, illustrated by Figure 3-4, we say the file (directory) is "linked" to the i-node.

In the i-node[12] there is a counter of how many links there are to this i-node. When the file is created the link counter is set to one. Each time another directory entry is linked to this i-node (through the *ln* command, for instance) the counter is incremented by one. When a link is removed (by the *rm* command or the *unlink* system call) the counter is decremented by one. If the counter is decremented to zero, all the blocks in the file are returned to the free block list, and the i-node is returned to the free i-node list.

---

[12] See articles INODE(4) (Microport SDS Vol. 2), INODE (F) (XENIX VRM), INODE(4) (AT&T PRM).

Figure 3-4

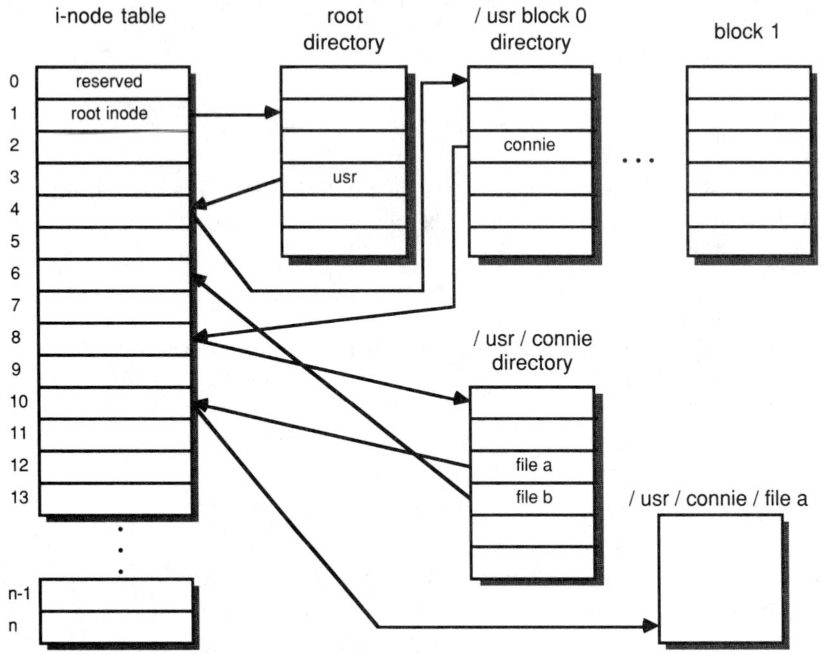

```
i-node table        root          / usr block 0
                  directory         directory        block 1

0  reserved
1  root inode
2                                    connie          ...
3                    usr
4
5
6
7
8                              / usr / connie
9                                directory
10
11
12                                  file a
13                                  file b       / usr / connie / file a
·
·
·
n-1
n
```

The s_inode array in the Super Block contains the numbers of up to *NICNODE* free i-nodes. When a free i-node is needed, the last i-node on the list is taken. If no free i-nodes are in the list, but there are free i-nodes in the system (as evidenced by the s_tinode variable), a new list is constructed by simply reading the actual i_node table sequentially until the free list is full, or there are no more free i_nodes to add.

When i-nodes are freed, the i-node number is put at the end of the s_inode array if there is room. If there is not room, the s_inode array is unchanged.

The i-node structure has the following elements in it, based on the structure found in */usr/include/sys/ino.h*:

Data objects in an i-node

di_mode   File type and security keys. This is a bit array that is described in Figure 3-5. The security keys can be changed with the command *chmod*.

Chapter 3   UNIX File System

Figure 3-5

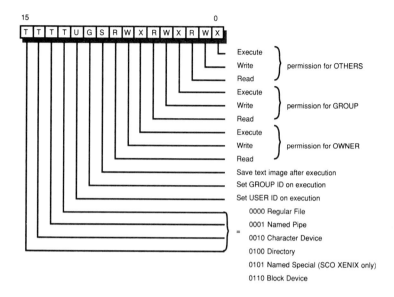

di_nlink	Number of links currently referencing this i-node. If this number is different from the actual number, the file system is in danger of crashing.
di_uid	The owner's User ID number. This number is defined in the file */etc/passwd*. It may be changed with the command *chown*.
di_gid	The owner's Group ID number. This number is defined in the the file */etc/groups*. It may be changed by the command *chgrp*, and is not necessarily the group number that might normally be associated with the User ID number in the previous field.
di_size	The size of the file in bytes.
di_addr	An array of up to 10 block addresses as they are used by the file. See below for how this array is used by files larger than 10 blocks.
di_atime	The date/time the file was last accessed.

di_mtime   The date/time the file was last modified.

di_ctime   The date/time the file status was last changed.

The following is a program that will read and dump the contents of any requested i-node, given the number of the i-node and the file system on which it resides.

```
1 0: /* dumpinode.c - dump the data from an i-node table
2 0*
3 0*     alan deikman 3/89
4 0*
5 0*     This program will take an i-node number and the name of a
6 0*     file system and dump all the data in the file system
7 0*     connected with the i-node.
8 0*
9 0*     Synopsis:
10 0*
11 0*          dumpinode <fs> <inode>
12 0*
13 0*     where <fs> is the device file of a file system and <inode>
14 0*     is an <inode> number.
15 0*
16 0*     */
17 0:
18 0: #include <stdio.h>
19 0: #include <fcntl.h>
20 0: #include <sys/types.h>
21 0: #include <sys/fs/s5param.h>
22 0: #include <sys/fs/s5filsys.h>
23 0: #include <sys/ino.h>
24 0:
25 0: struct   filsys   SB;            /* super block structure */
26 0: struct   dinode   I;             /* i-node structure */
27 0: int      fs;                     /* file system */
28 0: int      inode;                  /* i-node number */
29 0:
30 0: #define SECTOR  512              /* physical sector size */
31 0: int      block;                  /* the size of a block, as controlled
32 0*                                    by the s_type variable in the
33 0*                                    super-block */
34 0: long     iaddr;                  /* the address of the inode */
35 0:
36 0: main(ac, av)
37 0: int      ac;
38 0: char     **av;
39 0: {
40 1:    int i, j;
41 1:
42 1:    /* check arguments */
43 1:
44 1:    if (ac < 3) {
45 2:       fprintf(stderr, "Usage: dumpinode <fs> <inode>\n");
46 2:       exit(0); }
47 1:
48 1:    /* open the file system and get the super-block */
49 1:
50 1:    if ((fs = open(*++av, O_RDONLY)) < 0) {
51 2:       fprintf(stderr, "dumpinode: can't open %s\n", *av);
52 2:       exit(2); }
53 1:    lseek(fs, SECTOR * 1, 0);
54 1:    read(fs, &SB, sizeof(SB));
55 1:    if (SB.s_magic != FsMAGIC) {
56 2:       fprintf(stderr, "dumpinode: %s has a bad magic number\n", *av);
57 2:       exit(2); }
58 1:    if (SB.s_type == 1) block = 512;
59 1:    else                block = 1024;
```

Chapter 3   UNIX File System

```
 60 1:
 61 1:     /* calculate the address of the i-node and read it in */
 62 1:
 63 1:     inode = atoi(*++av);
 64 1:     iaddr = (inode - 1) * sizeof(I);
 65 1:     if (inode < 2 || inode > SB.s_isize * block / sizeof(I)) {
 66 2:     fprintf(stderr, "dumpinode: %d is not a valid inode number\n", inode);
 67 2:        exit(0); }
 68 1:     lseek(fs, (long) SECTOR * 4 + iaddr, 0);
 69 1:     read(fs, &I, sizeof(I));
 70 1:
 71 1:     /* dump i-node data */
 72 1:
 73 1:
 74 1:     printf("*** inode %d\n", inode);
 75 1:     printf("            mode bits: %8o\n", I.di_mode);
 76 1:     printf("      number of links: %8d\n", I.di_nlink);
 77 1:     printf("  owner user ID number: %8d\n", I.di_uid);
 78 1:     printf("  owner group ID number: %8d\n", I.di_gid);
 79 1:     printf("number of bytes in file: %8d\n", I.di_size);
 80 1:     printf("    time last accessed: %8x ", I.di_atime); tstr(I.di_atime);
 81 1:     printf("    time last modified: %8x ", I.di_mtime); tstr(I.di_mtime);
 82 1:     printf("          time created: %8x ", I.di_ctime); tstr(I.di_ctime);
 83 1:
 84 1:     /* print primary disk addresses */
 85 1:
 86 1:     printf("              disk addresses: ");
 87 1:     for (i = j = 0; i < 39; i += 3) {
 88 2:        iaddr = (I.di_addr[i]) | (I.di_addr[i + 1] << 8) | (I.di_addr[i + 2]) << 16;
 89 2:        printf("%7d ", iaddr);
 90 2:        if (++j > 6) {
 91 3:           printf("\n                          : ");
 92 3:           j = 0; } }
 93 1:     printf("\n");
 94 1:
 95 1:     /* done */
 96 1:
 97 1:     close(fs);
 98 1:     exit(0); }
 99 0:
100 0: /* function to print out time in ascii */
101 0:
102 0: #include <time.h>
103 0:
104 0: tstr(t)
105 0: time_t t;
106 0: {
107 1:     struct tm *clock;
108 1:     clock = localtime(&t);
109 1:     printf("%s", asctime(clock));
110 1:     return; }
```

The block array is used to locate the specific blocks in the file. If there are 10 or less blocks in the file, each array element will have a block address within it. If there are more than ten blocks, an "indirect" block is created with the last element of *di_addr*. This block will have, instead of file data, a table of up to an additional 256 block addresses (assuming a 1024-byte per block file system). When that number of block addresses is not enough, the second to last element of *di_addr* is used in a similar fashion. This continues until all the elements of the *di_addr* file are used for indirect blocks. If the number of blocks in a file are more than can be listed in indirect blocks, the file system will support double and triple indirect blocks.

The file system uses the *di_size* variable in the i-node structure to determine how many direct and indirect blocks are used. Note that in accounting for disk space consumed by the file, the indirect blocks must be taken into account.

Links to an i-node

We have seen that an i-node structure contains the number indicating the number of links to that i-node. Recall from the earlier discussion on links that there can be any number of file names within the directory structure that can reference a particular file. We can see this number from the command

```
ls -al /usr/spool/lp
```

which will produce a listing similar to the following:

```
drwxr-xr-x   7 lp     bin      320 Mar 16 06:55 .
drwxrwxr-x   8 root   bin      128 Feb 22 17:46 ..
prw-------   1 lp     bin        0 Mar 16 06:55 FIFO
-r--r--r--   1 lp     bin        4 Mar 16 06:50 SCHEDLOCK
drwxr-xr-x   2 lp     bin       32 Jun  2  1988 class
-rw-r--r--   1 lp     bin        3 Mar 14 14:43 default
drwxr-xr-x   2 lp     bin       80 Mar 15 20:32 interface
-rw-r--r--   1 lp     bin       33 Mar 16 06:55 log
drwxr-xr-x   2 lp     bin       64 Mar 14 14:43 member
drwxr-xr-x   2 lp     bin      240 Jun  2  1988 model
drwxr-xr-x   3 lp     bin       64 Mar 14 14:43 request
-rw-r--r--   1 lp     bin        3 Mar 15 20:43 seqfile
```

This is essentially a tabulated listing of part of the contents of every i-node that has been named in the directory. The first number on each line is the number of links to the i-node, one of which is the file name on the far right of the listing.

Links would not be necessary if everyone was willing to refer to a file by the i-node number only, in which case we could get rid of the whole directory hierarchy. It is unlikely that anyone would be willing to work this way.

Suppose we have an i-node number, and we wanted to find every link to that i-node? One way is with the following program:

```
 1 0: /* findlink.c - find links to i-node
 2 0*
 3 0*    alan deikman 3/89
 4 0*
 5 0*    This program will scan through all the directories in
 6 0*    file systems to find links to a given i-node number.
```

Chapter 3 UNIX File System

```
  7 0*
  8 0*     Synopsis:
  9 0*
 10 0*          findlink [<num> ..]
 11 0*
 12 0*     Where <num> is the desired i-node number.  If no <num>
 13 0*     given, findlink will scan for all possible <inodes>.
 14 0*
 15 0*     */
 16 0:
 17 0: #include <stdio.h>
 18 0: #include <sys/types.h>
 19 0: #include <dirent.h>
 20 0:
 21 0: main(ac, av)
 22 0: int     ac;
 23 0: char    **av;
 24 0: {
 25 1:    int i;
 26 1:    if (ac <= 1)
 27 1:       for (i = 1; i < 100; i++) findlink(i);
 28 1:    else while (--ac) findlink(atoi(*++av));
 29 1:    exit(0); }
 30 0:
 31 0:
 32 0: findlink(inode)
 33 0: int     inode;          /* i-node number to look for */
 34 0: {
 35 1:    printf("** INODE: %5d\n", inode);
 36 1:    scandir("/", inode);
 37 1:    return; }
 38 0:
 39 0:
 40 0: scandir(path, inode)
 41 0: char    *path;          /* directory to search */
 42 0: int     inode;          /* inode number */
 43 0: {
 44 1:    DIR   *dir;          /* current directory stream */
 45 1:    struct dirent *p;    /* current entry */
 46 1:    char  bufr[128];     /* pathname buffer */
 47 1:    short i;
 48 1:
 49 1:    if ((dir = opendir(path)) == NULL) return;
 50 1:
 51 1:    while ((p = readdir(dir)) != NULL) {
 52 2:       strcpy(bufr, path);
 53 2:       strcat(bufr, "/");
 54 2:       strcat(bufr, p->d_name);
 55 2:       if (p->d_ino == inode) printf("    %s\n", bufr + 1);
 56 2:       if (strcmp(p->d_name, ".") && strcmp(p->d_name, ".."))
 57 2:          scandir(bufr, inode); }
 58 1:
 59 1:    closedir(dir); }
```

Note that this program will automatically search all file systems for a given i-node number. There can be potentially one file for each file system. For example:

```
          findlink 32
```

can yield:

```
          ** INODE:    32
              /bin/mv
              /bin/cp
              /bin/ln
```

```
/usr/spool/cron/crontabs/adm
```

In this case the i-node 32 on the root file system has three links, and the i-node 32 on the /usr file system has one.

Free List

The interesting thing about the free list that UNIX uses is that it is a chain of blocks that are allocated out of the same space in which the users files are stored. This is unusual where operating systems in general are concerned. Usually the free block table is a bit-array of a fixed size stored on a reserved area of disk. The UNIX technique is better, for the following reasons:

1. It is fast. More than 95% of the time the file system programs can obtain the number of a free block by simply looking at the last entry in a table.

2. Disk space overhead is reduced. The free list structure does not need a reserved space.

The array *s_free* in the Super Block is a list of up to 49 free blocks. The first block, in *s_free[0]* is also a free block, but it is also the head of a chain of free blocks, each with an additional list of up to 49 free blocks. This chain is illustrated in Figure 3-3. Note that the block at the end of the chain has a zero in the first block address.

Now let's see how this is works. To get a free block, the following logic is used:

1. The free block is *s_free[--s_nfree]*. If that block number is zero, return an error because there are no more free blocks.

2. If *s_nfree* is zero, (it was just decremented in the preceding step), read the data that is in the free block into *s_nfree* and *s_free*. If *s_nfree* is still zero (it shouldn't be) repeat this step.

Simple and elegant! The reverse process is just as easy. To free a block:

1. If *s_nfree* is greater than or equal to NICFREE, copy *s_nfree* and the *s_free* array into the block that was just freed. Then set *s_nfree* to zero.

2. Set *s_free[s_nfree++]* to the block number that was just freed.

The clever thing is that if the free list in the Super Block is full when we want to free a block, the block that is to be freed can be automatically put to use as the head of the chain of free blocks.

Damaged File Systems

It is possible for this data structure to "break down," particularly when the system is shut down without updating the *super block* on the disk with the in-RAM copy. When this happens, the program *fsck* (file system check) is used to repair the damage by taking advantage of the redundancy of information in the file system.

When UNIX is booted certain checks are automatically made to see if the file systems were un-mounted in an orderly fashion. If not, the *fsck* program is run automatically.[13]

A number of error conditions are detected by *fsck*, which will produce a report of the files affected within the file system. What happens, however, when *fsck* detects an i-node that is not referenced by any directory entry? If *fsck* freed the i-node and the blocks associated with it, valuable files could be lost. What *fsck* does do is create a new directory entry in the *lost+found* directory, if any in the file system. The file is named after its i-node number within this directory. It is then up to the user to read this directory if any files have been lost after a system crash.

The *fsck* program operates outside the file system, and does not have the mechanism within it to allocate directory blocks. Therefore, if the *lost+found* directory does not exist, or if there is no spare room within the directory, the file cannot be created.

---

[13] A good description of the checks performed by the fsck program is given in the FSCK Chapter (Chapter 9) in the Microport Runtime System Manual. See also the FSCK(1) article in the Microport Runtime System Manual, and the FSCK(C) article SCO XENIX User's Reference.

4
The UNIX Bourne Shell

In UNIX, the line between the operating system and the "application program's" domain shifted noticeably from more traditional operating systems. This displacement made the core of the UNIX operating system smaller and more modular. What used to be considered "O/S code" has now been implemented in the same environment in which user application programs run.

The most significant of the UNIX O/S modules that are implemented as user-mode programs are those engines that converse directly with the user, passing requests to and from the internal operating system. Note how, as this relationship is diagrammed in Figure 4-1, the interfacing program wraps around the interior as a shell would a crustacean. The shell is the visible exterior of the UNIX the same way an oyster's shell is the visible exterior of that animal. This is how the "shell," the subject of this chapter, got its name.

Figure 4-1

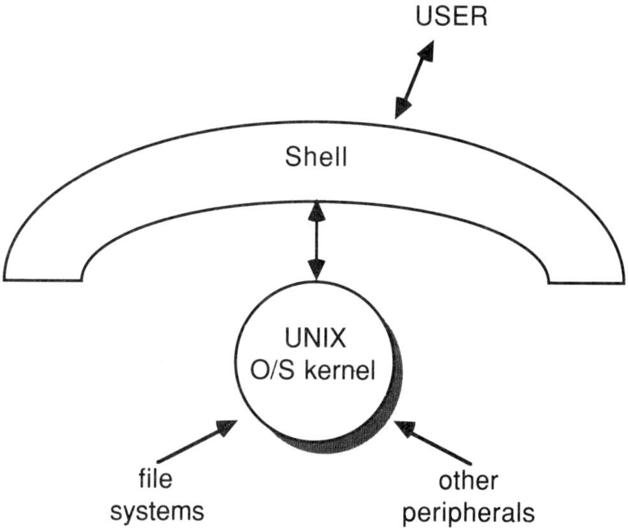

```
                USER
                 ↕
        ┌─────────────────┐
        │      Shell      │
        └───────↕─────────┘
              ╱   ╲
           ┌─────────┐
           │  UNIX   │
           │O/S kernel│
           └─────────┘
            ↗       ↖
         file        other
       systems    peripherals
```

Because the shell in UNIX is implemented as a protected mode user program, great latitude was enjoyed by the original designers and developers of the shell. Among other things, the shells are programmable, placing at the fingertips of the programmer a powerful new tool to use in developing application programs. The subject of shell programming is an extensive one, and far too broad to be completely covered by this chapter. What we will attempt is to get you started with the basics of the shell's theory and programming, leaving to the shell tutorials the simplest use of the shell. Once you have a feel for how the mechanisms work, the UNIX documentation on the shell is much easier to digest.

Since we have a choice of more than one shell, we will cover the Bourne shell[1] in this chapter, and the C shell in the chapter following.

I had resisted learning the programming of the UNIX shells for a long time. At long last, I was engaged in a project that absolutely required programming in Bourne Shell script, so I did learn how to program the UNIX shell, and found out I had been cheating myself all those years. I could have saved myself a lot of time in the past had I known then what I know now.

My resistance to programming in Shell script was born of a programmer's need to "have control" over a programming environment, and a thirst for "elegance" in the structure of the object program. There are a lot of things that you cannot do easily in shell script programs, and many well written shell scripts look, to put it bluntly, ugly, and are hard to read. By way of illustration, look at the following statement, which I use wherever I use a C shell:[2]

---

[1] See article SH(C) (XENIX VRM), SH(1) (Microport RSM), SH(1) (AT&T VRM).

[2] This statement is not really part of a program but a single statement that is put in the .cshrc file. This file is read by the C shell program whenever it is started. The command in the example, changes the interpretation of the cd command whenever it is typed in from that point on, in such a way that it changes the shell prompt each time the cd command is used to include the current working directory. This is similar to the DOS command:

```
PROMPT $P %
```

although DOS does not have the equivalent for the "!" object. See the next chapter on the C shell for more details.

Chapter 4 The UNIX Bourne Shell

```
alias cd 'cd \!* ; set prompt="! `pwd` % "'
```

The syntax and workings, if not the result, of this statement are difficult to explain, unless the reader already has a thorough knowledge of the syntax and parsing elements of the language in question. Without going into that (until later in this chapter) we can make the following observations that point out the problems with readability:

1. The dependence on many different special operators, or "meta-characters," such as the quote pair ('...'), quotes pair ("..."), and the back-quote pair (`...`).

2. The way certain meta-characters change with context so dramatically, such as the exclamation point (!) and asterisk (*).

3. The need for an "escape" character (the backslash).

4. The special significance of arbitrarily named objects, such as "prompt."

We could go on. This is a strong condemnation for a programming language. Any DP manager knows how important it is to be able to hire new programmers to modify old programs. On the other side of that, the sheer power of what you can do in shell programming is seductive. The initiated who know how to write such programs do so not out of perversity, but because of a need to get a job done. There are a lot of features to shell programming that make it attractive. Some of these are:

1. The ability to seemingly effortlessly integrate independently written programs in any language or mixture of languages.

2. Since it is interpreted (rather than compiled), the edit/test/debug cycle is short.

3. The easy accessibility of any feature or facility within the UNIX operating system.

On top of that, there is nothing to stop the professional programmer from writing well documented and organized code. Like it or not, shell programming is here to stay as long as UNIX itself is around. It has been said by more than one expert that to know the Bourne shell completely is to know UNIX completely. If so, we had best do a good job here.

In this chapter we will study the Bourne shell, which was the "original" shell developed with UNIX by Steve R. Bourne. In the following chapter we will look at the C shell, which was developed at UC Berkeley. The C shell shares many concepts with the Bourne shell, so the text which describes the C shell is dependent on the discussion of the Bourne shell which precedes it. If you want to learn about the C shell, I recommend that you read the part about the Bourne shell first.

Bourne Shell Basics

There are a few key concepts that are a prerequisite to understanding shell script commands. At the simplest level, the shell is simply a program into which you type commands when it prompts you. It then translates these commands into some action, whether it alters its RAM image in the system or makes a series of UNIX Operating System calls. Common commands, for example, are:

```
ls -l          (list the directory in long format)
cat food       (type out the file "food")
who            (list current users of the system)
```

In each of these commands, the shell would find an executable file of the same name as each of the commands, create a separate process, and run that program. Figure 4-2 shows the basic flow-chart of shell operation.

Start and initialize: The shell, when it is started, contains certain environment variables and parameters that were given it by the program which started it. These are used to set up the operation of the shell, which may be to take commands from a terminal, or, instead, a file. In addition, a file named *.profile* may be read in according to the rest of the flow chart before any other commands are taken from this source.

Obtain a command: A command is a series of words read in from the terminal or from an input file. The first of these words is taken to be the command name.

Figure 4-2

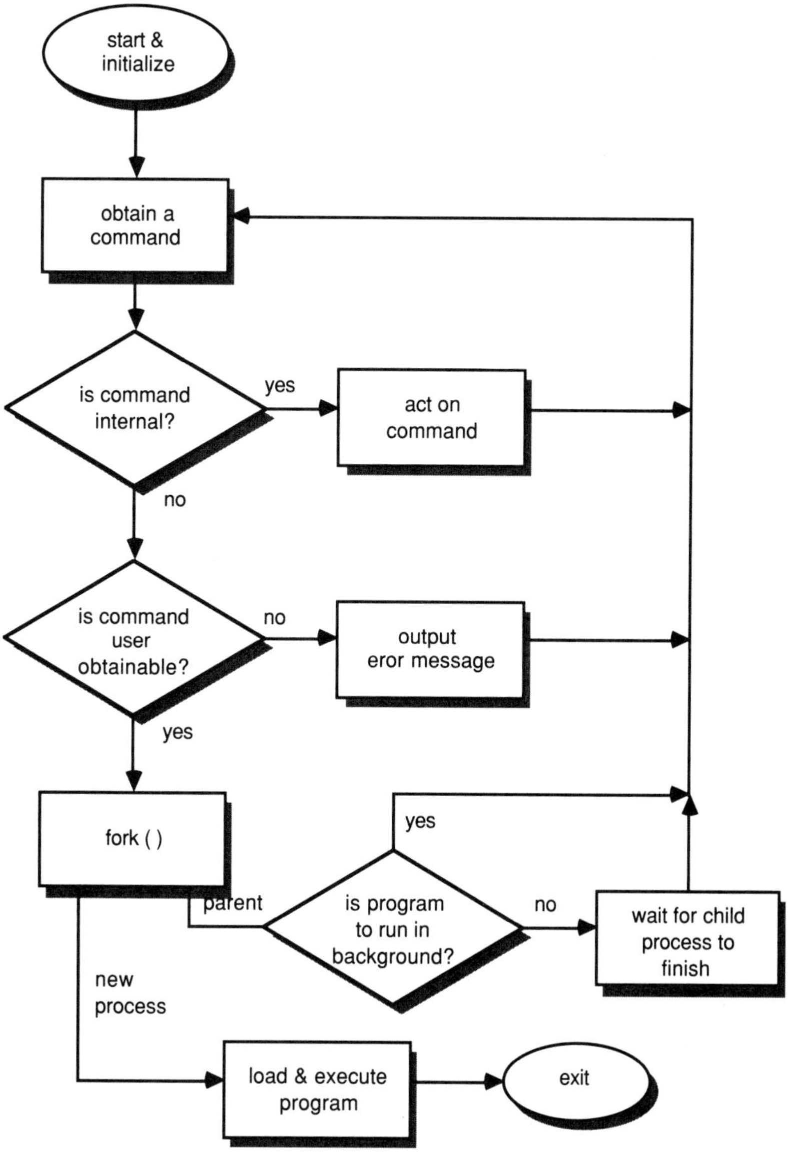
start &
initialize
obtain a
command
is command
internal?
yes
act on
command
no
is command
user
obtainable?
no
output
eror message
yes
fork ( )
yes
parent
is program
to run in
background?
no
wait for child
process to
finish
new
process
load & execute
program
exit

Is command internal? The command name obtained is compared against a list of commands the shell knows.

Act on command: The internal command is acted upon. One of the commands is *exit*, which will cause the shell to terminate. Other commands alter the control flow of a shell script program, and others change a data base of variables the shell keeps.

Is command obtainable? If the command was not internal, the command is assumed to be a file name in one of the directories named in the environment variable PATH. If there is no such file, or if there is a file that is not executable, this test fails.

Output error message. The error message is: "bad command or file name," which is annoyingly cryptic to novice users. However, the meaning is clear: the command is not the name of an internal command, and it is not a file name of a program that can be executed.

fork(): See Chapter 2, Forking, for a description of the fork process. From this point on, two processes are running: the "parent" process and the "child" process.

Is program to run in background? The parent process has the option of continuing processing in this program loop. It will do so, if an ampersand (&) terminated this command.

Wait for child process to finish: If the parent process is to wait, it will execute a *wait()* system call. See Chapter 2 for a discussion of this call.

Load and execute program: In the meantime, the child process, which starts out as a copy of the shell, performs one of the *exec* system calls to overwrite itself with the intended executable program. This new program then proceeds according to its own logic.

Exit: Sooner or later, the program being executed by the child process comes to a halt, voluntarily or not. When it does, and the parent process is still around, a signal is sent to the parent process, which will then finish waiting if that was what it was doing.

The flowchart serves primarily to illustrate the use of the *fork()* system call within the shell to execute, perhaps asynchronously, other programs. One of the things that was left out of the flowchart for simplicity is how the Input/Output is set up for each new process being created.

Shell Prompt

When the shell is being used interactively, (i.e. as a command interpreter), it sends out a "prompt" string each time it is ready for input. Initially, the $ character is used for a normal user and the # character is used for the super-user.

There is also a secondary prompt that appears when the shell is accepting additional lines of input that are necessary before it can execute the commands it has. Normally, the secondary prompt is the > character. The prompts can be changed to anything else the user desires by setting the PS1 and PS2 variables (See the section on shell variables that follows.) Unlike most texts documenting the shell, the *$* or *#* prompt character is omitted from the examples of commands that follow.

Meta-characters

Meta-characters are characters that have a special significance to the shell. The sub-sections of text that follow discuss the use of these characters, but we will start by presenting them all together in the following table:

Character	Name	Normal Use
;	Semi-Colon	Ends a command
&	Ampersand	Signifies background processing, or used with the < or > characters to change their meaning
(	Left paren	Starts enclosure of a list of commands are to be executed by a sub-shell
)	Right Paren	Ends enclosure started by Left paren
|	Pipe	Indicates a pipe
^	Carat	Older version of the pipe character.
<	Less-than	Signifies operation on an input file
>	Greater than	Signifies operation on an output file
\	Back Slash	Quotes the following character

:	Colon	Starts a comment
#	Pound Sign	Starts a comment
"	Double Quotes	Groups a string into a single word
'	Quote	Suspend interpretation of internal string
`	Back quote	Command substitution
$	Dollars sign	Variable (parameter) substitution
(new line)	Newline	Ends a command
(space)	Space	Ends a word
(tab)	Tab	Also ends a word

Any meta-character can be made to stand for itself, i.e. take on no special meaning, by "quoting" it. This is done by preceding it with a back-slash (\) character. This is useful in many ways that will be apparent later, but one that is germane is escaping the *newline* character. Normally a *newline* will terminate a command. However, for a long command we may want to break it up into several lines. This is done by quoting all the *newline* characters involved except the last. For example:

```
cat food furniture toys clothes \
houses books carpets
```

The backslash appears immediately before the *newline* character on the first line. That means that the three final words on the second line are included in the command.

Shell Pipelines

So what is a command? A command is simply a sequence of one or more words separated by "blanks." The first word is always treated as it is in the flowchart above. Blanks are a string of any combination of one or more spaces, tabs, or escaped newline characters.[3]

A "pipeline" is one or more commands, separated by the vertical bar (|) character. Some people make a practice of calling this character a "pipe." The significance of this terminology will be seen shortly.

---

[3] An "escaped new-line" is a *newline* character immediately preceded by a backslash (\). When editing a file, be careful to not allow any spaces or tabs to occur in the line between the backslash and the *newline*. If not, the *newline* character will be taken to be the end of the command, probably resulting in an error.

Figure 4-3 diagrams a process with a "standard input" and a "standard output." There is no rule that a process has to read from standard input or write to standard output (some don't do either), but if they do both they are called and can be used as a "filter." A filter takes an input stream, alters it in some way, and produces an output stream. Filters are fitted together in any combination with pipes, resulting in a pipeline. It is easy to see the mechanical allegory from which these names are derived.

Figure 4-3

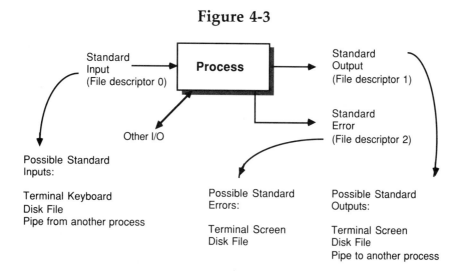

Look at your standard coffee maker. It has a reservoir of tap water, which is fed into the "standard input" of the pipeline. In good coffee makers this is a charcoal filter, which takes water at its input and (hopefully) purifies it to some extent. The output of this filter is connected by a pipe to the next stage: the heating coil. The heating coil is another kind of filter, which takes the water, heats it, and pumps it out the output end, into another pipe. This pipe dumps the water into the filter basket, which contains coffee grounds and a paper filter, the output of which is coffee.[4] The schematic of this mechanism is shown in the top part of Figure 4-4.

We can do the same thing with data. Suppose we have a program that adds a

---

[4] Note that the system that makes coffee relies on other inputs than what appears at the standard input, namely electricity and coffee grounds. Also, we have to empty the filter basket occasionally. The point is not to confuse "standard input" with "sole input" and "standard output" with "sole output."

name to the end of a particular file each time, say, that person calls into the office. People call at random times, so that our list looks like this:

>Ellen
>Ellen
>Connie
>Bernie
>Connie
>Ellen
>Huey

On a busy week, this list can go on for over a hundred entries. How then, can we get a simple alphabetical list of callers' names? With a pipeline like the one shown in the bottom half of Figure 4-4. The construction of the pipeline is simple: the three commands (filters) used are separated by pipe (|) characters. The shell does the work of issuing the *fork* and *pipe* system calls necessary to set up the processes.

The pipeline is one of the basic elements of shell programming.[5] The beauty of this facility is that all the processes are very simple in nature to understand, all run concurrently, and all don't need to have a separate copy of the data. In most other operating systems, this can only be accomplished by running the processes sequentially, thus creating scratch files where we use pipes.[6] In long pipes, this would be disastrous to overall throughput, because the file system would have to read in/read out all the data to the file system for each process. UNIX pipes, on the other hand, are very efficient because a process reading from standard input is merely suspended until data becomes available from the process feeding it from the other end.

---

[5] In Steve R. Bourne's book: The UNIX System, (Addison-Wesley) he gives credit to David McIlroy for the conceptualization of pipes and the development of the shell syntax by which we use them in UNIX today.

[6] In DOS, starting with Version 2.0, there is a little-used (at least as I have been able to observe) pipe facility, which emulates the UNIX pipeline workings by using scratch files.

Chapter 4 The UNIX Bourne Shell

Figure 4-4

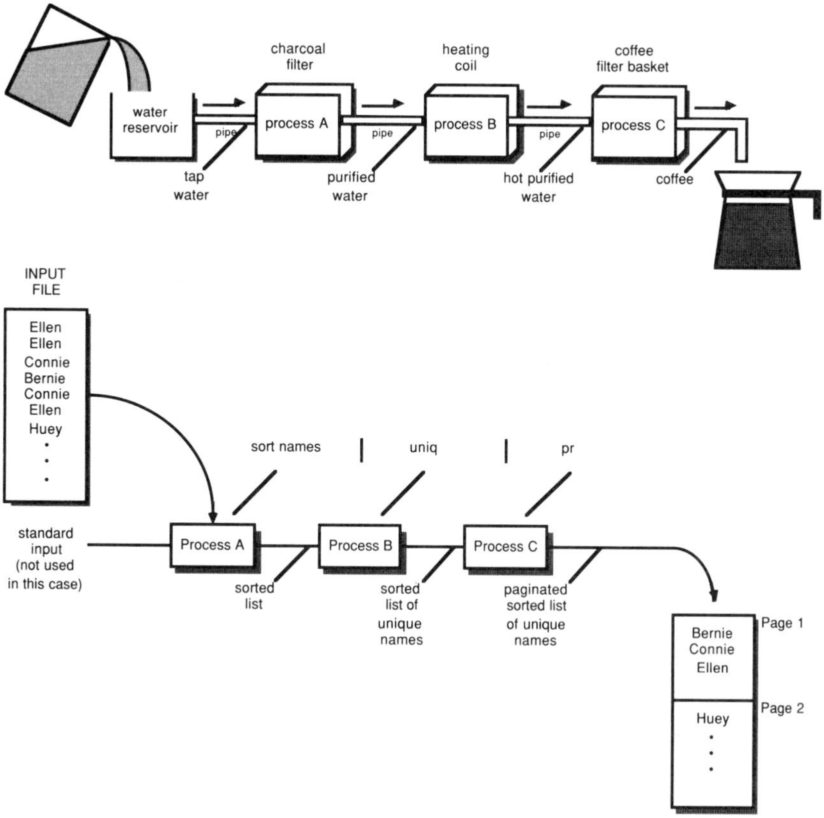

Command Parameters

Each command is supplied with a series of "parameters," which can be used at the option and the manner after the program's design. Most often the parameters are designed to provide the user (or calling shell script program) with options and data which control the program. The *pr* command, for instance, which we used in the preceding example to paginate a data file for printing, can be invoked in a variety of different ways:

```
pr                        to print 66 lines per page,
                          standard header

pr -h "July Listing"      to print with the page header "July
                          Listing"
```

103

```
    pr -d -h "July Listing"      to print with the page header "July
                                 Listing" double spaced

    pr -140 -d                   To print with 40 lines per page,
                                 double spaced
```

and so forth. All the characters on the command line are available to the *pr* program when it runs, arranged for it by the shell as a series of "words." The term "word" is used rather loosely here, because in the example above the string:

```
    July Listing
```

is considered one word because it is surrounded by double quotes. To understand how this mechanism is used by the program we can test it with the following C program:[7]

```
    main(ac, av)
    int   ac;
    char **av;

    {
        int i = 0;
        while (ac--) printf("%3d: %s\n", i++, *(av++));
        exit(0); }
```

This program loops on each parameter that is available to it, and outputs each one on a line by itself. Some examples (assuming the program name is *showit*) are:

---

[7] If this program is in the file *showit.c,* compile this program with the command:

```
    cc showit.c -o showit
```

[8] This is a useful feature in some cases, where the name by which a program is invoked is intended to change its operation. Consider the *ex/vi* editor. These are both the same program, only that it appears twice in the */bin* directory (by use of links). If the user uses an *ex* command, the program starts up in *ex* mode. However, if the user uses the *vi* command, the editor assumes visual mode at the start. (Once the program is started, the mode can be changed with typed in commands.) Another common use of this feature is that library error reporting routines can report the name of the program from which they were invoked.

Chapter 4   The UNIX Bourne Shell

Command	Output
showit one two -x	0: showit 1: one 2: two 3: -x
showit "Hello There" Hi	0: showit 1: Hello There 2: Hi
showit \"Hello There\" Hi	0: showit 1: "Hello 2: There" 3: Hi
showit	0: showit

Notice that the first parameter (the "zeroth") is always the name of the program itself,[8] so the program always has at least one parameter. The following parameters are copied after the shell performs a series of substitutions. These substitutions are:

1. Variable (parameter) substitutions, flagged by the $ meta character

2. Pathname generation characters, as indicated by the *, ?, and [meta characters

3. Command substitutions, generated by the ` (back-quote) meta character.

Each of these substitutions alter the line on which they appear before the shell attempts to execute the command. The result, which can be tested with the program above or the *echo* command, is passed to the program that is run as a series of words.

For "words" to contain blanks, such as the "Hello There" string in the example above, the string has to appear in double quotes. It is also possible to include a *newline* character in a parameter this way. Note that the double quotes do not appear as part of the parameter words. Another effect of the double quotes meta characters is that they will cause the shell to pass through backslash characters as a parameter. This is important to the *echo* command, because it interprets certain characters as commands if they are preceded by a backslash. The \c string will cause *echo* to not output a *newline* when it terminates its output. Writing:

    echo Input your data \c

would be a mistake because the shell will pass the string *c* as the fourth word. Instead we should type:

    echo "Input your data \c"

or

    echo Input your data \\c

To include double quotes in a parameter, they must be quoted:

    showit "\"Hello There\""

as in the example above, or:

    showit '"Hello There"'

which demonstrates the other grouping meta character, the single quote pair (' '). These can appear to be similar to the double-quotes, but are drastically different. Inside the single quote pair, every character is treated as if it were preceded by a backslash. That means no pre-execution operations, such as the variable ($ meta-character) or command substitutions (` meta-character) described later, are recognized in the string between single quotes. You can even have *newline* characters inside a single quote pair: For example:

    awk 'BEGIN { printf "List First Words" }
         { print $1 } ' file

This is actually one command. Because the *newline* at the end of the first line appears before the quote pair is terminated, it is treated as if it had a backslash in front of it. Note also that the *$1* string is not treated by the shell as a parameter reference, because it also is inside the quote pair. This example uses the awk command, which is a powerful report generating tool. awk is discussed in further detail in Chapter 8.

It is a syntax error to have unmatched single or double quotes.

Modifying Input/Output

Filters are useful because their inputs and outputs can be fitted to an arbitrary source and destination. As we have already seen, these sources and destinations can be:

1. a physical device, such as a terminal keyboard or screen,
2. a disk file, or
3. a pipe to or from another program.

The shell makes these connections for you. All you need to do is to supply the correct meta-characters in the proper places. The standard input is connected to the controlling terminal's keyboard and the standard output is connected to the screen by default. So if we type the command:

```
ls
```

which writes to the standard output, it will show up on the screen. For a program that reads from standard input, we would have to type input at the keyboard for it to respond. A trivial example is:

```
cat
```

If you typed this command and nothing else the shell would appear to have crashed. The *cat* command, in fact, has been started and is waiting for input. Anything you type, up to a CONTROL-D key (or whatever the EOF character is set to) will simply be copied to the standard output. Once the EOF is recognized, the *cat* program will terminate, and the shell will prompt for a new input.

We can also connect standard input and standard output (as well as any other input or output) to disk files. This can be done with the Less-than (<) and Greater-than (>) operators. If we type the command:

```
who > group
```

the file *group* would get the output that would otherwise have been sent to the screen. The file is created if necessary, but any previous file named *group* would have been over-written. If we had typed:

```
who >> group
```

then any previous file named *group* would be appended to, instead of overwritten. We could invent a command file that would be executed every half hour which had the two commands:

```
date >> who.history
who  >> who.history
```

When those two commands are executed, the current date and time, then the current list of who is logged in, is appended to the file *who.history*. Standard input is similarly treated, although the issue is somewhat complicated by the fact that most UNIX programs are designed to take parameters that name input files instead of standard input. If we want to sort the file names, for example, we could type either:

```
sort names
```

or the effectively equivalent:

```
sort < names
```

The *sort* program is designed in such a way that it will treat its parameters as file names of files to be input. If it finds no files, it will assume the data to be sorted will appear on the standard input. Which is better? The differences are so subtle as to be not worth mentioning. The first method is preferred where it is available because it is easier to type, and gives the opportunity to name more than one input file. On the other hand, you will eventually come across some filter programs where it is not an option. For those programs you will have to use the Less-than operator.

There is an interesting and useful facility in the shell actuated by the "<<" operator. This causes the shell's standard input starting on the following line to become the standard input of the program that is run. The << operator must be followed by a user invented word, which is used to flag the end of the input. A common use of this is to output screen loads of information with the *cat* program:

```
CLEAR=`tput clear`
DATE="`date`"
cat <<SCREEN
${CLEAR}Customer Data Base Menu                    ${DATE}

    1.  Edit Records
```

```
                    2.  Delete Records
                    3.  List Records
                    4.  Print Customer List

            Enter Option:

            SCREEN
```

The symbol *SCREEN* is an arbitrary name. Note how the *CLEAR* and *DATE* variables are available for reference within the edit stream. The result of the *cat* program is that the screen is cleared, and the menu is put on the screen with the date and time in the upper right hand corner.[9]   If, for some reason, we wish to avoid interpretation of the input,[10] we can quote any character of the word *SCREEN* as follows:

```
            cat <<`SCREEN`
```

A rather awkward (but often used nonetheless) extension of the << operator is to append the minus (-) character to it. This strips all leading tabs off the beginning of the input. I believe this was added to assist in making programs more readable, because the only use use for this I can think of is to allow you to indent the input text in the script by one or more tabs. The above example could look like:

```
            CLEAR=`tput clear`
            DATE="`date`"
            cat <<-SCREEN
                    ${CLEAR}Customer Data Base Menu            ${DATE}

                    1.  Edit Records
                    2.  Delete Records
```

---

[9] We could have placed a command substitution in the input stream as well, placing the string:

```
            `date`
```

inside the text sent to the *cat* program. I tend to avoid this, and use variables instead, because the variables can be used repeatedly without executing and re-executing the *tput* and *date* programs.

[10] The tput command provides a way to obtain CRT screen control strings in a device independent way. tput is documented in the TPUT(C) article in the SCO XENIX User's Reference Manual, and the TPUT(1) article in the Microport Runtime System Manual.

```
            3.   List Records
            4.   Print Customer List

     Enter Option:

     SCREEN
```

so that there is an unbroken column of white space between the *cat* command and the terminating *SCREEN* symbol. The text the *cat* program sees is stripped of any string of leading tab characters. Watch out, though, when editing scripts with *vi* are in auto indent mode. There is a big difference between a leading *space* and a leading *tab* character in this context. Your output may not look like your input, because *vi* will change any string of spaces it can into a tab character.

The Bourne shell gives us the ability to manipulate more than just the standard input and standard output file descriptors. We do this by prepending a digit to the < and > operators. The digit is the number of the file descriptor we wish to re-direct. One use for this is to redirect the standard error on a command so that it will go to a file instead of the screen. For example:

```
     cc blitz.c 2> blitz.err
```

will cause the error messages generated by the C compiler to be sent to the *blitz.err* file, which can then be examined later. I have not seen many examples of redirection of I/O redirection other than standard input, output, and error outside of script programming. Most programs written in C or some other compiled language that want to use other files will tend to open and close the files themselves. However, a script program needs this facility extensively. The file manipulation operators we have seen so far are:

<	Re-direct standard input
>	Re-direct standard output to over-write file
>>	Re-direct standard output to append to a file
<<	Re-direct standard input from following text
n<	Open for input on file descriptor *n*
n>	Open for output (*overwrite*) on file descriptor *n*
n>>	Open for output (*append*) on file descriptor *n*
n<<	Open for input on file descriptor n the text following

There are a few other operators available that we have not yet discussed.

Chapter 4 The UNIX Bourne Shell

These are:

    <&n   associate standard input with file open on file descriptor *n*
    <&-   close standard input
    >&n   associate standard output with file open on file descriptor *n*
    >&-   close standard output
    n<&*m*   associate for input file descriptor n with file descriptor *m*
    n<&-   close file on file descriptor *n*
    n>&*m*   associate for output file descriptor n with file descriptor *m*
    n>&-   close file on file descriptor *n*

In the above, the verb "associate" means "make equivalent," similar to the *dup2* system[11] call.

As shown earlier, standard input and standard output can be redirected to pipes, so that the output of one program is routed into the input of another. There are extensive examples of how to use this facility in the following text on programming the Bourne shell.

Shell Variables

The shell maintains a data base of variables, some of which it sets automatically, and others which have been set user or script commands that it has executed. For the most part, the variables (called "keyword parameters" in the shell documentation) act much like variables in other languages.

The most noteworthy attribute of shell variables is that they are always strings. There are no "numeric type" variables. You can store numbers in variables, and perform calculations on them with the *expr* command described later.

Another thing peculiar to shell syntax that takes some getting used to is that a variable reference looks different from a variable definition. When we set a variable, we use the very ordinary syntax:

---

[11] See articles DUP(2) (Microport SDS Vol. 2), DUP(2) (AT&T PRM), DUP(5) (XENIX PRM).

```
string="This is a String"
word=Thisisaword
number=234
```

Unquoted blanks are taboo when setting variables. If there were a blank before the equals sign, the variable name would be taken to be a command name. A blank after the equals sign causes other problems. A blank inside the string will cause the shell to start a new command. If we write:

```
word=This is a String
```

the shell will attempt to evaluate "is a String" as another command, after assigning the *string This* to the variable *word*. When we reference variables, we write commands that look like:

```
echo The value of string is $string
echo This word $word
expr $number / 10
```

When the shell receives the command line, it scans it for an unquoted dollar sign, and substitutes it with a value before interpreting the command. So our three example commands would return:

```
The value of string is This is a String
This word Thisisaword
23
```

A mistake that is easy to make until you get used to this syntax is writing:

```
count=`expr count + 1`
```

which does not work, because the *expr* program sees the three words "count", "+", and "1". What is needed is the value of the variable *count*, which is only obtained by writing:

```
count=`expr $count + 1`
```

The variable name in a reference can be enclosed in braces ({ }) to remove any ambiguity in the variable name. This is useful when the contents of a variable contain part of a filename we want to generate. If the variable month is set:

```
month="jan"
```

and a script gets to the point where it wants to remove a file ending in "ledger," we can use:

```
rm ${month}ledger
```

to do it. Without the braces the variable name would not be parsable. Note that braces were used an earlier example with the *CLEAR* variable, so that the next byte could show up in the first character position on the screen.

There are a series of other *$* operator variations, which are confusing in appearance, but invaluable when you need them. As for the syntax, well, we can call it strained at best. These variations test the current status of the reference variable, and perform some action if the variable was not previously set or the value was null.[12]

In all cases except the + modifier, if the variable was previously set and non-null, the value of the variable is interpolated as it would be in a simple reference. The + modifier causes the value of word to be interpolated. These modifiers, referencing *var* are:

Reference	Action if *var* not set or null
${var:-word}	Interpolate word
${var:=word}	Set *var* to word and interpolate the value of word
${var:?word}	Print value of word and terminate the shell. If word is null or omitted, output "parameter not set."
${var:+word}	Interpolate nothing

---

[12] By "null" we mean the a string without any characters in it. A variable set by the statement:

```
word=""
```

would be set, but have a *null* value. There are other ways that a variable can be null, most notably with positional parameters, described later.

To add to the fun, the colon (:) character can be omitted if you only want the test to be whether the variable was set or not. The implication in that case is that the *null* value is an acceptable interpolation.

The most obvious application of these forms of reference is to provide some sort of defaulting mechanism for positional parameters, which are described later.

The Environment

As with variables in other languages, shell variables may be considered either "local" or "global" in nature. A *local* variable and its contents are accessible only to the one shell that defined them. *Global* variables can be accessed not only by the currently running shell, but all shells and other programs that are started by the current shell.

Instead of calling these variables "global variables," the shell documentation says the "variable is in the environment" and the collection of all such variables is "the environment."

Many programs, including the shell itself, rely on variables obtained in the environment. A program that uses a CRT and is written to be device independent, such as the *vi* editor, consults the *TERM* environment variable to find out what protocol to use when talking to the terminal. It also looks to see if the environment variable *EXINT* is available, and if it is it executes it as an initialization string.

When a shell is first started, it inherits an environment from its "parent." Any of these variables can be modified by the shell, and subsequently added to the environment with the export command. The environment can be tested in a C program by using the *getenv()* function:

```
char *default = getenv("DEFDIR");
```

which will set the character pointer *default* to point to the value in the environment for variable *DEFDIR*. In the calling shell script, this value can be set up as:

```
DEFDIR=/usr/connie/accounts
export DEFDIR
```

and the invocation of the program can happen any time thereafter. Variables can be taken out of the environment with the *unset* command.

Command Substitutions

Many languages, mostly those that are interpreted rather than compiled, are capable of executing source code that is assembled at execution time. Shell scripts, however, are one of the few that have a primitive operator solely for this purpose. This is the back-quote (`) meta-character.

The string enclosed in a back-quote pair is evaluated as a shell command. Any output generated by that command to the standard output is assembled into a list of words and evaluated as part of the command in which the back-quote pair appeared. We used this before in setting the *CLEAR* and *DATE* variables.

The output within a back-quote pair is usually assembled as a list of words, even if *newline* characters appear within the output. An interesting exception to this shows up in our examples:

```
CLEAR=`tput clear`

DATE=`date`
```

The *date* command, in particular, returns a series of words that might have been equivalent to typing:

```
DATE=Thu Nov 26 16:28:53 PST 1987
```

which would not have worked, because *Nov* should have been taken as the start of a new command. However, this does not happen, and the *DATE* variable is assigned to the entire string.

For the most part, programs that generate lists, one word to a line, can be easily used for generating parameters to a program. A good example of this is the *find* command, which can name files according to certain criteria. We could type

```
rm `find / -user ellen -print`
```

which would remove every file in the system that belonged to the user *ellen*.

Pathname Substitution

Many commands are expected to take a list of file names as parameters. In many cases the list of names the user desires can be expressed as the set or a subset of the files that exist in the file system. Instead of forcing the user to type in each one, possibly using the *ls* command to discover them, the shell can look them up automatically given a "pattern" it can use to match them.

A pattern is a string of one or more characters, one or more of which is special character, matched against a specified set of files. Files that match are included in the command replacement of the pattern in the command string. The special characters are:

*	Matches any string, including the null string.
?	Matches any single non-null character.
[ ]	Matches any one character specified by the string between the braces.

Any character in the pattern that is not one of the above has to match the filenames being accessed. We can easily test any pattern by using the *showit* program described earlier in this chapter, or by the *echo* program which comes with UNIX. Examples of patterns are:

Template	Interpretation
*	All files
*.c	All files ending with ".c"
fool*	All files starting with "fool"
??	All two character file names
cash.???	All files that start with "cash." and end with three more characters
[abc]*	All files that start with either an "a," "b," or "c."
[am-z]???	All four character file names that start with an "a," or any character between "m" and "z" inclusive
[!fo]*	Any file that does not start with an "f" or an "o."

The bracket ([ ]) operator of patterns has been introduced by example. Inside the brackets, a string of characters will cause the bracket set to match one of any of the characters. If we have a series of characters, we can use the notation *a-b* to signify the inclusion of any one of the characters *a* through *b*, inclusive. The ! operator can be used to reverse the sense of the matches. That is [*!ald*] matches any character except "a," "l," or "d."

We will see later how to use patterns within a program script. In interactive command mode, many applications suggest themselves:

Command	Effect
vi *.c	edit (using vi, all the C programs in the current directory
rm *temp	remove every file in the current directory that ends in "temp"
ls -l [A-Z]*	produce a long-format listing of all the files in the current directory that start with a capital letter.

The period (.) character is treated a little differently than other characters in pattern matching by the shell. By a convention maintained by the shell and the *ls* command, files that start with a period (.) are normally considered "hidden" files. These files are normal files, except that they are not intended to be used except under special circumstances. For example, the *.profile* file, which is read by the shell at startup time, would normally only be accessed by the user when it has to be changed. It would be inconvenient to have this file show up inadvertently during routine pattern matches. For this reason files that start with a period at the start of a file name do not match unless it has been explicitly named.

A pattern can be used to search multiple directories as well. For example, if you wanted to look at everyone's *.profile* script, you could type:

```
cd /usr
more */.profile
```

The pattern used in the *more* command would generate a relative pathname for every directory (that the user has search permissions for) which has a *.profile* file in it. *more* would be presented with a list of pathnames on which it would operate.

Asynchronous (Background) Tasks

As shown in the earlier flow chart of the shell (Figure 4-2) the shell need not wait for a program it executes to terminate in order to proceed with the next command. The user selects this mode by terminating the command with an ampersand. When the shell does this, it will output the Process I.D. number of the new process that was thereby created.

The shell also sets the variable *!* to the same process number, allowing a shell script to save that number for use in a later command. You can use a *kill* statement to send a signal to that independently running process. For example:

```
server &              # start a server process
serverpid=$!          # record the process ID of server

#   (do other things)

kill -16 $serverpid # tell the server to do something
```

In the Chapter 2 discussion of signals we saw that the program that spawns one or more child processes can expect to get a signal in return. For this reason the shell keeps a list of the Process I.D. numbers of children it has spawned, so the *wait* command, if issued, knows what it is waiting for.

The user is cautioned to make sure that each program that is to be run in background has its outputs directed to some other destination than the terminal screen. If not, the output will be spewing out on the screen, indifferent to the other conversations going on there. As for input, a program that is run in background without a specific standard input other than the terminal defined will receive an EOF the first time it tries to read something. This will cause most programs to immediately terminate.

Bourne Shell Programming

So far we have touched upon a myriad of features of the Bourne shell, most of which are useful in interactive mode. That is the way the shell is most often used as a command interpreter. We will now turn our attention to the more powerful, complex, and useful side of the shell.

Shell programming is best learned by example, and here we will make an example of the use of each internal statement known to the shell. Along the way we will use a plethora of other commands which have not been introduced. We will do our best to explain them when this happens. Take careful note of the syntax pointers that come up. When a syntax error occurs in a shell script you are attempting to execute, you get a message which is perfunctory at best. About all you can count on is: "you did something wrong about here." Most often it turns out to be a missing semi-colon.

A shell script is necessarily in a disk file, which can be re-read as necessary during iterations of loops and branches. The program may be executed the same as any compiled-language program, by using its file name as the first word of a command. There is no difference between a script file and a regular text file, and they need not be prepared in any special way except as follows:

1. The "execute" mode bit must be set with the *chmod* system call or command.

2. If the Bourne shell script is to be executed from a command entered to a C shell, the first line should have nothing but a colon (:) character in the first position. This is the convention the C shell uses to distinguish C shell scripts from Bourne shell scripts.

To execute the shell script program, all the user does need do is type the name of the file in which the script resides, provided that the file resides in one of the directories on the search path list. The script can also be invoked from inside another script in the same way. Each time the user creates another shell script, the set of commands shell will accept has been increased.

Comments

Any programmer has been lectured about putting comments in programs. In the Bourne shell, we can start a line with a colon (:) or a pound sign (#) to indicate a comment. The comment ends with the next un-quoted *newline* character.

The colon (:) is actually not a comment indicator, but a *NOP* command. It must appear as the first word of a command to be effective. The side effect of the colon is that it will set the status variable, $! to zero. The # metacharacter can appear anywhere on a line.

Positional Parameters

A shell script program can be thought of as a subroutine with parameters. All the words on a command line are copied into "positional parameters," which are then accessible to the shell script. For example, the command:

```
add 15 12
```

will define three positional parameters:

$0	is set to	*add*
$1	is set to	15
$2	is set to	12

This will continue for any number of parameters. If our shell script *add* were:

```
: add two numbers
if test $# != 3; then    # if wrong number of parameters
  echo "Arg count"       # error message
  exit 1; fi             # exit
expr $1 + $2             # calculate two parameters
```

then the output of the above command would be

```
27
```

Note the use of the *$#* object in the *test* statement. This symbol is automatically set by the shell to the number of parameters available to the current shell.

Another object is *$**, (alternately *$@*), which is the same as saying $1 $2 ... for all the parameters that were specified when the shell was invoked or by the last *set* command. This is often handy when it is necessary to call another script or program with all the parameters given to the current script. See the discussion on the shift and set command later in this chapter.

Exit Status Codes

Every command, whether it be a loaded program, another shell script, or an internal shell command, terminates and leaves an "exit status code" that can be interrogated for a variety of purposes. It can be thought of as a return value from a subroutine, although it is limited to one number. The canonical use of the exit status code is to test whether a command executed successfully or not. In most cases a return of non-zero means an error, but in the case of the *read* statement, it may mean that either an error occurred or an EOF was encountered.

Exit status codes can be either implicitly or explicitly referenced. An explicit reference is:

```
mkdir test
echo "mkdir exited with: " $?
```

The *$?* symbol is replaced with the exit status code returned by the last completed command. Note that the *echo* command in our example would over-write this value, because *echo* itself will return an exit status code, which would most probably be zero. Explicit references are rare. Implicit references are done by the *if* and *while* statements, described below.

To write a script that returns an explicit exit status code, use the *exit* command, which can be any number:

```
exit 1
```

This will terminate the shell and return a 1 to the calling program. If your shell script terminates without an *exit* command, the exit status code will be that left by the last command executed. A C program can return an exit status code with the *exit()* function:

```
exit(23);
```

which terminates the C program.

for Statement

The *for* statement can be used to set a loop within a shell script. A control variable is set to successive items in a list and the commands within the loop are executed. There are two basic forms:

```
for name do list done
```

and:

> for *name* in *word* ... do *list* done

The first form sets the variable *name* to each value in the positional parameters, executing the commands in list once each time. This would allow us to make our *add* program more sophisticated, so it would allow any number of parameters. For example:

```
:   add numbers
sum=0

for number do sum="`expr $sum + $number`"; done
echo $sum
```

Now we could type:

```
add 15 2 9 31
```

and get:

```
57
```

The second form of the *for* loop works the same way, but uses a given list of values to set the variable *name* to when executing the commands in list. Most often the list is generated using a pattern.

Suppose all our C programs were written in such a way that the titles were on the first line. We could list all the titles with the program segment:[13]

```
for file in *.c; do
  echo "$file: \c"
  sed 1q $file
done
```

The shell would expand the object *.c into all the file names in the current directory that ended in .c. The result might look like:

```
main.c: /* General ledger main program */
```

---

[13] See article SED(1) (Microport RSM), SED(C) (XENIX VRM), SED(1) (AT&T VRM).

```
recread.c: /* read record routine */
recwrite.c: /* write record routine */
balsht.c: /* Balance sheet generator */
```

Note the use of the semi-colon in the *for* statement. It is necessary for the shell to know that the word *do* is not part of the word list. If we had written, for example:

```
for file in *.c do; do
  echo "$file: \c"
  sed 1q $file
  done
```

the loop would make its last iteration on a file named *do*. If the file *do* did not exist, a diagnostic message would be generated.

case Statement

The *case* statement can be used for selecting a series of program segments under the control of a variable. The general form is:

```
case word in caselist esac
```

where *caselist* is of the form:

```
pattern) list ;;
```

repeated for as many times as desired. Take care with the freewheeling syntax about which I complained at the beginning of the chapter, most notably the unmatched ")" character that terminates pattern, and the *;;* construct that terminates *list*. The control flow of the case statement is best described by example:

```
CLEAR=`tput clear`
cat <<-SCREEN
    ${CLEAR}Basic user options

        1.  who:   list users currently logged on
        2.  df:    list disk free space
        3.  mail:  mail to another user
        4.  exit:  exit shell
```

```
        Enter Option or first letter of command:

SCREEN

read ANSWER
case $ANSWER in

        1|w*)      who ;;
        2|d*)      df  ;;
        3|m*)      echo "Type name of user receive mail"
                   read ANSWER
                   echo "Type your mail"
                   echo "Terminate with a CTRL-D"
                   mail $ANSWER
                   ;;
        4|e*)      exit ;;
        *)         echo "Bad option"
                   exit 1 ;;
        esac
```

When this script executes, the user has the option of typing one of the digits of the menu options, or the first letter of the commands, such as "w," "d," and so forth. After the *case* statement, only the commands after the pattern that matches the value of *$ANSWER* will be executed. The case statement follows these rules:

1. The value of word is compared against each pattern in the order in which they appear. The commands after the first successful match are executed.

2. If control flows into a ;; symbol, the next statement executed is the one after the *esac* word. Note that a "break" statement or its equivalent is not needed as in the switch statement in C.

3. The patterns follow the same rules as the patterns in file name generation, except for the following:

    A. Two or more patterns may be specified, separated by a vertical bar (|).

    B. The period (.) and slash (/) need not be explicitly matched.

The *case* statement is useful, but care must be taken or else even simple scripts become unreadable. It is almost always advisable to limit the number of commands that appear between one pattern and the next.

if statement

The *if* statement in the shell does what *if* statements normally do in most languages, except that the Bourne shell has no operator primitives for doing arithmetic or comparisons. Therefore, the *if* statement is almost always used with the *test* command,[14] which returns a status code according to the test being made.

> The test command is documented separately from the shell, in the TEST(C) article of the *SCO XENIX User's Reference Manual,* and the TEST(1) article of the *Microport Runtime System Manual.*

The general format of the simplest *if* statement is:

    if list then list fi

We can also get more complicated with the form:

    if list then list elif list then list fi

and still worse is:

    if list 1 then list 2 elif list 3 then list 4 else list 5 fi

In each case the structure ends with the *fi* symbol. The *list* structure is simply a series of commands, each terminated by either a semi-colon (;) or a *newline*.

When *list* appears after an *if* or *elif* command, the return status code of the last command executed is tested to control the flow of the program. As we mentioned before, *list* in this case is most often a *test* command. Figure 4-5 shows a flow chart of how the *if* statement controls program flow.

The sub-structure:

    elif list then list

may appear as many times as necessary, although you may have trouble deciphering the resulting code later.

---

[14] See articles TEST(1) (XENIX VRM), TEST(1) (Microport RSM), TEST(1) (AT&T VRM).

Figure 4-5

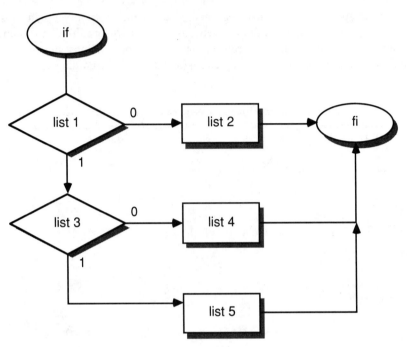

A few examples of the *if* statement are:

```
# test to see if post file is there.  if not ask user
# if we want to create it

if test -r post; then
   echo "post file is not there.  Shall I create it? \c"

   read ANSWER
   if test "$ANSWER" = "y"; then
      echo "Post stream created " `date` > post
      echo "Created post stream"
   else
      echo "Cannot continue"
      exit
   fi
fi
```

Syntax notes: The reason for the double quotes around the reference *$ANSWER* is that if the variable *ANSWER* is set to the *null* string, the *test* program will be sent a word with a *null* string. Otherwise a syntax error occurs. Also, note that because the *then* keyword is placed on the same line as the *test* command, the *test* command had to be terminated with a semi-colon. We could, if we wanted, code the *then* statement on the next line.

Be careful to precisely place the *fi* symbols. In our example above, the *else* statement was bound to the second *if* statement, following the rules C programmers use for such structures. Furthermore, don't forget to include the *fi* symbol for a simple one line *if* statement, such as:

```
if test ! -d temps; mkdir temps; fi
```

which will make the directory *temps* if it does not already exist. If you forget the trailing *fi* you could spend a lot of time debugging before you find the error.

while Statement

As with the *for* statement, the *while* statement can be used to perform iterations of a command list. The *while* statement is a very important feature in the shell language, because there is no "go to" statement or equivalent. Therefore, all iterative processing, including true and nominal infinite loops, is controlled by the *while* statement. The basic form is:

```
while list do list done
```

The coding and usage of each list is exactly the same as with the *if* statement, except that the process is repeated until the non-zero exit status code is returned by the first list.

The *while* command makes its test before evaluating any statements in the second list. Therefore, it is possible that the second list is never executed.

There are many uses for the *while* statement. One is to provide query iterations for user input:

```
while true; do                    # infinite loop
    echo "Input name of file: \c"
```

```
        read FILE
        if ! test -r $FILE; then
            echo "That is not a file I can read"
        else
            echo "Got it"
            break; fi
    done
```

which will repeat infinitely until a user types in a file name of a readable file. Note that the *true* statement always returns a zero exit status code, so that while *true* signifies an infinite loop, the loop is broken out of by the *break* statement.

Other Shell Features and Commands

We have discussed a large segment of the Bourne shell features and commands. Items that we have left out include signals, traps, and a number of the internal commands. A full treatment of all of these would be the subject of an entire volume all by itself. If you are self motivated, however, the foregoing material plus the articles on the shell in the UNIX/XENIX documentation should provide what you need to get started in shell programming.

5
The UNIX C Shell

In the previous chapter we discussed the "original" shell that was developed with UNIX. As with most software products, the Bourne shell left something to be desired in terms of features that were convenient to programmers. Programmers who were using UNIX wanted some additional "easier to use" features and this gave birth to the C shell at Berkeley while Bill Joy was there. The C shell, the vi editor and its by-product, the CRT-control library are considered his most important contributions to the UNIX user routines.

The C shell has many details in common with the Bourne shell, particularly the more conceptually basic meta-characters such as back-slash (\), quote ('), back-quote (`), pipe (|), and the ampersand (&). These all work as they do in the Bourne shell. This is one of the reasons I recommend any user starting with UNIX to learn the Bourne shell first before trying the C shell. The other reason is that there are many Bourne shell scripts delivered with the system[1], and trying to tune or alter them (which is inevitably necessary) as if they were C shell script won't work. In this chapter we will concentrate on some of the more major differences between the C shell and the Bourne shell:

   1. History substitutions.
   2. Alias substitutions.
   3. New syntax for variable substitutions.
   4. New file name expansion operator.
   5. C syntax and different commands.
   6. I/O redirection.
   7. Custom startup files.

There is also a job control facility that was implemented in Berkeley UNIX,

---

[1] Most notably, the /etc/rc file is a Bourne shell script that is executed when the system is first booted. Also, many elements of the line printer spooler that are changeable by the user are Bourne shell scripts.

which is not currently supported with either version of SCO XENIX or Microport UNIX.

The C Shell is documented by the CSH(C) article in the SCO XENIX User's Reference Manual, and the CSH(1) article in the Microport Runtime System Manual. The documentation for the job control facility of the C Shell appears in the Microport Runtime System Manual, with a caveat that it is not currently supported.

Most of these differences were made to accommodate the needs of the programmers who were using the C shell at the time it was developed. The additions make the shell easier to use, and it is the command interpreter of choice for most of those people introduced to it.

History Substitutions

This feature is very quickly appreciated by anyone who has to compose and type long series of commands that cannot be pre-programmed. The C shell remembers the commands that have been typed in and places them in a RAM data base called a "history." The user can refer to any command line currently stored in the history, re-submit it to the C shell, and optionally modify it without retyping the entire line.

Consider the case where you are in an edit/compile/debug cycle. We have to type the commands:

```
vi sub2.c                              # edit subroutine
cc sub2.c -o lexico lexico.o sub1.o    # compile and link
lexico < input > output                # run program
egrep 'date|DATE' output | more        # examine pieces of output
```

Like it or not, in many cases these same four commands might have to be repeated a dozen times before the file *sub2.c* is correct. With the history substitution feature of the C shell, however, we need not go through the work. If the above four commands have been entered, what we would actually have to type is:

```
!v
!c
!l
!e
```

The exclamation point (!) is the meta-character that invokes history substitutions. Typing:

```
!c
```

for example, is the same thing as saying, "re-submit the last command that began with the string c," which in this case means the last *cc* command. In the general case, *c* can be a multi-character string if necessary. This would be the case if our history was:

```
vi sub2.c                            # edit subroutine
cc sub2.c -o lexico lexico.o sub1.o  # compile and link
lexico < input > output              # run program
cat output                           # examine output
```

In this case, the *!c* string would re-submit the *cat* command. The user can access the *cc* command by typing:

```
!cc
```

Another way of accessing past *history* commands is by their "event number," which is a unique number assigned to each command line sequentially starting from 1. You can see all the command lines that are in the history and their event numbers by using the *history* command. For example, if the *history* command output:

```
25   vi unhook.c
26   rm *.o
27   make comsys
28   who
29   comsys &
30   ps -f
```

If we wanted to repeat the *vi* command we could type:

```
!v
```

or:

```
!25
```

which would be the same thing. Incidentally, the *history* command is useful

131

to verify past commands that have been typed in. I have in the past made errors in typing a series of complicated *mv* commands, and had files not end up where I expected them. The situation can often be reconstructed by looking through the command line history.

Another way of obtaining the event number is by modifying the *prompt* variable to include the exclamation point (!) meta-character in the *prompt* string. The C shell substitutes this character with the event number each time the *prompt* string is output. A most common form of this is:

```
set prompt="! % "
```

which will cause the C shell to prompt the user as follows:

```
25 %
```

where the "25" is replaced by the actual event number of the command line about to be typed.

Note that each command line is entered into the history before any substitutions are made. When they are re-submitted, the expansions are made again. For example, in the command series:

```
set x=square
echo fair and $x
set x=circular
!echo
```

The first *echo* command will output "fair and square," where the second *echo* command, even though it was a copy of the first one, would output "fair and circular."

The foregoing is the most trivial use of the history substitution feature of the C shell. By itself, it can save hours of typing time, and indeed many users of the C shell never use any further refinements of this facility. However, for those who want to get really elegant, it is possible to modify history substitutions to obtain greater conveniences. A thorough study of these modifiers could be covered in a chapter of this volume all by itself. To avoid that, we will describe some of the more useful, albeit mundane, applications.

The formulas that most often appear are:

Chapter 5 The UNIX C Shell

- Repeat the previous command. This can be done simply by typing:

    !!

    and the previous command will be repeated.

- Fix a substring in the previous command. Usually this is done just after the user receives an error message from a long command line. For example, if the command was typed as:

    ```
    echo We the peeple of the United States
    ```

    obviously we need to correct the misspelling. This can be done quickly by typing

    ```
    ^ee^eo^
    ```

    which would result in the "ee" being replaced by "eo," making the command correct. This is a special case of the history substitution command, and can be applied to any part of the command line being corrected.

- Type a new command with all the parameters the same as previous. For example, if we have a doubt about a complicated set of pathname substitutions, we can first test them by using the *ls* command:

    ```
    ls *.tmp ????xxx core
    ```

    which would list out all the file names that match the patterns given. We can then remove all the files listed by typing:

    ```
    rm !*
    ```

    which would copy all the parameters of the *ls* command and feed them to the *rm* command.

- Type a new command with the last parameter the same as previous. The above principle is sometimes convenient with only the last parameter. If for example we wanted to remove only the *core* file, we could type:

```
        rm !$
```

which is handy when the last parameter is difficult to type.

- Add a parameter to the previous command and run it again. Sometimes a parameter is forgotten. If the command

```
        cc -o main robot.c disk.c sub1.o sub2.o
```

produced a disk error because we forgot the object file *shoot.o*, we can quickly resubmit the corrected *cc* command by typing

```
        !! shoot.o
```

because *!!* will be expanded to the previous command.

The C shell provides a series of extension operators that can alter history substitutions. These are separated by a colon (:) from the ! operator and its event specifier, except that the colon is not necessary in the case were the extension begins with $, ^, *, 0, or %. Briefly, these are

0 - *n*	Word zero (command word) through word *n*
^	Synonymous with 1
$	The last argument of the event (see example above)
%	Matched word, which contains *s* in preceding specifier *?s?*
n-m	Word *n* through *m*
-*y*	Abbreviates *0-y*
*****	Same as *1-$* (see example above)
n*	Same as *n-$*
n-	Same as *n** except that the last word is omitted

All of the above operators select a specific word or series of words. There are further operators that can be applied to make certain alterations to the words that were selected. These further modifiers, also preceded by a colon (:), are

h	Removes trailing pathname component. For example, */usr/lib/libc.a* becomes

	/usr/lib/.
r	Removes trailing .* component. For example, *robot.c* becomes *robot*.
s/*a*/*b*/	Substitute *b* for *a*.
t	Removes all leading pathname components. This would obtain *libc.a* out of the pathname /usr/lib/libc.a.
&	Repeats the previous substitution.
g	Makes global changes.
p	Print command without executing.
q	Quotes words, which prevents pathname substitutions. For example, if an argument had a pattern character in it we could prevent pathname substitutions with this.
x	Will break up a quoted word into multiple words at the normal separation spaces.

Many of these operators seem to be too complex to be convenient in many cases. Most users would simply prefer to retype a command rather than go through the work of figuring out what strange sequence of characters made out of the above will correct the command. Besides, it often works out that correcting a command will turn out to be more typing than simply re-typing it. However, there are applications in certain programming sequences that are useful because the above operators work on other types of substitutions as well. For example, if we wanted to rename all the files that end in *.h* to *.c*, we can use the following:

```
foreach file (*.h)
    mv $file ${file:r}.c
    end
```

which is a case where the *:r* operator is applied to a variable name substitution.

The size of the history data base is controlled by the special variable *history*. If this value is not set to any number, no history data base is kept. Otherwise, the number of lines kept is the number which is assigned to the variable. Normally the history variable is set in the *.cshrc* file, described later.

Alias Substitutions

Another convenience feature of the C shell are alias substitutions. These allow very personalized customizations of the commands that can be typed into the C shell. Most often, *alias* commands are found in the *.cshrc* file that is executed by the C shell when it is started. The use of this feature from user to user can range from the very ordinary to the extremely obscure.

Basically, the user can invent new commands that are handled internally to the C shell, where the new command will be aliased, or made equivalent to, any other arbitrary string. Each time the new command is typed, the string is substituted and further processing by the C shell proceeds normally. A simple example that is often seen is:

```
alias ll ls -l
```

After this command has been processed by the C shell, any time the user types

```
ll
```

the full command *ls -l* is executed. The alias facility allows the user to make up his own commands that will be most convenient. A long-time DOS user, for example, might use the *alias* set:

```
alias dir ls -l
alias type cat
alias del rm
alias copy cp
alias edlin ed
alias ws vi
```

which might make life easier.

There are more advanced applications of the *alias* command. The example given at the beginning of Chapter 4 is one that I use habitually on every UNIX system I use:

```
alias cd 'cd \!* ; set prompt="! `pwd` % "'
```

This has the effect of causing the commonly used "change directory" command, *cd*, not only to change the current working directory, but to change the *prompt* variable to match. This helps a lot, particularly when four or more screens are in use and I am flipping between them. This example shows the use of the history substitution mechanism in use during aliasing. When I type:

```
cd /usr/tmp
```

with the above alias in effect, the string "\!*" is replaced with all the parameters in the *cd* command, the same as if the typed-in *cd* command was the previous command. Any of the history substitution operators can be used. Note that the back-slash character was necessary to prevent history substitution in the *alias* command when it was entered. Also, alias substitutions do not nest. If they did the above example would recursively loop, ultimately causing a stack error.

An alias can be removed with the *unalias* command, although I have rarely seen this done. Most of the time *alias* commands are confined to the *.cshrc* file, and are forgotten as soon as the C shell exits.

New Syntax for Variable Substitutions

C shell variables differ from Bourne shell variables in three ways:

1. Variables are set with the *set*, *@*, or *setenv* commands.
2. It is possible to have arrays named by a single variable.
3. New arithmetic, comparison, and testing operators have been defined.

The *set* and @ commands are used to create and reset variables to specific values in the C shell. The *set* command syntax is:

```
set
set name
set name=word
set name[index]=word
set name=(wordlist)
```

Just typing *set* by itself will cause a complete list of currently set variables to be displayed. The second form, which sets the variable *name* to the *null* string, is useful for signaling certain options to the C shell and other programs. For example, entering the command:

```
set noclobber
```

will cause the variable *noclobber* to be created, which the C shell takes as a signal to ask the user before wiping out any files implicitly with I/O redirection.

Arrays are possible with the final two forms of the *set* command. If we have a declaration:

```
set progs=(abc.c bgm.c arf.c)
```

the *progs* variable has three elements that can be referenced as follows:

```
$progs[1] $progs[2] $progs[3]
```

and you can change one of the words without altering the others by using the *set* command as follows:

```
set progs[2]=max.c
```

A special form of the variable *reference* will yield the number of words in the array stored in the variable, rather than the variable itself. This is:

```
$#name       or    ${#name}
```

Additionally, the existence of a variable can be sensed (without generating an error) by using:

```
$?name       or    ${?name}
```

which will result with a 1 value if the name is defined, 0 if it is not. The array facility of the C shell was created in such a way as to be consistent with the way that arguments are passed and used in C shell script files. Unlike the Bourne shell, which has special forms of the $ meta-character operator to access the parameters of the currently running shell script, the C shell simply uses the special variable *argv* for that purpose. For convenience, however, the C shell accepts the reference *$n* or *${n}* as equivalent to *argv[n]*, and *$** is the same as *$argv[*]*.

For setting specific values, the third form above of the *set* command can be used. If the value must contain blanks, tabs, or newlines, in the Bourne shell, we can set environment variables in the following fashion:

```
SOURCE=/usr/alan/source/tools
export SOURCE
```

The equivalent in the C shell is:

```
setenv SOURCE /usr/alan/source/tools
```

From the point of view of the called program, there is no difference. Note that for some reason there is no = character used in the *setenv* command. This may take some getting used to.

New Filename Expansion Operators

In addition to the *?*, ***, and *[]* meta-characters, the C shell also provides the *{}* and *~* meta-characters for file name substitutions. Actually, these new meta-characters are best thought of as "pattern generators," because the resulting words they produce are not dependent on the directory entries in the file system.

The meta character *~* is a shorthand for referring to the user's home directory as currently set in the variable *home*. This is mostly a convenience to those users who have to change their current working directories to other places and still use the files in their home directory fairly often.

To generate repetitious patterns, we can use the *{}* pair. The construct:

```
x{a1,a2,...,an}y
```

expands to:

```
xa1y xa2y ... xany
```

In practical application, say that you wanted to examine two files, *temp1* and *temp2* in a remote directory. You could type:

```
more /usr/tmp/temp1 /usr/tmp/temp2
```

but:

```
more /usr/tmp/temp{1,2}
```

would be easier. The *{}* meta-characters can be nested, with either themselves or other file name pattern matching characters.

C Syntax and Different Commands

The area in which the C shell differs most from the Bourne shell is in the area of new commands and operators. The Bourne shell relies on the *test* command and the *expr* commands to control the actions of the *if* and *while* commands. In the C shell there are primitives supported that handle these functions. For the most part these were designed in such a way that C programmers would be comfortable with them, although there are several that do not appear in C. The operators, in order of increasing precedence, are:

==	Test equality
!=	Test inequality
=~	Test against pattern match
!~	Test against pattern not matching
<=	Test less than or equal
>=	Test greater than or equal
>	Test greater than
<	Test less than
<<	Binary shift left
>>	Binary shift right
+	Add
-	Subtract
*	Multiply
/	Divide
%	Modulo
( )	Evaluation precedence

The equality and pattern matching testing assume their operands are strings, not numeric values. When comparing two numbers this will not be a problem as long as literals do not have leading zeroes and the values being compared are the results of expressions. The syntax of using these operators with variables takes some getting used to, particularly if you switch back and forth from C shell script to other high level languages. For example, it is easy to write:

```
@ count = count + 1
```

which generates an error, and what was really meant was:

```
@ count = $count + 1
```

The @ command is a special version of the *set* command that will parse and execute an expression and place the result in a variable. The other commands that will take an expression are *if*, *while*, and *exit* commands. Note that spaces are mandatory separators between operators and operands in C shell syntax.

It is interesting to note that both the SCO XENIX and the Microport articles on the C Shell say that literals starting with a zero (0) will be considered octal numbers. However, experimentation shows otherwise. The statements:

```
@ val = 0377 + 1
echo $val
```

yields a result of 378, rather than 256, which would be correct if 0377 was an octal number. This feature was probably so little used that nobody has bothered to report or correct the problem.

The parentheses operator has an extra application other than the usual altering of the order of evaluation in expressions. Some of the operators above have double meanings. For example, the >> operator means "right shift" in expressions, and as a C shell meta-character it means "redirect standard output (append mode)." Parentheses can be used to resolve the ambiguity. The statement

```
@ val = 300 >> 1
```

will assign the value 300 to *val*, and create (or append to) a file named 1 the output of the statement (which will be nothing). However, if we use:

```
@ val = (300 >> 1)
```

the variable *val* will receive the value 150. Note that the parentheses characters are exempt from the rule that operators must be surrounded by spaces.

Another operator that is available is the braces ({ }) pair, which allows certain test results to be used as an operator in an expression. The following forms are available:

Expression	Returns 1 (true)
{ -r name }	if shell has read access to file *name*
{ -w name }	if shell has write access to file *name*
{ -x name }	if shell has execute access to file *name*
{ -e name }	if file exists (assumes that the shell has search permission into each element of pathname)
{ -o name }	if owner of file is the same as the effective user I.D. of the shell
{ -f name }	if file is a disk file (as opposed to a directory or a special file)
{ -z name }	if file is zero length
{ -d name }	if file is a directory

In each of the above, *name* can be either a relative or absolute pathname, and the result of the expression is zero (0) if the test is not true, or if the file does not exist. Unfortunately, not all of the tests that are available with the test command have been implemented. However, another form of the { } operator is to allow the return status code of a command to be used as a true-or-false operator in an expression. This is of the syntax:

```
{ command }
```

where *command* is a series of words taken as a shell command, executed as such, and if the resulting exit status code zero (successful) a value of 1 is interpolated, zero otherwise. This is akin to the use of functions in other languages, except that only a zero or one value can be returned, and can be used to supplement the logical tests that are already supported by the C shell.

Be careful to note the difference between the braces ({ }) operator and the back-quotes (` `) meta-characters. The braces interpolate the exit status of the command into a 0 or 1. Consider the following program:

```
main() {
  printf("22");
  exit(5); }
```

If this program is compiled into the file *test1*, the expression:

```
@ x = { test1 }
```

will set the variable *x* to the value of zero (0), because *test1* returned a "failure" exit status code. The statement:

```
@ x = `test1`
```

will set *x* to the value 22. On the other hand, we can use:

```
test1 > /dev/null
@ x = $status
```

to set the variable *x* to 5, the real value of the exit status of *test1*.

C-like Syntax

Ostensibly, the C shell gets its name because it is closer to C in its command and structure rules, and the operators that are available. The other area of similarity is the names of the structured statements that are provided. However, the syntax of these statements is somewhat compromised. For example, in the general form of the *if* statement

```
if (expr1) then
    ...
else if (expr2) then
    ...
else
    ...
endif
```

and the *while* statement:

```
while (expr)
    ...
end
```

we can see that the keywords *then*, *endif*, and *end* take the place where braces ({ }) would be in the C language equivalents. This does not pose much of a problem, but care must be taken to use the proper keywords when coding a C shell script.

I/O Redirection

I/O redirection is the one area where I distinctly prefer the Bourne shell to the C shell. The C shell does not give operators for handling more than three file descriptors: standard input, standard output, and standard error. What's more is that when standard error (file descriptor 2) is re-routed, it is re-routed along with standard output.

The meta-characters supported for I/O redirection in the C shell are:

<*name*	Take standard input from *name*
<<*word*	Take standard input from shell input until line containing only *word* is reached
>*name*	Redirect standard output to *name*, erasing any previous file
>!*name*	Same as >*name* except that the variable *noclobber* is ignored
>&*name*	Redirect standard output and standard error to *name*, erasing any previous file
>&!*name*	Same as >&*name* except that the variable *noclobber* is ignored
>>*name*	Redirect standard output to *name*, appending to any existing file
>>!*name*	Same as >>*name* except that an error condition occurs and the file *name* does not exist
>>&*name*	Same as >>*name* except that standard error is also redirected
>>&!*name*	Same as >>!*name* except that standard error is also redirected
|	Pipe standard output to following command
|&	Pipe both standard output and standard error to following command

where *name* can be any valid relative or absolute pathname. Note that the variable *noclobber* can be set to make sure that no target file can inadvertently erased unless the ! meta-character is included.

One of the shortcomings of the C shell version of the I/O redirection as opposed to the Bourne shell method is that the C shell cannot be easily made to open another input file descriptor and read lines from it. For example, in the Bourne shell we can write:

```
exec 3< ifile
while read LINE <&3; do
  echo here is $LINE
done
```

which will read each input line in *ifile* and output them one-by-one. I have not found an easy way to do the same thing in the C shell. Also, in a case where we want to separate the standard output to one place and the standard error to another, we can write in the Bourne shell:

```
lexicon > lex.out 2> lex.err
```

in the C shell we have to type:

```
(lexicon > lex.out) >& lex.err
```

which actually invokes one more process (commands in parentheses are executed in a sub-shell) than does the Bourne shell version.

Custom Startup Files

Normally, when a C shell is invoked it checks for a file named *.cshrc* in its home directory (as indicated by the environment variable home) and reads that file as a C shell script. In addition, if the shell was started by the system login process, the file *.login* is executed first. These files allow user-specific customizations of the shells.

The *.login* file usually has commands used to set up the user's terminal correctly, check for mail, and other "login time" duties. The *.cshrc* often has all the alias and environment variable settings the user wishes. These files are normally set up with default files by the programs that SCO XENIX and Microport use to create new users.

6
Shell Programming Example

Now that we have looked at the UNIX shells and the *awk* programming language, we can develop a sample program in shell script. We can use this sample program as a basis of experimentation and extension to learn other ways of using shell script to solve programming problems.

When we program in C, Pascal, or other structured languages that are more closely tied with VonNeumann-type computers, we tend to think of microscopic loops and individual memory locations. In shell script we get away from that and think in terms of *streams* or *pipelines* of data. Our ability to do so seems to set our degree of success in shell programming. An example of this is that we can code a loop such as:

```
exec 4< atemp
i=0
while read LINE <&4; do
    i=`expr $i + 1`
    echo "${i}: $LINE" > atemp1
    done
exec 4<
```

This shell script segment will read lines from the file *atemp* and output them to the file *atemp1* with a line number at the beginning. Although this works, it is much more complicated than necessary. More than that, it is slow because the source-code lines are interpreted, once each time around the *while* loop. It is much better to code the line:

```
pr -t -n atemp > atemp1
```

which will do the same thing, but much faster.

The key is in how to use the standard filters, such as *cat*, *pr*, *awk*, *sort,* and others as provided as part of the UNIX */bin* and */usr/bin* directory. In a pinch we can implement our own filters for a special function in C, but it is endlessly surprising to see the things that can be done with just the standard set.

The following shell script programs show only a few inches of the miles you can travel with them. We chose the Bourne shell to write these programs, although it would not be difficult to convert these programs to the C shell if desired. With shell script, the hard part is getting started, and these examples suggest one way to formulate your own program.

Simple Bookkeeping Program

Our test program is a simple bookkeeping application, which maintains a data base of customers and respective ledger files. Each customer has two files in the current directory, of the names:

<number>.act   Account file containing name and address of the customer referenced by *<number>*.

<number>.lg   The ledger file associated with customer associated with *<number>*.

The symbol *<number>* can be any string that makes a legal file name in the UNIX file system. Many bookkeeping systems require the user to adopt a numeric-only identifier. Here the user can adopt any convention she wants.

In the *.act* file we will have one line for the full name of the customer, and up to three lines for address information. The *.lgr* file will have accounting records, one line for each transaction of the form:

```
<date>\t<description>\t<debit>\t<credit>
```

These are four fields separated by TAB characters. Any information can go into these fields (except the TAB character itself), although it is expected that the user will have to enter proper information. This is one improvement in our program that suggests itself, because most bookkeeping programs will enforce formatting rules on input data.

Although we could implement a series of commands that can be typed in at the shell prompt, we can make it easier for the user by presenting a menu. The bookkeeping program can be started by changing to the current directory and typing the command *menu* at the prompt. This file contains the following script:

```
1   #  menu - main menu for customer billing program
2   #
3   #  alan deikman 3/89
4   #
5   #  Set up useful variables
6   #
7   CLEAR=`tput clear`
8   BLINK=`tput blink`
9   NORMAL=`tput sgr0`
10  export CLEAR
11  export BLINK
12  export NORMAL
13  #
14  #  Output main menu until user quits
15  #
16  while true; do
17  cat <<SCREEN
18  ${CLEAR}DEMO PROGRAM FOR CUSTOMER BILLING
19
20
21                MAIN MENU
22
23          0.  Quit
24          1.  Edit a customer data file
25          2.  Post a charge/debit item
26          3.  Post a payment/credit item
27          4.  Print a statement
28          5.  Find an account given a search key
29          6.  Print ledger
30          7.  List accounts with non-zero balance
31
32
33  SCREEN
34  #
35  #  Get user's option
36  #
37  echo "          Enter Option: \c"
38  read OPTION COMMENT
39  #
40  #  if user decided to quit, do so
41  #
42  if test 0 = "${OPTION}"; then
43     echo Bye!
44     exit
45     fi
46  #
47  #  see if the user entered a legal command.  if so,
```

```
48    #  execute it
49    #
50    if test -x ${OPTION}.cmd; then
51       ${OPTION}.cmd
52    else
53       echo "\n\n\0007${OPTION} is ${BLINK}not${NORMAL} an option!"
54       echo "Press ENTER to continue"
55       read COMMENT
56       fi
57    #
58    #  send out menu again
59    #
60    done
```

The first thing this program does is set up some handy environment variables used to manipulate the screen. The statement:

```
CLEAR=`tput clear`
export CLEAR
```

allows the following programs to clear the screen by outputting the symbol *${CLEAR}* instead of invoking the *tput* program over and over again.

The next agenda item for the *menu* program is to output an option menu screen and get a response from the user. This should be a digit from 0 to 7. If the input is 0, the program exits. Otherwise, it checks for the existence of a file that has execute permission of the form *${OPTION}.cmd*. If the test is true, the program therein is executed, otherwise we generate an error message.

In most cases where we want a single word input from the user, we use the command

```
read OPTION COMMENT
```

The reason for two variables is that in the event the user accidentally types extra input, that input will be absorbed in the COMMENT variable, and not interfere with the evaluation of the variable OPTION.

This scheme makes it very easy to add commands to our menu. All we have to do is add a line to the menu itself, and create a corresponding *?.cmd* file with the program in it. Note that this program need not even be shell script if we wanted to use a compiled language instead.

Edit Customers

The first order of business for the user will be to create and modify customer *.act* files. This is easily done with the *1.cmd* program:

```
1    # 1.cmd - Edit a customer
2    #
3    #  Loop until a customer is edited or the user
4    #  quits
5    #
6    while true; do
7    cat <<SCREEN
8    ${CLEAR}DEMO PROGRAM FOR CUSTOMER BILLING
9
10
11                      EDIT CUSTOMER
12
13   SCREEN
14   #
15   #  Get user's input
16   #
17   echo "  Enter Customer Number or blank line to quit: \c"
18   read OPTION COMMENT
19   #
20   #  if user decided to quit, do so
21   #
22   if test "" = "${OPTION}"; then
23     exit
24     fi
25   #
26   #  see if the user entered an existing customer
27   #
28   CFILE=${OPTION}.act
29   if test -r ${CFILE}; then
30     echo "\n\n"
31     cat $CFILE
32     echo "\n\nIs this the customer you wanted? \c"
33     read OPTION COMMENT
34     if test "$OPTION" = y; then
35       vi ${CFILE}
36       fi
37     fi
38   #
39   #  If this customer does not exist, ask if we want to make a new one
40   #
41   if test ! -r ${CFILE}; then
42     echo "\n\n${OPTION} not found.  \c"
43     echo "Do you want to make this a new customer?  \c"
44     read OPTION COMMENT
45     if test "$OPTION" = y; then
```

```
46         echo "\n\n"
47         echo "  Enter full name of customer: \c"
48         read COMMENT
49         echo $COMMENT > $CFILE
50         echo " Enter street address line #1: \c"
51         read COMMENT
52         echo $COMMENT >> $CFILE
53         echo " Enter street address line #2: \c"
54         read COMMENT
55         echo $COMMENT >> $CFILE
56         echo " Enter street address line #3: \c"
57         read COMMENT
58         echo $COMMENT >> $CFILE
59         fi
60      fi
61   #
62   #   send out question again
63   #
64   done
```

This program gets input from the user and creates a variable called *CFILE* out of it that should be the name of the *.act* program. If that file exists, we output the contents of the file to verify whether this is the desired customer. If so, we will invoke the *vi* editor, letting the user edit the file as needed. Otherwise we make sure that the user wants to create this account, and input the needed fields.

This is a cheap way out of creating and editing data base files. In a real application we could code a program that would display a form on the screen and make sure that the application convention was being followed by the user. Nonetheless, this program will effectively maintain any list of customers.

Posting Debit/Credit Items

Once we have accounts established, we need to be able to place charges and payments in their *.lgr* files. This is done with menu options #2 and #3, which are very similar. The main difference is that a credit shows up in the fourth data-base field, and a debit is placed in the third data-base field. Accountants prefer to deal with positive numbers only, and this arrangement allows the distinction between a negative credit and a positive debit.

The debit item program is:

Chapter 6 Shell Programming Example

```
1    # 2.cmd - Post a debit Item
2    #
3    #  Loop until a user quits
4    #
5    while true; do
6    cat <<SCREEN
7    ${CLEAR}DEMO PROGRAM FOR CUSTOMER BILLING
8
9
10                     Enter Charges/Debit Items
11
12   SCREEN
13   #
14   #  Get user's input
15   #
16   echo "  Enter Customer Number or blank line to quit: \c"
17   read OPTION COMMENT
18   #
19   #  if user decided to quit, do so
20   #
21   if test "" = "${OPTION}"; then
22     exit
23     fi
24   #
25   #  see if the user entered an existing customer
26   #
27   CFILE=${OPTION}.act
28   LFILE=${OPTION}.lgr
29   if test -r ${CFILE}; then
30     echo "\n\n"
31     cat $CFILE
32     echo "\n\nIs this the customer you wanted? \c"
33     read OPTION COMMENT
34     if test "$OPTION" = y; then
35   #
36   #  enter debit items
37   #
38       while test "$OPTION" != ""; do
39         echo "          Enter date: \c"
40         read DATE
41         if test "$DATE" = ""; then
42            break;
43            fi
44         echo "  Enter Description: \c"
45         read DESC
46         if test "$DESC" = ""; then
47            break;
48            fi
49         echo "        Enter Amount: \c"
50         read OPTION
51         if test "$OPTION" != ""; then
```

```
52            echo "${DATE}\t${DESC}\t${OPTION}" >> $LFILE
53          fi
54        done
55      fi
56    fi
57  #
58  #  If this customer does not exist, advise user
59  #
60  if test ! -r ${CFILE}; then
61    echo "\n\n${OPTION} not found.  \c"
62    echo "Pres ENTER to continue"
63    read OPTION
64    fi
65  #
66  #  loop
67  #
68  done
```

And the credit program is:

```
1   # 3.cmd - Post a Credit Item
2   #
3   #  Loop until a user quits
4   #
5   while true; do
6   cat <<SCREEN
7   ${CLEAR}DEMO PROGRAM FOR CUSTOMER BILLING
8
9
10                  Enter Payments/Credit Items
11
12  SCREEN
13  #
14  #  Get user's input
15  #
16  echo "  Enter Customer Number or blank line to quit: \c"
17  read OPTION COMMENT
18  #
19  #  if user decided to quit, do so
20  #
21  if test "" = "${OPTION}"; then
22     exit
23     fi
24  #
25  #  see if the user entered an existing customer
26  #
27  CFILE=${OPTION}.act
28  LFILE=${OPTION}.lgr
29  if test -r ${CFILE}; then
30    echo "\n\n"
```

Chapter 6   Shell Programming Example

```
31      cat $CFILE
32      echo "\n\nIs this the customer you wanted? \c"
33      read OPTION COMMENT
34      if test "$OPTION" = y; then
35   #
36   #  enter debit items
37   #
38        while test "$OPTION" != ""; do
39          echo "          Enter date: \c"
40          read DATE
41          if test "$DATE" = ""; then
42            break;
43            fi
44          echo " Enter Check Number: \c"
45          read DESC
46          if test "$DESC" = ""; then
47            echo " Credit Memo Number: \c"
48            read DESC
49            if test "$DESC" = ""; then
50              break;
51              fi;
52            DESC="Credit Memo #${DESC}"
53          else
54            DESC="Check #${DESC}"
55            fi
56          echo "          Enter Amount: \c"
57          read OPTION
58          if test "$OPTION" != ""; then
59            echo "${DATE}\t${DESC}\t\t${OPTION}" >> $LFILE
60            fi
61          done
62        fi
63     fi
64   #
65   #  If this customer does not exist, advise user
66   #
67   if test ! -r ${CFILE}; then
68     echo "\n\n${OPTION} not found.  \c"
69     echo "Press ENTER to continue"
70     read OPTION
71     fi
72   #
73   #  loop
74   #
75   done
```

The credit-posting program also has a small amount of data formatting. It is assumed that any credit will either be a check or a credit memo, so that the description field will be always *Check Number #* or *Credit Memo #*. This could be modified to allow entry of cash receipts or other credit items.

Both these programs are convenient in the sense that the user can get back to the main menu quickly by simply hitting the ENTER key one or more times. This is done by the use if the statements

```
if test "${OPTION}" = ""; do
```

which will sense a blank line. Note the necessity of placing the symbol *${OPTION}* in double quotes. This is because if the variable is null, the *test* command will not evaluate properly, receiving the = as its first parameter.

Printing Statements

Now that we have entered customers, debit items, and credit items, we can check the balances of the accounts of individuals. This is done by *4.cmd*, which obtains a customer number from the user and invokes *awk* to output a statement.

This version of the program is output to the *pg* filter so that the results can be seen on the screen. It can be easily changed to the *lp* program to allow output to the system spooler.

```
1    # 4.cmd - Print a statement
2    #
3    #  Loop until user quits
4    #
5    while true; do
6    cat <<SCREEN
7    ${CLEAR}DEMO PROGRAM FOR CUSTOMER BILLING
8
9
10                Print a Statement
11
12   SCREEN
13   #
14   #  Get user's input
15   #
16   echo "  Enter Customer Number or blank line to quit: \c"
17   read OPTION COMMENT
18   #
19   #  if user decided to quit, do so
20   #
21   if test "" = "${OPTION}"; then
22      exit
23      fi
24   #
```

Chapter 6 Shell Programming Example

```
25    #   see if the user entered an existing customer
26    #
27    CFILE=${OPTION}.act
28    LFILE=${OPTION}.lgr
29    SFILE=${OPTION}.stm
30    if test -r ${CFILE}; then
31       echo "\n\n"
32       cat $CFILE
33       echo "\n\nIs this the customer you wanted? \c"
34       read OPTION COMMENT
35       if test "$OPTION" = y; then
36    #
37    #  print the statement
38    #
39          cat > $SFILE <<STATEMENT
40
41                              This Company Name
42                              123 Anystreet
43                              Anytown, ST 019233
44
45                                   `date`
46
47    STATEMENT
48          cat $CFILE >> $SFILE
49          awk -f 4.cmd.awk $LFILE >> $SFILE
50          pg $SFILE
51       fi
52    fi
53    #
54    #  loop
55    #
56    done
```

A variation of this program might allow the user to enter a range of customers, rather than viewing statements one-by-one. The above program will have to be modified to place the correct letterhead on the top of each statement. We use a simple awk program[1] to format and summarize the data lines:

```
1   BEGIN    { FS = "\t"
```

---

[1] Notice the odd construction *$3 + 0* and *$4 + 0* in the *awk* program. This was due to a bug that was discovered in the particular awk implementation I used to write this program. What happened is that in specific lines where there is no third or fourth field, *$3* and *$4* were evaluating as a non-null string. The expression used forced *awk* to reevaluate those fields as numerics, and come up with zeroes. This, of course, would not work if the garbage happened to look like a numeric. Your implementation should not have this bug.

```
2               printf "\n"
3               printf "Date       Description              Charge         Credit\n"
4               printf "--------   ----------------------   -----------    ------------\n" }
5         { if ($3 + 0 != 0) {
6                 printf "%8.8s %-22.22s %12.2f\n", $1, $2, $3
7                 DR += $3    }
8           if ($4 + 0 != 0) {
9                 printf "%8.8s %-22.22s %12s %12.2f\n", $1, $2, "", $4
10                CR += $4    } }
11  END     { if ( DR > CR ) {
12                printf "\nPlease pay your balance of %12.2f\n", DR - CR }
13            else {
14                printf "\nYou have a %12.2f credit.  No payment required.\n" CR - DR} }
```

Using the *printf* statement in *awk*, we can precisely format data lines, so that the variable fields in the data file are transformed into readable columnar text.

Find a Customer

One of the problems with our data-base structure is that it might be difficult to locate a particular customer's number. This is solved by the *5.cmd* program, which uses the *grep* program to run through all the *.act* files to come up with a list of possible account numbers. The program is:

```
1   # 5.cmd - Find a customer given a search key
2   #
3   #   Loop until a customer is edited or the user
4   #   quits
5   #
6   while true; do
7   cat <<SCREEN
8   ${CLEAR}DEMO PROGRAM FOR CUSTOMER BILLING
9
10
11                  FIND A CUSTOMER
12
13  SCREEN
14  #
15  #   Get user's input
16  #
17  echo "  Enter a search key or a blank line to quit: \c"
18  read OPTION
19  #
20  #   if user decided to quit, do so
21  #
22  if test "" = "${OPTION}"; then
```

```
23    exit
24    fi
25  #
26  #  scan files to see which it is
27  #
28  echo "\n\n"
29  echo "Account/Full Name"
30  echo "----------------"
31  for file in `grep -l "${OPTION}" *.act`; do
32    read NAME < $file
33    echo "${file}\t${NAME}"
34    done
35  echo "\nPress ENTER to continue\n"
36  read COMMENT
37  #
38  #  loop
39  #
40  done
```

The *grep* program provides us with the *-l* option for just this purpose. It produces a file name for each file that has a string matching the user input. Note that the input need not be part of the name, it could be part of the address. That makes this program useful for finding all the people who live in a specific zip code or city.

Print Ledger

Sooner or later the business will have to have an accounting of how it is doing overall. This can be done by a ledger/journal that sums together all the accounts to produce one number.

This is the most complicated of our sample programs, using *awk* several times to reformat and summarize data. The program is:

```
1   # 6.cmd - Print Ledger
2   #
3   echo ${CLEAR}LEDGER PRINT PROGRAM
4   #
5   #  Get user input
6   #
7   echo "\n\n"
8   echo "Enter earliest date of transactions in journal (YYMMDD): \c"
9   read FIRST
10    if test "$FIRST" = ""; then
11      FIRST=000000
12    fi
```

```
13   echo "  Enter latest date of transactions in journal (YYMMDD): \c"
14   read LAST
15   if test "$LAST" = ""; then
16     LAST=991231
17     fi
18   TMP1=lgr1.$$
19   TMP2=lgr2.$$
20   TMP3=lgr3.$$
21   #
22   #  Catenate all the ledger files together, adding a name field
23   #  at the end of each line
24   #
25   for lfile in *.lgr; do
26     echo Reading: $lfile
27     NUM=`expr $lfile : '\(.*\).lgr'`
28     awk 'BEGIN { FS = OFS = "\t" } \
29            { printf "%s\t%s\t%7.2f\t%7.2f\t%s\n", $1, $2, $3, $4, name }' \
30     name=$NUM $lfile >> $TMP1
31     done
32   #
33   #  Normalize the date field into YYMMDD format
34   #
35   cut -f1 $TMP1 | awk -F/ '{printf "%2.2d%2.2d%2.2d\n", $3, $1, $2}' > $TMP2
36   cut -f2-99 $TMP1 | paste $TMP2 - > $TMP3
37   #
38   #  Sort the file and produce the report
39   #
40   echo ${CLEAR}
41   sort $TMP3 | awk -f 6.cmd.awk first=$FIRST last=$LAST - | pg
42   #
43   #  Ask to clean files and exit
44   #
45   echo "Do you want to save the temporary files? \c"
46   read OPTION
47   if test "$OPTION" != y; then
48     /bin/rm $TMP1 $TMP2 $TMP3
49     fi
50   exit
```

In this program we have a series of pipelines that generate temporary files. The first step is to add a new field to the output data file so that we can trace the source of a transaction. This is done by feeding the first invocation of *awk* with a name variable. Note the use of the *expr* program to take a file name such as *xyz.lgr* and turn it into *xyz*. The result of this pipeline is placed in file *$TMP1*.

After that the dates that the user entered in the files, in the form MM/DD/YY must be converted to to YYMMDD format.[2] This will later allow the sort filter to properly sort all the transactions in their chronological order regardless of the year. This is done in two pipes, where the dates by themselves are stored in *$TMP2* and the final result is stored in *$TMP3*.

Finally, the data in *$TMP3* is sorted and fed to an *awk* program that produces the output. The *awk* program is:

```
1    BEGIN    { FS = "\t" }
2    NR % 20 == 1 {
3            printf "DEMO PROGRAM JOURNAL         Page %d\n\n", ++page
4            printf "Records from %s to %s\n\n", first, last
5            printf "Date       Account       Item                  "
6            printf "Debit        Credit        Balance\n"
7            printf "--------   ----------    --------------------  "
8            printf "-----------  -----------  -----------\n" }
9    $1 >= first && $1 <= last {
10           balance = balance + $3 - $4
11           printf "%8.8s %10.10s %-20.20s %12.2f %12.2f %12.2f\n", \
12             substr($1, 3, 2) "/" substr($1, 5, 2) "/" substr($1, 1, 2), \
13             $5, $2, $3, $4, balance }
14
```

The variables *first* and *last* are provided to make sure that only transactions within the desired period are listed.

At the user's option, the temporary files are saved so they can be examined. Looking at these files will give a better understanding of the *cut* and *paste* processes.

Print Customers with a Balance

One more useful program allows the bookkeeper to quickly analyze the accounts receivable. Often we simply need to peruse the list of all customers that have an outstanding balance to determine whether to take some action.

```
1    # 7.cmd - Print customers with a balance
2    #
3    echo "${CLEAR}DEMO PROGRAM FOR CUSTOMER BILLING"
```

---

[2] In the appendix on shell script examples, there is a *sed* program that also can do this.

```
 4    echo "\n\nCustomers with balance owing\n\n"
 5
 6    ( for file in *.lgr; do
 7        NUM=`expr $file : '\(.*\).lgr'`
 8        BAL=`awk -f 7.cmd.awk ${file}`
 9        if test "$BAL" -gt 0; then
10            read NAME < ${NUM}.act
11            echo "${BAL}\t${NAME}"
12        fi
13    done ) | pg
14  #
15  #   return
16  #
17    exit
```

Note the above use of the parentheses to enclose the *for* loop. This was done so that the *for* loop would be run in a sub-shell, and the overall output sent to the *pg* program. The *awk* program that produces a single number that is placed in *BAL* is:

```
1   BEGIN     { FS = "\t" }
2             { BAL += $3
3               BAL -= $4 }
4   END       { print BAL }
```

Summary

Obviously we have a long way to go before our collection of shell routines becomes a complete application. Hopefully, however, we have seen some of the ways that shell scripts can be used to implement quick and efficient programs. Consider the amount of C code, for example, that it would have taken to duplicate all the above shell scripts, and the difficulties that might have arisen in the debugging process.

The decision to use shell scripts as opposed to more formal languages is not always easy because it can feel like too much of a compromise for some systems analysts. Some project managers have used shell scripts for prototyping programs, then followed through with a compiled implementation. In any event, the option is there for those who want it, and the growing user base of UNIX systems makes it a better choice as time goes on.

7
Basic UNIX Utilities

In this chapter we visit the fertile field of commands that are available to the UNIX user. There are better than 240 commands listed in the AT&T and Microport manuals, and even more in the SCO XENIX manuals. I am convinced that less than one UNIX user out of a hundred knows them all, and, quite frankly, there is rarely any need to. I once worked with a programmer new to UNIX who developed an 800-line C program; and he only knew six commands (other than the login command and the command to start the developed program):

vi	Edit the program
cc	Compile the program
rm	Remove files
ls	List files in the directory
lp	Send file to the line printer
exit	Log off

He was a very focused individual. If he ever typed another command, it was while I was not looking, but he got the job done. I do not advocate this type of orientation, but at the same time, trying to swallow the whole of the UNIX documentation at once is counter-productive.

The problem is that in the documentation, applications development tools (such as *awk*, and *yacc*) are mixed in with system support programs (such as *crash* and *install*), along with interactive utilities (such as *vi* and *ls*).

This trend was started in the earlier UNIX systems where there were fairly fine lines between the "user," "applications programmer," and "systems programmer" communities. It does make UNIX difficult to learn at first. The key is to focus on the subset of commands that are needed right away, and learn the rest as the need arises.

This chapter does not attempt to reproduce all the information in the UNIX manuals. It will attempt to categorize the more commonly used commands, and provide hints as to how they are used. The UNIX shells, both the C shell and the Bourne shell, both use an environment variable named *PATH* which is used to locate commands. At a minimum, the *PATH* variable is set to:

```
setenv PATH /bin:/usr/bin:.
```

for the C shell, or:

```
PATH=/bin:/usr/bin:.
export PATH
```

for the Bourne shell. This tells the shell that for every command typed in or read from a file that is *not* a command understood by the shell itself, three directories will be searched for an executable file of that same name. In this example, the */bin* directory, */usr/bin* directory, and the current directory *(.)* will be searched in that order.

For practical purposes, it is irrelevant whether a particular command resides in */bin* or */usr/bin*. Usually, commands that are considered optional or high-level or not "true UNIX" are in the */usr/bin* directory. Originally, the */bin* directory contained all the commands. Later, when that directory got too large to be handled easily, the */usr/bin* directory was created. At system installation time, the operator has the option of placing the */usr/bin* directory on a different file system (or different disk drive) to distribute files more evenly between devices.

The system operator will also have the */etc* directory in the search path. Many of the commands that are intended to be executed only by the system operator are found there.

Here we divide some of the commonly used commands into the categories mentioned above. Note that there are some commands that may appear in more than one category, but that they are grouped this way because of how they are commonly used.

Interactive utilities	Used continually as the need arises in interactive sessions.
at	Execute commands at a certain time
cat	Catenate files
chmod	Change the security modes of a file
chown	Change the owner of the file

cmp	Compare two files
cp	Copy files
cpio	Copy groups of files
cu	Call another system
dc	Desk calculator
df	Display the amount of disk that is free
du	Display the amount of disk used
egrep	Search in a file for a string
fgrep	Fast search in a file for a string
file	See what type of file
find	Find files in the directory structure
grep	Search in files for a string
kill	Kill (or send a signal to) a process
ln	Make directory links
lp	Send file to the line printer spooler
lpstat	Get the line printer status
ls	List the contents of a directory
mail	Mail a message to another user
mesg	Allow or dis-allow messages coming in
mkdir	Make a directory
more	Peruse a file
mv	Move a file
od	Dump a file in octal (or other) format
pack	Pack files to save disk space
passwd	Change the user password
pwd	Get the present working directory
rm	Remove files
tail	See the last lines of a file
tar	Make or read a tape archive
unpack	Unpack a file
uucp	Copy a file to another UNIX system
wc	Count the words in a file
who	See who is on the system
write	Write a message to another user
Programming Tools	Programs that are used in the development of programs or documents.
ar	Make a file archive library
diff	See the difference between two files
ed	Simple editor

ex	Advanced editor
make	Make a file according to a set of rules
time	Time a command
vi	Visual edit a file (variant of ex)

Program Filter These commands are typically incorporated into shell scripts as part of programs being developed.

awk	Report generator
cat	Catenate files
col	Filter reverse line-feeds
comm	Get or reject lines common to two files
date	Get the date
echo	Echo a message to a terminal
expr	Evaluate an expression
join	Join two files according to a key
pr	Paginate a file for printing
sed	Stream editor
sleep	Suspend operation for an interval
sort	Sort lines in a file
tee	Send a file to two different destinations
test	Test conditions
uniq	Find the unique lines in a file

In addition, there are system utilities that are interactive commands normally used by the system operator in the maintenance and operation of the system.

There are many other commands that are available with UNIX. The sections that follow provide some usage and orientation notes for some of those listed above. Other chapters will discuss some of the commands not shown here.

at Command

One obvious use of this command is an alarm clock. If we enter the command string:

```
at 3PM
write alan
```

```
TIME TO FEED THE PARKING METER
^D
```

the command *write alan* will be executed at the next 3PM with the input shown. The benefit of this is obvious. You may schedule any string of commands to execute at any time.

cat Command

This is one of the most misunderstood commands by persons not familiar with UNIX. The name "cat" is short for "catenate," which is what this command is for. However, most people learn the command by one of its common uses, which is to simply display the contents of a file. For example:

```
cat food
```

takes the file *food* and sends it to the standard output, usually the terminal screen. Many DOS users (and I am one of them) are used to using the DOS TYPE command for this purpose, so we often alias the command type to *cat*.

The *cat* command is more useful in performing the function for which it is named, which is catenating files. In the command:

```
cat food dog > feddog
```

Places the file *food* in front of *dog*, and places the result on standard output, which is redirected to the file *feddog*. This can be done with any number of files.

Note that the standard input can also be placed in a stream. If, for example, we have a series of records that must be sorted, then output with a header that is contained in one file, and a footer that is contained in another, we can use the command:

```
sort records | cat header - footer
```

The sort command places its output on standard output, which is piped into the standard input of the *cat* command. The *cat* program will output the contents of header, the standard input, and footer to standard output in that order. By convention, the - symbol represents standard input.

cp, ln, mv Commands

The reason that these commands are shown together is that their syntax is exactly the same. They do, however, have three distinct functions:

cp Copy files: new files are made which are duplicates of old ones

ln Link files: new directory entries are made for existing files without removing the old directory entries

mv Move files: a new directory entry is made for a file, and the old directory entry is deleted. If the new directory entry is on another file system, the file is actually copied.

The general form of these commands (using *cp* for a prototype) is:

```
cp source destination
```

where *source* is one or more files or a directory (for *mv* only) and *destination* is either a file or a directory. The rules are:

1. If destination is a file, that file is unlinked. (Other links to the same file will remain)

2. If destination is a directory, then a new file will be created in that directory of the same name(s) as the source.

3. If source is more than one file, then destination must be a directory.

For a practical example, suppose you had a directory named *progs* in which you are writing a program, and you wanted to make a complete copy of all the C source in that directory for safekeeping before doing any more work. The commands:

```
mkdir save
cp progs/*.c save
```

would create a new directory named *save,* and copy all the files in the directory progs that end in .c into it.

For copying files, the *cp* command is more efficient than using the *cat* command.

du Command

The *du* command will report the number of disk blocks used by any directory hierarchy. One useful feature of the *du* command that is often overlooked is its ability to give you a map of a sub-directory hierarchy. The command *du*, executed in your own directory, might generate a report such as:

```
10    ./progs/c
32    ./progs
444   ./docs
486   ./
```

which shows us not only do we have 486 blocks in use, but that there are two sub-directories: *progs* and *docs*, and a directory *c* underneath *progs*. If you want to see the directory structure of the entire system, type:

```
du /
```

file Command

This command is often useful when you are attempting to explore a new directory. The file program makes several tests, and attempts to derive what type of file is being queried. Although file does not know about every file that exists, it can generally sense accurately the following file types:

- C source code
- ASCII data file (editable with *vi*)
- Binary Data (not executable object)
- Executable binary file
- COFF format file

You may often wish to type *file** instead of *ls*.

find Command

The syntax of this command can throw you until you get used to it.

However, this is one of the most useful tools in a large UNIX file system that is being used by many people. It is also helpful in any large directory/sub-directory structure where you need to find a specific set of files.

One common use of this is in a large time-sharing system, where it becomes necessary to recover all the disk space taken up by core files, which can be created inadvertently by users and left in the system. We can get a listing of every *core* file in the system with the command:

```
find / -name core -print
```

which will generate a listing of every pathname in the system that is named *core*. It is important to note that the *-print* option must appear at the end of this sequence in order for the results to be written to standard output. The syntax also allows us to execute a command on each file, such as:

```
find / -name core -exec rm {} \;
```

which will execute the *rm* command for each pathname found. Note that the string after the *-exec* is taken as a command that ends with the escaped (quoted) semi-colon, and that the *{}* symbol is replaced by the pathname(s) found.

Patterns may be specified after *name*. For example:

```
find / -name "*.c" -exec ls -l {} \;
```

will list in long *ls* format every C source code file in the system.

Other find options are available, including owner name, size of the file, and the last modification time.

grep, egrep, fgrep Command

With these commands we can search out data in files quickly and easily. The names of these commands are another "UNIXism" that throw a lot of newcomers. The term "grep" stands for "Get Regular Expression Pattern." Regular expression patterns are defined by the *ed* editor, which was the early UNIX line editor. Regular expressions were originally similar to the pathname patterns that are understood by the shell, useful for addressing specific lines in a file.

There are three versions of *grep,* depending on your specific need:

grep   Get Regular Expression Pattern
egrep Extended *grep:* allows multiple patterns
fgrep Fast *grep:* matches simple strings only.

For programmers working on a program that has many source files, the *grep* program can work as an instant cross-reference. If our C source code is in the current working directory, and we decide to change a certain symbol, we can use the command:

```
grep baseptr *.c *.h
```

to get a quick listing of every line in every C source code and include file in which *baseptr* appears. If we use the *-n* option to *grep* we will get the line numbers as well.

Of course, this technique will not work very well with a simple symbol named something like *i*. *Grep* would find every line with the letter *i* in every file. If necessary, you might try:

```
egrep "i=|i =" *.c *.h
```

which will obtain every line where *i* appears on the left of an operator that starts with =. *egrep* will search for either of the two patterns, one with a space after the *i* and one without. Note the use of the quotes *(")* to avoid the shell interpreting the pipe *(/)* and embedded space character.

If you are inconsistent in your coding style, and sometimes put two spaces after a symbol, those particular lines will be missed. In addition, you will also be confronted with every case where this appears with a symbol that ends in *i*. This makes a case for using global symbols only with significant names.

kill Command

The *kill* command is somewhat misnamed, because it has more than one function other than killing a process. Any signal (see Chapter 2) can be sent, although the most common signal is 15 which kills a process. Signal 15 is the default in the *kill* command.

When a background process is started by the shell, the process I.D. number is displayed. You can use that number or obtain the number from the *ps* command at a later time.

ls Command

This is perhaps the most commonly typed command. The result is a listing to standard output of some or all of the files in one or more directories, in one or more formats. The formats are controlled by options, and the most common are:

```
ls -l      Long list: most useful data on a file is shown.

ls -CF     Columnar list with file type encoded.  The F option causes a
           conventional character to be appended to each file name to
           indicate the type of file.  Slash (/) is used for directories,
           and asterisk (*) is used for executable files.
```

These versions of *ls* are so often typed, that many C shell users placed the following alias commands in their *.cshrc* files:

```
alias ll ls -l
alias l ls -CF
```

The long format includes the size of the file, the owner name, and the security mode bits (changeable with *chmod*) in the output.

Without parameters other than options, *ls* lists the files in the current working directory. Any parameters that are not listing options (those that start with -) may be files or directories. If a parameter is a directory, the contents of the directory are listed, rather than just the name itself. This causes the command:

```
ls
```

to be different from:

```
ls *
```

because the first form will not expand sub-directories, and the second form will. This action can be turned off with the *-d* option.

Another useful option to *ls* is the ability to sort directories. If we wish to see which files were modified most recently, we can type:

```
ls -lt
```

and most recently modified files will be listed first.

mkdir Command

This command is used to make a new directory. The most interesting thing about this command is that it executes in privileged mode, because that is necessary to make the appropriate *mknod()* system call to make a directory. This means that if you need to make a directory from within a C program, you will have to code

```
system("mkdir subdir");
```

rather than the more obvious *mknod()* system call.

more Command

Although the *cat* command is often used to examine the contents of a file, the *more* command is often more convenient. It will dump the contents of files one screenload at a time, rather than all the file at the maximum rate of the terminal. For a file that is more than 24 lines long (the size of a CRT terminal) this makes life easier.

At the end of each screen, *more* will pause, waiting for the user to press a key that will be taken as a command. Some of the commands are:

```
(space)   Output 24 more lines
[CR]      Output one more line
/         Search for text
!         execute shell command
```

Of course, pressing the interrupt key ([DEL], most commonly) will cause *more* to quit before displaying any more of the file. Using more is also more efficient than examining a file with any of the system editors, because the editors have to copy the file to a scratch space before they can begin processing.

od Command

For binary files, (those not editable with a character editor) the *od* command can be used to examine the contents of files. The output can be in octal, decimal, or escaped-character format.

There are other commands, explained in the next chapter, that are useful for examining specifically formatted files related to programming. These include *nm*, *ar*, and the debuggers.

pack, unpack, pcat Command

If you have a number of intermediate to large sized files, you can conserve disk space by using the *pack*, *unpack*, and *pcat* commands. These programs take advantage of the "wasted bits" common to many data formats, notably English language in ASCII, and can save up to 70% of the disk space by compression. For example, if you have a directory with a series of document files whose name ends in *.doc*, you can compress them with the command:

```
pack *.doc
```

Every file that can benefit from compression will be replaced by a file of the same name with a *.z* appended. To read these files, the *pcat* and *unpack* commands can be used. For example:

```
pcat thesis.doc.z | more
```

will list the packed file *thesis.doc* using the *more* command.

rm Command

The *rm* command can be very risky, because UNIX provides no facility for recovering an unlinked file. To make matters worse, the *-r* option will recursively unlink directories. So the super user could theoretically remove all the files in the system with the command:

```
rm -r /
```

Many users of the C shell place an alias for *rm* in their *.cshrc* file such as:

```
alias rm rm -i
```

which will cause *rm* to get a "y" confirmation before it unlinks any file.

8
awk

One of the shortcomings of the C programming language is its inability to handle variable length text information. This is not to say such jobs can't be done in C—most certainly they can. But to do so requires the programmer to make many decisions to allocate memory, read and parse input, format output, and possibly convert data from one form to another.

This type of job usually shows up in the task of report writing. Although C generates efficient object code, this can be odious programming indeed, particularly if you or your user is fussy about the style and appearance of the reports. In this chapter we will look at the *awk* programming language and how it can be used for report writing.

The language structure of *awk* was designed to save as much time for the programmer as possible. This makes many useful *awk* programs so short that they can be coded completely on the command line that invokes *awk*. For example, the command line:

```
awk '{ for (i = one; i <= NF; i++) print $i }' data
```

will take the text file *data*, and output each separate word in the file on its own line in the standard output. The *awk* program is fully enclosed within the single quotes as a single argument. Of course, we would not normally type such a line each time we needed it, but inside a shell script program this is perfectly acceptable.

If the *awk* program is too big for placing on the command line, it can be stored in a text file and invoked by:

```
awk -f report1.awk data
```

where the program is stored in *report1.awk* and the data is in the file data. I generally follow the convention of terminating *awk* programs with the string ".awk".

UNIX Programming on the 80386/80386, Second Edition

Input Record Structure

Before we go any further into programming *awk*, let's look at the data that *awk* is supposed to work on. Basically, the idea is to process data records that are stored as lines of text in an ordinary text file. In most systems other than UNIX, a data-base file is treated as "binary" information, which cannot be manipulated by a text editor.

This causes a problem for many systems analysts who are concerned about efficiency of data storage. If we look at a data record[1] such as:

```
1946     240643     16657
1950      63375      4409
1955     106173      5174
```

we can see that they are stored as text data in a minimum of 51 bytes, more depending on the number of spaces between the numbers. In binary, this data could be stored in 30 bytes or less by using 16-bit and 32-bit numbers.

This is not really a problem for smaller data files. But if it ever did become a problem, and we had to store data in binary, we do not necessarily rule out the use of *awk*, particularly as a report writer, because *awk* can be used as a filter. This means we could write a converter program to feed *awk* with data, and disk space for text form of the data need never be allocated. For example:

```
cvt.to.text bigdata | awk -f report2.awk | lp
```

If *bigdata* was a binary file, and *cvt.to.text* was a program that took that file and output it to the standard output as text lines, *awk* could run *report2.awk* on it without a problem and send it on the the line printer spooler.

An input file to *awk* is a series of records, each terminated by a "Record Separator." The default record separator, which can be changed by the *awk* command line or the program, is the newline character (\n). The end of file will also terminate a record.

Each record consists of any number, including zero, fields. Fields are strings of characters separated by "Field Separators." The default field separator is a

---

[1] The numbers shown are the number of male and female commissioned officers in the military for given years.

" ", which indicates any string of blanks or tabs. The beginning and the end of the record also mark the boundaries of the first and last fields, respectively. As with the Record Separator, the Field Separator can be changed by the program. Consider the following two lines in a file:

```
Clarence owes me $50
This word         and this word        are_far_apart
```

With the default settings *awk* would take these as two records, the first with four fields and the second with six fields. Note that the variance in number of spaces makes no difference.

It is often the case that we want to define our input file in such a way that blanks can exist within the fields. Most often this is done by setting the field separator to the tab character. In an *awk* program, as we will see later, this is done with the statement:

```
FS = "\t"
```

This not only allows space characters to appear within fields, but it allows the "skipping" of fields as well. Consider our sample data file:

```
01/02/89    436     Bigbank                 310.10      Auto
01/04/89            Nocturnal Aviation     -2325.29     Salary
01/10/89    437     PG&E                    213.17      Utility
01/10/89    438     Safeway                 129.33      Food
01/15/89    439     HS&L                   1350.50      Mortgage
01/15/89    440     Bigbank                   7.50      Bankcharge
01/18/89    441     Safeway                 239.33      Food
01/31/89    442     Draeger's                87.35      Food
02/02/89    443     Bigbank                 310.10      Auto
02/04/89            Nocturnal Aviation     -2325.29     Salary
02/10/89    444     Safeway                 399.33      Food
02/12/89    445     PG&E                    114.22      Utility
02/15/89    446     Bigbank                   7.50      Bankcharge
02/16/89    447     HS&L                   1350.50      Mortgage
02/20/89    448     Draeger's                82.34      Food
02/27/89    449     Safeway                  81.36      Food
03/02/89    450     Bigbank                 310.10      Auto
03/04/89            Nocturnal Aviation     -2325.29     Salary
03/09/89    451     Safeway                 129.26      Food
03/11/89    452     PG&E                    212.21      Utility
```

```
03/12/89    453     Safeway                 178.93      Food
03/15/89    454     HS&L                   1350.50      Mortgage
03/15/89    455     Bigbank                   7.50      Bankcharge
04/02/89    456     Bigbank                 310.10      Auto
04/02/89    457     Draeger's               159.33      Food
04/04/89            Nocturnal Aviation    -2325.29      Salary
04/15/89    458     PG&E                    119.69      Utility
04/15/89    459     HS&L                   1350.50      Mortgage
04/15/89    460     Bigbank                   7.50      Bankcharge
04/18/89    461     Safeway                 239.37      Food
05/02/89    462     Bigbank                 310.10      Auto
05/04/89            Nocturnal Aviation    -2325.29      Salary
05/05/89    463     Draeger's               122.12      Food
05/11/89    464     PG&E                    214.03      Utility
05/13/89    465     HS&L                   1350.50      Mortgage
05/15/89    466     Bigbank                   7.50      Bankcharge
05/19/89    467     Safeway                  89.81      Food
05/30/89    468     Safeway                 129.90      Food
06/02/89    469     Bigbank                 310.10      Auto
06/04/89            Nocturnal Aviation    -2325.29      Salary
06/08/89    470     PG&E                    115.80      Utility
06/13/89    471     Safeway                  29.90      Food
06/15/89    472     HS&L                   1350.50      Mortgage
06/15/89    473     Bigbank                   7.50      Bankcharge
```

This is a hypothetical check data file, where we have the following fields:

1. The check date
2. The check number
3. The payee
4. The amount, with negative number being deposits
5. A coded "transaction type"

Each field is assigned a number within the *awk* program, starting with the number one (within the program, fields are referenced by the symbols $1, $2, ...).

In our text, we cannot see the difference between spaces and tabs, so it will suffice to say that the only spaces that exist in our sample file are within the payee field, specifically the company name "Nocturnal Aviation."

You also might have noticed that the fields do not necessarily line up from line to line. This is because a tab character is displayed as a sequence of spaces calculated to place the next character at the *next* tab stop, rather than at a specific tab stop. If a longer data field, such as "Nocturnal Aviation" or "Safeway" causes the print position to move over the tab stop, the next field appears at the one following.

Note also that in some cases there are two tabs next to each other. Unlike the case where the space character is the Field Separator, *awk* determines that this condition indicates a null field.

So it is not easy to read our data file, although we can input and edit it fairly easily using the *vi* text editor. It is also easy to generate this type of file with another program.

In the descriptions that follow, we will use our check register data file to demonstrate some of the facilities of *awk*.

awk Program Structure

As we peruse the programming language of *awk*, we can observe many similarities to the C programming language. This is no accident. The creators of *awk* were all conversant in C. They wanted to make a language that was easy for *them* to use, yet could do things that were laborious in C. The carry-overs from C are:

1. Most of the operators found in C are available.

2. The *if*, *else*, *while*, and a few other keywords have the same meaning that they do in C.

3. The braces { } symbols can be used to make compound statements.

4. The *printf* function is available, although the *awk* syntax treats *printf* as a statement and not as a function.

There are a number substantial differences between C and *awk*. At first these seem annoying, because a lot of syntax errors can result when you first attempt to use *awk*. But after you get the feel of *awk*, the changes become more of a help than a hindrance. The differences are:

1. No user coded functions.

2. Although numbers are stored internally in binary, strings and numbers are interchangeable and can be used as an operand in any context.

3. Variables are not declared, and have no fixed type.

4. Although the semicolon will terminate a statement and allow a new statement to start on the same line, a newline will terminate a statement. You have to end a line with a backslash if you want to continue it onto another line.

5. There are some variables with special meaning,

6. There is no preprocessor to handle #*include*, #*define*, and the like.

One important aspect of *awk* to note is that the programs are *interpreted* rather than compiled. This allows *awk* to more easily manipulate varied data types, and also makes it possible to quickly access *awk* within shell scripts.

An *awk* program consists of a sequence of statements of

```
<pattern> { <action> }
```

There can be any number of such statements, but there must be at least one. In any statement, either *<pattern>* or *<action>* may be missing, but not both.

The job of *<pattern>* is to select which input records are to be processed by its corresponding *<action>*, and the job of *<action>* is to do something with each record selected for it.

Patterns

As the syntax of *awk* follows the C design with exceptions, the pattern object follows the design of the *ex* editor. If you know how to use pattern matching strings in the *ex/vi* editor, you also know most of the patterns in *awk*. The *awk* pattern can be one of the following:

Chapter 8 awk

<null> Match every record. This is the most common pattern, used when the action associated with it is to act on each record in the input file.

BEGIN Matches the record *before* the first record. The action associated with this pattern is often used to initialize variables or print out a header line.

END Matches the record *after* the last record. Useful for printing out summary lines. In some programs the action associated with this pattern is the only statement that prints anything.

/*<regexp>*/ Matches each record according to the pattern *<regexp>* (regular expression). We will describe regular expressions below.

<relexp> Matches when *<relexp>* (relational expression) is true. A relational expression will yield a true or false. We will describe relational expressions later when we investigate the operators available to *awk*.

A complicated *awk* program can be made easier to understand by careful selection of patterns. One could ignore the pattern facility altogether and simply program the action sequence to control itself with *if* statements—but this is a waste of the utility of *awk*.

A regular expression (*<regexp>* above) refers to a sequence of letters that can be compared against the input record according to certain rules to determine a match. Basically, a string of characters must match exactly. Some characters have special meanings:

. Matches any single character.

^ Matches only the character before the beginning of the line.

$ Matches only the character past the end of the line.

[*<str>*] Matches any single character that can be found in *<str>*.

+	Allows a repetition of the previous character.
*	Matches zero or more instances of the preceding character.
?	Indicates a match of zero or one occurrences of the preceding character.
|	Can be used to separate two regular expressions to form one that will match either.

The backslash character can be used to nullify the special meaning of any of the characters above. Some examples of patterns follow:

Pattern	Will Match	Will Not Match
/blast/	it was a blast blaster master	BLAST Blast it
/^The/	There she blows The Big Easy	Where is the disk Where is there
/conclude.$/	We conclude. We conclude?	conclude it now
/[Tt]he /	The stormy night He is the one	There we go THE stormy night
/b.g/	The big one will you bag it? caught in a bog nab grab	the berg Don't Bug Me
/ax*z/	az you wish axz xyaxxxxxxxz	a zebra zaxp
/hither|tither/	hither we go thither we went hither, thither	yonder

Keep in mind that patterns can also be relational expressions. We will explore this further in the discussion of *awk* operators.

Action Object

An *awk* action is a series of statements between a set of braces that looks somewhat like a segment of a C program. This program segment is invoked each time its associated pattern matches the current input record.

In the following descriptions, any reference to <*statement*> can be either a single statement or a series of statements enclosed in braces ({ }). Elements enclosed in brackets ([ ]) are optional. The statements recognized by *awk* are:

print [<*exp1*>, ... <*expn*>]

> Output a record, each <*exp*> in a separate field. The current value of the variable *OFS* is used to determine the proper field separator. If an <*exp*> evaluates to a numeric type, the format used is in the variable *OFMT*. If no expressions are given, the entire record is printed.

printf <*fmt*> [, <*exp1*>, ... <*expn*>]

> Output a formatted string, similar to the C-library *printf* function. The <*fmt*> is a string literal or expression, and follows the same rules as the C-library function, although *awk* makes sure there is a one-to-one correspondence between the expressions and the formatting operators in the format string. If not, a fatal error results.

while (<*expn*>) <*statement*>

> Execute <*statement*> while <*expn*> evaluates as non-zero.

for (<*exp1*>; <*exp2*>; <*exp3*>) <*statement*>

> Execute <*exp1*>, then loop through <*statement*> and <*exp3*> while <*exp2*> evaluates to non-zero. This syntax is very close to the C version of this statement.

for (<*var*> in <*array*>) <*statement*>

Execute <statement> once for each element in <array>, setting <var> to the index of successive elements. We will discuss *awk* arrays later. The syntax of this statement is closer to the Bourne shell version than the C version.

break

Break out of a *while* or *for* loop.

continue

Start next iteration of a *while* or *for* loop, without executing any further statements following on this iteration.

if (<exp>) <statement1> [else <statement2>]

Execute <statement1> upon <exp> evaluating to non-zero, and <statement2> upon <exp> evaluating to zero.

next

Abort the processing of the current input data record and start processing the next, beginning with the first pattern.

Since the syntax of these statements can be learned best by example, we will skip an extensive grammar. Let's now look at a practical example.

Check Register Output

The data file we presented earlier could have been input with a text editor, but it could also be the output of another program. Assuming that file is named *checks*, we can format it for output with the following *awk* program:

```
BEGIN           { FS = "\t" }
                { balance -= $4 }
NR % 10 == 1    { printf "\fCheck Register %40s Page %d", " ", ++page
                  printf "\n\n"
                  printf "Date     Check Payee              Debits     "
                  printf "Credits    Balance\n"
                  printf "-------- ----- ---------------- ---------- "
                  printf "---------- ----------\n" }
```

```
$4 < 0           { printf "%8.8s %5d %-15.15s %10s %10.2f %10.2f\n", \
                   $1, $2, $3, " ", 0 - $4, balance }
$4 >= 0          { printf "%8.8s %5d %-15.15s %10.2f %10s %10.2f\n", \
                   $1, $2, $3, $4, " ", balance }
```

If this program is in the file *checkreg.awk* we can get a check register by typing:

```
sort checks | awk -f checkreg.awk
```

And two pages of the resulting output are:

```
Check Register                                                  Page 1


Date      Check Payee              Debits    Credits    Balance
--------  ----- ---------------   ---------- ---------- ----------
01/02/89   436  Bigbank              310.10              -310.10
01/04/89     0  Nocturnal Aviat      325.29              2015.19
01/10/89   437  PG&E                 213.17              1802.02
01/10/89   438  Safeway              129.33              1672.69
01/15/89   439  HS&L                1350.50               322.19
01/15/89   440  Bigbank                7.50               314.69
01/18/89   441  Safeway              239.33                75.36
01/31/89   442  Draeger's             87.35               -11.99
02/02/89   443  Bigbank              310.10              -322.09
02/04/89     0  Nocturnal Aviat     2325.29              2003.20



Check Register                                                  Page 2


Date      Check Payee              Debits    Credits    Balance
--------  ----- ---------------   ---------- ---------- ----------
02/10/89   444  Safeway              399.33              1603.87
02/12/89   445  PG&E                 114.22              1489.65
02/15/89   446  Bigbank                7.50              1482.15
02/16/89   447  HS&L                1350.50                31.65
02/20/89   448  Draeger's             82.34                49.31
02/27/89   449  Safeway               81.36               -32.05
03/02/89   450  Bigbank              310.10              -342.15
03/04/89     0  Nocturnal Aviat     2325.29              1983.14
03/09/89   451  Safeway              129.26              1853.88
03/11/89   452  PG&E                 212.21              1641.67
```

Because the date and check number are at the start of each record, *sort* will place the records in date order, with checks sorted within a given date. This output is fed to *awk*, which sends its output under the control of *checkreg.awk*. Let's examine this program a piece at a time:

```
BEGIN          { FS = "\t" }
```

The *BEGIN* pattern causes this action to be taken before the first line is read. It causes a special variable that controls the Field Separator, *FS,* to be set to the TAB. As we have seen, this is critical to the proper interpretation of our data file.

```
               { balance -= $4 }
```

Because there is no pattern, this action occurs for each line in the input file. A variable called *balance* has the amount field, field 4, subtracted from it. This is how action items refer to the data within the record. Any field, from one onward, can be referenced as *$n* where *n* is the number of the field. *$0* is a special case that can be used to refer to the entire input record. All other *awk* variables, such as balance, can be assumed to be initialized to zero, and need not be declared.

```
NR % 10 == 1   { printf "\fCheck Register %40s Page %d", " ", ++page
                 printf "\n\n"
                 printf "Date      Check Payee              Debits    "
                 printf "Credits    Balance\n"
                 printf "--------  -----  ---------------- ---------- "
                 printf "----------  ---------\n" }
```

This pattern makes use of another special variable, *NR*, which is automatically set by *awk* to be the number of the current record, the first being 1. The pattern is true when *NR* module 10 is equal to one, in other words when *NR* is one, 11, 21, etc. The action item uses *printf* to print out the header for the page, starting with a form-feed character and incrementing the page number each time. Note that the syntax of the *printf* statement does not use parentheses as does the *printf* function call in C. Since this action is invoked only once every ten lines, starting with record #1, we get pagination of every ten lines. If we wanted a different number of lines per page, we could use another number besides 10 to divide into *NR*. No processing of a data input record is done here.

```
$4 < 0          { printf "%8.8s %5d %-15.15s %10s %10.2f %10.2f\n", \
                    $one, $two, $three, " ", 0 - $4, balance }
$4 >= 0         { printf "%8.8s %5d %-15.15s %10.2f %10s %10.2f\n", \
                    $one, $two, $three, $4, " ", balance }
```

Here we have two patterns and two actions to take care of two different types of records in our data input file. If the amount field, field 4 is less than zero, we consider it a credit and format the output line accordingly. Alternately, if the amount field is greater than zero we treat it as a debit item. We can refer here to the variable *balance*, which was set in the previous action item. All variables in *awk* are global in scope. The *printf* statement is used to impress a specific format on the output lines that matches the header in the previous section. Note that the backslash is used to extend the length of the source lines, because an unescaped newline would be assumed to end the statement.

awk Data Objects and Variables

As with most languages, *awk* data objects are either variables or literals, and there are two types: numeric and string. The convenient thing about *awk*, however, is that the two data types can be freely intermixed. If the context of a reference requires a string expression and we give a numeric expression, the numeric expression is translated into a string form to complete the operation. The opposite will also happen, where strings can be interpreted as numbers, with zero being the result for strings that have no numeric interpretation. For example:

Literal Object	Type	Numeric Value	String Value
0	Numeric	0	0
10	Numeric	10	0
934	Numeric	934	934
0.123	Numeric	0.123	.123
3E6	Numeric	3000000	3000000
" "	String	0	"abc"
	String	0	abc
"this text"	String	0	this text
"234"	String	234	234
"0.33"	String	0.33	0.33
"23E3"	String	2300	23E3

Variables can be user defined or defined automatically by *awk*. As we mentioned earlier, a variable need not be declared, it comes into existence when it is referenced. All you need to do for your own variables is to make sure that its name does not conflict with any of the keywords or preset variables set by *awk*. The format of a variable reference can be:

<identifier> A simple variable reference, either user defined or *awk* defined.

<identifier>[<exp>] A reference to an array, whose index is <*exp*>. (In this context the brackets are literal, and do not denote an optional element.)

$<exp> A reference to one of the fields in the current input record. As we mentioned in the example, <*exp*> is a numeric literal or a simple variable reference that indicates what field is to be accessed. Zero indicates the entire record, and *n* indicates the *n*th field.

Since all variables are global, one pattern/action pair can set data to be processed or output by a following pattern/action pair, as is done in our earlier example with the *balance* variable.

The preset, or special, variables that *awk* recognizes are:

NR The number of the current input record, the first being 1.

NF The number of fields in the current input record.

FS The input field separator. The special case of *space* (" "), indicates any string of blanks and tabs will be taken as a field separator. This is the default value. Any other character will cause only one instance of that character to be considered a field separator.

RS The record separator. By default this is the *newline* (*"\n"*) character. If it is set to *space*, the record separator is a blank line, making it possible to have multi-line records in a file.

$i The value of field *i* in the current record.

$0	The entire record taken as a string.
OFS	This value is the output field separator, which is a *space* by default.
ORS	The output record separator, which is a *newline* ("\n") by default.
OFMT	The output format for numerics in the print statement. By default this is %.6g.
FILENAME	The name of the current input file. Note that the awk command line could have been invoked with more than one file, and this variable can be used to separate the outputs.

You can reset the special variables at any time to make variances in the output of following statements, although this is more typically done in the action following the *BEGIN* pattern.

Arrays

Arrays in *awk* are useful, but can be overused. It is important to remember that *awk* is an interpreted language, and not well suited to handling large arrays. Still, arrays make possible certain operations such as collating or summarizing input records, as we will see in the following example.

As with any variable, memory for an array is allocated at the time of reference, and the special thing about *awk* arrays is that their subscripts need not be simple numerics. For example, we could have references such as:

```
sizes["Small"] += $2
sizes["Medium"] += $3
sizes[10] += $4
```

which would create the array sizes with three elements. Any previously unreferenced element in an array can be assumed to be zero.

Consider the following program:

```
BEGIN       { FS = "\t" }
            { amount[$5] += $4                    trans[$5] += 1    }
END         { printf "Type Code       # trx Total Amount\n"
              printf "--------------- ----- ------------\n"
              for (code in amount) printf "%-15.15s %5d %12.2f\n", \
                     code, trans[code], amount[code] }
```

when run with our earlier example data file, *checks* with the command:

```
awk -f quicksum.awk checks
```

the resulting output is:

Type Code	# trx	Total Amount
Utility	6	989.12
Auto	6	1860.60
Salary	6	-13951.74
Mortgage	6	8103.00
Food	14	2097.66
Bankcharge	6	45.00

In the *checks* file we had coded the fifth field to categorize the type of transaction that the record represented. Of course, if a field was mis-coded (for example, *Auto* was spelled *auto*) a new element would have been created in the arrays *trans* and *amount* and shown on the output.

If there are a lot of categories, *awk* will slow down considerably since each new assignment will require the interpreter to scan the entire arrays on each assignment or reference (not to mention reallocating memory as necessary). In this type of job, it is better to use the technique we will show later with the *glossary.awk* program.

awk Built-in Functions

Before we get into another example program, we can complete our description of *awk* by listing the functions and operators that awk makes available. Since the user cannot define functions in *awk*, this set is all that is available. The functions that yield numeric results are:

exp(<*exp*>)   The exponential of <*exp*>.

int(<exp>)   The integer component of <exp>.

log(<exp>)   The natural logarithm of <exp>.

sqrt(<exp>)   The square root of <exp>.

and the functions that yield string results or operate on string values are:

getline

>   Causes *awk* to read the next line. The values of *NF*, *NR*, and $*n*, are all updated. The function returns a one if an input record has been read, zero otherwise. Processing continues from the next *awk* statement. This differs from the *next* statement, where processing starts from the next pattern.

index(<exp1>, <exp2>)

>   Returns the character position of the string <exp2> within <exp1>.

length[(<exp>)];

>   The length of string <exp> is returned.

split(<exp1>, <identifier>, <exp3>)

>   This function separates the string <exp1> into elements of an array <identifier>, using <exp3> as the field separator. The subscripts for the new array are the ordinal number one, two, ... and the function *split* returns the number of elements placed in the array.

split(<exp1>, <identifier>)

>   Same as the previous version of *split*, but uses the current value of *FS* as the field separator.

sprintf(<fmt>, <exp1>, <exp2> ...)

>   Returns the formatted string in a manner similar to the *printf* statement.

substr(<exp1>, <exp2>)

Returns the remainder of the string <*exp1*> starting from character position <*exp2*>. The first character position is one.

substr(<*exp1*>, <*exp2*>, <*exp3*>)

Returns the substring of <*exp1*>, starting at <*exp2*> for length <*exp3*>. The first character position is one.

If a string processing problem is presented that cannot be easily handled by these functions, you might want to consider breaking up the *awk* program into two or more steps, perhaps using a utility other than *awk* for one of the steps, and piping the data between runs. Generally, this is preferable to writing long and complicated single programs.

Operators

All of the operators found in C are also available in *awk*, although *awk* operators have interpretations on string data types that would make no sense in C. Also, there are a number of new operators we will discuss first.

The first operator that bears mentioning is the string catenation operator. The operator has no symbol; it is simply invoked by placing two string expressions next to each other. So in the following program segment:

```
a = "There"
b = "Hi " a
```

The variable *b* is assigned the value "Hi There." This becomes useful in constructing or reconstructing output data. For example, the *awk* program:

```
{ print $1 $2, $3 "-" $4, $5 }
```

will take a five field input file and make a three-field file out of it by merging the first and second, and third and fourth input fields. The third and fourth fields will have a hyphen between them.

It is important to recognize the presence of the string catenation feature of *awk*, because the omitting of commas will cause this to occur where it is not intended, resulting in syntax and logic errors. In the *printf* statement

```
printf "%33s %d" $1, amnt
```

note that the comma is missing between the format string and what was intended to be the first data object to be processed by *printf*. What this will actually do is append the string *$1* to the end of the format string, and take *amnt* as the first data object. Programmers beware.

Another operator that does not appear in C is the pattern match operator, ~, and its derivative, negative pattern match *!~*. We have seen how *awk* processes patterns against the input record. These operators refine this facility and make it possible to use pattern matching within statements. The forms of this operator are:

```
<exp> ~ <pattern>
```

which evaluates to true if *<exp>* matches *<pattern>*, and

```
<exp> !~ <pattern>
```

which evaluates to true if *<exp>* does not match *<pattern>*.

These operators can be used in the pattern field as well as the action field. For example, if we want to scan our example data-input file for data transactions relating to automobile expenses, we can use the pattern:

```
$5 ~ /Auto/ { ... }
```

This guards against the possible match of the string *Auto* in other fields of the input record.

The list of operators that remain in *awk*, some of which we have seen and used already, are:

Assignment operators: = += -= *= /= %=
Increment operators: ++ --
Math operators: + - * / %
Grouping operator: ( )
Relational operators: < <= == != >= >
Logical operators: && || !

All these operators have the same meaning as they do in C.

Redirected Output

Sometimes it is useful for *awk* to send output other directions other than the standard output. For this the following operators are provided:

```
| "<cmd>"      Send output to command <cmd>

> "<file>"     Send output to file <file>

>> "<file>"    Append output to file <file>
```

These operators can be used in a manner similar to the shell. Note that they have meaning only on the *print* and *printf* statement. The use of the >> operator other than the > operator only refers to the overall *awk* run, not the individual statement.

Glossary Program

As a final demonstration of how to use *awk* within a shell program, we provide a quick glossary program that sorts and counts all the words in a text file. This is often useful for catching spelling errors and other aesthetics.

To facilitate this, we will have to add a C-program filter that will strip out all punctuation and special symbols, and covert all words to lower case. This can be done in the shell and by other means, but it is simple and efficient to do it in C. The C program, called *stripjunk.c*, is

```
 1 0: /* stripjunk.c - reduce all flotsam and jetsam from text file
 2 0*
 3 0*    alan deikman 2/89
 4 0*
 5 0*    This program is a filter that follows the following rules:
 6 0*
 7 0*    1.  The high bit of every byte is zeroed out (to handle
 8 0*        Wordstar type files)
 9 0*
10 0*    2.  Newlines are preserved, except where the last preceding
11 0*        byte was a hyphen
12 0*
13 0*    3.  Characters of isalpha(), apostrophe, and hyphen are
14 0*        preserved, converted to lower case
15 0*
16 0*    4.  The return character (\r) is suppressed (for DOS format files)
```

Chapter 8 awk

```
17 0*
18 0*       5.  A hyphen suppresses all successive output until an isalpha()
19 0*           is reached
20 0*
21 0*       6.  All other characters become spaces
22 0*
23 0*    */
24 0:
25 0: #include <stdio.h>
26 0: #include <ctype.h>
27 0:
28 0: main() {
29 1:    short c;              /* character */
30 1:    short pc = 0;         /* prior character */
31 1:
32 1:    while ((c = getchar()) != EOF) {
33 2:       c &= 0x7f;
34 2:       if (isalpha(c) || c == '\047') putchar(tolower(c));
35 2:       else if (c == '-' && isalpha(pc)) {
36 3:          putchar('-');
37 3:          while ((c = getchar()) != EOF && !isalpha(c));
38 3:          ungetc(c, stdin); }
39 2:       else if (c == '\n') putchar(c);
40 2:       else putchar(' ');
41 2:       pc = c; }
42 1:
43 1:    exit(0); }
```

Then we can use the shell command line to take the text of this chapter and turn it into a glossary:

```
stripjunk < awk.ws | \
awk '{ for (i = one; i <= NF; i++) print $i }' - | \
sort |\
awk -f cword.awk
```

The original text is in *awk.chp*, and after *stripjunk awk* is first invoked to strip all the whitespace characters off and break each word onto a separate line. Then sort can sort the words, and our *awk* program *cword.awk* can produce the output. The program is:

```
BEGIN           { word = "" }
word == $one    { count++ }
word != $one    { if (word != "") printf "%-16.16s %9d\n",\
                                   word, count
                  count = 0
                  word = $one }
```

```
END             { printf "%d different words found.\n", wc }
```

And the first page of resulting output is:

```
'                7
a              129
a-and            1
abc              2
ability          1
abort            1
about            4
above            2
acceptable       1
access           1
accessed         1
accident         1
according        2
accordingly      1
act              1
action          20
actions          1
actually         1
add              1
after            3
against          3
all             13
allocate         1
allocated        2
allow            1
allows           4
already          1
also            12
alternately      1
although         8
altogether       1
amnt             2
amount          10
an              16
analysts         1
and             84
annoying         1
```

```
another         8
any            18
anything        1
apart           1
appear          2
appearance      1
appears         1
append          2
are            40
argument        1
array           9
arrays          8
as             47
aspect          1
assigned        2
assignment      3
associated      4
assumed         3
assuming        1
at             13
auto           11
```

9
Spooler

One of the most difficult things to make run smoothly in a timesharing system is a large capacity, shared printer. In a single-user environment, or one where there is one printer for each user, the person who enters a command that activates the printer can schedule and supervise the printer.

Nowadays, more and more computer buyers are going with laser printers. A laser printer is quieter, faster, produces better quality output, and can handle graphics and automatic forms generation. But they are relatively expensive: from $2,000 to $10,000 or more. Consequently, most budget managers will want to get as much use out of a single printer as possible. This also holds true even if the system printer is a $200 special.

If a printer is serving any more than one user, even if those users are at adjacent desks, someone must handle the arbitration and at least the "electronic maintenance" of the printer. It is up to the computer itself to handle these tasks:

1. Make sure that print jobs are not printed on top of each other. If a print request is received and another print job is in process, collect the output and print it when the printer becomes available. This action is called "print spooling."

2. Make sure that the printer is loaded with the right type of paper before a job starts.

3. Make sure the interface between the printer and the computer is set up properly, including the right communication speed and parity setting.

4. Account for the usage of the printer.

5. Print page separators between jobs for easy separation of jobs when there is more than one in the output bin. These are called "banners."

6. Reset the printer before each job, so that each job's output will be done starting from a known state in the printer. Many printers have special font and graphics modes that, once set, must be reset to perform normal text printing.

7. Notify users when certain events occur.

The UNIX spooler system helps a system manager with all these tasks. If this facility is properly set up, all the UNIX users hooked up to the system or the network should be able to invoke print jobs without regard to the present status of the printer. This should lead to a more efficient work environment.

In this chapter we will study the standard line printer spooler provided with UNIX. In addition to understanding how to use the printer more efficiently, we can also learn from the implementation techniques that were invented so this facility could be implemented. Some aspects of these methodologies can be used in implementing other UNIX subsystems.

Daemons

A good design for a line printer spooler considers that print requests can come from many different sources at unpredictable times. If a program is to respond to this, it will have to be available all the time and be uninterruptable by any user except the super-user. It will also have to have complete command of the resource to be shared, in this case the serial or parallel communication port to the printer, to prevent accidental or intentional misuse.

Therefore, it stands to reason that the central, arbitrating program of the line printer system will have to be a privileged (i.e., super-user) program. This program has to be available to accept data and requests, processing or rejecting them according to its own rules.

We also want the spooler system to run without operator intervention, at least in the routine cases. It is also desirable to not necessarily have a super-user logged in at some terminal just so users can access the printer.

In UNIX, this type of situation is addressed with a *daemon*. A daemon is simply a process that runs without interaction or even attachment to any user or system terminal. It is normally designed to take as little processor time or resources as possible, so that overall system performance or throughput is not affected.

In UNIX System V.3 the central line printer daemon is the program in the file */usr/lib/lpsched*. (In older versions of UNIX you might see */usr/lib/lpd*) When not otherwise active, *lpsched* will sleep on a *read()* request to the named pipe */usr/spool/lp/FIFO*. Any program wishing to issue a line printer request can do so by writing to the pipe FIFO. The *lpsched* program will read this request and act on it as appropriate.

Spooler System Files and Directories

Before describing further how the daemon works, it helps to look at the files the printer spooler programs use. Conveniently, these are stored in the directory */usr/spool/lp*. The subdirectories and files used are:

./lp/request	Every request that any user makes creates a file in this directory. The file has the job number in it. Also, a copy of the data file to be printed is stored in here.
./lp/qstatus	A data file that stores the current status of the printer queue.
./lp/pstatus	A data file that stores the current status of each printer.
./lp/model	A directory of sample shell programs for different makes and models of printers. These programs are potentially modified and copied to the *./lp/interface* directory when a new printer is added to the system. They are not directly accessed by the print spooler.
./lp/member	For each printer in the system, there is a file which stores the device that corresponds to that printer.
./lp/interface	A directory of the shell programs that are used as output interfaces for each printer served by the print spooler. These programs do any necessary filtering of files according to the needs of the actual printer being served.

./lp/class	For each printer "class," a file exists in this directory to name all the specific printers that belong to each class.
./lp/default	This file names the default printer. All print requests not otherwise directed will go to this printer.
./lp/outputq	A data file containing the current information on the output queue.
./lp/FIFO	This is the named pipe through which the *lpsched* daemon accepts its requests.
./lp/SCHEDLOCK	A file used for interlocking access between daemons.
./lp/oldlog	The log file from the prior initialization of the *lprinter* scheduler.
./lp/log	A history of print activity from the last time the scheduler was started.
./lp/seqfile	A data file containing the number of the last job.

The *lp* Command

A user that does not have responsibility for managing the system will want the easiest access mechanism possible. In UNIX, this is accomplished with the *lp* command. Whenever any user wants to perform output, he simply creates a process with the program in */usr/bin/lp* and tells it were the data is. From a shell command, we might type

```
lp -dlaser xoutput
```

which will send the data in the file *xoutput* to the destination *laser*. If the -d option had not been specified, the destination stored in the file */usr/spool/lp/default* would have been used. Alternately we can generate output by:

```
awk -f xl.awk infile | lp
```

When *lp* does not have any parameters, it assumes it will be taking input from the standard input. This makes it easy to invoke the line-printer spooler from a program, as in the example that follows:

Chapter 9   Spooler

```
1 0: /* ptable.c - Print an arithmetic table to the lp spooler
2 0*
3 0*     alan deikman 3/89
4 0*
5 0*     This program demonstrates a simple method of sending output
6 0*     directly to the line-printer spooler from a program.
7 0*
8 0*     */
9 0:
10 0: #include <stdio.h>
11 0:
12 0: int     Pipe[2];          /* two file descriptors returned by pipe() */
13 0: FILE    *out;
14 0:
15 0: main() {
16 1:    int pid;
17 1:
18 1:    /* create a pipe */
19 1:
20 1:    if (pipe(Pipe) < 0) {
21 2:       fprintf(stderr, "ERROR: cannot open pipe\n");
22 2:       exit(2); }
23 1:
24 1:    /* now fork into two processes */
25 1:
26 1:    if ((pid = fork()) == -1) {
27 2:       fprintf(stderr, "ERROR: cannot fork\n");
28 2:       exit(2); }
29 1:
30 1:    if ((pid = fork()) == -1) {
31 1*       output of the pipe, and then execute the line-printer
32 1*       spooler with the desired options */
33 1:
34 1:    if (pid == 0) {
35 2:      close(0);
36 2:      close(Pipe[1]);
37 2:      if (dup(Pipe[0]) != 0) {
38 3:         fprintf(stderr, "ERROR: dup in child failed\n");
39 3:         exit(2); }
40 2:
41 2:      /* invoke the printer spooler for destination test, with
42 2*         a title "Math Table", and an instruction to send mail
43 2*         to the user of this process when it has been printed */
44 2:
45 2:      execl("/usr/bin/lp", "lp", "-dtest", "-m",
46 2:                            "-tMath Table", (char *) 0);
47 2:      fprintf(stderr, "ERROR: cannot call the printer spooler\n");
48 2:      exit(2); }
49 1:
50 1:    /* the parent process will output the table data to the input
51 1*       of the pipe */
52 1:
53 1:    close(1);
54 1:    if (dup(Pipe[1]) != 1) {
55 2:       fprintf(stderr, "ERROR: dup failed\n");
56 2:       exit(2); }
57 1:    table(stdout, 1, 20);
58 1:
59 1:    /* close out the pipe so that lp command will get
60 1*       an EOF */
61 1:
62 1:    close(1);
63 1:    close(Pipe[0]);
64 1:    close(Pipe[1]);
65 1:
66 1:    /* done */
67 1:
68 1:    exit(0); }
```

```
69 0:
70 0:
71 0: #include <math.h>
72 0:
73 0: table(file, start, end)
74 0: FILE    *file;          /* file stream to output */
75 0: int     start;          /* starting integer */
76 0: int     end;            /* ending integer */
77 0: {
78 1:     register int i;
79 1:     register double f;
80 1:
81 1:     fprintf(file, "    i        sqrt(i)      log(i)              exp(i)\n");
82 1:     fprintf(file, "-----  ------------  ------------  ------------------\n");
83 1:     for (i = start; i <= end; i++) {
84 2:         f = i;
85 2:         fprintf(file, "%5d %12.7f %12.7f %18g\n", i, sqrt(f),
86 2:                 log(f), exp(f)); }
87 1:
88 1:     return; }
```

The *lp* program does not access the printer port directly. Instead, it places its output and requests its files in the directory */usr/spool/lp/request* and signals the *lpsched* daemon by writing a short message to */usr/spool/lp/FIFO*.

If possible, *lp* will not make a separate copy of the data to be printed. This can be done by linking the file to be printed into the */usr/spool/lp/request* directory. After the file is printed the link is removed. When *lp* does this the user must be sure not to alter the files before they are printed.

It is not possible for *lp* to simply create a link if its input is on the standard input or another file system from */usr*. In this case, a new file is made in the *request* directory, which is then deleted after it is printed.

Printer Classes and Multiple Destinations

The *-d* option on the *lp* command gives the user the capability to redirect the output to any of a number of destinations. This is not only useful for when there are multiple printers, but is also useful for only a single printer.

A different printer destination does not necessarily mean a different physical printer. It might be desirable to create a different printer destination on the same physical printer for the following reasons:

1. A different type of paper is to be loaded instead of what is normally loaded.

2. A different printer mode is required. For example, many laser printers can print in "landscape" or "portrait" mode.

3. This job is a lower priority job.

The system manager can create a different printer destination for each of these categories by using the *lpadmin* command. The printer destination itself can be controlled by using *enable* and *disable* commands when jobs of a specific type are to be run.

Sometimes there is more than one printer that can satisfy a category of requests hooked into a system. If this is the case, a printer class can be created and named as a destination when the user does not care which of the printers in the class will be actually used to print the output.

Printer classes can be set up by the *lpadmin* command described below.

Other Commands for Users

The line printer spooler subsystem also provides users with a series of other commands that will allow them to control their own jobs:

enable <*destination*>

> Enable printer <*destination*>. The named printer will process jobs. Any jobs in the queue for that destination will start printing.

disable <*destination*>

> Disable printer <*destination*>. The named printer will not process any more jobs after the current ones.

cancel <*job*>

> Cancel job <*job*>. The named job will be taken from the output queue, and can be aborted in the middle of a printout. If this command is executed by the system manager, mail will be sent to the user with a note that the job had been canceled.

lpstat   [*-t*]

> Get the status of all the jobs in the output queue. If the *-t* option is given, list out all the printer destinations and their status.

The *lpadmin* Command

The *lpadmin* command is used to set up printer destinations and classes. Note that this command is usually placed in the */usr/lib* directory, so to invoke it you will have to type the complete path name. It has three primary options:

-p<*printer*>

>Change a parameter associated with the named printer destination. If the printer destination does not exist, it will be created.

-x<*printer*>

>Removes the named printer from the system.

-d<*printer*>

>Makes the named printer the system default.

The <*printer*> referred to above is a destination that can be named in the *lp* command. This can be either a printer or a class of printers. The above operations are augmented with the following options:

-c<*class*>

>The named printer is inserted into the named class. The printer class is created if necessary.

-r<*class*>

>The named printer is removed from the named class.

-v<*device*>

>The printer is associated with the named device, for example */dev/tty02*.

In addition to creating the printer destination, the system manager will have to supply an interface program. This program is described later in this chapter.

Chapter 9 Spooler

Other Commands for the System Manager

These commands are provided in the /usr/lib directory. Since this directory is not normally in the search path, these commands are often invoked by typing their absolute path name.

lpsched

>Start the line printer daemon. If the spooler system was shut down, this command can be used to restart it.

lpshut

>Shut down the spooler subsystem. This is necessary for most of the *lpadmin* commands to work. Note that the *lp* command will still be able to take requests, but they will not be processed until *lpsched* is started again and the printers are enabled.

accept <*destination*>

>Allow the named destination to accept *lp* requests.

reject <*destination*>

>Do not let *lp* accept any more requests for the named destination.

The Printer Interface Program

Each printer destination has what is called an *interface* program. An interface program is a shell script that may perform any or all of the the following functions:

1. Prints out a banner page that identifies the following output by user name, file name, date, and time.

2. Sends appropriate initialization strings to the printer.

3. Sets up the communications port attached to the printer with the appropriate values.

209

4. Invokes a filter that will process the data from the user into a form suitable to sending to the printer. In many cases, this is simply the *cat* command.

5. Repeat step #4 in order to make multiple copies as requested by the user.

The shell script is invoked automatically by the scheduler daemon for each job processed. This gives the system manager tremendous flexibility in supporting various printers and configurations of the same printer.

The interface program is found in the directory */usr/spool/lp/interface* in a file of the same name as the destination printer. When invoked, the scheduler provides the program with four or more parameters by setting up a command line such as:

```
sh interface/<iface> <request> <user> <copies> <file>...
```

where:

<iface>   is the name of the interface program.

<request>   is the unique identifier assigned to the print job. Usually this is of the form *p-n*, where *p* is the printer destination, and *n* a number taken from *seqfile*. In the shell script this can be referenced as *$1*.

<user>   is the user login I.D., referenced as *$2*.

<copies>   is the number of copies requested, referenced as *$3*.

<file> ...   are the files to be printed.

The system manager is expected to set up interface programs appropriate to the needs of the installation. If you are working with a single-user system, or a low-volume printer, it is likely you will want to dispense with banner pages. You can copy the shell script in the directory */usr/spool/lp/model* that most closely matches your needs. You may modify it as necessary. In the system that was used to write this book I used:

```
# basic line printer interface without frills
# for parallel printers
    copies=$4
```

```
          shift; shift; shift; shift; shift
          files="$*"
          i=1
          while [ $i -le $copies ]
          do
             for file in $files
             do
                /usr/spool/lp/interface/basiclp < "$file" 2>&1
             done
             i=`expr $i + 1`
          done
          exit 0
```

Note the use of a special filter called *basiclp*. This was written to efficiently process characters for the laser printer being used. This is because the parallel device driver I was using was very simple and could not expand tabs or insert \r characters before \n characters, which is what the laser printer I was using needed. The C program for this filter is as follows:

```
 1 0: /* basiclp.c - basic line printer filter
 2 0*
 3 0*    alan deikman 3/89
 4 0*
 5 0*    This filter will process data files for printing on a
 6 0*    parallel line printer.  The processes are as follows:
 7 0*
 8 0*        1.  Tab characters are expanded to spaces up to
 9 0*            8 space tab stops
10 0*        2.  \n is translated to \r\n
11 0*        3.  The last character is guaranteed to be \f
12 0*        4.  Multiple \f are suppressed
13 0*
14 0*    */
15 0:
16 0: #include <stdio.h>
17 0:
18 0: main() {
19 1:    register short c;
20 1:    register short pc = 0;
21 1:    register short col = 0;
22 1:
23 1:    while ((c = getchar()) != EOF) {
24 2:
25 2:      /* newline character */
26 2:
27 2:      if (c == '\n') {
```

```
28  3:          putchar('\r');
29  3:          putchar('\n');
30  3:          col = 0; }
31  2:
32  2:      /* form-feed character */
33  2:
34  2:      else if (c == '\f') {
35  3:          putchar('\r');
36  3:          if (pc != '\f') putchar('\f');
37  3:          col = 0; }
38  2:
39  2:      /* tab character */
40  2:
41  2:      else if (c == '\t') {
42  3:          do {       43  4:          putchar(' ');
44  4:            col += 1;
45  4:          } while (col & 0x7);  }
46  2:
47  2:      /* any other character */
48  2:
49  2:      else {
50  3:          putchar(c);
51  3:          col += 1; }
52  2:
53  2:      pc = c; }
54  1:
55  1:  /* make sure we ended in a \f */
56  1:
57  1:  if (pc != '\f') {
58  2:      putchar('\r');
59  2:      putchar('\f'); }
60  1:
61  1:  /* done */
62  1:
63  1:  exit(0); }
```

If the printer is attached to a serial port, it is likely that a special baud rate, parity, and other parameters will be needed. In that case, the interface shell script should have a command such as

```
stty 4800 opost onlcr otab3 0<&1
```

which will set the serial port to 4800 baud, with \r characters added to \n characters, and tabs expanded. This would make the above filter for the simple parallel port unnecessary.

Chapter 9   Spooler

Summary

The UNIX line printer spooler can be very convenient, or in simple systems it might just get in the way too much. For single user systems, it is often the case that users simply redirect their output to the /dev/lp device file, and ignore the spooler altogether. The facility of being able to do something else while the printer is printing can be duplicated by running jobs in background or by jumping between virtual screens.

For larger systems, where printer sharing takes place, the UNIX printer spooler can be configured to meet almost any situation. Properly used, the spooler system is seen as a necessity.

10
C Programming Under UNIX

It is hard to imagine UNIX without the C programming language. There are plenty of programming languages other than C available for UNIX, but the fact remains that C is the concept building block of UNIX. This Chapter covers the basic commands and programming tools used to develop C programs. These tools also work for other languages, but are best demonstrated with C.

C Compiler—*cc* Command

Most compiled languages have two phases to the process of converting a source program to the executable object: 1) compile, and 2) link-load. C under UNIX is no different, although the command *cc*,[1] which compiles C programs, will automatically invoke the loader (the *ld* command, described later) if not otherwise directed.

The *cc* command is easy to use and best described by progressive example. If your source file is in the file *wordwrap.c* it can be compiled with:

```
cc wordwrap.c
```

This will automatically compile and load the program, placing the executable object in *a.out*. If any errors or warnings occur during either compilation or loading process, the appropriate messages will be sent to the standard error device. If the message is a fatal error (such as a syntax error in the C program) no output will be sent to *a.out*. If we wanted the executable output in some other file than *a.out*, we can use the *mv* command to rename the file, or use the *-o* option to the *cc* command line as follows:

---

[1] See articles cc(cp) (XENIX PRM), cc(1) (Microport RSM), cc(1) (AT&T PRM).

```
cc wordwrap.c -o wordwrap
```

This places the executable object in the file *wordwrap*. The *-o* option can be placed anywhere on the *cc* command line, as long as the target file name is placed immediately after it. Note that the name of the target (*wordwrap*, in this example) need not have anything to do with the names of the source files.

The *cc* command allows the compilation of more than one file at a time, simply by including the name of the files on the command line. The command line:

```
cc piston.c head.c bearing.c crank.c cylinder.c -o engine
```

in this case, the C compiler is run for five source files, and the result is placed in the target file *engine*.

In such multiple source file programs, however, it is usually more convenient to compile each component separately, and load them all together in a separate command. This way, if we change one of the source files, we usually need not spend the time to recompile all the elements that did not change.

By the convention used by the loader and compiler programs on UNIX, the intermediate "relocatable object" files are stored in files suffixed with *.o*. These files, which otherwise would be discarded by *cc* after the loading phase, can be saved by the *-c* option. For example, the command lines:

```
cc -c piston.c
cc -c head.c
```

will create the files *piston.o*, and *head.o*, which can then be later loaded in a separate command line. For example:

```
cc piston.o head.o bearing.c crank.c cylinder.c -o engine
```

will compile the other three files, *bearing.c*, *crank.c*, and *cylinder.c*. If there are no errors *cc* will then pass the names of all five *.o* files to the loader. Note that the order of the files on the command line are not important on the *cc* command line.

There need not be any files to compile on the *cc* line. If all the files given

Chapter 10 C Programming Under UNIX

are object files, no C compilations are done and the loader is invoked directly. The C programmer need never type a loader (*ld*) command directly, although this is sometimes done in special cases. The *cc* command is more convenient to use than the *ld* command for the reason that the C library files are automatically passed to the loader by the *cc* program, and the files are submitted to the loader in the correct order.

Sometimes it is useful to support several different versions of a program in a single source file, and to choose which version at compilation time. This is what the *-D* option is for, which is the equivalent of the C pre-processor *#define* statement. By using the *#ifdef* and *#ifndef* directives, we can select and deselect segments of code in the source program. We can also specify other parameters. For example, if we have the C program segment:

```
#ifdef SINGLE
float matrix[MSIZE][MSIZE];
#else
double matrix[MSIZE][MSIZE];
#endif
```

we can choose at compilation time whether the symbol matrix is declared of type float or of type double, and what size it is. If this segment is in the file *invert.c,* then the command line:

```
cc -o invert -DSINGLE -DMSIZE=20 invert.c
```

will compile the program with matrix defined as a 20x20 matrix of single precision floating point numbers. If we use:

```
cc -o invert -DMSIZE=18 invert.c
```

matrix will be 18x18 double precision numbers. The C preprocessor gives us other directives we can use for compile-time code modification.

For debugging, the compiler can generate programs with additional information in it to allow the *sdb* debugger to locate source code while the program is running. To activate this feature, the *-g* option is used on the *cc* command line which compile the program to be debugged. For example:

```
cc -g piston.o head.o bearing.c crank.c cylinder.c -o engine
```

will recompile the same .c files as before, but for those files, the executable

217

file *engine* will have the tags necessary to trace pieces of code back to the original lines in the original source files. Note that this will not be true of the functions within *piston.o* and *head.o*. If the the code in either of those files needs to be debugged, it is advisable to recompile them.

In many programming problems, there is more than one way to structure a program, and it is possible that one division of tasks between subroutines is better than another. To help make optimization decisions it is often useful to be able to monitor how much time was spent in each subroutine and how many times each subroutine was called. The *-p* option on the *cc* command line generates an executable program that automatically keeps track of this information. For example:

```
cc -p invert.c -o invert
invert < matrix > result
prof invert
```

The executable program *invert* is generated by the *cc* command line, which includes a special version of the system libraries that were also compiled with the *-p* option. The invert program is executed, with matrix as the input and result as the output. When the invert program finishes execution, the *monitor()* library function is automatically called, generating the file *mon.out*. This file is interpreted by the *prof* program.[2]

Because the SCO XENIX C compiler and the Microport C compiler come from such widely different origins,[3] most of the other options to the *cc* command line between the two systems are different. The options we have covered so far are common between the two. The following table briefly describes the other options available for the XENIX *cc* command line. Note that many of these options are similar to those that are available in the Microsoft C for DOS product (version 3.0 and later).

---

[2] See articles PROF(CP) (XENIX PRM), PROF(1) (Microport RSM), PROF(1) (AT&T PRM), MONITOR (9S) (XENIX PRM), MONITOR(3C) (Microport RSM), MONITOR(3C) (AT&T PRM).

[3] SCO XENIX, because it comes from Microsoft, uses a version of the the Microsoft C compiler originally developed for DOS. This compiler supports many more options for memory models and code optimization options than does the C compiler used with the Microport, which is the AT&T "pcc" portable C compiler.

SCO XENIX System V *cc* options

Option	Description
-C	Preserves comments in preprocessor.
-compat	Makes object compatible across various version of XENIX
-CSmode	Enables/disables common sub-expression compression. The values for mode may be ON or OFF
-d	Displays compilation phase names as they occur
-dos	Generates executable output for DOS.
-E	Runs the C preprocessor, and sends the result to the standard output.
-F*num*	Sets the size of the stack to num bytes.
-Fa*name*	Creates an assembly listing in file name. If name is not specified, *source.s* is used.
-Fc*name*	Creates a merged C source and assembler listing file in file name, or *source.L* if name is not specified.
-Fe*name*	Same as -o name.
-Fl*name*	Creates a source listing in file name, or *source.L* if name is not specified.
-Fm*name*	Creates a memory map from the *ld* loader in file name, or file *a.map* if name is not specified.
-Fo*name*	The object file will be placed in file name.
-FP*mode*	Specifies DOS floating point support option.
-Fs*name*	Creates a C source listing in file name, or *source.S* if name is not specified.
-i	Creates a separate program segment from data segment in the small model. (see Chapter 13).
-I*path*	Add directory path to the list of directories to be searched for files reference by *#include* statements.
-K	Remove stack probes from a program.
-l*name*	Search library name for unresolved function references.
-L	Creates an assembler listing file for each source file. The generated file names will be the same as the source file except for the extension will be *.L*.
-LARGE	Use the compiler that executes in the large model. This may be necessary for large programs.
-M*string*	Sets the program model and instruction set for the executable program. The string may be any non-conflicting combination of the following:

219

s	Small model
m	Medium model
l	Large model
h	Huge model
e	Allow extended keywords (near, far, etc.)
0	Generate code for 8086
1	Use instructions found in 80186
2	Use instructions found in 80286
3	Use instructions found in 80386
b	Reverse word order for double words
tnum	Allocate items larger than num in new segment
d	Do not assume stack segment is equal to data segment
-n	Same as -i

-NDname	Set data segment to name.
-nlnum	Sets maximum length of external symbols to *num*.
-NMname	Sets the module name for each compile source file to name. If name is not given, the name of the source file would be used.
-NTname	Set the text segment name to name. The default is *source_TEXT* for middle and large model programs, and *_TEXT* for small model programs.
-Ostring	Object code optimizer. The string parameter may one or more of the following characters:

d	Disables optimization (default).
a	Relaxes alias checking.
s	Optimizes code for space.
t	Optimizes code for speed.
x	Performs all optimizations.
c	Eliminates common expressions.
l	Loop optimizations.

-P	Leave the preprocessor output in file(s) the same name as the source file(s), except with suffix .i.
-pack	Pack all structures.
-r	Use the incremental loader.
-S	Creates an assembly source listing in a file the same name as the source file, except suffixed with .s.

Chapter 10 C Programming Under UNIX

-SEGnum	Sets the maximum number of segments.
-u	Removes all manifest defines. See -U
-Uname	Removes the "manifest define" name. Manifest defines are compile time symbols that are automatically set by the compiler for use by conditional compilation directives. These defines identify what type of compiler, system, and memory model are being used.
-Vstring	The value string is copied to the object file.
-w	Prevents all warning messages. Same as -W0.
-Wnum	Sets warning message level. For the following warnings, the value *num* can be:

0	No warning messages
1	Program structure and overt type mismatches
2	Strong type mismatches
3	All automatic conversion

-X	Remove standard directories from search for #include files.
-z	Displays passes without executing them.
-Zpnum	Aligns data structures on num bytes, which may be 1, 2, or 4.
-Zi	Same as -g.

The AT&T and Microport compiler does not support as many memory models or optimization options. The options that are found are much more in line with those found in other UNIX systems.

Interactive Systems UNIX and Microport System V *cc* options

Option	Description
-E	Run only the C preprocessor, and send the result to the standard output.
-O	Optimize the object code.
-P	Run only the C preprocessor on the input file(s) and leave the result in corresponding files suffixed with .i.
-S	Generate assembly source code without compiling.
-g	Include data for the *sdb* debugger in the object files.
-V	Display the version of the compiler, optimizer, assembler, and/or link-editor that is invoked.
-Wx,args	Pass arguments to various programs within the C

221

compilation process. The *args* parameter is a series of words, separated by commas, that are passed to the program indicated by *x*:

p	preprocessor
0	1st pass of compiler
2	optimizer
a	assembler
l	link editor

-Yx,dir   Specify the location of the various section(s) of the C compilation process. The directory dir is specified for the section(s) or resources defined by string *x*. The possible values for *x* are:

p	preprocessor
0	1st pass of compiler
2	optimizer
a	assembler
l	link editor
S	start-up routines
I	default directory for *#include* directives
L	First default library searched by *ld*
U	Second default library searched by *ld*

-#   Output information about the execution of *cc*:

-#	Output the name of each part.
-##	Add the full pathname.
-###	Output the name and pathname, but do not execute.

-Mx   Select the memory model. *x* is one of:

s	Small model, 16-bit addressing
l	Large model, 32-bit addressing

The small model is the default.

The options for both SCO and Microport that control the memory and instruction model require some discussion. By default, we obtain the "small, pure" model, which allows us 64KB of text (program) space, and up to 64KB to be shared by the data and the stack. On both SCO XENIX and Microport UNIX these limits can be changed with the -*M* element on the command line, although there are important programming considerations. See Chapter 12 for details.

The Loader—*ld* Command

The loader, or the "link editor" has the job of combining relocatable object files into a single file which is itself either relocatable or executable. A typical example of *ld* activity is shown in Figure 10-1. As explained earlier, normally the *ld* command is automatically executed by the *cc* command, so we will usually discuss loader options as if they were *cc* options.

The loader takes two forms of input: 1) the object output of a compiler, the assembler, or another run of the *ld* command that had combined other inputs, and 2) object libraries created with the *ar* command (see next section).

The object data format of the loader is *a.out*[4] format, which is used for both input and output. In an executable program, however, there should be no undefined externals.

There is one important difference between the loader used by SCO XENIX and the one used by Microport V/AT. The XENIX loader will iteratively search all libraries until it is unable to resolve any undefined externals by doing so, where the Microport loader will only search a library once.

The Archive Program

The UNIX facility for libraries of object files is the *ar* "archive" program.[5] The archive program can combine more than one file, not necessarily object files, into a single file which can be referenced as a unit.

---

[4] By convention, the file name a.out is the default output of the loader. For that reason, the format of executable files is documented in the A.OUT(F) article in the SCO XENIX User's Reference Manual, and the A.OUT(4) article in the Microport Software Development System Manual Vol II.

[5] See articles AR(cp) (XENIX PRM), AR(1) (Microport RSM), AR(1) (AT&T PRM).

Figure 10-1

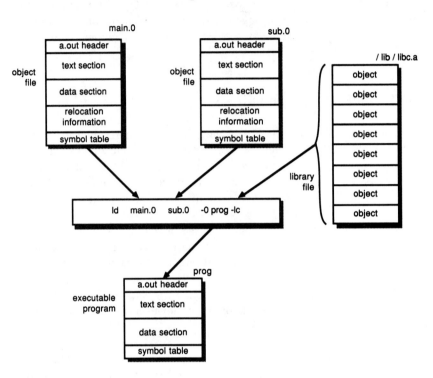

If we have four object files, we can make a library out of them with the command:

```
ar r libu.a piston.o cylinder.o head.o
```

which will create the new library *libu.a*. If *libu.a* had already existed, this command would have replaced any existing occurrence of those object files in the library. If the object files did not exist in the library, they are added at the end.

In cases where the order of object files are important, we can modify the r command key parameter with either *a* or *b* to specify where in the library a new object file is to be put. This is the case where one object file has unsatisfied externals that are defined by another object file. For example, in our library created above, the command:

```
ar ra piston.o libu.a crank.o
```

would place the file *crank.o* in the library *libu.a* after the file *piston.o*. To reverse the process, we can use the *x* option to extract files from a library. For example:

```
ar x libu.a cylinder.o
```

will create the file *cylinder.o* from the copy found in the library. This is not often done, although this makes it possible to reference particular object module in a *cc* command line. We might want to do this in a special circumstance where we do not wish to automatically load the remainder of the file that is referenced by *cylinder.o*.

To get a table of contents of the archive file we can type:

```
ar t libu.a
```

to get a short listing, or:

```
ar tv libu.a
```

to get a long listing, which includes all the information that would be presented by the *ls -l* command.

To use an object library, all that is needed is to mention the library name in the *cc* command line. For example, if we have a subroutine library that was made with the command:

```
ar r graphics.a line.o circle.o arc.o grid.o spline.o
   point.o
```

we could compile a program and use the library with:

```
cc graph.c -o graph graphics.a
```

More typically, libraries are named with the convention:

```
libxx.a
```

where *xx* is replaced with a letter or letter combination that represents the library. The *ld* (as well as the *cc*) command line understands the option *-lxx* to mean *libxx.a* in the directories */lib* or */usr/lib*.

The *Make* Utility

The *make* program quickly becomes indispensable when developing a C program with more than one source file. *Make* automatically issues the minimum number of commands necessary to "make" a particular object, given the current state of its defined components. It does this by interpreting a dependency tree and the current last-modification times of all the files involved.

Consider a program that has three source files:

```
main.c
sub.c
defs.h
```

We can compile and load the whole program with the command:

```
cc main.c sub.c -o prog
```

which will compile two C source code files and load them into the executable file *prog*. However, if we are modifying the code in *sub.c*, but not *main.c*, why should we recompile *main.c* each time? It would make more sense to do the following:

```
cc -c main.c
cc sub.c main.o -o prog
```

The first line creates the file *main.o*, and the second command compiles only *sub.c* and includes *main.o* in the load process. The next time we modify *sub.c* we only need to issue the second command again, and avoid recompiling *main.c*. Of course, if we then find out we have to modify *main.c* the reverse process is necessary. We could maintain both *.o* files in the program, recompile each source code file when it is modified, and then load the result with:

```
cc main.o sub.o -o prog
```

This works for a two or three source code file program, but what happens when there are a half dozen or more files to keep track of? A mistake could cause an obsolete object file to be loaded with the program, and cause undetected trouble for a long time. Even if such a thing did not happen, it's a bore to keep retyping the commands to compile and load files.

The *make* program solves that problem.[6] The inter-dependency of the source-to-object files is described by the programmer in the "make file," named by default *makefile*. In our previous example we could have a *makefile* whose contents are as follows:

```
main.o:    main.c defs.h
           cc -c -O main.c

sub.o:     sub.c defs.h
           cc -c -O sub.c

prog:      main.o sub.o
           cc main.o sub.o -o prog
```

This file tells *make* the following:

1. The *main.o* file is dependent on the files *main.c* and *defs.h*. To make *main.o*, issue the command:

    ```
    cc -c -O main.c
    ```

2. The *sub.o* file is dependent on the files *sub.c* and *defs.h*. To make *sub.o*, issue the command:

    ```
    cc -c -O sub.c
    ```

3. The file *prog* is dependent on *main.o* and *sub.o*. To make the file *prog*, issue the command

    ```
    cc main.o sub.o -o prog
    ```

Now, each time the programmer wishes to update the program *prog*, all he needs to do is type the command:

```
make
```

and *make* will examine the last modification times of each of the files involved, and issue the appropriate commands. If either *main.c* or *def.h* was modified more recently than *main.o*, the *cc* command will be automatically

---

[6] See articles MAKE(C) (XENIX VRM), MAKE(1) (Microport PRM), MAKE(1) (AT&T PRM).

executed to compile *main.c*. A similar action is taken for *sub.o*. After that, if the prog file's last modification is compared to that of both *main.o* and *sub.o*, and the *cc* command is executed if appropriate.

If it turns out that no file needs to be "made," the *make* program will announce "prog is up to date" and do nothing more.

Once the make file is properly set up, *prog* will always be built with the most up-to-date pieces. Note that if the file *defs.h* is modified, both *main.c* and *sub.c* will be compiled. In more complex situations, *make* can save hours of the programmer's time.

In simpler situations, the inter-dependency of files is so obvious, that make does not actually need much of that information in *makefile*. For example, *make* will assume that a *.o* file can be made out of a *.c* file. For example, the *make* file:

```
graph:      x.o y.o aa.o
            cc -o graph x.o y.o aa.o
```

will work provided that the *x.c*, *y.c*, and *aa.c* exist. To make things even easier, a variable/macro facility is provided. The same file can be written as:

```
OBJ=x.o y.o aa.o

graph:      $(OBJ)
            cc -o graph $(OBJ)
```

so that if the list of object files needs to be changed, only the *OBJ=* statement needs to be edited.

The SCCS Utility

For large programming projects, ones that have many revisions and source files that must be kept organized, the SCCS (Source Code Control System) is provided with UNIX. SCCS is a collection of programs that allow multiple versions of a file to be maintained within a single UNIX file, complete with revision history. SCCS makes it possible to recover any version of a file, not just the most current version.

SCCS is implemented as a series of programs that are installed in the system libraries. The major programs, briefly, are:

admin	Create and administer SCCS files (make an *s-file*).
delta	Make a change to an SCCS file (integrate an edited *g-file* into the *s-file*).
get	Get a version of an SCCS file (make a *g-file* out of an *s-file*)
prs	Print (sections of) an SCCS file
cdc	Change Delta Commentary

The SCSS programs are documented in the ADMIN(CP), DELTA(CP), GET(CP), PRS(CP) and CDC(CP) articles in the SCO XENIX Programmer's Reference Manual, and the SCCS file format is documented in the SCCSFILE(F) article in the SCO XENIX User's Reference Manual. In addition, a well written guide to SCCS may be found in Chapter 3 of the SCO XENIX Programmer's Guide Part I. In the Microport manuals, the articles ADMIN(1), DELTA(1), GET(1), PRS(1), and CDC(1) are in the Runtime System Manual, and the SCCS file format may be found in SCCSFILE(4) in the Software Development System Volume II. The Microport tutorial Chapter on SCCS is in Chapter 7 of the Software Development System Volume I.

The use of SCCS imposes a file-usage protocol on the user in order to keep control of access to the master file. The master file, which is always named with an *s.* prefix,[7] is never accessed directly by the user. Instead, an editable copy of the file of one version of the master file is created by the get command. Once that file has been edited (by whatever means) the changes are reintegrated into the master file with the *delta* command.

The data flow is pictured in Figure 10-2.

When maintaining a large and complex program text file, it is important to keep track of which versions were created when, and for what reason. It is also often helpful to be able to retrieve previous version, and "branch" versions, that are special to a particular purpose.

---

[7] As opposed to a suffix, which is more typical in UNIX.

Figure 10-2

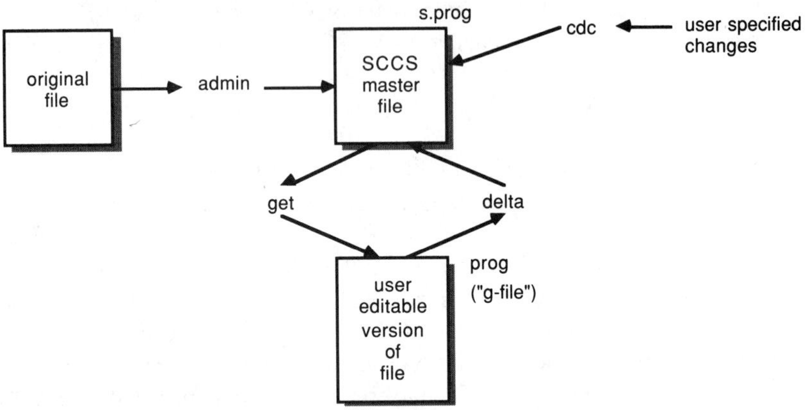

```
                          s.prog      cdc ←── user specified
                         ┌──────┐   ←──           changes
 ┌──────┐              │ SCCS │
 │original│ ── admin ──→│master│
 │ file  │              │ file │
 └──────┘              └──────┘
                        ↙      ↘
                      get      delta
                        ↘      ↙
                       ┌──────┐   prog
                       │ user │  ("g-file")
                       │editable│
                       │version│
                       │  of  │
                       │ file │
                       └──────┘
```

SCCS does this by maintaining a "delta table" within the master file. A delta is a change or set of changes to an original file. No restrictions are made on the size of the change, which means that the entire file could be replaced, or that one character in one line may be different.

Each delta is identified by a number which has up to four parts:

R	Release
L	Level
B	Branch
S	Sequence

For example, a delta labeled 3.1.2.2 may be read as "Release 3, Level 1, Branch 2, Sequence 2." Typically, the hierarchy of numbering is not used past the second level except for very complex programs. Proper use of delta numbering, coordinated between the program pieces and the program's documentation, is helpful in maintaining published software.

SCCS inserts special keywords in the source files to help identify the origin and history of the file. These keywords are based on the "SID" (SCCS IDentification) string. You will often see this string in many of the source files (such as shell scripts and C program source segments) that are delivered with the UNIX system. If you see the string:

```
/* @(#)3.1 */
```

in a C program, the file you are looking at was generated out of the Release 3 Level 1 delta of an SCCS master file. The *@(#)* string is a key which programs can use to find the SCCS I.D.

It is recommended that you start with the SCCS tutorial documentation when learning SCCS. I find it is most useful after the "first cut" of a program has been established, rather than with the pre-release versions. For example, if we have finished release 1 of a program that has the two parts *invert.c* and *solve.c* without using SCCS, we convert the programs to SCCS format with:

```
admin -r1 -iinvert.c s.invert.c
admin -r1 -isolve.c s.solve.c
```

The files *invert.c* and *solve.c* can be disposed of until we need to compile or change the program. The new files *s.invert.c* and *s.solve.c* will be created with no write permissions.

Suppose we now need to change the *solve.c* file, and we are going to create a new level. We get the most current version of the file with:

```
get -e s.solve.c
```

which will create the file *solve.c*, which has read and write permissions. Now we can edit the file with *vi*, recompile, and test the program. When we are done, we incorporate the changes into the SCCS file with the command:

```
delta -r1.1 s.solve.c
```

The delta program will prompt the terminal for comments which will be related to the new delta, which will be 1.1. Once that is done, the changes are incorporated into the the *s.solve.c*. Note that delta does not need to be told about the file *solve.c*.

After this point, we can retrieve either version of the file with get commands that specify the SID we wish. This can be carried out to any level.

The SCCS programs support many more options, including the concurrent maintenance of two versions of a given file, and a substitution facility to allow version dependent strings to be automatically updated in the source files. The best way to learn SCCS is to simply start using it.

11
Named Pipes

In Chapter 3 we described a named pipe, or a *FIFO* file. In this chapter we will develop the *system daylog* utility that uses a named pipe.

A system daylog is merely a file or series of files that makes chronological records of events as they happen. The daylog files in our system are simply text files, in a specific format that makes them easy to pass through utilities such as *grep* or *awk*. A typical series of daylog entries might be:

```
09:54:15 alan      vt01  3382 glentry.
09:54:34 george    ty03  3354 plsort. end. 5442 records
09:54:55 tina      ty02  3381 mainmenu.
09:55:12 alan      vt01  3382 glentry. end. 2 records added
09:55:13 tina      ty02  3394 oentry.
```

For those who are used to poking around in a UNIX system, this type of data file will be almost self-explanatory. Some parts are less obvious, so we will describe each field:

1. Time of event.
2. Name of the user who invoked the program.
3. Last four characters of the terminal name.
4. The process I.D. of the process that made the log entry.
5. A *free form* field made by the program making the log entry.

This last field can make the overall system daylog much more effective by following a universal convention. This will become apparent when we see how these data files are used.

The system daylog programs keep a separate file for each day of activity in the */usr/syslog* directory. In most cases, this keeps any individual file from becoming too large, and it alleviates the necessity of a *date* field within the data itself. The name of the file is simply the month and date in numeric format, as appropriate, such as "0713" for July 13.

When the /usr/syslog directory becomes too large, it is easy to archive and delete a month's worth of activities with a set of commands such as:

```
cd /usr/syslog
/bin/ls 06?? | cpio -ov > /dev/rdsk/f0
rm 06??
```

which will remove all of June's records from the system after making a *cpio* floppy.

Use of Daylog Files

The more large and complex a programming project or application is, the more useful a system daylog becomes. When you have dozens or even hundreds of different routines in shell script, C, and other compiled languages, and all are being used by multiple users, procedural and systemic bugs can be hard to find. This is doubly true if the bug is intermittent. An example command the programmer might enter is:

```
grep vt03 /usr/syslog/0810 | grep judy
```

which will scan the daylog for all the activity on August 10 by user "judy." If the report came up with:

```
10:53:05 judy     vt01    282    mainmenu.
10:53:15 judy     vt01    283    glmenu.
10:53:33 judy     vt01    283    gltrx.
10:55:47 judy     vt01    283    gltrx. end. 6 records
10:56:07 judy     vt01    288    glsorttrx.
10:56:34 judy     vt01    288    glsorttrx. end. 6 records
10:56:35 judy     vt01    291    glmrgtrx.
10:58:00 judy     vt01    283    glmenu. end
(etc.)
```

We can see that Judy invoked the main menu program *mainmenu*, then from that invoked *glmenu* (General Ledger), and from that invoked the *gltrx* (G/L transaction) program. A little over two minutes later *gltrx* ends, reporting that Judy had entered six records. These records were sorted by the the program *glsorttrx* in 27 seconds. (27 seconds to sort six records? Suspicious.) Then the program *glmrgtrx* (Merge Transactions) was called. Aha! The *glmrgtrx* program never made a "termination" entry. This means that it must have aborted abnormally, and probably never did the work it was supposed to.

If the programmer followed the proper daylog conventions, the applications programmer/troubleshooter now need rely on detailed verbal reports or observations of end users. It is unlikely that a non-programming user will observe or place any relevance on a briefly flashed message such as *sh: cannot shift* or something equally obscure. In our example above, the user *Judy* probably reported that she entered some new transactions, and they never showed up on the journal output. Using the system daylog, the programmer can quickly isolate which program never terminated properly. The investigation can continue with:

```
cd /usr/syslog
grep glmrgtrx. 08?? | pg
```

which will quickly come up with a report of when *glmrgtrx* was run, by whom, and in each case whether it terminated properly or not.

Other uses of the system daylog are that it can keep a record of the usage of each program. This can uncover bottlenecks or assist in analyzing the overall efficiency of the computer. For example, if the application is order-processing, and the order entry program makes a daylog entry every time an order is processed, a quick perusal of the daylog can quickly determine how many orders per unit time are processed and who processed them.

One by-product of usage accounting is the possibility of royalty calculations. If you wrote a program that you charge for on a "pay-as-you-use" basis, you can use the system daylog to record usage, then every so often generate a billing, using the system daylog as input.

Another aspect of the daylog is security. If the only way for a user to access a database is through one of the application programs, and that program makes daylog entries, an automatic record is kept of who accessed or altered the data, and at what time. From the point of view of the applications programmer, the daylog reporting is strictly voluntary. Of course, for anyone using the program and who does not have access to the source code, the reporting mechanism is transparent and involuntary.

UNIX Programming on the 80286/80386

The FIFO Queue

The requirements of our system daylog system are twofold: 1) it must be easy to use for the programmer, and 2) it must be inviolate as far as accidental or intentional corruption is concerned. This second requirement is more difficult, and is solved by the use of a named pipe and the normal UNIX security mechanism for files.

The system-wide named pipe we use is called */usr/syslog/FIFO*. This file and the *syslog* directory in which it resides must belong to either the super-user (root) or a user who is entrusted with managing the system daylog. Normally, the system manager who has super-user access performs this chore. The directory and FIFO may be created as:

```
cd /usr
mkdir syslog
chmod 0755 syslog
cd syslog
mknod FIFO p
chmod 0622 FIFO
```

by the super-user and the system log directories are ready to use. First, let's look at the program pieces that drive it.

The Daylog Subroutine

The daylog subroutine is simple to operate. It takes one parameter, a string that is the free-form field to be entered by the process into the log file. This function can be added to one of the system libraries or included by explicit reference when compiling the program that uses them. The program listing follows:

```
1  0:  /* daylog() - generate message in the daylog system
2  0*
3  0*     alan deikman 3/89
4  0*
5  0*     This function provides a programmer interface to the daylog
6  0*     system.  The daylog system will accept general messages
7  0*     from any number of sources, format them, and submit them for entry
8  0*     into the system daylog.
9  0*
```

Chapter 11 Named Pipes

```
10 0*    The program syslog will operate the other end of the FIFO.
11 0*
12 0*    */
13 0:
14 0: #include <stdio.h>
15 0: #include <time.h>
16 0: #include <sys/types.h>
17 0: #include <fcntl.h>
18 0:
19 0: daylog(s)
20 0: char    *s;              /* message to transmit */
21 0: {
22 1:   time_t t;                      /* current time in seconds from epoch */
23 1:   struct tm *clock;              /* structure version */
24 1:   int   pid;                     /* process I.D. to report */
25 1:   char  user[L_cuserid];         /* user name */
26 1:   char  *p, *getenv(), *ttyname();
27 1:   int   i;
28 1:   char  Logfile[128];
29 1:
30 1:   /* verify directory */
31 1:
32 1:   if ((p = getenv("SYSLOG")) != NULL) {
33 2:     strcpy(Logfile, p);
34 2:     for (p = Logfile; *p; p++);
35 2:     if (*--p != '/') strcat(Logfile, "/"); }
36 1:   else strcpy(Logfile, "/usr/syslog/");
37 1:   strcat(Logfile, "FIFO");
38 1:   if (access(Logfile, 2)) {
39 2:     fprintf(stderr, "ERROR, cannot access SYSLOG system\n");
40 2:     return; }
41 1:
42 1:   /* get current time */
43 1:
44 1:   t = time((long *) 0);
45 1:   clock = localtime(&t);
46 1:
47 1:   /* get terminal name, if any */
48 1:
49 1:   i = 0;
50 1:   p = " ";
51 1:   do {
```

```
52 2:       if (isatty(i)) {
53 3:         p = ttyname(i);
54 3:         while (*p) p++;
55 3:         p -= 4; }
56 2:       } while (*p = ' ' && ++i < 3);
57 1:
58 1:    /* if first character in the message is a *, report the parent
59 1*       process I.D.  otherwise use this process I.D. */
60 1:
61 1:    if (s[0] == '*') {
62 2:      pid = getppid();
63 2:      s++; }
64 1:    else pid = getpid();
65 1:    cuserid(user);
66 1:
67 1:    /* open file and print message */
68 1:
69 1:    i = open(Logfile, O_NDELAY | O_WRONLY | O_APPEND, 0);
70 1:    if (i < 0) {
71 2:      fprintf(stderr, "ERROR: cannot open SYSLOG file\n");
72 2:      return; }
73 1:    sprintf(Logfile, "%2.2d:%2.2d:%2.2d %-8.8s %-4.4s %5d %s\n",
74 1:          clock->tm_hour, clock->tm_min, clock->tm_sec,
75 1:          user, p, pid, s);
76 1:    write(i, Logfile, strlen(Logfile));
77 1:    close(i);
78 1:
79 1:    /* done */
80 1:
81 1:    return; }
```

The *daylog()* function formats a message line, then simply does a write to the file */usr/syslog/FIFO*, which is the named pipe we created earlier with the *mknod* command. If the environment variable SYSLOG is set, it is assumed to name an alternate directory to use.

If this function attempts to execute and there is no program that has the FIFO open for reading, the *daylog()* function will simply print an error message and return to the calling program. The log message itself will be lost.

In general this should not be a problem because the *syslog* program, shown later in this chapter, will always have the named pipe open for reading. However, if this is not acceptable, it is possible to modify the *daylog()* program to automatically invoke a child process that makes an *exec()* call to create the *syslog* process. I preferred to leave this out, because if the system is having difficulty to the point that *syslog* cannot operate, we don't want to have dozens of attempts to recreate it.

Any program in the system can make log entries in the standard format by using the *daylog()* function. Note that earlier we created the file *FIFO* with the mode bits set to *0622*, which allows anyone write access but not read access. Although a rogue process could possibly write unformatted messages to the file *FIFO*, it could not take anything out again unless it had read access to the pipe.

In the normal case, a skeleton example of how to use the *daylog()* function might be:

```
char bufr[128];
int  nf;

main() {

    daylog("cleanup.");

    ....

    sprintf(bufr, "cleanup. end. %d files removed", nf);
    daylog(bufr);
    exit(0); }
```

which will take care of all the basic log reporting needed to detect usage, abnormal aborts, and execution timing on a long-term basis. For a longer, more complex program, other calls to the *daylog()* function can be provided to add more information to the system daylog.

The *log* Program

The *daylog()* function works for compiled programs, but what about shell scripts? For this we provide a simple main program, compile it, and place it in the */usr/bin* directory. This program is:

```
 1 0: /* log.c - Create a log entry from the command line
 2 0*
 3 0*    alan deikman 3/89
 4 0*
 5 0*    This program calls the daylog() function to add a line to
 6 0*    the system log from a shell line.
 7 0*
 8 0*    Synopsis:
 9 0*
10 0*         log [<msg> | -f <file>]
11 0*
12 0*    Where <msg> can be any message and <file> is the name of a file
13 0*    to read into the daylog.  <file> may be - for standard input */
14 0:
15 0:
16 0: #include <stdio.h>
17 0:
18 0: char    msg[64] = "*";           /* message to send (note that a leading
19 0*                                     asterisk signals the daylog program
20 0*                                     to use the parent process I.D. rather
21 0*                                     than the running process I.D. */
22 0:
23 0: main(ac, av)
24 0: int     ac;
25 0: char    **av;
26 0: {
27 1:    int i, len = 1;
28 1:    char *p;
29 1:    FILE *f;
30 1:
31 1:    /* loop for all parameters */
32 1:
33 1:    while (--ac > 0) {
34 2:
35 2:      /* if we have an -f option, treat the next component as a file
36 2*         name and read the lines of the files from it */
37 2:
38 2:      if (!strcmp(*++av, "-f")) {
39 3:        if (--ac == 0 || **++av == '-') f = stdin;
40 3:        else if ((f = fopen(*av, "r")) == NULL) exit(0);
41 3:        while (fgets(msg + 1, 60, f) != NULL) {
42 4:          for (p = msg + 1; *p && *p != '\n'; p++);
```

```
43  4:            *p = 0;
44  4:            daylog(msg); }
45  3:          fclose(f); }
46  2:
47  2:      /* if a parameter to copy to the log message overruns the limit
48  2*         send out the line and start a new one */
49  2:
50  2:      else if (len + (i = strlen(*av)) > 63) {
51  3:        daylog(msg);
52  3:        msg[1] = 0;
53  3:        msg[0] = '*';
54  3:        len = 1; }
55  2:
56  2:      /* add the current parameter word to the message string */
57  2:
58  2:      else {
59  3:        if (i > 63) *av[63] = 0;
60  3:        if (len != 1) strcat(msg, " ");
61  3:        len += i;
62  3:        strcat(msg, *av); } }
63  1:
64  1:    /* dump any residual message and quit */
65  1:
66  1:    if (len > 1) daylog(msg);
67  1:    exit(0); }
```

As with any other program that uses *daylog()*, this program must be compiled and loaded with a reference to the *daylog.o* file. It can then be placed in the */usr/bin* directory, which will be in the search path of most shell scripts.

Note that the messages passed to *daylog()* by the log program are preceded with an asterisk (*). This is to signal *daylog()* to format the process I.D. of the *parent* process instead of the current process. This is more useful for logging messages in shell script programs.

A skeleton example of a program might be:

```
# cleanup - Cleanup user files
#
log cleanup.
nf=`/bin/ls ${tmpdir} | wc -l`
```

241

```
/bin/rm -r ${tmpdir}
log cleanup. $nf files removed
```

This can be expanded to any length. Another application of the log program might be:

```
df | awk '{printf "df. %5s %d\n", $1, $4}' | log -f
```

This will make a report of the current disk space free on all the file systems. This command can be executed by *cron* at regular intervals, which can be useful in determining peak disk load conditions.

This program can be used not only by shell scripts, but by users at the shell prompt as well. For example,

```
log T. Williams called
```

might be a useful way to record that specific event. However a series of *alias* commands in the C shell might make this more useful by forming a conventional format:

alias rcv log rcv. $*
alias call log called. $*

where the *rcv* command can now be used when phone calls are received and *call* could be used when phone calls are made. There are some office environments, such as attorney offices, where phone-call tracking is important.

The *syslog* Program

The one last piece to the system log program is the daemon that receives all the messages and places them in log files. This program, *syslog*, can be invoked by the */etc/rc* script that is executed at startup time, or placed in the */etc/inittab* file to be started when the system is placed in various states. See the chapter on system administration for descriptions of these procedures.

```
1 0: /* syslog.c - System log facility
2 0*
3 0*    alan deikman 3/89
4 0*
5 0*    This program reads from a FIFO and generates entries in a series
```

Chapter 11 Named Pipes

```
 6  0*      of log files to keep a system log of process activity.  The input to
 7  0*      the FIFO is one or more incarnations of the daylog() program.
 8  0*
 9  0*      The files written by this program are in the form /usr/syslog/mmdd,
10  0*      where mmdd is the current month and day.
11  0*
12  0*      This program should be run at system startup.  If it is killed
13  0*      for some reason, it can be restarted at any time without adverse
14  0*      effect.
15  0*
16  0*   */
17  0:
18  0: #include <stdio.h>
19  0: #include <fcntl.h>
20  0: #include <unistd.h>
21  0: #include <sys/types.h>
22  0: #include <sys/stat.h>
23  0: #include <time.h>
24  0:
25  0: char    Ldir[40] = "/usr/syslog/";   /* System log directory */
26  0: char    Bufr[256];                   /* general purpose buffer */
27  0: int     Fifo;                        /* FIFO file descriptor */
28  0: int     Logf;                        /* Log file descriptor */
29  0: short   Mon;                         /* current month */
30  0: short   Day;                         /* current day */
31  0:
32  0: main() {
33  1:    int i;
34  1:    char *p, *getenv();
35  1:    time_t t;                         /* current time in seconds from epoch */
36  1:    struct tm *clock;                 /* structure version */
37  1:
38  1:    /* switch to non-default directory if directed */
39  1:
40  1:    if ((p = getenv("SYSLOG")) != NULL) {
41  2:       strcpy(Ldir, p);
42  2:       for (p = Ldir; *p; p++);
43  2:       if (*--p != '/') strcat(Ldir, "/"); }
44  1:
45  1:    /* check to make sure the FIFO file exists.  if it does not,
46  1*       execute a mknod call to create it */
47  1:
```

```
48  1:    strcpy(Bufr, Ldir);
49  1:    strcat(Bufr, "FIFO");
50  1:    if (access(Bufr, R_OK)) {
51  2:      unlink(Bufr);
52  2:      umask(0);
53  2:      if (mknod(Bufr, S_IFIFO | S_IRUSR | S_IWUSR |
54  2:                      S_IWGRP | S_IWOTH, 0)) {
55  3:        fprintf(stderr, "ERROR: Cannot create %s\n", Bufr);
56  3:        exit(2); } }
57  1:
58  1:    /* open FIFO file. We assume that it has already been created
59  1*       by the prior code */
60  1:
61  1:    if ((Fifo = open(Bufr, O_NDELAY | O_RDONLY, 0)) < 0) {
62  2:      fprintf(stderr, "ERROR: Cannot access %s\n", Bufr);
63  2:      exit(2); }
64  1:    printf("System log started for %s\n", Bufr);
65  1:    fflush(stdout);
66  1:
67  1:    /* loop for all messages coming from FIFO */
68  1:
69  1:    logopen();
70  1:    while ((i = read(Fifo, Bufr, 256)) >= 0) {
71  2:
72  2:      /* get current time and determine if the date changed. If it
73  2*         did, open a new log file */
74  2:
75  2:      t = time((long *) 0);
76  2:      clock = localtime(&t);
77  2:      if (clock->tm_mon != Mon || clock->tm_mday != Day) {
78  3:        if (Logf > 0)
79  3:          write(Logf, "SYSLOG file closed\n", 19);
80  3:        close(Logf);
81  3:        logopen(); }
82  2:
83  2:      /* write message out. if there was no message, sleep for a bit */
84  2:
85  2:      if (i > 0) write(Logf, Bufr, i);
86  2:      else sleep(30); }
87  1:
88  1:    /* this should never really happen */
89  1:
```

```
 90 1:     printf("SYSLOG in directory %s terminated.\n", Ldir);
 91 1:     exit(0); }
 92 0:
 93 0:
 94 0: logopen() {
 95 1:
 96 1:     char fnam[48];
 97 1:     time_t t;                    /* current time in seconds from epoch */
 98 1:     struct tm *clock;            /* structure version */
 99 1:
100 1:     /* format the new file name string */
101 1:
102 1:     t = time((long *) 0);
103 1:     clock = localtime(&t);
104 1:     sprintf(fnam, "%s%2.2d%2.2d", Ldir, 1 + clock->tm_mon, clock->tm_mday);
105 1:     Mon = clock->tm_mon;
106 1:     Day = clock->tm_mday;
107 1:
108 1:     /* open file, creating if necessary */
109 1:
110 1:     if ((Logf = open(fnam, O_WRONLY | O_APPEND | O_CREAT,
111 1:                      S_IRUSR | S_IWUSR | S_IRGRP | S_IROTH)) < 0) {
112 2:        fprintf(stderr, "SYSLOG ERROR\007: cannot open %s\n", fnam);
113 2:        fprintf(stderr, "SYSLOG terminating.\n");
114 2:        exit(2); }
115 1:
116 1:     return; }
```

This program should be the only process that will have write access to any of the files in /usr/syslog, so no corruption of any daylog files can occur.

Note that the *open()* call has the *O_NDELAY* bit set. When this bit is set, any call to *read()* on the associated file descriptor will not block the process regardless of whether any data was available within the FIFO. This requires us to insert a *sleep(30)* call at the end of the read loop so that *syslog* does not consume an inordinate amount of CPU time looking for messages in the pipe.

This means that when a message is posted by the *daylog()* program up to 30 seconds can elapse before the syslog program will process it. Other messages that arrive before *syslog* awakes will be processed quickly, because *sleep()* is not called unless the previous *read()* returned a zero. If your application has a higher volume of daylog traffic, it might be advisable to lower the 30-second sleep time, even though the operating system will make sure that no data is being lost.

Why not simply open the FIFO without *O_NDELAY* being set? That way, the *read()* will simply block until data is available, eliminating the need to go through a poll/sleep cycle. Actually, this does not work in our case. The problem with this approach is that the *open()* call blocks the process until some other process calls *open()* with write access to the pipe. Then, when that process closes the file, the *read()* call in s*yslog()* returns immediately every time, with a return value of zero. We would have to have a *sleep()* call anyway.

Summary

A named pipe is useful in providing a funnel through which many divergent programs can place requests for a service. This daylog system and the line printer spooler demonstrate this utility. The funnelling effect simplifies the overall programming and provides the security of the UNIX file system to the application. However, the transmittal of data is one-way and is suitable for situations where there is one process reading and one or more processes writing. Before committing to a named pipe approach, I advise examining alternatives, namely the message passing utility and shared memory.

12
Shared Memory

A programmer realizes that one of the functions of the operating system is to manage system RAM memory in such a way that every process is treated individually and equally. On the other hand, there are applications where it is the best plan to intermix processes, i.e., memory address space. Of course, any usable program will have to do this in an orderly fashion and there are further considerations of not violating system security.

The UNIX shared-memory facility allows any number of processes to access common blocks of memory. In this chapter, we will develop a simple application that uses shared memory.

Most applications that are candidates for the shared-memory approach will have a "real-time" aspect to them.[1] In other words, it is critical that data move from one process to another as fast as possible. Another attribute is the situation where there can be any number of receiving processes for a single transmitter process.

The Shared Memory Model

In the normal process model, there will be only one process that has read and write access to memory space. For the text (object code) segments, it is common to have more than one process with read access, but this is transparent to any process and presents no programming considerations. After all, there is no way for a process to detect if another process read data from a memory segment.

When we build a shared memory application, we want to have one or more segments that can be read and written to by more than one process, as pictured in Figure 12-1.

---

[1] Note that UNIX is not properly a "real-time" operating system, but its performance when properly programmed is good enough to successfully run many real-time applications.

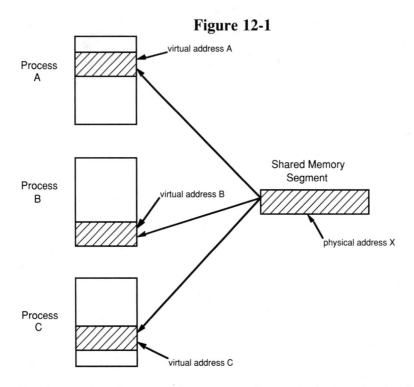

Figure 12-1

In this case, there is a segment of memory that can be both read and written by more than one process. The effect of write operations is that certain memory locations of other processes can change contrary to the logic of those processes.

The easiest way to access shared memory from a C program is through the use of character pointers. (type *char *$) The *shmat()* operating system call returns a pointer to the region of shared memory. The programmer can create any type of structure to use in the shared memory region:

```
        typedef struct sms {

           (type declarations)

        } SMS;

        SMS *S;

        ...
```

```
                S = (SMS *) shmat(...);
```

And future references to the shared memory can take place through pointer *S*.

Race Conditions

Shared memory involves coordination between processes, and this can generate what is known as a *race* condition. Race conditions are where two processes, possibly with the same program, perform what is known as a "test and set" operation. Consider the following program segment, where *sms->flag* is an integer object in shared memory that, when not zero, signifies that a particular resource is in use:

```
     if (!sms->flag) {        /* is resource in use? */
        sms->flag = getpid(); /* no, let's use it by marking
                                 it with our PID */
```

The intent of the programmer is for the *if* statement to evaluate to true only if the resource is free. If it is free, we will mark it as *in use* and no other process following the same rules will touch it. But this is wrong! Note that there is a delay between the time that *sms->flag* is tested and when it is set. The delay involves a couple of machine instructions including a quick call to the kernel to get the process number. What is happening during that time?

The race condition is this: Process A evaluates the *if* statement and it comes up true. Then, sometime between that time and before the *sms->flag* is set, Process A is either preempted by a higher priority process or its time slice runs out. Before Process A is allowed to execute again, Process B evaluates the same *if* statement, and comes up with a true result. After this point the situation degenerates, because the logic of the program in both Process A and Process B will assume that they each have the resource allocated to them.[2]

In systems with more than one CPU, it is not even reliable to make a process the highest priority and lock it in memory. It is possible to have the same program running on another CPU at the same instant!

In shared memory applications, the resources often allocated first are portions of the shared memory itself. This is true of our example program later. In

---

[2] Race conditions also occur with programming device handlers, described later in this volume. Device handlers have access to any amount of "shared" memory.

this program, we sidestep the race condition by recoding the above test-and-set operation as follows:

```
do {
    if (!sms->flag) sms->flag = getpid();

    ...

} while (sms->flag != getpid());
```

What this does is retest the result of the set operation to make sure that the assignment statement really *took hold*. Note that this is still not a perfect solution. The mechanism can still be defeated in the case where Process B evaluates the *if* statement, comes up true, then Process A executes the assignment statement and the *while* statement, then Process B executes again, and executes its assignment and *while* statement.

The only 100% solution to this dilemma is the use of semaphores, which are provided for this purpose. In order to simplify our example program, we will use the *do/while* loop, which will work correctly better than 99% of the time in actual practice.

Polling Loops

Although shared memory is efficient for transmitting data from one process to another, it can lead to a programming inefficiencies. One area where this turns up is in how a receiving process is to detect the arrival of data. Assuming that the integer *flag* in the structure *sms* (Shared Memory Segment) will be changed by the transmitting process when the data is ready, we could set up a loop such as:

```
while (sms->flag);
```

which will loop indefinitely until the object changes value from zero. This will consume a lot of CPU time that could be used for more productive work. Alternatively, we could try:

```
while (sms->flag) sleep(2);
```

which will consume much less CPU time but is still wasteful and will compromise the response time of the receiving process up to two seconds.

One method of getting around this problem is with the use of semaphores, another is with the use of signals. In our example program that follows, we use signals to activate processes that are waiting for activity to occur in the shared memory segment.

The Shared Memory Key and Identifier

There can be more than one application that uses shared memory in the system, and one application might have more than one use for shared memory. This means that programs that require shared memory must identify *which* shared memory segment is to be used. This is done by a Shared Memory Key.

The Shared Memory Key is a number of type *key_t*, (as defined in */usr/include/sys/types.h*) that uniquely identifies an application. This number, however, is not enough for us to use shared memory.

To actually access shared memory, we must use the Shared Memory Key as a parameter to the *shmget()* system call to obtain what is called a Shared Memory Identifier.

The Shared Memory Identifier is another number, of type *int*, that identifies a shared memory segment that is actually in use in the system at this time. This number is what is used to access the shared memory through the *shmat()*, *shmdt()*, and *shmctl()* system calls. If a shared memory segment is destroyed and then recreated, the Shared Memory Identifier may not be the same for a given key.

Shared Memory Security

The operating system implements a form of security that is similar to the file system security. Users are placed in three categories: the owner, the group of the owner, and everyone else. When a process creates a shared memory segment, it specifies the type of access permitted to each of the categories of users. The type of access can be read access, write access, or both.

The values of the type flags are defined by the */usr/include/sys/ipc.h* file, which defines the following compile time symbols:

```
        SHM_R           for Read access
        SHM_W           for Write access
```

These bits are shifted left by six bits for owner permissions, three bits left for group permissions, and zero bits for other permissions. The flags value:

    ((SHM_R | SHM_W) << 6) | ((SHM_R | SHM_W) << 3) | SHM_R | SHM_W

specifies read and write access for all users.

The Shared Memory Operating System Calls

There are four operating-system calls defined for the shared-memory operations. We will describe them briefly and then go on to a sample of their use.

shmget(key, size, shmflag)

>This is the function call that will get the Shared-Memory Identifier based on the given key, creating the shared-memory segment if necessary. It is roughly analogous to the *open()* system call. The *size* parameter indicates the desired size of the shared-memory segment, and the *shmflag* parameter gives the read/write permission bits and the *IPC_CREAT* flag.

shmctl(shmid, cmd, buf)

>This function call provides the mechanism to interrogate the status of the shared-memory segment, change its read/write permission bits, or lock or unlock the segment in memory. It also provides a command to remove the shared memory segment from the system, which disallows any further access. This call is roughly analogous to the *ioctl()* system call.

shmat(shmid, shmaddr, shmflg)

>A process will use this call to make a shared-memory segment part of its address space. The process will have already found the Shared-Memory Identifier and placed that in the *shmid* parameter. Although it is normally best to allow the operating system to pick the address at which the segment will be addressed, the *shmaddr* can be used to select an address. The *shmflg* parameter is used to control this operation.

shmdt(shmaddr)

> This call will detach the shared-memory segment that is attached at the specified location. Any further access to that segment will result in a memory address error.

These calls provide a simple interface for shared-memory applications. From an example we can see how to work thcm.

The *chatter* Program

One area where shared memory is definitely the best approach is in real-time communications. In UNIX, we have the *write* command where we can send messages to one another, but this does not work for a group discussion.

The *chatter* program, below, uses shared memory to create a "chatter board," where anything any user types is shown on all displays. Our program allows up to eight users to talk this way.

The first thing *chatter* does is attempt to create a new memory segment, with the key of 13. If it turns out that the shared memory segment already exists, all it needs to do is attach it and proceed. On the other hand, if the process turns out to be the creator, it assumes the responsibility for destroying the shared memory segment when it is no longer in use. If the user of the creating process signs off the chatter board before all other users have logged off, it uses *fork()* to create a background process that waits around until no other users are using the segment, and then destroys it.

If, for some reason, a shared-memory segment has been created in the system before the first rendition of *chatter* has been run, we can use *chatter -k* to force the program to kill the segment after it is done.

We use the *curses* subroutine library to manage the scrolling of the eight user windows on the screen. See the chapter on terminal programming for more information on how this subroutine library works.

```
1  0: /* chatter.c - Run a chatter board
2  0*
3  0*    03/89  Alan Deikman
4  0*
5  0*    This program demonstrates the use of shared memory in the
6  0*    implementation of a multi-user chatter box.  Up to eight users
```

```
 7 0*       can invoke this command to sign on to the chatter box.
 8 0*
 9 0*       The user input terminal is placed into raw mode and each time
10 0*       a character is typed signals are sent to all the other logged
11 0*       in processes so they can update their displays.
12 0*
13 0*    */
14 0:
15 0: #include <errno.h>
16 0: #include <stdio.h>
17 0: #include <sys/types.h>
18 0: #include <sys/ipc.h>
19 0: #include <sys/shm.h>
20 0: #include <signal.h>
21 0: #include <curses.h>
22 0:
23 0: /* structure used in shared memory segment.  each user logged on will
24 0*       have one of these structures */
25 0:
26 0: typedef struct {
27 1:    int    pid;                    /* process ID of logged in process */
28 1:    char   user[L_cuserid];        /* user name */
29 1:    short  in;                     /* next byte into the buffer */
30 1:    char   bufr[160];              /* up to two lines of buffer */
31 1:    } Box;
32 0:
33 0: /* globals */
34 0:
35 0: key_t   Key = 13;     /* shared memory key */
36 0: int     Shmid;        /* shared memory ID */
37 0: Box     *S;           /* shared segment pointer */
38 0: short   Index;        /* the index of this user */
39 0: int     Mode = 0;     /* mode recorder */
40 0: WINDOW  *win[8];      /* one window for each user */
41 0: int     users[8];     /* the last known list of all users */
42 0: short   Out[8];       /* next character out of each bufr */
43 0:
44 0: main (ac, av)
45 0: int     ac;
46 0: char    **av;
47 0: {
48 1:    int    i, c;
49 1:    void sigrun();
50 1:
51 1:    /* attempt to attach to an existing memory segment */
52 1:
53 1:    if ((Shmid = shmget(Key, 8 * sizeof(Box), 0666)) < 0) {
54 2:      if (errno != ENOENT) {
55 3:         perror("chatter shmget1");
56 3:         exit(2); }
```

Chapter 12 Shared Memory

```
57 2:
58 2:     /* create shared memory segment */
59 2:
60 2:     printf("Creating shared memory segment\n");
61 2:     Mode = -1;
62 2:     if ((Shmid = shmget(Key, 8 * sizeof(Box),
63 2:                         IPC_EXCL | IPC_CREAT | 0666)) < 0) {
64 3:       perror("chatter shmget2");
65 3:       exit(2); } }
66 1:   printf("Shared memory ID = %d\n", Shmid);
67 1:
68 1:   /* attach the shared memory segment */
69 1:
70 1:   S = (Box *) shmat(Shmid, (char *) 0, 0);
71 1:   if ((int) S == -1) {
72 2:     perror("chatter shmat");
73 2:     exit(2); }
74 1:   printf("Shared memory attached at: %8X\n", S);
75 1:
76 1:   /* check to see if anyone is logged in.  If not, let's take
77 1*      responsibility for killing this segment when we're done. */
78 1:
79 1:   for (i = 0; i < 8 && S[i].pid; i++);
80 1:   if (i >= 8) {
81 2:     Mode = -1;
82 2:     printf("Unused segment detected\n"); }
83 1:
84 1:   /* If the user specified a -k option, kill the segment when
85 1*      we're done. */
86 1:
87 1:   if (ac > 1 && !strcmp(*++av, "-k")) Mode = -2;
88 1:
89 1:   /* if we created this segment, zero it out */
90 1:
91 1:   if (Mode) {
92 2:     register int i = 0;
93 2:     register char *p = (char *) S;
94 2:     while (i++ < 8 * sizeof(Box)) *p++ = 0; }
95 1:
96 1:   /* now search for a Box to park our pid in.  This marks it as
97 1*      ours.  We have to read what we wrote to circumvent any
98 1*      race conditions if two processes are trying to hit this
99 1*      one segment at the same time */
100 1:
101 1:  do {
102 2:    for (Index = 0; Index < 8 && S[Index].pid; Index++)
103 2:      printf("Process %5d is logged in\n", S[Index].pid);
104 2:    if (Index >= 8) printf("Sorry, the chatterbox is full. Try later.\n");
105 2:    else {
106 3:      S[Index].pid = getpid();
```

```
107 3:         printf("Logging on as user #%d.  Our pid=%d\n", Index, getpid());
108 3:         sleep(2); }
109 2:      } while (Index < 8 && S[Index].pid != getpid());
110 1:   for (i = 0; i < 8; i++) Out[i] = S[i].in;
111 1:   cuserid(S[Index].user);
112 1:   printf("Hit RETURN to continue"); getchar();
113 1:
114 1:   /* set the function to handle signals, then announce our arrival to
115 1*      everyone else */
116 1:
117 1:   signal(SIGUSR1, sigrun);
118 1:   sigall();
119 1:
120 1:   /* initialize the curses window environment */
121 1:
122 1:   initscr();
123 1:   scrollok(stdscr, FALSE);
124 1:   noecho();
125 1:   raw();
126 1:   for (i = 0; i < 8; i++) {
127 2:      mvaddstr((i * 3) + 1, 0, "--------------------------------------");
128 2:        addstr(              "--------------------------------------");
129 2:      win[i] = newwin(2, 80, (i * 3) + 2, 0);
130 2:      scrollok(win[i], TRUE); }
131 1:   mvaddstr(0,  0, "ChatterBOX program V 1.0");
132 1:   mvaddstr(0, 50, "Press @ to log off");
133 1:   refresh();
134 1:
135 1:   /* now loop on user input */
136 1:
137 1:   do {
138 2:     errno = 0;
139 2:     c = getch();
140 2:
141 2:     /* if we did not escape the getch() from a signal, process the
142 2*        input character into the buffer */
143 2:
144 2:     if (!errno) {
145 3:       S[Index].bufr[S[Index].in++] = c;
146 3:       if (S[Index].in >= sizeof(S[Index].bufr)) S[Index].in = 0;
147 3:       sigall(); }
148 2:
149 2:     /* see if anyone dropped off or came on the list of logged-
150 2*        on users.  if so, update the "background" screen */
151 2:
152 2:     for (i = 0; i < 8 && S[i].pid == users[i]; i++);
153 2:     if (i < 8) {
154 3:       for (i = 0; i < 8; i++) {
155 4:         users[i] = S[i].pid;
156 4:         if (S[i].pid)
```

```
157  4:              mvprintw((i * 3) + 1, 40, "%16.16s %5d", S[i].user, S[i].pid);
158  4:            else mvprintw((i * 3) + 1, 40, "(Logged Out)-----------"); } }
159  2:        refresh();
160  2:
161  2:        /* scan all the boxes for output and send anything found */
162  2:
163  2:        for (i = 0; i < 8; i++) while (S[i].in != Out[i]) {
164  3:          wechochar(win[i], S[i].bufr[Out[i]]);
165  3:          if (++(Out[i]) >= sizeof(S[index].bufr)) Out[i] = 0; }
166  2:
167  2:      } while (!(errno == 0 && (c == '@' || c == EOF)));
168  1:
169  1:    /* return terminal to prior state */
170  1:
171  1:    endwin();
172  1:
173  1:    /* remove us from the active users */
174  1:
175  1:    S[Index].pid = 0;
176  1:
177  1:    /* detach the shared memory segment */
178  1:
179  1:    if (!Mode) {
180  2:      if (shmdt(S)) {
181  3:        perror("chatter shmdt");
182  3:        exit(2); }
183  2:      printf("%d Shared memory detached\n", getpid()); }
184  1:
185  1:    /* if this process was the one that created the chatterbox, fork
186  1*       off another process that sticks around to remove it when it
187  1*       is no longer used */
188  1:
189  1:    printf("%d Mode = %d\n", getpid(), Mode);
190  1:    fflush(stdin);
191  1:    if (Mode) {
192  2:      if (fork() == 0) {
193  3:        printf("%d Waiting for segment to become unused\n", getpid());
194  3:        fflush(stdin);
195  3:        if (Mode != -2) do {
196  4:          sleep(10);
197  4:          for (i = 0; i < 8 && !S[i].pid; i++);
198  4:        } while (i < 8);
199  3:        shmdt(S);
200  3:        shmctl(Shmid, IPC_RMID);
201  3:        printf("%d Shared memory segment released\n", getpid()); } }
202  1:
203  1:    /* done */
204  1:
205  1:    printf("%d Done\n", getpid());
206  1:    exit(0); }
```

```
207 0:
208 0:
209 0: /* catch signals */
210 0:
211 0: void sigrun(sig)
212 0: int sig;
213 0: {
214 1:
215 1:    if (sig != SIGUSR1) {
216 2:       printf("sigrun caught signal %d\nABORT!\n", sig);
217 2:       exit(2); }
218 1:
219 1:    /* reset signal */
220 1:
221 1:    signal(SIGUSR1, sigrun);
222 1:    return; }
223 0:
224 0: /* send signal to all other processes */
225 0:
226 0: sigall() {
227 1:    register int i;
228 1:    for (i = 0; i < 8; i++) if (S[i].pid && i != Index) kill(S[i].pid, SIGUSR1);
229 1:    return; }
230 0:
```

In our program we eliminate the problem with polling by using the *getch()* call to block the process until a character is read or a signal is received. Any process that changes the display will send a signal to all other processes so they can update their displays.

Summary

Shared memory is a valuable facility, but must be used with caution. As a general rule, shared memory should be used only when there is no alternative—when, for example, system messages, named pipes, or semaphores will not handle the job and shared file access would be too slow.

13
Mass Storage Programs

We have already examined the way UNIX handles disk-drive mass storage through its file system structures. In the UNIX environment, mass-storage devices may also be accessed directly by programs, without any structure imposed by the file system in the UNIX kernel. This is done by performing file I/O system calls such as *open()*, *read()*, and *write()*, to special device files associated with the device.

One type of device that is always accessed this way is the tape drive, which is designed to store large quantities of data on a removable media. This is the type of device used for backing up system files for security, and transferring files from one system to another.

To a program running in the UNIX environment, the tape device will appear to be a file that:

    a) can be very large (more than 20MB) in the case of tape,
    b) does not take disk space from any of the mounted file systems,
    c) cannot be randomly accessed, except for rewinding (*lseek()* to location 0), or search for end-of-file (*lseek()* to end-of-file).

We can store a file on tape by executing the *cp* command:

```
cp data /dev/mt0
```

where */dev/mt0* is the file name of the first tape device on the system. After this command is done, the contents of the file *data* will be stored on the magnetic tape. However, there will be no other information on the tape, about the file's original name, dates, owner, or anything else. When the tape is read, the person would have to enter a new *cp* command and know what the correct file name would be.

It is also unlikely that the file *data* would fill even a measurable fraction of the capacity of the tape device. With most tape drives, it is possible to add another file after the end of the first one, and then another one after that, but the shortcomings mentioned above apply to each. Since the UNIX kernel imposes no file structure on the tape device, it is up to a user-mode program to do so. Such a program would be able to read a group of files (specified by the user), collect all the pertinent information about them including the contents of the files, and combine all the files into one data file. This single data file could be written out to the tape device. For reading, the same program would be able to interpret it's data structures to allow the user to restore one, several, or all files back into the UNIX file system with the file names, owner's names, dates, etc. intact.

Several programs are provided with UNIX that perform this function. They were written at different times for different purposes, but the basic concept is the same. These are:

1. *dump* and *restore*. This program is provided with XENIX, but not Interactive Systems UNIX or Microport System V/AT. (Warning: there is a completely different program provided with Microport V/AT that is named dump) The dump program can make "incremental" dumps of the file system, where a particular run dumps only the files that have changed since the last time the program was run.

2. *tar*. Similar in syntax and operation to the *ar* archive program (see Chapter 8), tar provides the same convenience with the archive being stored on tape. The primary advantage of *tar* is that it is easy to extract specific files from the archive, and the archive can be "updated," rather than re-written.

3. *cpio*. This program provides easy access to files, and can be easily driven by any other program that can write pathnames to standard output. The Microport *install* program uses this format.

4. *dd*. This program is provides certain block and character translations for an unstructured file on a mass storage device.

Secondary mass storage devices include 1/2" tape drives, 1/4" tape drives, floppy disk drives, and hard disk drives. All of these devices are treated the same by the programs described in this chapter. The three primary uses of these media are:

1. **Backups of files.** Copies of part or all files on a file system can be copied in case of a systems failure.

2. **Transfer of files between systems.** Software for sale, including the UNIX system itself, is distributed this way. This is often the best way of moving data from one computer to the other.[1]

3. **Auxiliary mass storage.** Some programs process data too large to be contained within the file system. For example, a form letter generating program could produce letters for a mailing list that data file from tape.

Traditionally, the secondary mass-storage media was magnetic tape, the most popular at the time UNIX was invented being the 1/2" reel-to-reel type. These devices are very cost efficient on larger systems (minicomputers and mainframes) because of their huge capacity, high reliability, and the high transfer rates possible. For UNIX on the smaller systems, the IBM AT compatible 80286 and 80386 units, 1/2" tape is relatively rare. Instead, lower cost and lower performance devices such as 1/4" cartridge tape and floppy disks are used. The programs that are provided with UNIX are same as those designed for the 1/2" tape drive.

Note, by the way, that each of these programs can direct their outputs and inputs to any file, not just a tape drive or a floppy disk drive. This makes the programs useful for other purposes than backup and restore, such as performing a complex copy operation from one file system to another.

dump/restor

The *dump* and *restore* programs have become less popular for the smaller AT class of systems, mostly because *tar* and *cpio* have had features added to them

---

[1] There is a potential problem with transporting files from one system to another when using tar. On the archive, the user and group number are stored as integers which are taken directly from the i-node entry (see Chapter 3) for the file. These numbers are normally translated into user names and group names by the */etc/passwd* and */etc/group* files, respectively. The difficulty occurs when files are read off of a *tar* archive onto another system where the user and group numbers are defined differently. Usually this is little more than an annoyance, although it is possible for a user who had just read a tape or a disk written on another system to not be able to access the files just created. To circumvent this problem, *tar* provides the *o* option, which resets the user and group number to the effective I.D. of the *tar* process.

that make them easier to use.[2] *dump* is designed to treat an entire file system as a single backup unit, and to provide the fastest backup method for the entire disk.[3]

The command to backup the entire hard disk for the default file system is:

      dump 0u

After this creates a complete backup, the date of the backup will be stored in the file */etc/ddate*. (Note that this means that only the super-user can use *dump*). After this point, it is only necessary to dump the files that have changed since the prior dump. This can be done with the command:

      dump 1u

which will dump all the files that have changed since the *dump 0u* backup was made. The file */etc/ddate* is consulted as to the cut-off modification time.

In a similar fashion, we can then dump all the files that changed since the prior dump *1u* with dump *2u*. The sequence suggested by the manual is:

      1 2 1 3 1 2 1 4 1 2 1 3 1 2 1 5 . . .

The idea being that the minimum amount of disk or tape writing takes place at each backup session.

The *dump* program is written in such a way that it has difficulty with "end of volume" indicators on tape and disk drives. When writing to the typical UNIX device driver for tape, and the end of the media is reached, dump does not know how to recover. For this reason, *dump* must be told what the size of the media is so that it can anticipate the end-of-media before it happens,

---

[2] Another reason that *dump/restor* was more popular in the past has to do with the way those systems were distributed and installed. On a UNIX distribution tape, there were programs that could be booted directly from tape and executed. These usually included stand-alone versions of a hard disk format program, *mkfs*, and *restor*. UNIX was first booted by executing the stand-alone version of *restor* to copy a bootable file system from the tape to the disk. For UNIX/XENIX on the 80286/80386, the distribution itself is a mountable media, so the standard versions of the hard disk format and *mkfs* routines can be used, and files can be copied to the hard disk with any of the programs.

[3] See articles DUMP(C) (XENIXVRM), RESTORE(C) (XENIX VRM).

and ask the operator to mount a new reel (disk).

To recover files, the *restor* program is used. Generally, an entire file system is restored at one time, although it is possible to extract specifically named files. When restoring an entire file system, the most recent dump level should be used last. For example:

```
/etc/mkfs /dev/hd2 10000
restor r /dev/hd2         # the level 0 is restored
restor r /dev/hd2         # the level 1 is restored
restor r /dev/hd2         # the level 2 is restored
```

The *dump* and *restore* programs are the fastest way to change the size of a file system. This is done by creating a complete dump tape of the file system, then recreating the file system by using *mkfs*, then using *restor* to copy the files back.

tar

The *tar* program is popular on XENIX systems because it is easier to use and understand than *dump* and faster than *cpio*.[4] Also, the distribution floppy disks for XENIX that are designed to be read with the *install* program are written in *tar* format. The options and operation are similar to the *ar* program, although the *r* (replace) and *u* (update) options are difficult to implement. (There is no random file access on tape drives, or floppy disks being used as if they were tape drives) For this reason, XENIX does not provide the *u* option, and Microport cautions the user against it's use.

There are a couple of differences between the *tar* program in XENIX and the *tar* program in Microport. SCO has added better multi-volume support and the F option, which allows *tar* to accept a list of names to process from a file instead of relying on the names in the command line. However, the file format is the same so tar can be used to transfer files between XENIX and Microport should the need arise.

The basic *tar* file format is shown in Figure 13-1. The "link information" in the file header is used when *tar* detects multiple links to a single file. When this occurs, only a header is written which contains the original pathname to

---

[4] See articles TAR(C) (XENIX VRM), TAR(1) (Microport RSM), TAR(1) (AT&T VRM).

the file and the new pathname. No data blocks are written in this case.

To aid in efficiency, *tar* provides an option to combine up to 20 data blocks into a single write operation. When writing to tape, it is almost always desirable to write the largest blocks possible. To backup up the entire system, the command:

```
tar cfb /dev/ct0 20 /
```

will start at the root directory, and recursively work its way down all subdirectories to back up all files. To make incremental backups with *tar*, the technique varies depending on whether you are using XENIX or Microport.

On Interactive Systems and Microport, the *u* option can be applied to add any newly modified or created files to an archive tape or disk set. Although it is easy to use, this option can be slow. For XENIX, you can use the F option to process a list of file names generated by the find command. This technique is similar to how the *cpio* command is used in the next section

cpio

The *cpio* program is the most general purpose utility for making and reading multi-file volumes. Interactive Systems and Microport software distribution floppies are written in *cpio* format.[5]

There are three modes in which *cpio* operates, as directed by its first option word:

- *-o* **Output mode**. A list of file names is taken from standard input to make the *cpio* archive on standard output.
- *-i* **Input mode**. The output of a previous cpio archive is read on standard input, and files which match patterns on the command line are extracted.
- *-p* **Pass mode**. Standard input is read to obtain a list of path names of files that are conditionally copied (or linked) to a new directory.

---

[5] See articles CPIO(C) (XENIX VRM), CPIO(1) (Microport RSM), CPIO(1) (AT&T VRM).

Chapter 13 Mass Storage Programs

Figure 13-1

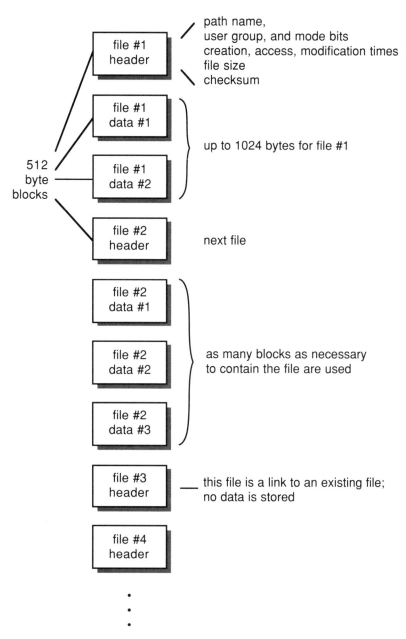

Generic Multi-file Data Structure Used by Both *cpio* and *tar*

265

When creating a backup, the *cpio* program depends on some other program to generate path names on which to operate. The two most common are *ls* and *find*. For example, to make a backup disk of the current directory, one of the commands:

```
/bin/ls | cpio -ov > /dev/rfd          # XENIX version
/bin/ls | cpio -ov > /dev/rdsk/fd      # Microport version
```

can be used.[6] If *cpio* detects a write error on the floppy disk (or tape if you happen to be using tape) it will prompt for a "new" device on which to continue writing.

In development projects, I often keep of list of "approved" pathnames in a special file which is maintained manually with the editor. This way, when scratch or temporary files get created, they do not automatically get written to the backup tapes. Also, there is no reason to waste backup media space with intermediate object files that might be left around. In these cases, the backup command is usually:

```
cpio -ov < dumplist > /dev/rdsk/fd
```

The *find* command is an alternative way to generate file names with certain types omitted. This might be safer if *dumplist* changes rapidly. To list the files on a *cpio* tape, the command:

```
cpio -itv < /dev/rdsk/fd
```

is used to display the files. The *-i* option to *cpio* may be thought of as the reverse of the *-o* option. By removing the *t* in the command line above, the files listed will be actually created instead of simply listed.

However, in most restore operations, more options are needed. For example:

```
cpio -idvum < /dev/rdsk/fd
```

is more common, because the *d* option will create new directories if they are needed, and the *u* option will over-write files that are more recent than the version that are on the archive, and *m* will cause *cpio* to create the files with the modification time that they had before they were written out the the floppy disk.

---

[6] The reason I use */bin/ls* instead of plain *ls* is that most of the time the *ls* command is aliased to a more complex form of the *ls* command. (usually the -CF options). Specifying the full pathname to *ls* circumvents the *alias* mechanism.

Because the *cpio* program is so often used with the *find* command, the *find* program has a special form that simplifies commands. For example, the command:

```
find / -name "*.c" -print | cpio -ov > /dev/rfd
```

which will backup every file in the system that ends in *.c* is equivalent to:

```
find / -name "*.c" -cpio /dev/rfd
```

The *find* program can be used to implement an incremental backup scheme that allows partial backups to be performed. The following shell script (in the file *full.back*) can be used to make the original, full backup set:

```
:
#    make full backup with cpio
#
#    syntax:
#
#            full.back > /dev/rdsk/fd
#
date > /etc/full.back.time
date > /etc/part.back.time
find / -type f -print | cpio -o
```

and the following script, *part.back*, can be used to backup all files that have changed since the last partial backup:

```
:
#    make partial backup with cpio
#
#    syntax:
#
#            part.back > /dev/rdsk/fd
#
find / -type f -newer /etc/part.back.time -print | cpio -o
date > /etc/part.back.time
```

The options to the *find* command allow many variations of this script, including backups specific to individual users and file types. Another use of *cpio* is to copy a complete or partial directory hierarchy with a single command. This is the *p* mode mentioned above. For example, if we wanted to grab a copy of all of a specific user's files and copy them to a new directory for safekeeping, we might type:

```
mkdir /tmp/george
cd /usr/george
find -name "*" -print | cpio -p /tmp/george
```

The structure of the *cpio* file that was created includes blocks of control information (which contain the name, size, and i-node data for a file), interspersed with the data of the files themselves. Normally, this control data is written in binary, much in the same format as it appears in the i-node (*see* Chapter 3). However, should a bad block develop on the media (we will discuss this below) it is useful to have the control information written in printable ASCII. The *c* option in *cpio* does this.

dd

This program is somewhat lower level than *cpio* or *tar*. The *dd* program is not designed to handle multiple files within a file.[7] Instead, it is useful for processing and converting data files, sometimes using it as a filter for either *cpio* or *tar*. If you are transferring data to and from an operating system that is not DOS or UNIX, you will likely end up using *dd*. The *dd* program performs various conversions, and can "block" or "un-block" data as required.

One useful conversion performed by *dd* is byte swapping. On certain other computer architectures or devices, notably Motorola 68000 based systems, the order of bytes within a 16-bit word is reversed from what they are on the 80286 or 80386. For example, the string:

```
The quick brown fox jumps over the lazy dog
```

becomes:

```
hT euqci krbwo nof xujpm svoret ehl za yod g
```

where every two bytes are swapped. Most people will want to fix this, which can be done by using the *conv* option of *dd*. When reading a *tar* tape from a system that does this, the following command can be used:

```
dd if=/dev/rmt0 conv=swab | tar xvf -
```

The *dd* program reverses the bytes. Similar conversions can also be made for translation between EBCDIC (Extended Binary Coded Decimal Interchange

---

[7] See articles DD(C) (XENIX VRM), DD(C) (Microport RSM), DD(1) (AT&T VRM).

Code) and ASCII.

When using the UNIX file system, the block size is for the most part transparent to the program. However, with tape devices the hardware sometimes imposes a data-block size limitation. Typically, the block size will be large (tape becomes more efficient the larger the block size). With such media, it is not always possible for the program to read an arbitrary number of bytes. For example, if the tape is positioned at the beginning of a 1024 byte block, and the program performs a *read()* operation of 200 bytes, the remaining 824 bytes in the block will be discarded. If this is the case, *dd* can buffer the blocks. The command:

```
dd if=/dev/rmt0 ibs=1024 | prog
```

will allow the program *prog* to process its standard input as if it were any normal file. This action is also important for streaming tape drives, where the largest possible block size is desirable. For example:

```
tar cf - . | dd obs=8192 > /dev/rct0
```

Another useful feature of *dd* is the ability to grab certain sections of a file. For example, suppose you wished to copy the second and third block of a floppy disk:

```
dd if=/dev/rdsk/fd of=boot bs=512 skip=1 count=2
```

The UNIX file boot would contain the requested two blocks. This feature can also be used to skip around parts of a tape or disk file which has bad blocks. (This always happens when you least expect it and can least afford it.) The tape drive hardware can often skip over a block without actually reading it. So if you get the message:

```
Tape drive error
```

or something similar in your *cpio read* operation, try the following:

```
dd if=/dev/mt0 bs=yyy skip=xxx | cpio -ivd
```

where *xxx* is the block number of the first *cpio* control block after the bad block, and *yyy* is the block size. Remember earlier, where we suggested the the *c* option to *cpio* would write the control information in printable format? This is where it is most useful, because you will probably have to hunt and search for the position of the next readable control block. The block size will be either 512, or 5120 if the B option was used to create the tape.

14
DOS Support

UNIX and DOS are currently in competition for much of the same market. We have, in earlier chapters, discussed the relative merits of each operating system for each application. However, when using UNIX on 286- and 386-based systems, often the same computer has to be shared with a DOS environment. The reason for this is that there are thousands of useful, commercially available programs for DOS that have not yet appeared for UNIX or XENIX. Even if a DOS program does not have to be used, it is often the case that a UNIX user has to access data written by a PC in DOS format.

There are three links between DOS and UNIX we will discuss in this chapter:

1. UNIX and XENIX can read and write DOS media.
2. XENIX has the capability of generating programs that run in the DOS environment.
3. Locus Computing and Interactive Systems both have products that allow DOS programs to run as a UNIX sub-process.

DOS Media Access

Both Microport and XENIX provide commands that allow the user to read and write DOS media. The commands for Microport are:

doscat	similar to the *cat* command for DOS files
doscp	similar to the *cp* command for DOS files
dosdir	lists DOS directories in DOS format

for XENIX, the list is more extensive:

doscat	similar to the *cat* command for DOS files
doscp	similar to the *cp* command for DOS files
dosdir	lists DOS directories in DOS format

dosformat Formats a DOS diskette
dosls   lists DOS directories in *ls* format
dosmkdir performs a DOS *mkdir* function
dosrm   performs a DOS *del* function
dosrmdir performs a DOS *rmdir* command

The commands in both systems use the DOS convention of providing a disk drive letter followed by a colon to specify on which physical device a file is located. In DOS, typical assignments are:[1]

A: First floppy disk drive
B: Second floppy disk drive
C: Hard disk drive #0
D: Hard disk drive #1

In the XENIX and Microport commands, a DOS file name is recognized by the presence of a drive letter and a colon. For example, the command:

```
doscp data/afile A:afile
```

is a copy command from UNIX to DOS, whereas:

```
doscp A:/word/infile .
```

is a copy command from DOS to UNIX. When interpreting a DOS file name, both systems apply the following rules:

1. All lowercase letters are mapped into upper case.

2. Slash characters are used (/) (as in UNIX) instead of back-slash (\) characters (as in DOS) to separate path-name elements. Most UNIX users will find this more convenient, particularly since backslash has a special meaning to the shell.

3. DOS limitations of the file name size apply. In DOS, a file name can have no more than 8 characters, with an optional period (.) and three more characters.

---

[1] The commands used by XENIX for DOS media access are documented in the DOS(C) article in the SCO XENIX User's Reference Manual. Microport provides the DOSCAT(1), DOSCP(1), and DOSDIR(1) articles in the Runtime System Manual.

The DOS access programs have a method of mapping the DOS drive letters that appear on their command lines to physical devices. The XENIX approach is to provide the directory specifications in the /etc/default directory in the file *msdos*. This file, in the usual installation, has the lines:

```
A=/dev/rd0
B=/dev/hd0d
C=/dev/hd1d
```

which maps the drive letters A, C, and D, into the first floppy disk, the first and second hard disks, respectively. Currently, XENIX provides support only for the 48TPI DOS formats (360KB capacity).

Microport makes use of links to specify which DOS drive letters correspond to which node names. For example, if the first floppy disk drive (drive A) is to be normally accessed as a 96 TPI drive (1.2MB format) the link can be created with the command:

```
ln /dev/rdsk/fd096 /dev/dos/a
```

The DOS commands look in the directory /dev/dos for a special file of the same name as the drive letter. Other letters may be assigned to different formats. For example, the DOS drive letter B can be used to access the same disk drive in 48 TPI (360KB) format if the link

```
ln /dev/rdsk/fd048 /dev/dos/b
```

has been made. Therefore, if we type:

```
dosdir A:
```

a 1.2MB floppy disk directory will be listed, or if we type:

```
dosdir B:
```

a 360KB floppy disk directory will be listed.

DOS and UNIX have similar directory structures, although typical file formats are different. The conventional difference between UNIX and DOS files that needs the most attention from the user is how text files have their lines terminated.

In DOS, each line in a file (that can be edited with a text editor) is terminated with a *CR* and *LF* sequence (two bytes with the hexadecimal values 0x0D and 0x0A). In UNIX, the convention is to simply terminate a line with the "newline" character, which is the same as *LF* (hexadecimal 0X0A). If a text file is transferred from DOS to UNIX without translation and examined with the *vi* editor, each line would have a CONTROL-M character at the end of the line. Similarly, a UNIX text file transferred to DOS without modification will confuse most programs that expect a *CR* character before the *LF*.

For this reason, the XENIX DOS access commands provide the *-m* options to perform the necessary conversion, and the Microport routines provide the conversion unless the *-b* option is given. For example, to list out a source program that is stored on the hard disk drive, we would type:

```
doscat -m c:life.c          # XENIX
doscat c:life.c             # Microport
```

On the other hand, if we wanted to copy a binary data file without conversion, we would use:

```
doscp -r c:datafile .       # XENIX
doscp -b c:datafile .       # Microport
```

XENIX/DOS Cross Development

Because the SCO XENIX system had its roots in Microsoft, the company that developed DOS, the C compiler it uses is very closely related to the C compiler Microsoft markets for DOS systems. This allowed the easy development of a cross-compilation system that allows DOS programs to be developed under XENIX.

On the *cc* command line, the *-dos* option will tell the compiler to produce object files compatible with the DOS development library provided with XENIX. The loader invoked will also generate a file that can be loaded and run in the DOS environment.

Not all the library functions available to C program that run under XENIX are available to DOS programs, and there are several routines provided by XENIX for the DOS environment that have no counterparts in the XENIX environment. For instance, the XENIX library for DOS includes the *bdos()*

function to allow direct access to DOS system calls. There are also functions to provide direct access to I/O ports and other resources not found in the XENIX user environment.[2]

Locus DOS/Merge and Interactive Systems VP/IX

Locus Computing Corporation and Interactive Systems have both developed products that allow the user to run DOS programs on a UNIX system. Locus has two products: one for the 80286 called DOS/Merge 286 and one for the 386 called DOS/Merge 386. Interactive Systems Corporation has developed VP/IX, which is exclusively a 386 product.

At this time, SCO XENIX does not have the capability of running DOS programs.

The problem posed by having DOS and UNIX run in the same system at the same time is quite complex. Many DOS application programs, to say nothing of the DOS Operating System itself, are written as if they were the only software running on the computer, with exclusive access to CPU and I/O device resources. DOS/Merge and VP/IX use the memory protect features of the 80286 and the 80386 CPU chips to provide an environment that "looks like" an 8088 (or 8086) based PC, including access to the memory mapped ROM and video boards.

Because the 80286 does not provide any "virtual machine" mode, DOS/Merge 286 actually sets up the user process in unprotected mode, setting up the current memory map to properly locate the ROM BIOS[3] and memory mapped video boards. The program can also execute I/O instructions. This means three things:

1. the DOS environment can only exist on the system console
2. there can be only one DOS environment active in the system

---

[2] The functions provided for DOS are documented in the (DOS) articles in the SCO XENIX Programmer's Reference Manual.

[3] BIOS is an acronym for Basic I/O Services. Every PC or AT compatible system provides a set of hardware dependent subroutines in ROM at a special set of memory locations. DOS makes extensive use of the BIOS.

3. the DOS program can crash the system by executing mis-behaved programs

DOS/Merge 286 requires an involved modification the the UNIX kernel, because new low-level operating system calls have to be added to allow the management of a special process for DOS. A side effect of this is that it is not always possible to install additional device drivers (which otherwise could be installed) on a DOS/Merge kernel.

Obviously, DOS/UNIX on the 286 has some heavy limitations. It does provide a way out, however, for certain 80286 installations that have to have some DOS access. However, on the 80386 things are quite different. The 80386 has a special mode, called "Virtual 8086 mode" where the program running is provided with an almost exact 8086 environment. This gives the operating system complete control over what the program does.

Conclusion

Although advanced technology hardware and software has eroded the line between UNIX and DOS, the line will still be there. DOS was implemented with the idea that there would be a single user on the computer, and UNIX was designed to serve as many users as the available CPU power could provide for.

If the available software written for DOS and software written for UNIX serve different functions, at least we have the choice of accessing both on the same hardware. Rather than detracting from each other, both operating systems can now support each other, because the applications written for each operating system can access data originating on both sides of the fence.

15
Basics of 80286 Architecture

In this chapter we examine the basics surrounding the Intel 80286 CPU chip and how it is used in the IBM AT and compatible computers. Although UNIX rarely requires knowledge of assembly language or the hardware used, it is often helpful when programming in C to be aware of the environment in which the program is executing. If you are writing a device driver, you will at least need to know about how I/O is accomplished at the hardware level.

The Intel 80286 CPU is the base of the IBM AT and the IBM PS/2 model 50. Because of its upward compatibility with the 8080 (and 8086), which was used in the IBM PC, the IBM AT had available to it a vast library of popular, market-ready programs. That added to the fact that the 80286-based AT offered a significant performance increase over the PC made the architecture immensely successful in the market. An uncountable number of manufacturers have made 80286 based systems that are IBM AT compatible, and the result is an installed base of over 5,000,000 computers.

A vast majority of those systems were purchased to run the DOS programs that work on the older IBM PC. This was possible because when the Intel 80286 processor is reset, it acts (from a software standpoint) exactly as if it were a 8086 (or 8088) processor. However, there are a number of things that are different about the 80286 from the 8088 if the software loaded chooses to use them. The major changes were the addition of memory protect and virtual memory, which allowed the implementation of multi-user operating systems such as UNIX.

In this chapter, we will concentrate mainly on the "80286 mode" that is seen by the user program under UNIX. All user processes and the UNIX kernel run in this mode. The "real" mode of the 80286, which is when it appears to be an 8086, is not used by UNIX except when the system is first being started. We will also discard an extensive discussion of how the memory-protect mechanism (through the GDT, or "Global Descriptor Table," and the LDT, or "Local Descriptor Table") is operated in favor of describing how the effect looks to the application program. The UNIX kernel provides for us all the low-level routines necessary for changing the virtual-memory environment.

Figure 15-1

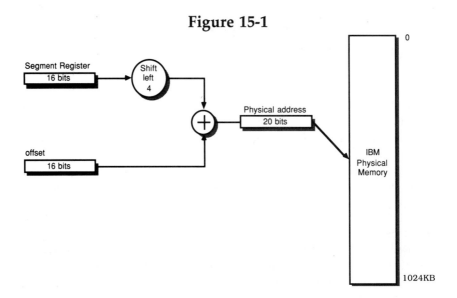

The Major Intel Microprocessors

8080   The basic Intel processor, with the "8 bit" instruction set. This chip was largely overshadowed in the market by the more successful Z80 microprocessor from Zilog.

8086   The original "16 bit" processor from Intel. Although the addresses generated by instructions are 16 bits wide, by using segment registers (see Figure 10-1) 20 bits of addressing can be generated.

8088   An "8 bit" architecture version of the 8086. Sixteen bit operations, external to the chip itself, were executed in two 8-bit sections. This was the engine used in countless IBM PCs and IBM PC clones. A more efficient chip that was software compatible with the 8088 was the NEC V20 series chips.

80186 A higher performance 8086, with some instructions and addressing modes added. The chip also included a number of support circuits (transparent to software) that are not found on

Chapter 15 Basics of 80286 Architecture

the 8086/8088. This was only used in a small handful of general purpose PC clones and products, being more favored for use as a dedicated microprocessor controller whose software could be developed on the IBM PC.

80286 This chip implements the full instruction set of the 8086, with new instructions and memory protect at a higher speed. This chip is the one used in the IBM AT and the countless clones of the IBM AT. Although this CPU may execute as if it were an 8086, in cannot provide a virtual 8086 environment for a protected mode program.

80386 The major technology "32-bit" chip running at unprecedented speeds. This processor has two major features of interest:
  1) 32-bit registers and operations, and
  2) backwards compatibility with the 8086 and 80286 in protected mode. This processor is described in the next chapter.

In our examination of the 80286, we will discuss various elements of the processor's design. We are assuming you already know a little about how vonNeumann theory based computers operate. In such computers, there are the following elements to examine:

1. The register set.

2. The memory system.

3. The Instruction set.

4. The I/O mechanism.

The 80286 is not significantly different from most other CPU systems, except in the concept of segment registers. Our purpose here is to provide a basis for understanding how the specific implementation of the 80286 affects the UNIX program and kernel environment, and certain C program structures. For specific details, refer to the *Intel 80286 Programmer's Reference Manual*.

80286 Register Set

The Intel 80286 provides an array of 16-bit registers for machine instruction use, as shown in Figure 15-2.

Figure 15-2

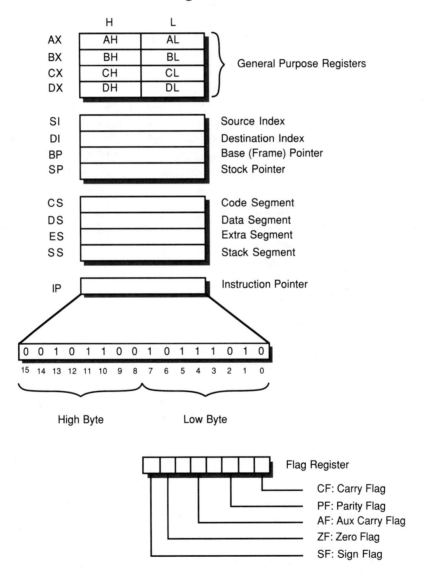

Chapter 15 Basics of 80286 Architecture

We will refer to the registers by their assembly-language symbols. There are five groups of registers, whose functions are described briefly as follows:

1. *AX, BX, CX,* and *DX*: These are the "general purpose" registers that programs use to hold temporary results. For the most part, these registers can be used interchangeably at the programmer's (or compiler's) discretion, although there are instructions that assume certain assignments. This was done to reduce the number of instruction op-codes that had to be built in the chip.

    Additionally, each 8-bit half of each 16-bit register can be addressed as independently for 8-bit operations. For example, the *BH* register is the upper 8-bits of the *BX* register, as shown in the figure.

2. *SI, DI, BP,* and *SP*: These registers each have a special purpose, although *SI* and *DI* are often used as a holding register when all four of the general purpose registers are in use.

    The *BP* and *SP* registers are central to a program's environment. The *SP* register points to the object that is currently at the "top" of the stack. The *BP* register gives us a reference to find the top of the stack for the routine that called the current routine. The use of these registers is best described in the context of how they are used.

3. *CS, DS, ES, SS*: The segment registers. All memory addressing is done relative to one of these segment registers. Basically, the value in the register indexes a table which tells the hardware where the base of a memory segment is. This action is illustrated in Figure 15-3.

    The segment registers are set up by the UNIX kernel in the user's processes. Although the user's program can change the values in the segment registers, the memory protect mechanism provided by the 80826 will allow only a specific list of values to be used. If an attempt is made to reference a segment which is not permitted, a "Segment Violation" error occurs.

    Each segment register serves a different purpose. The following section on the 80286 memory system describes how these registers are used.

4. *The Instruction Pointer.* This register indicates the address of the next instruction to be executed. It is automatically incremented by the hardware when instructions are decoded, and set to new values when jump, branch, and subroutine call statements are executed.

5. *The status flags register.* This collection of bits are automatically set and reset by the processor when arithmetic instructions are executed. Conditional branch instructions alter the program's sequence based on these registers.

The contents of all the registers mentioned above are under control of the program being executed at the time. There are a number of "control flags" and special registers which only privileged (unprotected) programs can change. These flags control access to certain operations such as I/O instructions and control register load/sort operations that user programs are not supposed to execute.

80286 Memory System

The physical memory of the 80286 is modeled as a single dimensioned array of bytes, each with a unique address. The first byte's address is zero, and the last byte's address is $2^{24} - 1$. Any amount physical RAM memory may be installed, although UNIX requires a minimum of 640KB to run. Referencing undefined physical memory locations results in an error (the value of undefined memory is always −1, or 0xFFFF).

On IBM AT compatible architectures, 393,216 bytes (384 x 1024) of the physical memory model starting at address 655,360 (640 x 1024) are reserved for the use of ROM memory, video buffers, and other memory mapped I/O devices. Also, the lowest memory locations are used for interrupt vectors.

The lower memory (those with addresses less than 640KB) are generally used by the operating system, although no other restrictions on the use of RAM memory is made by the 80286 architecture.

Single or multiple byte objects may be stored at any memory location, although it is generally more efficient to start multiple byte objects at an even address. This is because most memory systems built of 80286 processors are organized to transfer 16 bit words in a single operation. Simple objects used in the C language are:

Chapter 15 Basics of 80286 Architecture

Object	C type	Bytes
Single byte	char, unsigned char	1
Word[1]	short, unsigned short	2
Double word	long, unsigned long	4
Single precision	float	4
Double precision	double	8

More complex objects can be made up using these elements in structures or arrays. Such multiple-element objects are defined and interpreted by the high-level language compiler, not the 80286 architecture.

When storing multiple byte values in memory, the least significant byte is always stored in the lower memory location. For example, the 16 bit value 0x5C2F stored at address 0x2000 will be stored with 2F in location 0x2000 and 0x5C in location 0x2001. This is "backwards" from some other 16-bit architectures which store the most significant byte first. Storage of 32-bit long words is done in a similar fashion.

The "low byte first" arrangement is easier to visualize in the following code segment:

```
{
char *p, *q;
short i;
long dw;

i  = 0x5C2F;              /* assign a short */
dw = 0x44332211;          /* assign a long */
p  = (char *) &i;         /* p points to 0x2F */
q  = (char *) &dw;        /* dw points to 0x11 */
printf("%x %x %x %x %x %x\n", *p, *(p + 1), *q, *(q + 1),
                              *(q + 2), *(q + 3));

}
```

The output generated by the *printf* will be:

---

[1]Note the absence of *type int*. We use short in this context because the C language uses 32 bits for type in the large model programs, and 16 bits for type in the small model. The keywords short and long are always unambiguous, and refer to 16-bit and 32-bit integers, respectively.

```
2f 5c 11 22 33 44
```

which shows that the least significant bytes are stored in the lowest memory addresses.

Character strings are usually stored with the "leftmost" character occupying the lowest memory location. Because an address on the 80286 is necessarily a byte address, this provides the most natural convention for subscript calculations on character arrays.

Segment Registers and Memory Addressing

Segment registers are the area in which the 80286 differs most from other machine architectures that support UNIX. This design is primarily the result of the need to support the 8086 instruction set, which in turn was required to support the even earlier 8080 instruction set.

The problem addressed by segment registers is that the 8086 and 80286 instruction set is only capable of directly generating a 16-bit memory address. This would normally limit the programmer to addressing 64KB (65,536 bytes) of memory. By separating the data space from the instruction space, as is done on the higher end DEC PDP-11s, we could address 128KB. This is thought of as too small of a program environment for DOS, UNIX, and many user programs.[2]

One way of getting around this problem is to allow instructions to generate more than 16 bits of address. Although this could be done, it is generally wasteful to do so because instructions take more memory and take longer to

---

[2] It is somewhat ironic that the earlier UNIX systems were implemented on PDP-11s that had no way to address more than 128KB (64KB instruction, 64KB data) of memory. Many of these systems are still in operation. However, the thirst for more computing power (i.e. larger memory address spaces) caused the wholesale migration of UNIX from the PDP-11 to the VAX, Motorola 68000, and other CPUs that had instruction set that generate more than 16 bits of address. Later on, later versions of UNIX were then ported backwards to the PDP-11. The 80286, although nominally constrained to 16-bits of address, has all the capabilities and more than the PDP-11 in terms of it's program environment. Yet the public image of UNIX on the 80286 is that of an elephant riding a mouse. Hopefully this misconception will change eventually.

fetch from memory. The approach used by the 80286 is to use segment registers.

All memory references either explicitly or implicitly refer to one of the four segment registers. The value in the segment register, as shown in Figure 15-3, controls where in physical memory a specific access will be directed. Each segment register is used differently as follows:

CS register: This is the "code" (the UNIX term is "text") segment that contains the instructions to execute. Whenever an instruction is fetched from memory to execute, the CS segment is used. The CS register is changed whenever a "far" jump is executed. (See the section below on "near" and "far" objects).

DS register: This is the main "data" segment, which is used by default during memory accesses. Any memory-to-register or register-to-memory access that does not explicitly refer to another segment uses the segment indicated by this register.

Figure 15-3

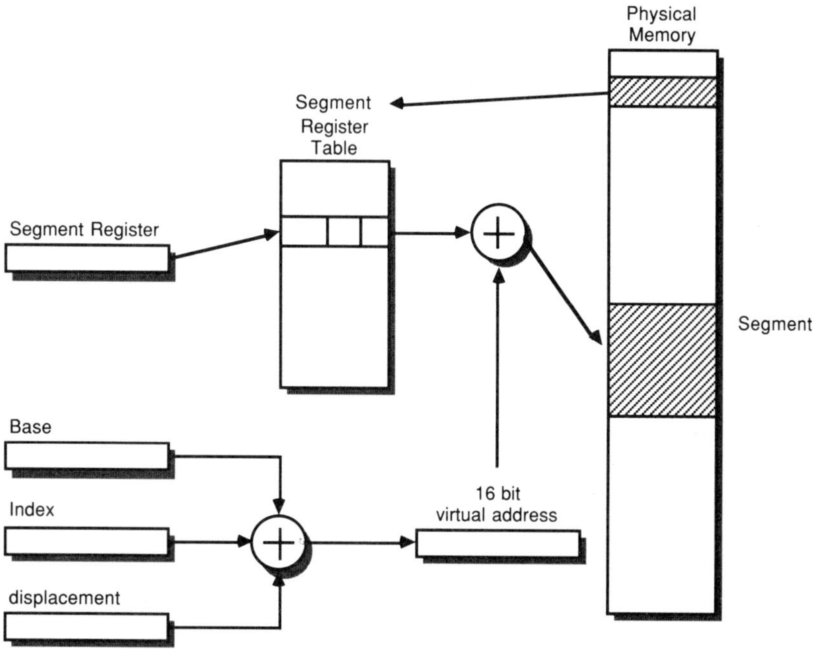

ES register: This is the "extra" segment, provided to make inter-segment data transfers possible. Actually, there are a few instructions that use this segment register by default. Normally, however, this segment can be used by any instruction can use the DS register.

SS register: The data stack is placed in this segment. Any *PUSH* or *POP* operation automatically uses the *SS* register. It is very rare in UNIX for a user program to change the *SS* register, which is set up by the kernel when an *exec()* system call is done.

The operating system divides physical memory up into segments. Segments can be of any size up to 64KB. Generally, segments contain only machine instructions or only data, although a process may have up to 65,535 segments or as many as allowed by the operating system. On UNIX, this limitation is governed by the amount of physical RAM memory available for user programs. The program run by the process can switch segments by loading different values into the segment registers.

Instruction Set

The instruction set of the 80286 is simple in concept and implementation. If you already know assembler language on any other typical minicomputer or microprocessor, you should not have any difficulty with the assembly language of the 80286. Of course, much of the design of UNIX is oriented to the concept that you need never program in assembly language, but it is sometimes helpful to know some of what is going on "behind the scenes."

Instructions are coded as a series of bytes, with an optional segment override prefix, a one or two byte op-code, and a series of optional parameters depending on the nature of the op-code. The instructions are grouped into the following categories:

1. **Data Transfer**: These instructions include the MOV instruction, which performs transfers from register to memory, memory to register, and register to register.

    Also included are the *PUSH* and *POP* operations, which transfer registers to the stack and vice versa.

Chapter 15 Basics of 80286 Architecture

2. **Arithmetic**: Standard binary arithmetic instructions are provided, which specify operations from register to register or memory to register.

   Certain arithmetic opcodes require the use of specific general purpose registers, and combine two 16-bit registers to store a 32-bit result.

3. **Logic**: The logic instructions include shift operations, and Boolean logic functions.

4. **String Manipulation**: The string instructions allow manipulation of a character array of data. These instructions make use of the SI (Source Index) and DI (Destination Index) registers to indicate the locations of the string operands. The C compiler does not generate these opcodes directly, because they do not easily map into C statements.

5. **Control Transfer**: The conditional and unconditional jump instructions, and the subroutine call and return instructions are in this category. The unconditional jump and subroutine call instructions allow inter-segment calls, which is the method the program uses to change the contents of the CS register. The conditional jump instructions must jump to a location in the same segment.

   Also provided are special *LOOP* instructions, which allow simple coding of loops. The *ENTER* and *LEAVE* instructions provide easy setup and take-down of the data stack when a subroutine is entered and returned.

6. **I/O instructions**: I/O instructions (described below) allow data to be transferred to and from I/O ports. These instructions can only be executed in unprotected mode.

7. **Processor Control**: These instructions include the setting and clearing of flags, including the Interrupt Enable flag, which is privileged.

8. **Protection Control**: All these instructions execute at a privileged level. These allow the setting and reading of special registers that control the memory access and protection mechanism of the 80286.

UNIX Programming on the 80286/80386, Second Edition

In assembly language, all instructions are assigned an opcode mnemonic, which may be prefixed by an instruction modifier and followed by one or more operands as appropriate. The syntax is best demonstrated with the most common instruction, the *move* instruction, in all its various forms:

```
MOV  AX,BX        ; MOVE THE CONTENTS OF BX TO AX
MOV  CH,AL        ; MOVE THE CONTENTS OF CH (HIGH PART OF CX)
                  ; TO AL (LOW PART OF AX)
MOV  CX,352       ; MOVE THE VALUE 353 TO THE CX REGISTER
MOV  DX,VAR       ; MOVE THE CONTENTS OF THE VARIABLE VAR TO DX
MOV  AX,[BP+6]    ; MOVE THE CONTENTS OF THE MEMORY LOCATION
                  ; ADDRESSED BY THE BASE POINTER + 6 (IN THE
                  ; STACK SEGMENT)
MOV  VAR,SI       ; MOVE THE SI REGISTER INTO THE CONTENTS OF THE
                  ; VARIABLE VAR
```

Note that the operations above that reference the variable VAR assume that the DS register is set up properly, because that is the segment register used by default. It is possible, however, to use the ES register to allow inter-segment accesses:

```
MOV  AX,ES:VAR    ; GET THE CONTENTS OF VAR FROM EXTRA SEGMENT
MOV  SUM,AX       ; STORE IN VARIABLE SUM
```

Many instructions can operate on either 8-bit or 16-bit values. Although the actual op-code is different for these instructions, the assembler deduces the proper operation from the names of the operands. For example, when the AL is referenced, which is an 8-bit register, the 8-bit instruction is used. One of the more interesting instructions of the 80286 set is the REP instruction loop. Certain 80286 instructions are designed to be executed repetitively. One example is the MOVS instruction, which move the contents of the memory location pointed to by the SI register in the DS segment to the location pointed to by the DI register in the ES segment. After the move, both SI and DI are either decremented or incremented (depending on a control flag that can be set).

The MOVS instruction will perform the above operation once. However, if we prefix it with a REP instruction, it will execute repeatedly, each time decrementing the CX register by one. If the CX register becomes zero, the loop is escaped. We have an example of these instruction later. Another set of instructions of interest are the CALL and RET instructions, which provide the means to set up nested subroutines. The CALL instruction simply pushes the address of the next instruction on to the stack, and jumps to the indicated address. The RET operation pops the value off of the stack into the IP register, effectively returning control to the instruction after the CALL.

Typically, the program will implement a protocol using the BP register and the stack for local storage and parameters. This will be seen in Chapter 13. The CALL and RET instructions can be more complex when the subroutine being called is in a different segment than the routine executing the CALL. In this case, referred to as a "far" subroutine call, the current value of the CS register must also be pushed in addition to the offset within the segment. Also, the called routine must also execute a "far" RET instruction that will re-load the CS register with its old value. If the CALL and RET are not properly matched, the program will crash.

C programs and 80286 assembly language Note that with only four general purpose registers, there are limitations to the register-assignment optimizations the C compiler can use. Also, care should be taken when using the C storage class register. Because the general purpose registers are at a premium, the compilers generally use the SI and DI registers for storing register variables. The SI and DI registers are used in some instructions that are not easily mappable from C. In the case of a string move, such as:

```
char *p, *q, i;

i = 310;            /* number of bytes to move */
p = source;         /* source array */
q = dest;           /* destination array */
while (i--) *p++ = *q++;
```

could be mapped into the assembly language equivalent:

```
MOV   CX,310        /* number of bytes to move */
MOV   SI,source     /* source index */
MOV   DI,dest       /* destination index */
REP   MOVSB         /* perform the move */
```

where the actual *while* loop is encoded down to the two instructions *REP* and *MOVSB*. Note that the usage of the CX, SI, and DI registers are all predetermined by the 80286 instruction set. However, most C compilers will not be able to make this mapping in actual practice. Instead, a loop using a conditional jump is constructed.

The C compiler does take advantage of some of the programming aspects of the instructions and how they affect general purpose registers. For example, the C program segment:

```
    short i, j;

    j = i >> 8;
```

will not generate a shift instruction. Rather, the assembly language result is:

```
    XOR  AX,AX      ; Generate a 16 bit zero
    MOV  AH,i+1     ; Move the high byte of I into the high byte of AX
    MOV  j,AX       ; Move 16 bit register AX into J
```

This is faster than the shift operation, and in circumstances where the value of *i* is already in a register, it will be even faster. Of course, if the shift amount is a variable, the shift instruction will have to be used. A complete list of the 80286 instructions is provided in the *Intel 80286 Programmer's Reference Manual*.

The Stack

The 80286 machine language makes heavy use of the data stack which is stored in the region of memory indicated by the segment register. The stack provides temporary storage and subroutine return-address information. The stack is accessed with the following three registers:

1. The *Stack Segment* (SS) register, which indicates the memory segment currently being used for the stack,

2. The *Stack Pointer* (SP) register, which points to the object currently at the top of the stack, and

3. The *Base Pointer* (BP) which points to the calling routine's top of stack. It provides a fixed reference into the stack area for the purpose of locating automatic storage for the currently executing procedure and the parameters to the procedure.

Any instruction which uses the SP or BP registers automatically use the segment specified by the SS register. For UNIX processes, there is normally only one stack per process. Because the stack is in its own segment, we need not worry about the stack "growing into" other program or data space, crashing the program. In Chapter 13 we will see how the stack is used by the C program environment.

I/O on the AT Compatible 80286

Data to and from the 80286 is accomplished by I/O instructions which can transfer a string of bytes to and from an entity known as an "I/O port." An I/O port is a device which responds to the 80286 when I/O instructions are executed. Each I/O device is assigned its own number by the hardware system designer.

The I/O instructions are:

IN	Read word (or byte) from device
OUT	Write word (or byte) to device
INS	Input string from device
OUTS	Output string to device

The instructions specify the I/O port either as an immediate operand, or take the value in the DX register as the number of the I/O port.

When we discuss the writing of device drivers, we will see how these instructions are accessed from C by special subroutines provided for this purpose. All the I/O instructions and capabilities on the 80286 are privileged operations, and may be performed only by the UNIX kernel.

When an IN or OUT instruction is executed, what happens is defined by the external device that was addressed. Sometimes actual data is passed to and from the device, other times only control information. Most devices define more than one I/O port to make this distinction.

Most I/O devices have the capability of interrupting the CPU. This happens when the device needs attention, or when it is signaling the end of a data transfer. The processor can be used for other tasks until the interrupt occurs.

If necessary, device interrupts can be masked out by setting a control bit. When the interrupt does occur, the processor is forced to do a special subroutine call to an interrupt handler, suspending whatever task was executing at the time. The interrupt handler is in effect a subroutine, which executes at the highest privilege level. Its job is to read status values set up for it in designated memory locations and act on them, translating them into IN and OUT instructions which will set up the device for the next operation, if any. When finished, the interrupt hander executes the special IRET instruction, which is similar to the RET instruction, except that it restores the privilege and memory-map status that was in effect when the interrupt occurred.

Certain high speed devices, such as disk drives and tape drives, transfer too much data to be efficiently passed through IN and OUT instructions. A disk drive[3] will typically transfer at least 512 bytes of data with one request. If each byte had to be handled by an IN or OUT instruction, the overhead would be excessive. To get around this problem, the IBM AT compatible architectures have special devices called "DMA" (Direct Memory Access) controllers.

A DMA controller implements a channel directly between the high speed device and memory. When a transfer is to be done, the device driver program sends instructions to the device via OUT instructions to I/O ports defined for that purpose. The actual transfer can then take place at the device's own rate, and the processor can be used for other tasks. When the transfer is done, the I/O device will interrupt the processor. The status of the transfer can be monitored with IN instructions.

---

[3] Interestingly enough, the IBM AT hard disk controller does not use DMA. The floppy disk controller does.

16
Basics of 80386 Architecture

The 80386 is the long awaited answer by Intel to the justifiably popular Motorola 68020 series of micro-processors. The architecture of the 80386 breaks the limitations of its predecessors with a vengeance. The highlights of this chip are:

- it is fast (16 & 20 mega-hertz operation)

- it is a true 32-bit processor, with 32 bit registers and data paths

- it has virtual memory capabilities

- it has virtual machine capabilities, where multiple and simultaneous operating systems can be implemented

- it is upwardly compatible with the 80286 and 8086

This last fact is the reason the 80386 has become so popular so quickly. All the other features have been available in competing CPU chips for years before Intel had the 80386 ready. However, the majority of end-user systems being produced are being purchased for DOS applications. This high volume creates a market condition where sophisticated hardware is available at a very reasonable cost, and with it the Operating Systems such as UNIX.

The 80386 does something of a tap-dance to enhance the 80286 instruction set while maintaining binary compatibility. This was mostly done by using the undefined operation codes on the 80286 and giving them definitions on the 80386. Any instruction that works on the 80286 will have the same effect on the 80386, with certain minor variations.[1] Also, in some control

---

[1] These variations are very unlikely to come up in actual practice. For example, it is possible to generate a "17 bit" address with 80286 instructions by using a base register and an offset. On the

registers, "reserved" bits in the 80286 now have defined counterparts in the 80386.

In this chapter we will focus primarily on the differences between the 80286 and the 80386, and how they affect our C programs. Actually, the changes had been made in such a way as to cause very little difference from the point of view of the C programmer, except that 32-bit operations will occur faster, with fewer instructions.

Register Set

The set of registers for the 80386 is a superset of those found in the 80286. As seen in Figure 16-1, the general and special purpose register, and the instruction pointer, have been extended to 32 bits. Interestingly enough, the segment registers are still 16 bits, although there are two more of them. We will examine the segment register scheme later.

The registers are all used the same way they are on the 80286, except the programmer (or compiler) now has the option of encoding 32-bit operations. For example, the C program segment:

```
long i, j;

j = i + 3;
```

can be translated as:

```
    MOV   EAX,I        ; GET THE VALUE OF THE I
    ADD   EAX,3        ; ADD 3
    MOV   J,EAX        ; STORE THE VALUE INTO J
```

instead of the following:

```
    MOV   AX,I         ; GET THE LOWER 16 BITS OF I
    MOV   DX,I+2       ; GET THE UPPER 16 BITS OF I
    ADD   AX,3         ; ADD 3 INTO LOWER 16 BITS
    ADC   DX,0         ; PROPAGATE ANY CARRY
```

80286, such an address would "wrap around," ignoring the 17th bit. On the 80386, which normally deals with 32 bit instructions, the address would extend past the 64KB limit.

```
        MOV   J,AX              ; STORE LOWER 16 BITS OF J
        MOV   J+2,DX            ; STORE UPPER 16 BITS OF J
```

which is what the 80286 has to do. The 16 bit version will work on the 80386 as well, as will the 8 bit instructions, but clearly there is an advantage when working with 32 bit numbers.

Figure 16-1

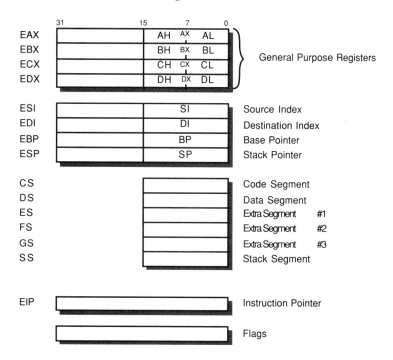

When referring to a 32-bit register, the assembly language convention is to prefix the 16-bit register name with an "E" (for Extended).

Memory Architecture and Segment Registers

As mentioned earlier, the 80386 adds two segment registers to the original set of 80286 segment registers. This allows a single instruction to access two additional segments without loading any segment registers.

The segment registers are 16-bits, which allows (theoretically) the usage of 65,536 different segments. Each segment can be be up to 2^{32} bytes long so that the effective virtual memory limitation is 2^{32+16} bytes or 2^{48} bytes. This is a total of 2.81 x 10^{14} bytes. Even with video disk technology, it is difficult to imagine a physical RAM that would approach this size.

Recall that segment registers were originally designed to work around the 16 bit address limitation of the 8086/80286 instruction set. Now we have an instruction set that can generate addresses of 32 bits, or up to 4,294,967,295 (2^{32}-1) bytes. It would seem that this is practically no limitation at all, and hardly needing the machinations of a segment register scheme to increase addressing capability.

One answer is to ignore the segment registers completely. We can set all the segment registers to the same value, which index the same page, and we can have a "flat" memory architecture where instructions, data, and stack all share the same memory space. This is the model of many standard computers, and this is what the UNIX C compilers call the "small" memory model for the 80386. The AT&T Portable C compiler (pcc), which is the one Microport uses for the System V/386, compiles in no other model. We will discuss memory models in Chapter 18.

However, by doing so we throw away certain other features segment registers give us other than increased memory access. Having code segments separate from the data and stack segments, for example, allow the UNIX kernel to allow text (i.e. code segments) to be shared among multiple processes. This saves memory and, more importantly, swapping time.

Another advantage of segment registers is that, when used properly, they can increase execution speed by allowing the coding of smaller address operands. For example, if we have a program with the following array declarations:

```
int   mat1[256][192];
int   mat2[256][192];
```

we will allocate 98,304 bytes of memory. This is too much to be addressed by 16-bit address and operand calculations, except where mat1 is in a segment addressed by ES and mat2 is in a segment addressed by FS. If that is the case, all addressing can be done with 16 bits, which makes the index variables smaller, and hence fetched to and from memory faster.

Instruction Set Differences

Although the actual bitwise encoding of instructions is somewhat convoluted, the 80386 instruction set is a natural outgrowth of the 80286/8086 instruction sets. Some differences are important to note when reading assembly language programs:

1. It is possible to select one of two additional segment registers, GS and FS.

2. The default operand size may be 32 bits long, depending on the setting of a control in the segment descriptor of the code segment.

3. The stack segment may have either a 16 or 32 bit pointer, depending on the setting of a control bit in the descriptor of the stack segment.

A complete description of the 80386 instruction set may be found in the Intel 80386 Programmer's Reference Manual. From a C programmer's standpoint, these considerations are taken care of by the choice of a memory model, which we will discuss in Chapter 18.

17
Floating Point

As is common with microprocessors, the Intel 80286 and 80386 support a math coprocessor to speed floating-point calculations. Historically, floating-point arithmetic logic has been "optional" when ordering computer hardware. The reason for this is that some installations never (or rarely) need to perform floating-point calculations, so that leaving out the added cost of the extra hardware is an advantage to those users who do not need it.

When the 80287 or the 80387 is installed, certain instruction codes are added to the basic instruction set, and an additional set of registers designed for floating-point numbers become available through that instruction set. The map of floating point registers is shown in Figure 17-1.

Figure 17-1

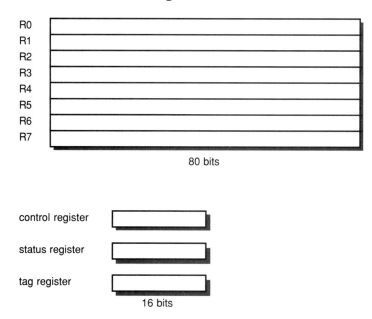

When the floating-point math coprocessor is not there, it can be simulated with subroutines that use the integer arithmetic hardware inherent in the basic processor's instruction set. The UNIX kernel contains the code which does this. In such a system, each floating point operation causes a "invalid op-code" trap, which the UNIX kernel takes as a signal to invoke the routines that emulate the math co-processor. This method enables us to use only a single version of the executable binary for systems with or without the math co-processor installed.

For the 80286 processor, the 80287 math-coprocessor chip is used. On 80386 based systems, some designs allow the use of the 80287, others use the 80387, and some allow one or the other. In addition, some allow a third-party math coprocessor called the Weitek 1167, which requires a special compiler and support from the operating system.

Floating point numbers in C are type float, which is "single precision" using 32 bits, and double, which is "double precision" using 64 bits. These formats and the range of values that can be represented are shown in Figure 17-2. Each number has three components:

1. the sign bit, which indicates whether the value is positive or negative

2. the exponent

3. the mantissa, which is a normalized binary number

Note that single precision has only six digits of precision guaranteed. This means that the number 9,999,999 cannot be stored with complete accuracy. Also, since all calculations are actually done in the 80-bit extended precision format, there is very little time difference between single precision and double precision operations. The only real difference is the overhead of loading the values to and from the floating point registers. For these reasons, it is recommended that only type double be used in C programs. The extended precision format is not accessible to C programs.

Floating point arithmetic on the 80287 and the 80387 follows closely the IEEE[1] standard for binary floating point computations. This standard describes certain exception conditions. Not all exception conditions are

---

[1] This is the IEEE Standard 754-195, *IEEE Standard for Binary Floating Point Arithmetic*, IEEE Computer Society Press, Washington DC 1985.

fatal, although those that are are trapped by the UNIX kernel and result in a signal to the process that incurred the exception.

Figure 17-2

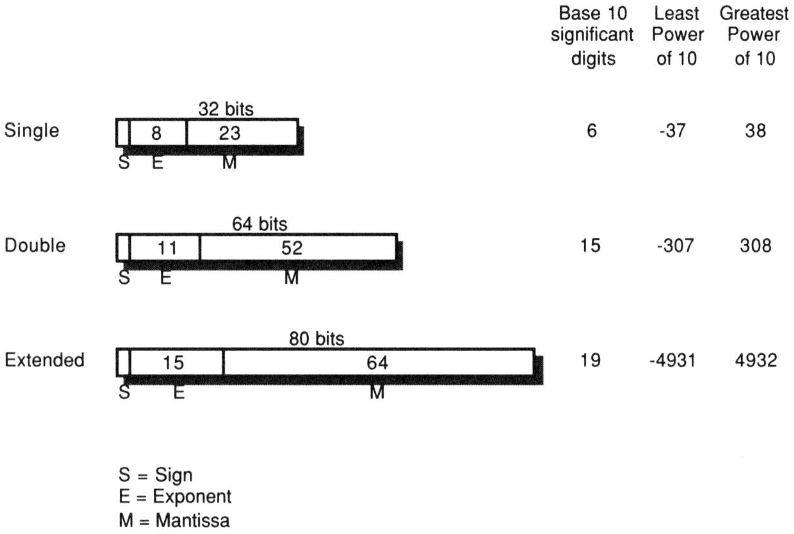

	Bits	Base 10 significant digits	Least Power of 10	Greatest Power of 10
Single	32 bits (S=1, E=8, M=23)	6	-37	38
Double	64 bits (S=1, E=11, M=52)	15	-307	308
Extended	80 bits (S=1, E=15, M=64)	19	-4931	4932

S = Sign
E = Exponent
M = Mantissa

1. **Inexact Result.** Not all rational decimal numbers can be expressed in binary. For example:

    ```
    double i, j;
    i = 1.0;
    j = i / 3.0;
    ```

    would assign the non-terminating binary value 0.01010101 . . . to the variable *j*. For most programming purposes, this is thought to be harmless, although it is the main reason commercial programs (accounting systems, in general) do not use floating-point arithmetic.

2. **Numeric Underflow.** This occurs when the result of a floating-point operation is non-zero, yet lies between the greatest negative and least positive values. This can generally occur when dividing a small number by a very large one.

3. **Division by Zero.** This exception will cause a process to terminate, unless it has enabled the catching of the division by zero signal.

4. **Numeric Overflow.** This occurs when the result of a floating-point operation is greater than the greatest positive number, or less than the least negative number.

5. **Invalid Operation.** This exception should never occur when programming in C. Invalid operations include the use of a non-defined register, or the calculation of a negative square root.

18
Segment Register Programming

In this chapter we discuss the most significant aspects of UNIX/C programming that is different from the Intel 80286 and 80386 to the other architectures that have supported UNIX.

In the previous two chapters we have seen how the 80286 and 80386 support the instruction set of the 8086, which was limited to its 16-bit address component size. This had the carry-over of segment register addressing, which was again limited to 16 bits on the 80286, but then extended to 32 bits on the 80386. The programmer for the 80386 need not be concerned with segment registers at all. Essentially the processor has the capability of 32-bit "flat array" addresses, equivalent to a VAX or Motorola 68000 based system.

Before leaving segment register considerations completely behind, let us consider the facility they represent.

With C under UNIX for the 80286 and 80386, the programmer has a choice of which memory model to select. The following models are available:

Model	Compiler Option for SCO	Compiler Option for Microport
Impure Small	-Ms	(not available)
Small (pure)	-Ms (with -i to ld)	-Ms
Middle Model	-Mm	(not available)
Large Model	-Ml	-Ml
Huge Model	-Mh	-Mh

Note that SCO currently does not support anything but the "small" model for 80386 compilations. This is because the 80386 supports segments that are up to 2^{32} in size, which is effectively unlimited. However, we can select other models when compiling for the 80286, which can be run on the 80386 using SCO XENIX.

The programming differences between the various models are mostly taken care of at a low level by the compiler. In each model it is important to be aware of how memory is used, and with it pointers and pointer arithmetic. Each model is described as follows:

> **Impure Small** The text, data, and stack segments are all the same, as shown in Figure 18-1. Although there is only one segment for the kernel to keep track of for this process, it is impossible to share the text portion between processes, because the program will have write access to the text area within the segment. In the 80286, all pointers are 16 bits in size, limiting the aggregate total of all memory space to 64KB. In the 80386, all pointers are 32 bits.

Figure 18-1

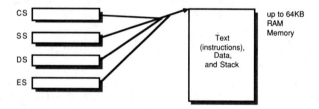

> **Small** This is the same as the Impure Small model above, except that the text segment has been separated so that it can be shared between processes. This is the default model, because it allows the greatest address space possible within the 16-bit address limitation,[1] as shown in Figure 18-2. In such cases, the process has read-only access to the text segment.
>
> **Middle Model** The middle model is one step between the Small and Large models, allowing more than one segment for

---

[1] It might have been possible to provide an extra 64KB of data space by allocating another segment, and assigning it to the ES register. This could not been made transparent to the programmer, however, because pointer arithmetic would be impossible to define within 16 bits.

text, but keeping only one for the data and stack areas. This allows programs of virtually any size, but only 64KB total for both data and stack. In this model, pointers to the text area (pointers to functions, mostly) are 32 bits long, while pointers to an object in the data area are 16 bits. This model is not available for 80386 programs.

Figure 18-2

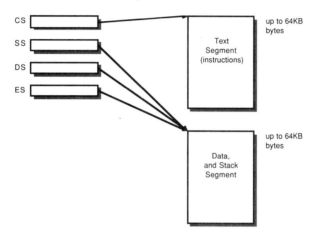

Large Model   In this model, all pointers are 32 bits long, and any number of segments are allocated to the text and data areas, as shown in Figure 18-3, although only one is allocated to the stack. Pointers have two parts: the upper 16 bits, which contain the segment, and the lower 16 bits, which contain the offset within the segment. Due to the way pointer arithmetic is handled (which we will discuss below) there is a limitation of 64KB on any single data object or array. This is the model for most large programs on the 80286. The 80386, which does not have a 16 bit limitation, does not need this model.

Huge Model   The huge model is designed to work around the limitations of the Large Model. Again, all pointers are 32 bits wide, except that now arrays can be greater than 64KB. However, there is a penalty to be paid in the form of more complex pointer arithmetic.

Figure 18-3

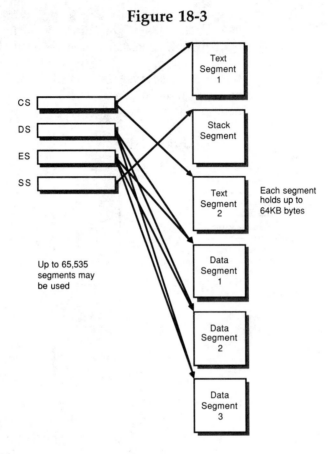

Stack Segment

The C programming language relies heavily on the program stack for both nested subroutine vectors and temporary storage. On the 80286 and 80386 running in the large model (with 32-bit pointers), a special segment will be allocated for the use of the stack through the Stack Segment (SS) register. On the small memory models, the Stack Segment will be the same as the Data Segment to allow direct addressing of objects on the stack through 16 bit pointers.

The Stack "grows" in a downward direction. This means that in the small memory models, it is necessary to allocate stack space in high memory, and hope that it does not "crash" into data objects that are allocated in lower memory but are not part of the stack. When this occurs we call it a "stack

Chapter 18   Segment Register Programming

overflow." For models where there is a separate stack segment, the memory-protect feature of the processor will alert the operating system when a stack overflow occurs, and a controlled abort of the program will occur.

Normally, items are pushed on the stack when a function (or subroutine) is called, and popped off the stack when a function (or subroutine) returns. Figure 18-4 shows an example subroutine and the map of the stack's configuration while it is executing.

Figure 18-4

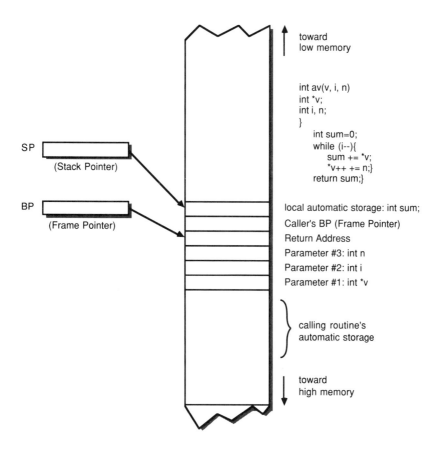

When a subroutine is called, the following occurs:

1. The parameters to the subroutine are pushed on the stack in reverse order.

307

2. A subroutine call is made to the entry point of the subroutine, which pushes the return address on the stack.

3. The subroutine pushes the caller's BP (Frame Pointer) onto the stack. The current SP (Stack Pointer) value then becomes the new BP (Frame Pointer).

4. The subroutine allocates its temporary storage (automatic local variables) on the stack, after checking to make sure the stack has not overflowed.

5. The subroutine executes.

6. The temporary storage for the subroutine is released by moving the contents of the BP (Frame Pointer) register into the SP (Stack Pointer) register.

7. The caller's BP (Frame Pointer) register is restored by a POP instruction.

8. The subroutine exits with a RET instruction. There are variations of this theme between the various memory models, because the size of the data objects (the return address and the pointer parameters) change in size between models. However, the principle remains the same in how the stack is used.

32-Bit Pointer Arithmetic

In any except the small model, the compiler has to accommodate the possibility of 32-bit pointers. As we have seen, in the 80286 a 32-bit address has two parts: 16 bits for the segment number and 16 bits for an offset within that segment. For example, if we have the C code segment:

```
char *p;

p = (char *) 0x000F1234;
```

in the large model, p points to offset 0x1234 in segment 0xF. In the large model, it is often necessary to load the DS or the ES register before accessing a particular variable or memory location. This is a fairly expensive operation, even though the compiler attempts to retain segment register values within the register set across operations. To make operations more efficient, the code generated by the compiler still uses 16 bit arithmetic on the offset portion only. This is what causes the limitation of 64KB of array sizes.

Any array, structure, or program must be contained wholly within one segment in order for the pointer arithmetic to remain valid.

In the huge model, pointer arithmetic is extended to 32 bits. Whenever pointer arithmetic occurs, the code must check to see if a segment boundary has been crossed. If so, the segment number is adjusted. This causes additional overhead with every pointer calculation, so the huge model should be avoided unless there is no other way to make a particular program work.

The Near and Far Keywords

In order to accommodate segment register considerations, two new keywords have been added to the C language: *near* and *far*. These keywords are valid for modification of data object declarations as follows:

```
int i;              /* default integer */
int far i;          /* integer in a far segment (the integer is 16
                       bits, and pointer to the integer must be
                       32 bits) */
int near i;         /* integer in a near segment */
char *p;            /* default pointer */
char far *p;        /* pointer to a far object (32 bits) */
char near *p;       /* pointer to a near object (16 bits) */
```

Most often, the keyword far is used in small and medium model programs where the default is type near, and the keyword near is used in large model programs, where the default is type far.

These type of declarations are useful when performing "mixed model" programming, which is described later. First, let's look at why we should bother with mixed mode programming.

309

Execution Speed

A program that can work using only 16 bits for addresses or data should do so. Why? Because no matter how fast or efficient a processor is, it will always be faster if you give it half the work to do. Consider, for example, the following C code segment:

```
char bufr[32];
char *p;

{
    for (p = bufr; *p && p < bufr + sizeof(bufr); p++);
}
```

The for loop will set the pointer p to the first null byte in the array bufr, or the last byte of bufr. The machine instructions that will be executed (assuming that the compiler optimizes the loop by placing the variable *p* in a register for the duration) will be as follows:

Step 1: Move the address of *bufr* into a register. This register will be called register-p.

Step 2: Compare the byte in memory addressed by register-p to zero. If it is equal to zero, go to Step 4. Compare register-p to the constant value that is bufr + sizeof(bufr). If register-p is greater or equal, go to Step 4.

Step 3: Increment register-p by one. Go to Step 2.

Step 4: Store register-p into the memory location assigned to the character pointer *p*.

Now what is the difference in this loop between using the large model and the small model? In the 80286 small model, all the operations are 16 bits wide. That means, for instance, register-p can fit into any one of the sixteen bit registers (whichever the compiler chooses) and access the array bufr through the DS (Display Segment), which is set to only one value all the time the program is executing. Only two bytes are accessed in memory for Step 1, above, and Step 4, above.

Chapter 18   Segment Register Programming

In the large model, Step 1 and Step 4 are 32-bit operations, requiring the loading and storing of the ES (Extended Segment) register. Fortunately, there is no added inefficiency regarding Step 3, the incrementing of register-p, because the 64KB restriction on array sizes allows the compiler to assume that only the lower 16-bits of the Segment/Offset pair needs to be incremented. All-in-all, nine more bytes are accessed than in the small model.

This does not seem like much. Because our compiler is smart enough not to store a value into the character pointer *p* on every iteration of the loop, the code is much more efficient than it could have been no matter which memory model we used. However, if this code segment is part of a subroutine that is called on every line of input, and there are 10,000 lines of input, we have accessed no less than 90,000 bytes in RAM memory that never needed to be accessed. We might as well have added the code line:

```
for (i = 0; i < 30000; i++);
```

at the beginning of the program, which would read about 90,000 bytes of RAM as instructions. No reasonable programmer would do this. The situation becomes much worse if the 32-bit operations occur on the inside of loops, such as in:

```
char bufr[32];
char *p;

{
    for (p = bufr; *p && p < bufr + sizeof(bufr); p++)
        checkdig(p);
}
```

Here, the large model compilation must generate instructions that push 32-bits on the stack and store the current value in the memory location *p* on each iteration of the loop. The small model requires only 16 bits. Now we have a big multiple of the 90,000 extra operations we had supposed earlier.

The hardware we are using these days is sufficiently fast that the difference would never likely be observed for the milder cases. Many programmers will never need to think about the optimization of their programs at this level, except to select the most efficient memory model for their particular program.

311

As a general rule, try the small model first. You would be surprised to see how large a program can fit into the small model. If it does not fit, you might consider restructuring the program so that it does.

Mixing Memory Models

Suppose that we have a program that will fit into the small model, except for one or two large data structures. We can make the overall program more efficient by simply compiling the program under the small model, while declaring the object to be accessed in a far segment. For example if the declarations:

```
int ix, jx;
char flags[60][60];
double far matrix[60][60];
```

were compiled into a small model program, all the accesses to flags, ix and jx would occur with 16 bit addresses (accessed through the DS segment), while accesses to matrix would occur in a far segment. This is far more efficient than compiling the entire program into a large model, which would require a 32-bit operation for every access.

The above does not work for 80386 programs. The reason is that only the "small" model is supported for the 80386, in which case the addressing arithmetic is all done with 32 bits anyway. The curious thing about this arrangement is that it is possible for a specific program to run faster when compiled for the 80286 than it is for the 80386. To explore this, you can compile the program both ways, then run the program each time with the *time* command from the shell.

The *brk()*, *sbrk()*, and *brkctl()* System Calls

Once a process has started, there is no difference between the small and large models in memory allocation or management from the point of view of the UNIX kernel. There is nothing stopping a small model program from allocating additional segments through the *brk()* and *sbrk()* system calls on Microport and the *brkctl()* system call in XENIX.

Normally a programmer is encouraged to use the *malloc()* call and additional routines for additional memory. In the case where we want to access

Chapter 18 Segment Register Programming

additional segments in a small model program, *malloc()* will not do the job. This is because there is a different version of *malloc()* for every memory model, and the small model version knows nothing about additional segments.

In the small model, we use the *far* keyword to identify pointers that are used to access far segments. Any pointer so defined must be handled with care, because it cannot be passed as a parameter to a small model function that is not expecting a 32-bit pointer. This means, for example, that a *far* pointer cannot be used as a parameter to *printf()*, as in the following:

```
char far *p;

printf ("String: %s\n", p);
```

which will yield undefined results.

For Microport, *sbrk()* can be used to allocate new segments. The parameter to *sbrk()* is the amount of memory allocate. This may be a negative number if the program wishes to free memory. Memory is always added to (or taken from) the end of the last data segment, in a similar fashion to a single-segment memory architecture.

The difference is that when *sbrk* finds that the requested amount of memory is greater than the amount remaining in the last segment, a new segment is allocated. The reason for this is to make sure that a new data object (presumably *sbrk()* was being called to allocate memory for a single object) resides fully within one segment. However, this may mean that there might be some "unused" memory at the end of the prior segment, which is unavailable.

For example, in the series of *sbrk* calls:

```
char far *p;
char far *q;
char far sbrk();
unsigned int j = 48000;

p = sbrk(j);
q = sbrk(j);
```

at least one of the of the two *sbrk()* calls is guaranteed to allocate a new segment, because both of them together allocate more than 64KB of memory. Suppose the allocations prior to the first sbrk were such that p was allocated to a new segment. In that case *q* will also be placed in a new segment, leaving a 64KB - 48,000 (17,536) byte gap that is unused.

The *brkctl()* call in XENIX is somewhat more flexible while still being easy to understand. The XENIX kernel keeps track of any number of segments that a process has currently allocated to it, and each one can have any amount of memory. It always returns a far type pointer, and understands three commands, as defined by the file *sys/brk.h*:

BR_ARGSEG   The user is providing *brkctl()* with an existing far segment. The return value will be to either find the status of that segment, or change the current amount of memory allocated to that segment.[2]

BR_NEWSEG   The user is requesting a new segment.

BR_IMPSEG   The user wishes to obtain or release memory relative to the last segment currently assigned.

An example of where *brkctl()* is used is where one or more large arrays are added to a small model program. In the example above, we used the loader to allocate a static area of memory. We can accomplish close to the same thing at run time with:

```
#include <sys/brk.h>

double far *matrix;
char far *brkctl();


{
        matrix = (double far *) brkctl(BR_NEWSEG,
                            (long) 60 * 60 * sizeof(double),
                            (char *) 0);
        if (matrix == (double far *) 0) {
```

---

[2] The brkctl() system call is documented in the BRKCTL(S) article of the SCO XENIX Programmer's Reference Manual.

```
            fprintf(stderr, "Memory not available\n");
            exit(1); }

    }
```

the difference is that matrix can only be referenced as a single-dimensioned array. We can later free that memory by the statement:

```
brkctl(BR_ARGSEG, (long) -60 * 60 * sizeof(double), matrix);
```

which will increment (in a negative direction) the memory allocated to the segment assigned to matrix.

If the above seems to be too much work for the project at hand, it might be worthwhile to use the large model on the 80286, or the small model on the 80386. Although the resulting program might not be as fast, it also will tend to be easier to debug, particularly in cases where memory is allocated and deallocated dynamically.

19
Programming Terminals

It is time to tackle a very messy subject, the programming of terminals. In this day and age we expect a high level of sophistication from our programs. At least, they must provide a convenient visual human interface in order to sell well.

The traditional UNIX user interface is of the "think-and-type" mode, where the user has to think of a command, then type it, press the ENTER key, and wait for a response. This is opposed to the "look-and-point" interface, which involves windows, icons, and a mouse pointing device. Look-and-point is becoming more popular, and is appearing on the higher end UNIX based workstations now being produced by Sun Microsystems, Apollo, and others.[1] However, for UNIX on the 286/386, it is still a think-and-type world, except where our application programs provide something else. For example, when entering a database record, we could provide the series of C statements:

```
printf("\n * * * PHONE LIST RECORD * * *\n\n");
printf("Enter customer last name: ");   scanf("%s", cust.last);
printf("       Enter first name: ");    scanf("%s", cust.first);
printf("      Enter Phone Number: ");   scanf("%s", cust.phone);
```

and so on. This makes use of the "scroll mode" of a CRT screen and is about the only way of performing this function over a printing terminal. The problem with this way of doing data entry is that the user cannot see all of the fields at one time, and it will usually be hard for a non-programming user to get used to visualizing the whole record and the current data within it. For this reason, most buyers prefer a "screen-mode" program, which

---

[1] These UNIX workstation systems allow the user to open several windows on a large screen, each one acting as an independent CRT screen of a user specified size, and providing a mouse to switch between them. This is a very handy environment for developing programs, because you can keep reference materials, several editing sessions, and a running version of the program in view all at once. We can come close to this environment in SCO XENIX and Microport System V because they allow virtual screens, which can be switched between at a single keystroke.

presents a form on the screen which can be filled in, and edited by moving the cursor about with special keys. The display might appear as:

```
------------------------------------------------------
|                                                    |
|        * * * PHONE LIST RECORD * * *               |
|                                                    |
|    Customer last name:                             |
|              First name:                           |
|            Phone Number:                           |
|                                                    |
|                                                    |
------------------------------------------------------
```

The cursor would then be positioned after the "last-name" field for the user to type, then move to the next field, then so on until the last field. Additionally, the cursor would be prevented from moving to any "illegal" position on the screen, overwriting part of the form.

CRT Basics

Let us review how a typical alphanumeric CRT screen is designed. Figure 19-1 shows such a terminal hooked up to a computer over a serial (sometimes called RS-232) line. Characters typed at the keyboard get sent to the computer, and are usually encoded by the ASCII (American Standard Code for Information Interchange) code. Each letter or key is assigned a number.

Most characters sent from the computer, in the same ASCII code, are displayed on the CRT screen. The CRT screen is divided up into (usually) a matrix of 25 rows and 80 columns. Each matrix position can hold one character, which might be set to special attributes such as boldface or blinking.

Where the next character appears depends on the current position of the "cursor," which is a marker displayed on the screen in one of the positions. When a character is displayed, the cursor moves one character to the right, or if the last character on the line is reached (depending on the make and mode of the terminal), down to the next line at the extreme left of the screen. Some characters are not displayed, but control the operation of the CRT. Some of these are the carriage return, new line, bell, and others. For more complex functions, combinations of characters are used. The problem is that different makes of terminals respond differently to control codes.

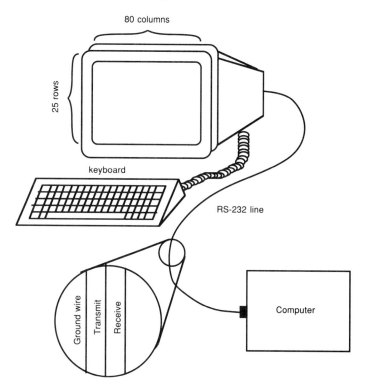

Figure 19-1

A "clear screen" command for a Televideo 920 will display garbage on an ANSI compatible terminal, and it won't understand the "clear screen" command for a ADDS terminal. We will see how UNIX deals with this problem later.

The name RS-232 is the name of a standard that defines a method of communications between two devices. The full standard provides a number of signals, some of which are not used except in special circumstances, and fall outside our discussion here. At a minimum, there are three wires between the computer and the terminal:

1. Send data, which transmits characters from the terminal to the computer.

2. Receive data, which transmits characters from the computer to the terminal.

3. A ground wire, to provide a voltage reference.

RS-232 also may provide signals which allow one device (either the computer or the terminal) to keep the opposite device from sending data. This is desirable when the terminal needs time to "catch-up" with all the instructions given it already. On a modern CRT device, this is rare because the terminal provides an input buffer that will cover most conditions.

When these wires are not used, a different method is available, called "XON/XOFF" protocol. XON refers to the ASCII character control-Q (hexadecimal 11) and XOFF is the ASCII character control-S (hexadecimal 13). If a device is operating in XON/XOFF protocol mode, it will stop sending data whenever a XOFF is received, and start again when an XON is sent. Since the XON and XOFF characters are sent over the Send Data/Receive Data lines, no additional wires are needed to provide this type of "handshaking."

The IBM AT Compatible Console

The IBM AT console does not use RS-232 communications. Instead, the keyboard has its own special I/O ports to the CPU and the screen has its own I/O ports. In addition the RAM memory that is used to refresh the image on the CRT screen is available as directly addressable physical memory to the 80286/80386. This allows very high speed data transfer.

However, for the purposes of this chapter we can treat the IBM AT console as any other CRT terminal device. This is because when UNIX was ported to the 80286/80386 environment (and when XENIX was written), a special device handler for the console terminal was added to the kernel. This device handler emulates an RS-232 device, and also allows the user to switch between several "virtual" screens. We will study device handlers in later chapters.

The *termcap* Data Base

Given the design of CRT hardware, in order to implement "look-and-point" menus and data entry screens, we will need the following facilities:

1. A way to instruct the CRT to perform certain functions, such as "clear screen," "move cursor to x, y," among others.

2. Control over character echo, to keep the user from typing characters that might "corrupt" the display.

In the earlier chapters on shell programming, we demonstrated the use of the *tput* command to generate programs that manipulate the CRT screen independent of which terminal they were actually run on. In this chapter, we describe how this is done from the C programming perspective. First, a bit of history.

The university environment in which UNIX grew up had a plethora of different CRT terminals, all of which more or less communicated with RS-232, but each used a completely different protocol or set of "control codes," described above, to control them. This was because many project budgets, administered for different reasons, contributed to the institutional pool of hardware before UNIX even arrived on the scene. The result was that the new UNIX systems were plugged into whatever terminal devices were at hand, or purchased for a special purpose. Many terminals were printing devices, including the venerable old Teletypes Model 30 and 35, the Diablo printing terminals, and the Texas Instruments Silent 700. The early makes of CRT terminals were Hazeltine, ADM (Lear Siegler), Datapoint, and others who are now not around.

In the early days, the CRT terminals were used primarily as if they were printing terminals which did not waste paper. There was no difference in the programming or usage procedures associated with a printing device as opposed to a CRT device. Indeed, this is much the way we use terminals now; with a "cursor" that moves from left to right, and a screen which "scrolls" when the cursor is moved one line lower than the bottom.

By the way, this is the reason that some of the UNIX documentation and naming conventions refers to the terminal as a "Teletype." The device file naming convention for both SCO and Microport feature *tt* (for "teletype") as part of their names. The generic device assigned to the current process is */dev/tty*. When much of UNIX software was originally written it was better than even odds that a true Teletype was on the other end of the line. It wasn't long before the development of CRT screen oriented programs arrived, which required the use of a CRT rather than a printing device. Undisputably the most important of these was the *vi* editor, which was built as a superset of the *ex* editor.[2] The *vi* editor was popular because it facilitated the composing of programs directly on the terminal. In *vi*, as opposed to a line editor such as *ex* or *ed*, the programmer is presented with an on-screen copy (at least 24 or so lines) of what was in the file at the time. In more recent years, this feature has been called WYSIWYG (What You See Is What You Get) in word processing programs. This made the task of text editing much easier, and boosted programmer productivity.

A problem existed, however, for the development of *vi*. With all the different CRT terminals available, how do make a program that will work the same on all (or at least most) of them? Upon examination, the CRT terminals all did have a few things in common:

1. They used the ASCII code.
2. They had a fixed number of rows (usually 24) and fixed number of columns (usually 80) in which a single character could be placed.
3. They had a CTRL key, which allowed access to the non printing ASCII characters.
4. There was a set of CRT commands, such as "clear screen," and "address cursor," which, although were not implemented the same on all CRTs, did at least exist on all of them.

Most CRTs had other special features, which the manufacturers put in for reasons of their own, such as "insert character," and "bold," and other commands which are useful, but not necessarily available on all terminals. One approach to this problem is to define a "generic command" subroutine library which would provide a transparent interface to the application (*vi*). The subroutine library could be re-implemented for each terminal type, then a different version of the program could be generated simply by re-loading. This was quickly adjudged undesirable, because that would mean the UNIX installation would have to have 20 or 30 different versions of vi loaded on the system. This would be wasteful of disk space. A slight variation of this turned out to be the solution. Instead of making the subroutine library different, simply have it interpret a data base which could be edited with an ASCII editor, specially designed for this purpose. This was done, and the result can be found in the file */etc/termcap*. Another landmark contribution of UNIX to computer science was born.

---

[2] Note that the *vi* and *ex* editors are actually one and the same. The *ex* editor has a "visual mode" which is invoked automatically when the command line that called the editor starts with *vi* instead of *ex*.

The /etc/termcap file is a specially formatted file that provides one "line" for each terminal. The line identified one or more names for the terminal, then all of the escape codes that could be mapped into the "generic command set."[3]

The last step was how to tell the subroutine library which termcap entry to use. This is done by setting the shell environment variable *TERM* to a string which matched any of the names identified in the /etc/termcap file. If the name was not found, the subroutine library would abort the program with an error message. For the C shell, this can be done with:

```
setenv TERM ansi
```

or for the Bourne shell, the commands:

```
set TERM=ansi
export TERM
```

may be used. Typically, the TERM variable will be set by the .login (for C shell) or .profile (for Bourne shell) script files.

The *terminfo* Data Base

It was a logical step to make this subroutine library available to other programs as a programming tool. The termcap data base worked so well that it was not long before there were over a hundred terminals defined in the data base. The termcap file became too large to quickly scan each time a new process was started. This, and other considerations, cause the conversion of the data base to the terminfo data base, which stores each terminal information set in a separate file. The current versions of UNIX use the terminfo files, although there are remnants of the older termcap system to be found here and there in the system.

---

[3] The termcap file is described in the TERMCAP(M) article in the SCO XENIX User's Reference Manual. The Microport System V does not provide a termcap article, because the newer System V releases are leaning towards the phasing out of terminfo.

SCO XENIX supports both *terminfo* and *termcap*.⁴ The terminfo data base is a series of directories and files in the directory */usr/lib/terminfo*. The name of each terminal is the name of a file within a sub-directory that starts with the same letter. For example, a common terminal is *vt100*. The terminfo file for this type of terminal is stored in */usr/lib/terminfo/v/vt100*. Because there are potentially so many files, the "first letter" directory convention is used to keep the size of the directories manageable.

Because the *terminfo* files are stored in binary, a compiler was made to convert the file from an editable form. The compiler is named *tic*. It is unlikely that a programmer will ever need to create a new entry, because either SCO XENIX or Microport System V comes with entries for virtually every terminal imaginable.

Curses Library

The subroutine library that is used to access the terminfo data base is called *curses*. To aid in programming the C include file *curses.h* is provided, which defines the data structure used.⁵

The *curses* package provides a somewhat lengthy list of functions that a running program can use, which are listed in Appendix B. An easier way to understand *curses* is by example. We will briefly describe the theory of how *curses* works here, then provide an example program. This program, available on floppy disk in the companion disk to this book, has many elements in it which can be expanded upon to implement any data base application.

One of the most advanced features of *curses* is the ability to manipulate several "windows" on a single screen. A new window may be introduced at any time, and displayed on the screen at any position. If a previous window

---

[4] The terminfo file is described in the TERMINFO(M) and TERMINFO(F) articles in the SCO XENIX User's Reference Manual, and the TERMINFO(4) article in the Microport Software Development System Vol. II Manual.

[5] The curses package is described in the CURSES (S) article in the SCO XENIX Programmer's Reference, and the CURSES(3) article of the Microport Software Development System Vol. II Manual, with a tutorial introduction in Chapter 15 of the Software Development System Vol. I Manual.

was already there, it is over-written on the display, similar to laying down a scrap of paper on top of a cluttered desk.

The difference between the desk-top and the CRT is, that once you take away the new window, what was underneath is lost. The *curses* library is a facility that takes care of this.

The way this is done is that *curses* maintains a data structure that simulates what is actually on the CRT screen as of the actual last physical output. When a user program wants to write to the CRT, it does so through *curses* functions, but the output data bytes are not sent directly to the CRT. Instead, they are sent to a "virtual" CRT screen. The actual output occurs when a special routine called *wrefresh()* is called. This function compares what is on the virtual CRT with what is on the simulated CRT screen (which should be what is actually on the physical CRT screen), and generates the output necessary to make them the same, using the terminfo data base to generate the correct control codes. This activity is block diagrammed in Figure 19-2.

Figure 19-2

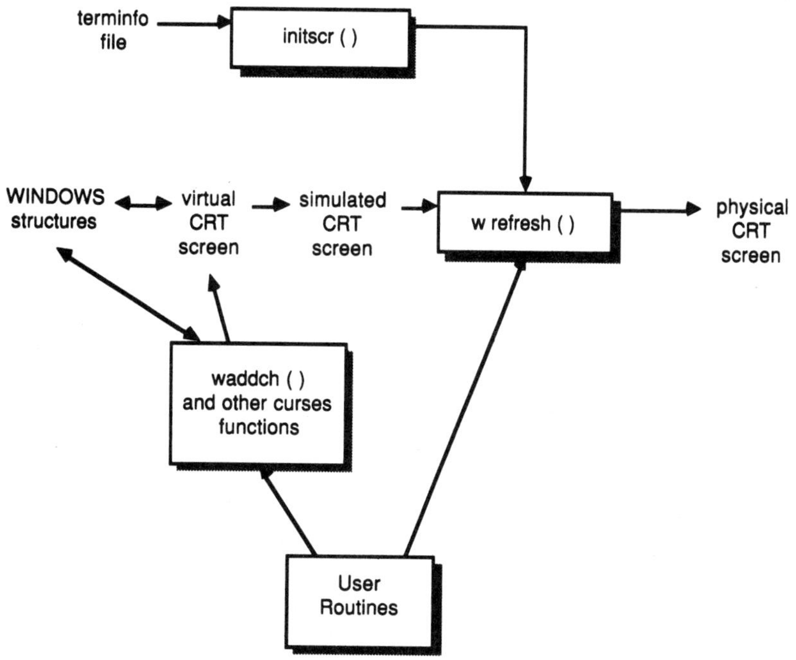

The data structure accessed by the user is typedef'ed to the keyword *WINDOW* in the file *curses.h*. All the output routines send data to a window (as well as the virtual screen). For convenience a number of macros are defined that send data to the "default" window *stdscr*, which is automatically created for us. For example,

to add a character to a window, we call the function:

```
WINDOW *win;
int chr;

waddch(win, chr);
```

If we wanted to add a character to the standard screen, we could use:

```
int chr;

addchr(chr);
```

where the function call expands to:

```
waddchr(stdscr, chr);
```

The *curses.h* file has many such variations, all described in Appendix B. Our sample program, presents the user with a menu. A menu option can be selected by pressing the up-arrow or down-arrow key until the desired option appears in reverse video, and pressing the ENTER key. Alternately a digit may be pressed. Note that no ENTER key is required with this method.

Option #1 allows the user to enter data into the record structure *rec*, which contains a number of character array fields. Options #2 and #3 allow the user to read or write this record to a data file, (named capp.dat) to make this a complete (albeit simplistic) data base application. The major functions in the sample program are briefly described as follows:

```
main()
```

> After initializing the curses library, the main program performs the major loop in the program on the *menu1()* function. After *menu1()* returns a zero (because option #0 was selected) the curses function *endwin()* is called, which resets the terminal.

Chapter 19 Programming Terminals

`menu1()`

    The main menu is displayed, then a loop is performed until the user selects an option.

`enter_rec()`

    The data base record is displayed, and the sub-function *rec_fld()* is called in a loop which terminates when the ENTER key is pressed on the last field. The loop control variable is fld, which indicates which field "number" is being processed now. The *rec_fld()* function is driven with the fld variable.

`fio()`

    Perform I/O on a single field. Note that the character echoing and backspace key are processed all within this function. There are many improvements and variations that I have left out of this sample program to keep it to a reasonable size. Some improvements that might be suggested are more advanced editing keys, "picture templates" that restrict the form of data to be input, a special version for YES/NO fields and other special types.

`read_rec()`
`write_rec()`

    These routines implement the read/write record options on the main menu. The fixed file *capp.dat* in the current directory is created if necessary.

`uhelp()`

    This routine demonstrates the creation and use of a new window through the *newwin()* function. The parameters to uhelp() indicate a file in which the help text might be found. If the file is not there, an error message results. The help message overlays the data screen underneath it. When the user acknowledges the help message, the screen is restored to its former state.

When compiling this program, the command line:

```
cc capp.c -o capp -lcurses
```

should be used. To run the program simply type the *capp* command.

The Terminal Device Handler

The curses subroutine library insulates the programmer from having to know much about how the process interacts with the terminal I/O handler. However, it is useful to know some of how to work the device driver at the lower level, should the need ever arise to program a non-CRT device through a serial port attached to the system.[6]

Normally, terminal I/O is accomplished through buffers, as show in Figure 19-3. The device handler, linked in with the UNIX or XENIX kernel, provides many services for the terminal, including echo, backspace rub-out, and special character mapping such as carriage return to newline. In addition, the characters are collected until a "line end" character is input. The entire line can then be passed to the process using a single read request. Some of the characters that have special meaning are:

Name	Default	Function
erase	#	Remove one character to left on input line
kill	@	Erase all characters on input line
intr	DEL	Send signal 15 to current process(es)

This mode is called "cooked" mode. In situations where the program is to exercise complete control over the screen, without the possibility of user interference (short of pulling the plug) these actions are undesirable. They can be disabled by turning on "raw" mode.

---

[6] The programming of the terminal device handler is described in the TERMIO(M) article in the SCO XENIX User's Reference Manual, and the TERMIO(7) article in the Microport Runtime System Manual.

Figure 19-3

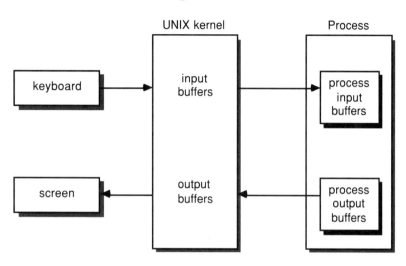

In raw mode, characters are passed from the keyboard to the process issuing the read request one-by-one as they occur. This means that the process controlling the terminal might be scheduled and entered for each and every character. (If there are more than one characters in the buffer by the time the process is scheduled, it will usually process all the characters until the input buffer is empty). To see how this action works, try the following program;

```
#include <stdio.h>

main() {
  unsigned c;

  while ((c = getchar()) != 'X')
  printf("%2.2x %3d %c\n", c, c, c);
  exit(0); }
```

When this program is run with the terminal port set to cooked mode, an entire line can be typed in, with corrections, and the corrected line is typed out again, one character per line. The program does not respond until a newline, formfeed, or a return is entered. Now run the program again after the command:

```
stty raw
```

which turns off cooked mode. The program will respond each time a single character is pressed.[7] Note that you cannot even interrupt the program with the DEL key, because it is interpreted as a character like any other. A incorrectly working program can lock up a terminal this way, with the only recourse being to issue a *kill* command from another terminal, or forcing a logout with a line disconnect. In following chapters we will outline the writing of a device driver for terminal devices. By doing so, we can examine the functions that can be performed by the terminal device handler.

Listing

```
1  0: /*title capp.c - Curses application example
2  0*
3  0*    Alan Deikman 1/88
4  0*
5  0*    This program provides an example of using the curses package
6  0*    in a simple menu/data entry application.  Two techniques
7  0*    of data entry are demonstrated:
8  0*
9  0*         1.  Menu with "highlight" or number selection
10 0*         2.  A protected field data entry form
11 0*         3.  A help key
12 0*
13 0*    To make this program small enough to use as an example, we
14 0*    will leave a number of the menu options not implemented.
15 0*
16 0*    */
17 0:
18 0: #include <curses.h>
19 0: #include <ctype.h>
20 0:
21 0: /* data record */
22 0:
23 0: struct datarec {
24 1:    char   last[25];           /* Last name of client */
25 1:    char   first[20];          /* First name of client */
26 1:    char   middle[20];         /* Middle name */
27 1:    char   address[30];        /* Street Address */
28 1:    char   city[25];           /* City name */
29 1:    char   state[2];           /* State abbreviation */
30 1:    char   zip[10];            /* Zip code */
```

---

[7] Our sample program quits when a capital *X* is pressed. To turn off raw mode, enter the command:

    stty cooked

Chapter 19 Programming Terminals

```
31 1:    char  phone[14];           /* Phone Number */
32 1:    } rec;
33 0: int recn;                     /* current record number */
34 0:
35 0: #define ENTER '\n'            /* our own input terminator */
36 0: #define HELP  1               /* define help key as CTRL-A */
37 0:
38 0: /*subtitle main program
39 0*
40 0*    The main program shows how to initialize and de-initialize the
41 0*    curses package.  In this example, we will have to perform
42 0*    echoing ourselves, so that we can implement DOWN ARROW and
43 0*    UP ARROW functions.  We will also have to provide character
44 0*    editing (erase & kill).
45 0*
46 0*    */
47 0:
48 0: main () {
49 1:
50 1:    int opt, menu1();
51 1:
52 1:    initscr();                 /* tell curses we are here */
53 1:    keypad(stdscr, TRUE);      /* we will use the keypad */
54 1:    scrollok(stdscr, TRUE);    /* OK to scroll on main screen */
55 1:    noecho();                  /* we will handle echoing */
56 1:    raw();                     /* we will process all charcters */
57 1:
58 1:    /* loop on the main menu function, which will return an integer
59 1*       telling us which option was selected */
60 1:
61 1:    while (opt = menu1()) switch(opt) {
62 2:       case 1: enter_rec();       break;
63 2:       case 2: read_rec();        break;
64 2:       case 3: write_rec();       break;
65 2:       case 4: no_opt("Four");    break; }
66 1:
67 1:    /* return terminal to prior state */
68 1:
69 1:    endwin(); }
70 0:
71 0: /*subtitle menu1 - Main menu
72 0*
73 0*    These routines display the main menu, then lets the user
74 0*    select an option by either using the arrow keys, or by
75 0*    pressing a digit to select a number which corresponds to
76 0*    the option desired.
77 0*
78 0*    */
79 0:
80 0: int menu1() {
81 1:
```

```
 82 1:    int opt;                /* current option */
 83 1:    int key;                /* current key input */
 84 1:
 85 1:    /* output basic screen */
 86 1:
 87 1:    clear();
 88 1:    mvaddstr(0, 0, "Main Menu for sample program");
 89 1:    mvaddstr(3, 5, "Select One of the options below");
 90 1:    for (opt = 0; opt < 5; opt++) menu1_opt(opt, A_NORMAL);
 91 1:    move(18, 0);
 92 1:    addstr("You may select your option by pressing UP ARROW");
 93 1:    addstr(" or DOWN ARROW\n");
 94 1:    addstr("and pressing ENTER, or press the number");
 95 1:    addstr(" corresponding to your\n");
 96 1:    addstr("choice.  Press the CTRL-A key for help");
 97 1:
 98 1:    /* now loop until a choice is made */
 99 1:
100 1:    opt = 0;
101 1:    do {
102 2:      menu1_opt(opt, A_STANDOUT);
103 2:      key = getch();
104 2:      menu1_opt(opt, A_NORMAL);
105 2:
106 2:      /* user pressed an option number */
107 2:
108 2:      if (key >= '0' && key <= '4') {
109 3:        opt = key - '0';
110 3:        key = ENTER; }
111 2:
112 2:      /* user pressed help key */
113 2:
114 2:      else if (key == HELP) uhelp("cappmain", opt);
115 2:
116 2:      /* user pressed an arrow */
117 2:
118 2:      else if (key == KEY_UP)   opt = opt > 0 ? --opt : 4;
119 2:      else if (key == KEY_DOWN) opt = ++opt % 5;
120 2:
121 2:      /* error */
122 2:
123 2:      else if (key != ENTER) uerror("That key is not defined");
124 2:
125 2:    /* loop until the ENTER key is pressed (or simulated) */
126 2:
127 2:    } while (key != ENTER);
128 1:
129 1:    /*  return the option value */
130 1:
131 1:    menu1_opt(opt, A_BLINK | A_BOLD);
132 1:    attrset(A_NORMAL);
```

```
133 1:    sleep(2);
134 1:    return opt; }
135 0:
136 0: /* output an option on the main menu */
137 0:
138 0: menu1_opt(opt, att)
139 0: int    opt;            /* option number to display */
140 0: int    att;            /* attribute to display option */
141 0: {
142 1:    attrset(att);
143 1:    move(5 + opt, 5);
144 1:    switch (opt) {
145 2:       case 0:  addstr("0.  Quit Program");                    break;
146 2:       case 1:  addstr("1.  Edit Data Record");                break;
147 2:       case 2:  addstr("2.  Read Data Record");                break;
148 2:       case 3:  addstr("3.  Write Data Record");               break;
149 2:       case 4:  addstr("4.  (Function Not Implemented)");      break; }
150 1:    refresh();
151 1:    return; }
152 0:
153 0: /*subtitle edit record routine
154 0*
155 0*     This routine demonstrates one technique for displaying and
156 0*     allowing input on a data entry form.  The first step is to
157 0*     display the form with the current data in the data record.
158 0*     Then, a loop is entered which makes successive calls to
159 0*     rec_fld(), which edits a single field and returns the code
160 0*     of the key the user pressed to terminate editing of the
161 0*     field.  Based on that return value, one of several actions
162 0*     are taken:
163 0*
164 0*          KEY_UP:       Go to previous field (roll to last)
165 0*          KEY_DOWN:     Go to next field (roll to first)
166 0*          ENTER:        Go to next field, terminate if on
167 0*                        last field
168 0*          HELP:         Invoke uhelp()
169 0*
170 0*  */
171 0:
172 0: #define NUMFLD 8        /* number of fields on this screen */
173 0:
174 0: enter_rec() {
175 1:    int    fld;            /* current field number */
176 1:    int    key;            /* last key pressed */
177 1:    int    rec_fld();      /* field subroutine */
178 1:
179 1:    /* output screen with current data */
180 1:
181 1:    clear();
182 1:    mvaddstr(0, 0, "Data entry form for curses sample program");
183 1:    mvaddstr(21,50, "Enter CTRL-A for help");
```

```
184 1:      for (fld = 0; fld < NUMFLD; fld++) key = rec_fld(fld, A_NORMAL);
185 1:
186 1:      /* now start at the first field, and loop until the user presses
187 1*         the ENTER key at the last field */
188 1:             .
189 1:      fld = 0;
190 1:      do {
191 2:         key = rec_fld(fld, A_REVERSE);
192 2:
193 2:         /* now interpret the key used to escape the field */
194 2:
195 2:         switch (key) {
196 3:
197 3:           case ENTER:    fld++;                                      break;
198 3:           case KEY_UP:   fld = fld > 0 ? fld - 1 : NUMFLD - 1;       break;
199 3:           case KEY_DOWN: fld = ++fld % NUMFLD;                       break;
200 3:           case HELP:     uhelp("capprec", fld);                      break;
201 3:         }
202 2:
203 2:      } while (fld < NUMFLD);
204 1:
205 1:      /* done with input, return to main menu */
206 1:
207 1:      return; }
208 0:
209 0: /* the function of the rec_fld() routine is to call the fio()
210 0*     subroutine for a selected field in the data entry screen.
211 0*     We use the macro FIO() to help get all the parameters to
212 0*     fio() on a single line on each field, which makes it easier
213 0*     to compose and edit the program.
214 0*
215 0*  */
216 0:
217 0: #define FIO(row, col, label, icol, str) \
218 0:         return fio(row, col, label, icol, str, sizeof(str), att);
219 0:
220 0: int rec_fld(fld, att)
221 0: int     fld;             /* Field Number */
222 0: int     att;             /* curses screen attributes to display
223 0*                             field with.  If att != A_NORMAL, a
224 0*                             user edit is performed */
225 0: {
226 1: switch (fld) {
227 2:
228 2: case 0: FIO( 5, 5, "  Last Name: ", 30, rec.last);
229 2: case 1: FIO( 7, 5, " First Name: ", 30, rec.first);
230 2: case 2: FIO( 9, 5, "Middle Name: ", 30, rec.middle);
231 2: case 3: FIO(11, 5, "    Address: ", 30, rec.address);
232 2: case 4: FIO(13, 5, "       City: ", 30, rec.city);
233 2: case 5: FIO(15, 5, "      State: ", 30, rec.state);
234 2: case 6: FIO(17, 5, "        Zip: ", 30, rec.zip);
```

```
235 2:     case 7: FIO(19, 5, "     Phone: ", 30, rec.phone);
236 2: }}
237 0:
238 0: /*subtitle fio() - Field I/O routine
239 0*
240 0*    This routine performs all the field I/O for each field.  It
241 0*    operates in two modes:  output only (where att == A_NORMAL),
242 0*    and output/input/output (where att != A_NORMAL).  The user
243 0*    sees the field that is to be edited as attribute att (which
244 0*    can be anything but A_NORMAL).  When input is done, (signaled
245 0*    by the user pressing a recognized field termination key), the
246 0*    field data is output again in format A_NORMAL.
247 0*
248 0*    The data is stored in parameter dat, which is treated as a
249 0*    character array of length len.  Note that a null in this
250 0*    array is assumed to terminate the data in the field (only
251 0*    printable characters are allowed), but the output may not
252 0*    be null terminated.  This is the usual way records with
253 0*    fixed sized fields are stored.
254 0*
255 0*    */
256 0:
257 0: int fio(row, col, lab, icl, dat, len, att)
258 0: int     row;            /* row of input */
259 0: int     col;            /* column of field */
260 0: char    *lab;           /* label of field */
261 0: int     icl;            /* column of input */
262 0: char    *dat;           /* data field */
263 0: int     len;            /* length of field */
264 0: int     att;            /* attributes of field */
265 0: {
266 1:    int i;       /* index into current field (subscript to dat) */
267 1:    int c;       /* current character received */
268 1:
269 1:    /* if we are in an output phase, simply output the field,
270 1*       the data, and return the ENTER value. */
271 1:
272 1:    attrset(att);
273 1:    if (att == A_NORMAL) mvaddstr(row, col, lab);
274 1:    move(row, icl);
275 1:    for (i = 0; i < len && dat[i]; i++) addch(dat[i]);
276 1:    while (i++ < len) addch(' ');
277 1:    refresh();
278 1:    if (att == A_NORMAL) return ENTER;
279 1:
280 1:    /* if we are in an input phase, move the cursor to the first
281 1*       position of the input field.  For each character typed,
282 1*       place the character in the output field and move to the
283 1*       next, unless we are at the end of the field.  If a
284 1*       recognized field terminator character is received, finish
285 1*       the input */
```

```
286 1:
287 1:    move(row, icl);
288 1:    i = 0;
289 1:    do {
290 2:       c = getch();
291 2:
292 2:       /* if the character is printable, enter the data into
293 2*          the record, taking care not to overflow the field. */
294 2:
295 2:       if (isprint(c)) {
296 3:          dat[i] = c;
297 3:          addch(c);
298 3:          refresh();
299 3:          if (++i >= len) {
300 4:             i = len - 1;
301 4:             move(row, icl + i); } }
302 2:
303 2:       /* process a backspace key by blanking the current
304 2*          character and the previous character (if any) and
305 2*          blanking both on the screen. */
306 2:
307 2:       else if (c == KEY_BACKSPACE || c == 8) {
308 3:          dat[i] = ' ';
309 3:          if (i > 0) dat[--i] = ' ';
310 3:          mvaddch(row, icl + i, ' ');
311 3:          addch(' ');
312 3:          move(row, icl + i);
313 3:          refresh(); }
314 2:
315 2:       /* loop unless we are finished with this field */
316 2:
317 2:    } while (c != ENTER && c != KEY_UP && c != KEY_DOWN &&
318 1:             c != HELP);
319 1:
320 1:    /* output field with normal attributes, and return the key
321 1*       that caused the termination of the above loop */
322 1:
323 1:    fio(row, col, lab, icl, dat, len, A_NORMAL);
324 1:    return c; }
325 0:
326 0: /*subtitle read_rec(), write_rec() - Data base I/O
327 0*
328 0*    These routines provide access to a simple data base in
329 0*    the current directory in a file called capp.dat
330 0*
331 0*    */
332 0:
333 0: read_rec() {
334 1:    int c;
335 1:    long pos;                    /* lseek position */
336 1:    int dfile, disp_recs();      /* data file descriptor */
```

```
337 1:
338 1:    /* display current data base */
339 1:
340 1:    clear();
341 1:    mvaddstr(0, 0, "READ RECORD:  Current data base entries");
342 1:    dfile = disp_recs();
343 1:
344 1:    /* ask user which record is to be read */
345 1:
346 1:    mvaddstr(15, 0,
347 1:          "Press a key, 0 through 9, to read the corresponding\n");
348 1:    addstr("record.  Press any other key to abort ");
349 1:    refresh();
350 1:    c = getch();
351 1:
352 1:    /* read the selected record, if any.  If the record does not
353 1*       exist, create a blank record */
354 1:
355 1:    if (c >= '0' && c <= '9') {
356 2:      pos = (long) (recn = (c - '0')) * (long) sizeof(rec);
357 2:      if (lseek(dfile, pos, 0) != pos ||
358 2:          read(dfile, &rec, sizeof(rec)) != sizeof(rec))
359 2:              strncpy(rec, " ", sizeof(rec)); }
360 1:
361 1:    /* close file and return */
362 1:
363 1:    close(dfile);
364 1:    return; }
365 0:
366 0: /*  the write_rec() routine displays the current data base, then
367 0*      asks for which record to over-write */
368 0:
369 0: write_rec() {
370 1:    int c;
371 1:    long pos;                      /* lseek position */
372 1:    int dfile, disp_recs();        /* data file descriptor */
373 1:
374 1:    /* display current data base */
375 1:
376 1:    clear();
377 1:    mvaddstr(0, 0, "WRITE RECORD:  Current data base entries");
378 1:    dfile = disp_recs();
379 1:
380 1:    /* ask user which record is to be read */
381 1:
382 1:    mvaddstr(15, 0,
383 1:          "Press a key, 0 through 9, to write the corresponding\n");
384 1:    addstr("record.  Press any other key to abort " );
385 1:    refresh();
386 1:    c = getch();
387 1:
```

```
388 1:    /* write the selected record, if any. */
389 1:
390 1:    if (c >= '0' && c <= '9') {
391 2:      pos = (long) (recn = (c - '0')) * (long) sizeof(rec);
392 2:      if (lseek(dfile, pos, 0) != pos)
393 2:        uerror("Cannot write that record");
394 2:      else write(dfile, &rec, sizeof(rec)); }
395 1:
396 1:    /* close file and return */
397 1:
398 1:    close(dfile);
399 1:    return; }
400 0:
401 0: /* display the current data base.  We are assuming, for this
402 0*    sample program, that the data base is no more than 10
403 0*    records */
404 0:
405 0: #include <fcntl.h>
406 0:
407 0: int disp_recs() {
408 1:    struct datarec rec;
409 1:    int i;                 /* current record */
410 1:    int dfile;             /* file descriptor */
411 1:
412 1:    /* open file, creating it if necessary */
413 1:
414 1:    if ((dfile = open("capp.dat", O_CREAT | O_RDWR, 0666)) < 1) {
415 2:      uerror("Cannot open file.  ABORTING PROGRAM");
416 2:      endwin();
417 2:      exit(2); }
418 1:
419 1:    /* loop through all records in data base, and output last
420 1*       name, first name, and phone number to allow the user to
421 1*       make a choice */
422 1:
423 1:    for (i = 0; i < 10 &&
424 1:               read(dfile, &rec, sizeof(rec)) == sizeof(rec);
425 1:               i++) {
426 2:      if (recn == i) attrset(A_BOLD);
427 2:      mvprintw(3 + i, 0, "%2d: %-20.20s %-20.20s %-14.14s", i,
428 2:                          rec.last, rec.first, rec.phone);
429 2:      if (recn == i) attrset(A_NORMAL); }
430 1:    while (i < 10) mvprintw(3 + i, 0, "%2d:", i++);
431 1:    refresh();
432 1:
433 1:    /* return file descriptor */
434 1:
435 1:    return dfile; }
436 0:
437 0:
438 0: /*subtitle uerror() - Announce user error
```

Chapter 19 Programming Terminals

```
439 0*
440 0*    This routine sends the error message to the last two lines
441 0*    of the screen and rings the bell.
442 0*    */
443 0:        .
444 0: uerror(msg)
445 0: char    *msg;
446 0: {
447 1:    /* send out message */
448 1:
449 1:    beep();
450 1:    attrset(A_BOLD | A_BLINK);
451 1:    mvaddstr(23, 0, msg);
452 1:    attrset(A_NORMAL);
453 1:    mvaddstr(24, 0, "Press any key to continue");
454 1:    refresh();
455 1:
456 1:    /* wait for user to acknowledge, then clear the screen */
457 1:
458 1:    getch();
459 1:    move(23, 0);
460 1:    clrtobot();
461 1:    return; }
462 0:
463 0: /* fake option */
464 0:
465 0: no_opt(opt)
466 0: char    *opt;           /* name of option deployed */
467 0: {
468 1:    char bufr[80];
469 1:    sprintf(bufr, "Option %s is not yet implemented", opt);
470 1:    uerror(bufr);
471 1:    return; }
472 0:
473 0: /*subtitle uhelp() - Generate help sub-window
474 0*
475 0*    This routine opens a new window and scrolls a help message
476 0*    through it.  The help message is taken from a file.  This
477 0*    is done for two reasons:
478 0*
479 0*        1.  It makes it easier to modify help messages
480 0*        2.  The text of all the help windows (which may be
481 0*            extensive) are not carried around in the RAM image
482 0*            of the program, making the program smaller and
483 0*            reducing system swap overhead.
484 0*
485 0*    The first line of the help file is taken to be four integers
486 0*    which define the size of the window to be displayed.
487 0*    (parameters to newwin())
488 0*
489 0*    */
```

339

```
490 0:
491 0: uhelp(bas, num)
492 0: char    *bas;   /* base file name */
493 0: int      num;   /* file name extension */
494 0: {
495 1:     WINDOW *win;
496 1:     FILE *hfile;
497 1:     char  fnam[16];
498 1:     int lines, cols, row, col, c;
499 1:
500 1:     /* if file is not available, give error message */
501 1:
502 1:     sprintf(fnam, "%s.%d", bas, num);
503 1:     if ((hfile = fopen(fnam, "r")) == NULL) {
504 2:         uerror("Help not available at this point");
505 2:         return; }
506 1:
507 1:     /* create a new window */
508 1:
509 1:     fscanf(hfile, "%d %d %d %d", &lines, &cols, &row, &col);
510 1:     win = newwin(lines, cols, row, col);
511 1:     scrollok(win, TRUE);
512 1:
513 1:     /* output the data in the file */
514 1:
515 1:     wmove(win, 0, 0);
516 1:     while ((c = getc(hfile)) != EOF) waddch(win, c);
517 1:     fclose(hfile);
518 1:
519 1:     /* wait for the user to press a key */
520 1:
521 1:     waddstr(win, "\n Press any key to continue ");
522 1:     wrefresh(win);
523 1:     wgetch(win);
524 1:
525 1:     /* kill the window, and cause the main screen to be re-output */
526 1:
527 1:     delwin(win);
528 1:     touchwin(stdscr);
529 1:     refresh();
530 1:
531 1:     return; }
```

20
UNIX System Administration

System administration has been a sore spot with UNIX from the point of view of the DP manager. UNIX does provide a fair number of tools for the system manager to use, but it requires specific knowledge of them, and methodologies are not always clear.

A case in point is the */etc/passwd* file. This file is used by the *getty* program (the one that performs logins for the users) and others to identify which users are known to the system. It is a file of a specific format that may be read by any process in the system (we describe this file later in this Chapter). In the original UNIX systems, the system administrator had to know the format of the file, and how to use the editor (*ed*, *ex*, or *vi*) in order to maintain it. At the time when UNIX was young the chances were that the systems administrator was also a systems programmer, making this not much of a problem. On the other hand, when you are delivering a turnkey applications system which must be maintained by a non-programming group of users, this becomes another matter.

To make things easier, both Interactive Systems SCO and Microport have added programs to the standard set of UNIX programs that perform these low level functions with either high level commands, such as *mkuser* (XENIX), or a system of menus, such as *sysviz* (Microport).

For a single (or few) user UNIX system, which is likely with UNIX on the 286/386, the problem is much easier. Overall, the task of the system administrator is to maximize usage of the system while keeping all the various users out of each other's hair. If there is only one user, this just means getting and keeping the system up and running.

For our purposes, we can define the job description of the system administrator to have the following responsibilities:

1. Installing the system, including:
    the basic system
    optional software packages
    additional disk devices
    additional tape devices
    additional terminal devices

2. Controlling access to the system, including:
    user names
    group names
    access to specific devices
    printer spoolers

3. Controlling access to particular programs, such as:
    the *cron* facility
    the *uucp* facility

4. Allocating disk space.

5. Making backup tapes (disks).

6. Diagnosing system problems and taking appropriate action.

SCO XENIX and UNIX, although they are very similar at the low level, provide different high level mechanisms to perform these functions. We will examine each of these functions of the system manager and see how they are accomplished.

Installing the Initial System

Most of these procedures are so specific to Interactive Systems UNIX, Microport UNIX, and SCO XENIX, that the actual procedure is best left up to the manuals and release notes that come with the system. The vendors have done their best to make the installation as easy as possible, even to the extent of sacrificing flexibility. The problem is that there are quite a few things going on during the installation process, and the installing shell script, while convenient, keeps the knowledgeable operator from knowing things that he should know.

The basic method of how the systems are installed is that the user is provided with a "boot disk," off of which a special version of the UNIX (or XENIX)

Chapter 20 UNIX System Administration

kernel can be loaded. This boot disk has a very abridged version of the overall operating system, with just a special shell script and the bare minimum of utilities necessary to allow it to run.

Once the boot floppy is started the initial shell script takes over and prompts the operator for what it needs to know. The procedures from there on are different between SCO and UNIX, although what happens is basically the same. The steps are:

1. Partition the hard disk drive, and install a boot block program on the drive.

2. Do a bad-track surface scan on the partition set aside for UNIX (XENIX).

3. Perform the divvy operation, dividing up the UNIX/XENIX partition into a root file system, a swap device, and an optionally separate user file system. The user has to make some decision on the size of these disk areas.

4. Perform a *mkfs* command on each mountable hard disk file system, which creates the super-block, i-node table, and free list.

5. Mount the root file system and copy the basic system kernel, a few utilities, and a "stage-two" installation shell script onto it.

6. Have the user reboot the system, this time from the hard disk. At this time the "stage-two" shell script takes over.

7. Copy the rest of the UNIX base utilities from the floppy disk to the hard disk.

8. Perform the optional program loading procedures, loading the software development system, the text development system, or other software packages. After these steps are done, the system is ready for the super-user to start it up and set up the user logins. The system will then be ready for use.

That's actually all there is to it. The reason that I took the time to note these steps is because the installation procedures seem very mysterious and complex until you get used to them. If you are ever going to install more than one system, it is a good idea to know what is going on. If something goes wrong during the process and you have to start over, you can waste a lot of time performing steps that do not need to be redone.

For example, if you found out too late that you made a bad choice in the size of either the swap area or the root file system, it is likely that the only way you can recover is to start the whole installation over again. However, there is no need to repeat the bad track scan if this happens. New users are strongly advised to do things the "standard way," i.e., take the defaults on most questions, until they gain some experience.

Installing Optional Software Packages

Optional software packages fall roughly into two categories:

1. Those delivered by the original software manufacturer. (SCO for XENIX and Microport for UNIX.)

2. Those provided by a third party developer.

The distribution software that is delivered by the original vendors follow the standard software installation procedures for that system. Third party software might or might not use the standard procedures, so you will have to check the documentation that comes with it.

The standard procedure for software installation is different between Microport and SCO. Microport supports a simple shell script installer called *installit*, and SCO has the more elaborate custom program.

The custom program in XENIX works by maintaining a data base file of all the files in a particular package. The three packages in the data base from the start are:

1. Operating System
2. Development System
3. Text Processing System

The data base for these three sets are found in */etc/base.perms*, */etc/soft.perms*, and */etc/text.perms*. For other packages, custom expects to read a data base in from the first diskette of the distribution software to a file in the directory */etc/perms*. The custom program is a very powerful system administrative tool, because it lets the user "de-install" packages if necessary, and to quickly take an inventory of which package components are installed.

The *installit* program in Microport is simpler, although completely automatic installation procedures are possible. When the user enters the command *installit*, he is prompted for the first diskette of the distribution media. The *installit* script then reads, in cpio format, the first set of files which, if they are named right, are treated as script files to be executed. When the script files execute, they perform any tasks necessary to the installation of the software that needs to be done other than the actual copying of the files.

Adding Hard Disk Drives

The original installation will perform the necessary installation of the second hard disk drive if it was available at that time. For a adding a hard disk after the rest of the system has been up and running, the following needs to be done:

1. Low-level format the drive.
2. Partition the drive.
3. Divide up the partition given to UNIX with the divvy program (usually with the secondary disk drives the entire drive is used for a single file system).
4. Perform a *mkfs* on each file system.
5. Add the file systems to the mount table and add the commands to the */etc/rc* file so that the file systems will be mounted automatically when the system is booted.

The nodes in the */dev* directory will have already been created in the original system installation.

All of the above functions are performed automatically by the *mkdev* command in XENIX. For Microport, the Installation instructions have a procedure for adding the second hard disk.

Adding Tape Devices

Tape drives, by necessity, are supported by the manufacturers of the tape drive hardware. Each manufacturer has its own installation procedure, some of which are carried out automatically, others require the user to type all the commands.

To install a tape drive device handler on Microport, you will need the "Link Kit," which is installed separately from the basic operating system. In following chapters, we will describe the link kit and how it works.

Controlling Users and Groups

The UNIX kernel recognizes and enforces two levels of system security: The super-user, and all other users which we call "regular users." A super-user process can perform any action without regard to security checks, which is necessary to performing many system administrative tasks. A regular user process may only execute those functions allowed to "non-privileged" processes and access files for which security access is granted.

Recall that each process has a real User ID (UID) and Group ID (GID), plus an effective User ID and Group ID associated with it. Each ID is a number which is defined and identified by the *letc/passwd* and *letc/groups* file, respectively. The super-user UID is always zero, which is a constant within the kernel.

The effective UID of a process is consulted whenever a "super-user-only" operation is attempted. A small number of the system calls are of this type, and are noted in the documentation whenever this is the case. Both the effective UID and GID of a process are examined for many of the file-system operations, such as *open()*, *exec()*, *link()*, and others to see if the process has the permission to perform the requested access. We will discuss these permission bits later, but first let's see how the UID and GID are defined.

The *letc/passwd* and *letc/group* files are text files. All fields may be edited using a text editor, except for the password field. This field is usually changed with the *passwd* command, which brings up an interesting subject.

Access to UNIX is controlled by passwords. That means that somewhere in the system, the passwords that users type in must be stored. In order for this to be effective, the passwords must be kept secret, so where do we store the password where gremlins cannot find it?

One possible solution is to store them in a file with no read permission (see below) to any user except the super-user. The problem with this is that a

Chapter 20 UNIX System Administration

hacker could easily purloin and copy a backup tape, then extract a list of passwords quite easily. It would also be possible to get at the password file through the special device file assigned to the disk drive, by scanning the entire disk. If that were locked off from user access, there are other methods. The point is, no matter how well protected the password program might be, once it is compromised, everything is compromised.

The solution in UNIX is to store the passwords in "encrypted" form, right in the /etc/passwd file which every process has read access to. The encryption algorithm inputs a string (the user's password) and outputs a seemingly unrelated complex string. The trick is that the algorithm cannot be inverted, at least not easily. Even one bit of change in the input usually results in a wildly different output. The *passwd* program and the program that performs logins and getty have the same subroutine linked into them. These programs, while they cannot yield what the passwords are, can nonetheless tell whether a given password is correct.

The /etc/passwd and /etc/group assign names to each defined UID and GID, and are used by many programs, (*ls*, for instance) to translate these numbers into names. This means that if a UID or GID is reassigned to another user, any files in the system with those numbers will be immediately inherited.

The control of access to files is accomplished with the chmod command (or the *chmod()* system call within a program).[1] Recall from Chapter 3 (Figure 3-3) that each file has associated with it an array of bits which identify which types of access by various users are allowed. There are three types of access, and three types of users. The type of users are:

Type	chmod symbol	Description
User	u	Any process with the effective UID the same as the owner of the file.
Group	g	Any process with the effective GID the same as the GID that is in the i-node for this file.
Other	o	Any process.

There are three types of access that may be allowed or masked out for each type of user. These are:

---

[1] See also CHMOD(1) (Microport RSM), CHMOD (C) (XENIX VRM), CHMOD(1) (AT&T VRM).

347

chmod/ls symbol	Description
r	Read access.
w	Write access. This also allows the deletion of any data in the file.
x	Execute access. For files in text format, an exec() call may be executed with this file as the object. This flag is also used by the shell to identify a script program from other text files. If the file is a directory, this flag is used to allow a process to scan the directory.

Only the owner or the super-user can change the mode bits associated with a file. This is true even if the file is in another user's directory, so it's possible that a user can have files in his own directory that he cannot change. This feature allows the super-user to set up special *.login* and *.profile* files for the shells to execute when the user logs on, but cannot change. However, if the user has write access to the file, he can delete it, then recreate it under his own name.

User Access to Privileged Programs

The *chmod* program allows access to a number of bits in the i-node not mentioned above. These are "set UID on execution" and "set GID on execution." If an executable file (not a shell script) has these bits set, the process that performs an *exec()* call with the file as an object has it's effective UID and GID changed (respectively) to match those of the owner of the file. Most often, this is done to allow the user to perform specific functions that only a super-user can do without giving the user super-user access. For example, the *passwd* command, which is reasonable for a user to access, must operate in privileged mode in order to successfully change the */etc/passwd* file. With the "set UID" bit set on the */bin/passwd* file, and if the */bin/passwd* file is owned by the super-user (UID zero), it can do this and terminate. Once it terminates the user has no more privileged access.

Obviously, only well-behaved programs with strictly defined functions defined with the system security in mind should be used like this. But this facility provides the needed loophole in the system security that allows limited access to the user of privileged operations.

Chapter 20 UNIX System Administration

Access to Specific Devices

Because devices appear to be files in UNIX, and have an i-node assigned to them, the security controls that apply to files also be used for devices. Generally, these devices will be of the following types:

System hard disk There is rarely any need for a user to read this device, and read permission should not be allowed if there are files in the system to which should not be read. This is because any knowledgeable user can easily write a program to read a file outside the system checks. If write access is allowed, the user may even write a program to change files to give himself super-user access.

User hard disk The same applies to this disk.

Swap Disk Usually, read access to this disk is allowed because the *ps* program uses it.

System memory The *ps* program also reads this file.

DOS partition Generally, this file, if there is a DOS partition on the hard disk, should be open to any user.

Floppy disk drives These devices are often used as if they were tape drives on small systems, but may also have file systems on them that can be mounted with the mount command. Also, DOS floppies might be mounted.

Tape drives Each installation will have its own requirements on the access to this type device. Usually, however, this is only used for system backup, which is done by the super-user anyway.

If you are managing a system with many users on it, particularly in an "educational" environment, you should be aware of the security holes these files represent. For most business installations without dial-in modems, these issues should not cause great concern, although the system manager should know about them, just in case.

UNIX Programming on the 80286/80386, Second Edition

Allocating Disk Space

The UNIX system does not provide any real-time check on the usage of hard disk space. When a user is logged on, he can create and expand files on any file system he has write access to, until the file system has no space left in it.

Obtaining larger and larger disk drives are no solution, because of the natural law that the demand for disk space will always grow to fill the space available (like gas in a vacuum). Since a UNIX system has no facility for controlling disk space usage among users, the task falls to the system administrator.

This is not an oversight on the part of the UNIX system designers. A decision was made at an early point in time that attempting to check each and every disk allocation request for overflow against a limit would introduce prohibitive overhead. Every block allocation would also have to be tallied to some user. To add to that, many programs (including compilers, editors, and the sort routine, among others) rely on scratch files which might grow to be quite large during execution, but are deleted as soon as the program terminates. It would be unbelievably frustrating to have the system utilities abort each time the disk limit was temporarily over-reached.

What the system manager can do is monitor the disk space usage on a timely basis, (every night, for example) and advise each user of their actual verses authorized usage. This can be automated to a certain extent. One method is to have a file in /etc called *disk.auth*, which contains a list of all the directories in /usr and their disk block limits. For example:

```
/usr/alan    300
/usr/connie  600
/usr/ellen   800
```

We will make the assumption that this file is sorted. Now we can run the following shell script via *cron* every night at 1:00 AM (or some other time):

```
du -s /usr/* | awk ' { print $2, $1 } ' | join - /etc/disk.auth | \
awk'{ if ($2 > $3) printf "%s exceeds by %d\n", $1, $2 - $3 }' - | \
mail root
```

which will run the actual disk usage, compare it to the authorizations in the *disk.auth* file, and send a message to the root regarding any directories whose actual disk usage exceeds their authorizations. When the root user next comes into the office and logs in, he or she can take action as is appropriate. It is easy to see how this program could be expanded to cover other file systems, and automatically send mail to users regarding their usage.

There are certain directories and that bear watching even though there are no users directly responsible for them. Certain system programs automatically append data to these files. These are:

/tmp	Junk left over from aborted user programs. Most programs that come with UNIX that use the /tmp directory are good about cleaning up after themselves.
/usr/tmp	Junk left over from aborted user programs. See comment above.
/etc/wtmp	Login/logoff information.
/usr/adm/pacct	Per-process accounting records.
/usr/lib/cron/log	Status log of commands executed by *cron*.
/usr/adm/errfil	Hardware error logging information.
/usr/adm/ctlog	A history log of who has used the *ct* command.
/usr/adm/sulog	A history of who has executed the *su* command.
/usr/adm/Spacct	Files left over from a failed accounting run.
/usr/spool	This directory contains all the data that is spooled to the line printer, through the *uucp* system, or via user mail. Sometimes mail is sent automatically to the *user adm* and root (as in the example above) which should be checked and purged occasionally.

If any of these directories seem to be overlarge, or they have increased in size, you should examine them and purge files that are no longer being used, or are overflowing.

UNIX Programming on the 80286/80386, Second Edition

Making Backup Tapes (Disks)

The method used for making backups of the system depends on what hardware is available and the preference of the operator who has to make the backups. In Chapter 13 we looked at some of the programs that can be used for backup tapes.

Sometimes it is a requirement in an installation that the person who performs the backup is not a privileged user. All the "backup" operator needs to be able to do is start the process, and load and unload the removable media as requested. If this is the case, one method for providing this type of access is to provide a login that automatically executes a specific shell script or program that performs the backup.

Diagnosing System Problems

The most difficult task required of the system operator is handling the condition where system problems come up. The two types of problems that might occur are either hardware or software, and it can often be difficult to tell which is which. I am happy to say that there are amazingly few software problems within SCO XENIX or Microport UNIX, particularly after a system has been completely installed. Most of the "bugs" are known and documented, and are not of the sort that make the system unusable. In the several hundred hours I have spent writing C programs on both systems, I have yet to experience a system crash caused by a system bug.

As for hardware, fortunately most subsystems are designed to be able to detect problems within itself, and report them to the operating system. The most typical failure that must be contended with is the occurrence of new bad blocks on the hard disk drive, although no device is immune. If the device is a peripheral, such as a keyboard, monitor, or floppy disk drive, the solution should be fairly obvious, and fixed by swapping components.

Errors that occur within the CPU, memory, and disk controller system are a tougher nut to crack. Whenever a hardware malfunction happens, messages are automatically generated on the console to be interpreted by the system operator. Since these messages can change between releases in the operating system, I cannot provide you with a comprehensive list. A "panic" condition can arise when the UNIX kernel has reach a point from which there is no logical way to proceed. When this happens, the system console will get a PANIC message, along with a dump of certain registers and memory

Chapter 20 UNIX System Administration

locations, and stop. The best action to take is to write down whatever information there is on the screen, and attempt to restart the system by rebooting.

If the system successfully starts again, try to run the software that was running at the time the system crashed. This should be done several times to exercise the system thoroughly. If the system does not panic again, it is possible you have an intermittent hardware problem, and you will have to wait and see what happens over time. This is the worst type of problem to have, because until you can demonstrate the failure, there is little that a hardware or software technician can do about it.

The best type of computer problem to have is one that can be repeated exactly. This allows the technician to quickly focus on the hardware component that is failing, because he will start replacing or removing possible offending components until the problem goes away. When calling for hardware service or software assistance, keep this in mind.

21
Device Drivers

One of the most remarkable things about the computers we use today is the versatility in the way they can be used. There seems to be no end to the different types of applications that show up every day. What fuels this wildfire is the easy accessibility to hardware that is made possible by today's low computer prices.

The hardware that is accessible is not just the computer itself, but peripheral devices as well. These devices include disk-drive subsystems, serial-terminal controllers, modems, video systems, special mass-storage devices, and digital/analog signal I/O. All of them, assuming they are hardware compatible, fall into two categories:

1. Software compatible with some other product supported by the operating system. This means that the new device works without any software modification. Most makers of peripherals will try for this first, although the specification for a particular device might be such that this is impossible.

2. Not software compatible. In this case the maker of the peripheral device must modify the operating system to accommodate the new product.

For the makers of most peripheral products for the IBM AT compatible 80286/80386 systems, the operating system to work on first is DOS. This is because there are more than ten times the number of DOS systems in operation than there are UNIX or XENIX. This may change, but it is most often the case that a product is supported by, or with DOS and not XENIX or UNIX. Also, some manufacturers do not have access to programmers who can implement the support to make their product work with UNIX.

If the product is supported, either through being on the list of supported products by Interactive Systems SCO or Microport (whichever you are using) all you need to do is buy it and perform the installation procedure in the documentation that comes with it. However, if the product is not currently supported and you wish to use (or sell) it, you will have to write your own custom "device driver." This chapter describes the anatomy of a device driver under XENIX and UNIX, and in following chapter we will provide an example of an actual device driver.

Definition of a Device Driver

Most operating systems, and UNIX is one of these, can be configured to work with a variety of different devices. However, in most installations there is only a subset of all the possible I/O devices actually present.[1] Since each type of device needs its own software in the kernel to drive it, which takes up valuable RAM space, we need a way to "leave out" unwanted device drivers, or better yet only include the ones we actually need.

To see how this is done, remember that the UNIX kernel is simply a program, albeit a complex one, which is compiled with many subroutine and function modules written in both C and assembly language. Unlike most programs, however, there are two differences:

1. The kernel is designed to run in an absolute, machine environment rather than under another operating system. This requires a special format of executable file, generated by a special option on the *ld* command line, and a special technique to load and execute the program at bootstrap time.

2. The kernel is designed in such a way that it can be recompiled and reloaded with new (and a variable number of) device drivers without access to most of the source code of the UNIX kernel.

A device driver is a software module which is loaded with the UNIX/XENIX kernel, which performs the function of interfacing the kernel to the physical device, as shown in Figure 21-1. Any given kernel will have a number of device drivers, each operating separately and dedicated to servicing a specific device.

In UNIX, the device driver module is a series of functions and data structures usually written in a single C/assembler source file. There is no

---

[1] In the case of UNIX on the 80286/80386 it is not even possible to have all the supported devices installed on one system. This is because there is a limited number of DMA channels and Interrupt Request (IRQ) lines available on the IBM AT I/O bus.

main() function in a device driver. Instead, a number of the functions are called as subroutines by the rest of the UNIX kernel at strictly defined times for specific reasons. These functions are called "entry points," and one of the best ways of understanding how device drivers work is to examine the entry points and see how and when they are called. Later in this chapter we will discuss all the entry points to a device driver.

Figure 21-1

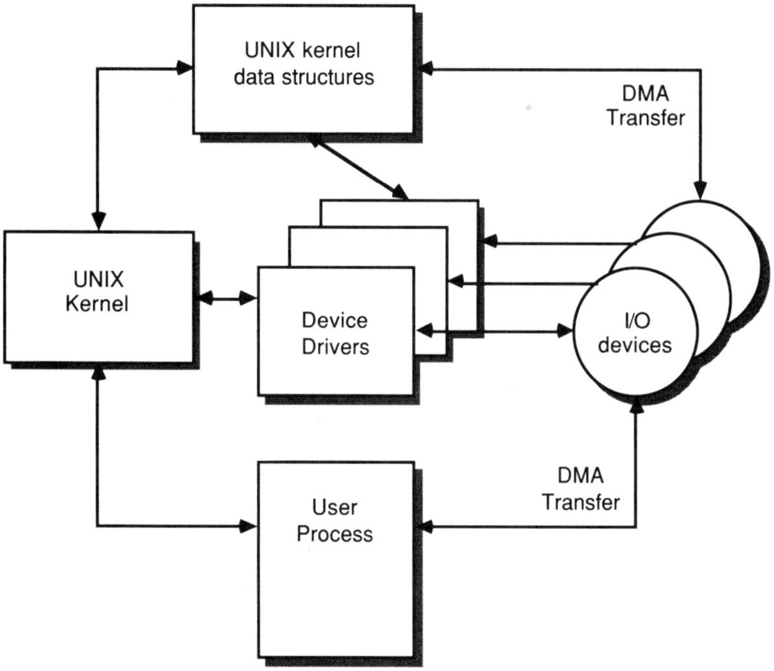

Device Driver Models

There are two basic types of device drivers: 1) Character Devices, and 2) Block Devices. In general, any device which transfers data in fixed size blocks must be driven with a block device driver. Devices which input and output variable sized streams of bytes are character devices.

Character devices are typically terminals, printers, and other devices which do not have file systems on them. The device drivers for character devices interact directly with user processes, with all the buffering and processing controlled by the driver itself.

Block device drivers are usually operated independently of the user processes, although that is where most I/O requests are originated. A block device is most often a random-access device, although tape drives which are not random-access, are usually block devices. The drivers for block devices interact with the UNIX/XENIX kernel, which in turn services the user process. The reasons this is done is so that:

1. A block device may have a file system on it.

2. The kernel can perform block caching, plus blocking/unblocking services for both the driver and the user process.

The differences between character and block device drivers will emerge when we discuss the kernel data structures and the device driver entry points.

Major and Minor Device Numbers

The nature of many peripheral devices is such that the device is divided into a "controller" and a "device." The controller contains most, or at least a large section of the electronics and is capable of operating one or more devices. This is true even though it is possible for two or more devices attached to a single controller to be operated completely independently of each other. This type of design reduces the cost associated with adding devices to a system.

For example, a disk drive might cost $450, and the disk drive controller which is necessary to operate it costs $250. If the need arises for a second disk drive, it is often possible to hook up the new disk drive to the same controller and not have to purchase another.

UNIX device drivers are modeled after this principle. It would not make sense, from either a logical or cost standpoint, to have a separate device driver for two or more devices that are exactly the same. Instead, we actually write our device driver to service a controller in such a way that we can support more than one device hooked up to it. It might be more accurate to call device drivers "controller drivers."

Recall from Chapter 3 how there are special files created with the *mknod* command that are used to access devices. Each special file, or "node," has associated with it a major device number and a minor device number. The UNIX kernel uses the major device number to select which device driver to call when performing I/O on that node. The minor device number is simply a parameter to the device driver, which is usually used to select which actual device out of the several being serviced by the device driver to use.

Often there is a secondary use for the minor device number. When viewed as a byte of eight bits, a device driver may place a special interpretation to specific bits in the byte other than the selection of a device. If, for example, we have a line printer device driver, with two line printers being controlled by it, we might reserve the 128 (27) bit to select "page eject on close" mode. The nodes might be created as follows:

```
mknod /dev/lp0 c 9 0
mknod /dev/lp0e c 9 128
mknod /dev/lp1 c 9 1
mknod /dev/lp1e c 9 129
```

At this point the user can select which type of operation is desired by choosing the pathname of the node that corresponds. If the command:

```
cat datafile > /dev/lp1e
```

is used, the device handler 9 would be called with the parameter 129, which indicates the second line printer with the flag set to cause a page eject after the device is closed.

A similar technique is used when accessing a tape drive, where the option exists as to whether to rewind after an operation or not. The interpretation of the minor device number is wholly up to the device driver writer.

The UNIX Kernel

In addition to performing the service of calling the device driver at appropriate moments, a device driver treats the UNIX kernel as a "black box" library of subroutines that provide access to data structures and hardware functions. The reason this is done this way is fourfold:

1) To avoid having to program a device driver in assembly language, the UNIX kernel provides functions that perform low-level I/O and instructions not otherwise available in C.

2) To avoid unnecessary duplication of code. Although the devices supported can be very different, there are many obvious functions that many device drivers will have to perform.

3) To allow different device drivers to share limited resources, such as RAM memory buffers.

4) To provide a way for the device driver logic to control the kernel with respect to process scheduling.

A by-product of this arrangement is that it makes it easier to implement a bug-free device driver. Many of the kernel-provided routines have to manipulate complex data structures, not to mention the virtual memory hardware of the CPU. The less of this type of code the device driver writer has to implement, the less chance there is of introducing a bug into the system.

Because the device driver is part of the kernel, its logic is responsible for the integrity of the operating system. It must not interfere with data structures or activities outside of its realm, and it must be written to support the "policy" of the operating system. This policy can best be stated: "Do what needs to be done and get the CPU back in the hands of the user where it belongs." The functions that are made available to the device driver logic help support these goals.

The User Process

The user process is, of course, the originator of all I/O activity once the UNIX kernel is booted.[2] In most cases, it is also the origin or destination of data that is being handled by the device driver. There are three possible paths for data to take between the device driver and the process.

1. Direct from the device to the process. This is only possible with DMA devices (described later) such as disk drives and tape drives. It requires the device driver to lock the target RAM region within the

---

[2] Remember that some "user" processes are actually parts of the UNIX operating system.

process in physical memory for the transfer, (as opposed to being swapped out) which it can do with a special request to the kernel.

2. Through buffers managed by the device driver. Data may collect in these buffers due to the varying rates of I/O. For input, when characters become available, the device driver "wakes up" the user process so that data may be read. If the process is not reading data, the device driver will have to attempt to stop the device from sending any more data until some process does actually read the data and empty the input buffers. On output, the user process is put to sleep if it is sending characters at a rate faster than the device can receive and the buffers become too full. When they do empty, the process will "awaken" again.

3. Through buffers managed by the kernel. This will occur whenever the process executes *read()* and *write()* system calls on disk files within a UNIX file system. The pool of buffers that the kernel manages act like a caching system which reduce the number of actual disk accesses necessary.

There are two areas of the user process that are of interest to the device driver. One is the process' virtual address space, which will have the target/destination region for I/O activity, and the "u-area," which is a data structure which the kernel uses to manage and schedule the process. The u-area contains, among other things, I/O base pointer (into the process' virtual address space) and a byte count of the current *read()* or *write()* call.

The UNIX kernel provides a number of service routines, described later, which allow the device driver to access the process' virtual address space and u-area as necessary.

The UNIX Kernel Data Structures

The UNIX kernel maintains a number of data structures, and there are a few that are of direct interest to the device driver. They provide temporary storage for I/O operations that can be used by other drivers. It is usually best to make use of these kernel-supplied structures rather than reserving RAM space just for the device, because when the device is idle there will be more RAM available for the rest of the system.

On the other hand, some devices which are very heavily used will always be requesting the same amount of data space from the kernel all the time anyway, so why not allocate it as a static buffer within the device handler? It will sometimes work out that this is more efficient, because then the overhead associated with allocating/deallocating buffer space will not be spent. An example might be a line printer driver in an installation which will almost always be printing through it, rather than intermittently as is usually the case.

There are two types of buffers that a driver can use, each meant for a particular type of device. It is unlikely that one driver will use both types, although there is no solid rule against it. In either case, the storage space comes from a system wide pool of memory that must be shared between all the device handlers. Therefore, it is up to the device driver logic to exercise restraint and impose an upper limit on the amount of data storage allocated to a particular device.

The first type is the "clist" structure, which is a linked-list FIFO queue of characters. Serial terminals and printer ports often use this type of buffer because their requirement is often variable in nature. A terminal can be idle for a long time, even when it is logged in, and then have a "screenload" dumped to it by the controlling process. Also, the service functions provided by the kernel are conducive to the way that such devices work. The *clist* structure is defined by the file */usr/include/sys/tty.h*.

The other type is called a "buf" structure, which is somewhat more complicated, and is defined by the file */usr/include/sys/buf.h*. The *buf* structure has a pointer within it that is used to address the data block assigned to the device handler, plus other variables interpreted by both the kernel's file system and the device handler. Commands to the device handler from the kernel (on behalf of the user processes) are stored in the *buf* structure. This is the reason that the *buf* structure is used by any device that is structured by the kernel's file system.

To understand how *buf* structures are used, it is important to know the separation of functions between the device driver for a disk drive and the UNIX/XENIX kernel file system, which imposes the file system structure within the data blocks that the device driver handles. Keep in mind that the device driver for a disk driver only passes disk blocks from physical sectors to and from designated regions in RAM memory without reading what is inside them. Any given block might be the super-block, a part of the i-node table, a directory file, or part of a user file. To the device driver it is all the same, and it is up to the UNIX kernel to ask for and deliver the blocks it and the user processes will need.

The Device Handler Structures

The device handler can define data structures for its own use, and they will not be accessed or manipulated by any other part of the system. These structures can be as complex or as simple as the writer desires, although it is advised to keep them as small as possible to conserve RAM space.[3] The device handler's structures appear as global variables to the *ld* loader during the link-loading process that produces the kernel, so it is a good idea to keep their names as unique as possible, using the naming convention described later in the descriptions of the entry points.

Local variables and structures are used for the following reasons:

1. As status flags for communications between the interrupt routine and the rest of the handler.

2. As critical, non-shared buffers for I/O.

Normally, there will also be a number of structures available to the device driver that are not really private to the device driver. One example is the process' u-area, which may be accessed through the global structure *u*.[4]

The Sleep/Wakeup Mechanism

The purpose of most of the logic of a device driver (and much of the logic in any multi-user operating system) is to make the most effective use of the CPU while waiting for comparatively slow I/O operations to take place. Since the device driver's function is to interact directly with a device on behalf of the rest of the operating system, it must be the code that "knows" a requested operation will take a long time and the CPU should be made available for another purpose.

---

[3] On older UNIX systems running on the PDP 11, the kernel had a physical limit of 64KB for code and 64KB data space. This limitation no longer applies, but it is still desirable to make our device drivers as RAM efficient as possible.

[4] The u-area structure is defined by the include file *<sys/user.h>*

Additionally, the device driver also knows when a event has occurred that should signal the continuance of some suspended operation. This usually occurs during an "interrupt" which is explained later. Two kernel support routines are provided for this purpose. They are called *sleep()* and *wakeup()*.

The *sleep()* routine will save the status of the currently executing process, then suspend its execution. The scheduler is then invoked, which searches for some other runnable process to execute. The process remains suspended until the device handler calls the *wakeup()* function, which will tell the scheduler that the process can now be executed. This may not happen immediately, but will happen when the scheduler is entered and no processes of higher priority are ready to executed.

The *sleep()* and *wakeup()* functions are described in greater detail in Chapter 22.

Device Driver Entry Points

We will now look at the device driver entry points, and how and when they are used. Each entry point is simply a C function with a special name, with a prefix which identifies the driver, and a suffix which names the entry point. The device driver prefix is usually a two letter code. For example:

hd	Hard Disk drive
fd	Floppy Disk driver
tt	TeleType (Asynchronous Communications Adapter)
lp	Line Printer (parallel port)

and so forth. So, for the line printer controller, the entry points might be:

lpinit()	/* Initialize lp device */
lpopen()	/* Open lp device */
lpwrite()	/* Write lp device */
lpclose()	/* Close lpdevice */

It is a good idea to stick to the naming convention to avoid possible symbol definition collisions with other modules in the kernel. I prefer to make a device driver with a prefix that ends in an underscore character, such as *xx_*. The two-letter convention got started in the days when the compiler/loader had a more restrictive limit on the number of characters allowed in an external name. In the rest of this chapter, we will use the prefix *xx_* which will be substituted with an actual prefix in a real device driver.

Not all the entry points are required for all drivers. Which will be included is controlled by the requirements of the device being serviced.

xx_init()

If a device needs to be "set up" before it is used, this entry point is called at the time the UNIX kernel is just being booted. This also allows the driver to initialize any local data structure it might need later, as shown in Figure 21-2.

Note that some of the functions performed by *xx_init()* might also be performed by *xx_open)*, which follows.

xx_open() and *xx_close()*

The *xx_open()* entry point is called each time any process issues an *open()* call to this device driver. This allows the driver to initialize the device and driver defined status bits, if necessary, as shown in Figure 21-3. The device driver might also return an error for one reason or another, one of which might be the attempted open of a device that was exclusively opened by another process.

The *xx_open()* entry point has three parameters, as follows:

```
xx_open(dev, flg, cb)
int    dev;       /* minor device number */
int    flg;       /* open mode flags */
int    cb;        /* 0 for character device, 1 for block device */
```

The *flg* parameter is similar, but not exactly the same as, the *oflag* argument that is passed to the open system call. The definition is found in the file */usr/include/sys/file.h*.

Figure 21-2

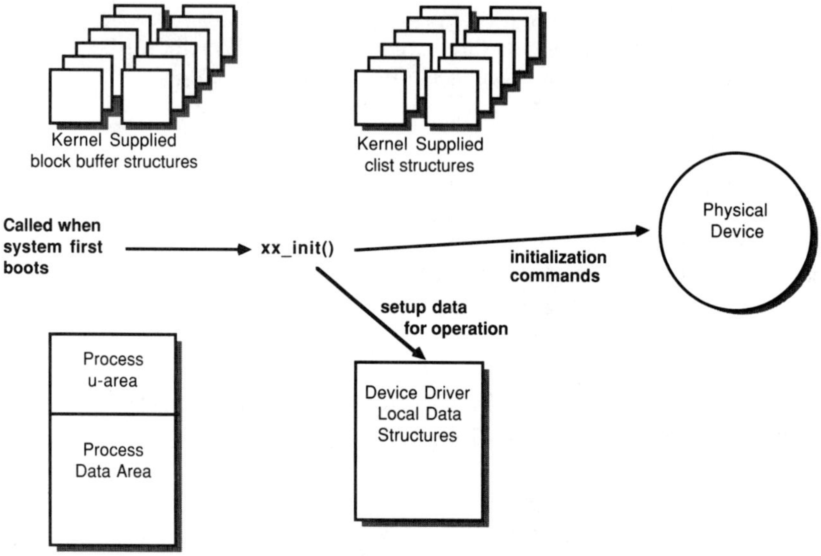

Kernel Supplied block buffer structures

Kernel Supplied clist structures

Called when system first boots → xx_init() → initialization commands → Physical Device

setup data for operation → Device Driver Local Data Structures

Process u-area

Process Data Area

Figure 21-3

Kernel Supplied block buffer structures

Kernel Supplied clist structures

Called when user process performs open() or close() system call → xx_close() xx_open() → reset commands → Physical Device

open status changes → Device Driver Local Data Structures

Process u-area

Process Data Area

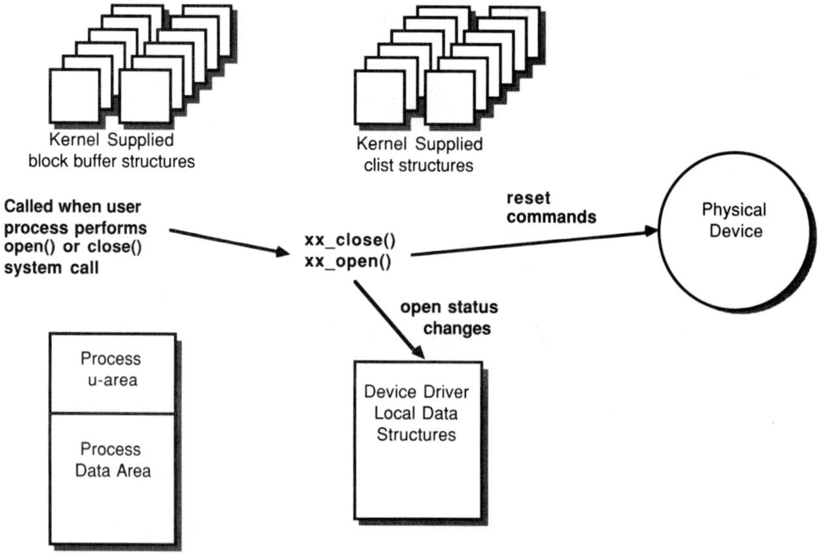

Note that *xx_open()* is not called when a process performs a *fork()* or *dup()* system call and has this device driver open. Therefore, there is no way for the device driver to be able to count how many has the device open. Fortunately, the kernel does that for us, and the entry point *xx_close()* is used only when the last process performs a *close()* system call.

The *xx_close()* entry point may be used to reset the device, free buffer space, and render the device inactive until the next time it is opened again. Its parameter is simply the minor device number.

xx_read()

As shown in Figure 21-4, the *xx_read()* entry point is used to initiate, and in some cases complete, a read activity when a user process makes a *read()* system call. Data will be passed directly to the process' address space, and the device driver may put the calling process to sleep if it is unable to complete the request.

If read activity is not already enabled, *xx_read()* must do so. When the device is ready with data, the *xx_intr()* routine will be called, and *xx_read()* will have to leave a message in its local data structures to advise it what to do with the input.

It might be possible that input activity has already occurred before *xx_read()* is called. In this case, the *xx_read()* routine will simply pass characters to the user process from the device driver managed buffers. The *xx_read()* routine is called with one parameter, the minor device number.

xx_write()

The *xx_write()* routine is the counterpart to *xx_read()*, and operates in the same fashion as shown in Figure 21-5. If output activity is not already occurring, this routine will initiate it, usually by sending the first byte or word to the output port. If physical output is already in progress, this routine will simply add the new characters to the end of the output buffer and return.

In either case, the *xx_intr()* routine will receive control when the device is available for the next unit of output. If the process fills the output buffers past some device driver defined limit, this routine will put the calling process to sleep until the buffers are empty or close to empty. The *xx_write()* routine is called with a single parameter, the minor device number.

Figure 21-4

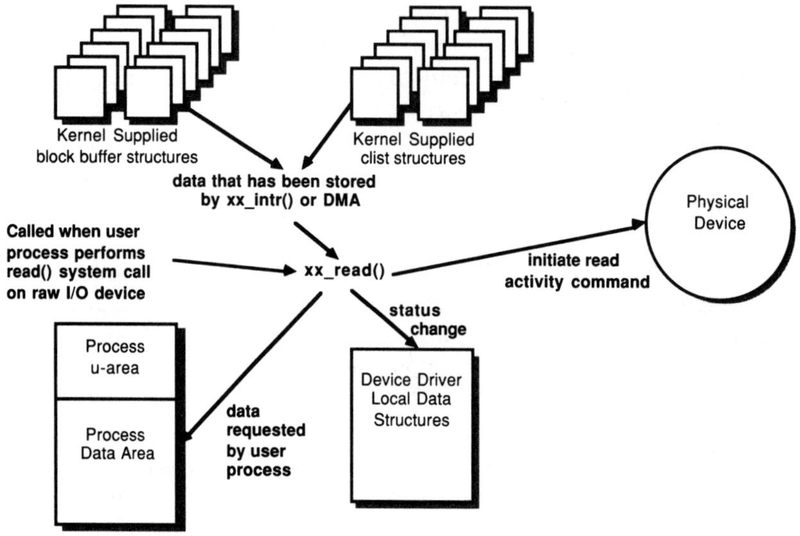

Figure 21-5

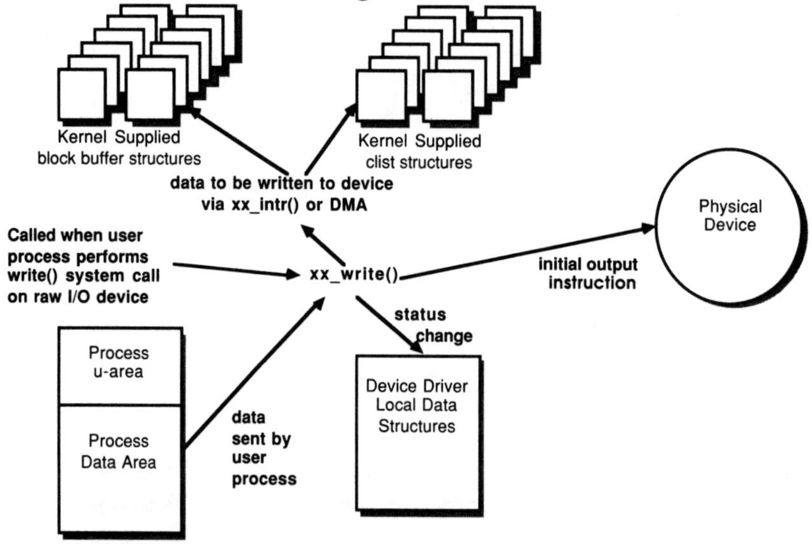

xx_strategy()

This entry point is only used for block I/O device drivers. The kernel calls *xx_strategy()* whenever it requires the input or output of a data block on a block device. It does not interact with any single user process.

Recall from the discussion on kernel supplied data structures that the kernel maintains a pool of block buffers. Each of these block buffers may be assigned to a different task, and many of them hold pieces of user data files.

When a user process executes a *read()* or *write()* system call to a data file or a block device, the device handler is not necessarily entered. If the data area requested happens to be in a block buffer in RAM already, the kernel makes a transfer between the buffer and the process directly. If, on the other hand, the data area is not available, the kernel assigns a block buffer to it and calls *xx_strategy()* to obtain it, as shown in Figure 21-6.

Note that on many file systems *read()*, *write()*, and *open()* calls, a number of disk accesses occur that are transparent to the user process. These accesses include i-node table and directory fetches, among others. The *xx_strategy()* routine for the disk drive is how the kernel makes these requests.

Figure 21-6

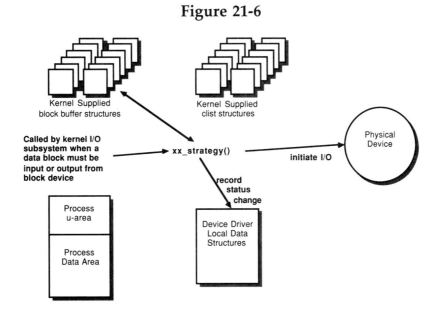

xx_intr()

The most interesting routine from a programming logic standpoint is the *xx_intr()* entry point. This routine can be entered at any time, if the system's and device's interrupts have been enabled and a device status change causes the interrupt. We will discuss the various interrupt protocols later, although the details for any particular device will be found in that device's programmer's reference manual.

In any case, when an interrupt occurs and *xx_intr()* is entered, it is generally one of two conditions:

1. An I/O transfer has completed, or

2. A miscellaneous status change has occurred.

The activity that results is shown in Figure 21-7. There is no way for an interrupt routine to interact directly with a user process, because it is possible that at the time the interrupt occurred the process is no longer in RAM memory. It might even not be in existence.

Figure 21-7

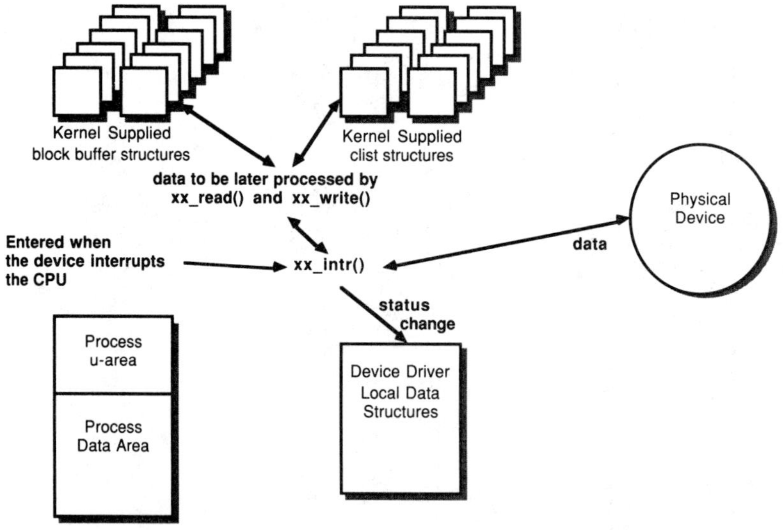

When coding the rest of the device handler, it is important to note what static memory locations can be changed by the *xx_intr()* routine. Care must be taken to defuse "race conditions" that might arise when both *xx_intr()* is modifying a location and another routine is making a logic decision based on the same location.

For example, consider the following statement:

```
if (condition) sleep(reason);
```

which means if *condition* is true, the calling routine's associated process will *sleep*. What happens when *condition* is true during the if evaluation, but turns false while the *sleep* routine is being called? The process will not receive the associated "wakeup" call from the *xx_intr()* routine, because the wakeup will already have been sent. For this reason, it is better to code the following:

```
int x;

x = splx(7);        /* disable interrupts, save previous priority */
while (condition) sleep(reason);
splx(x);            /* re-enable interrupts to previous level */
```

This covers all the bases. Using the *while* statement instead of the *if* statement ensures that condition is re-examined when a wakeup occurs, preventing a premature wakeup from confusing the logic.

xx_ioctl()

The *xx_ioctl()* entry point corresponds to the *ioctl()* system call that processes may make to control an I/O device. The definition of what the *xx_ioctl()* routine does is completely up to the writer of the device driver. Its function is shown in Figure 21-8.

Figure 21-8

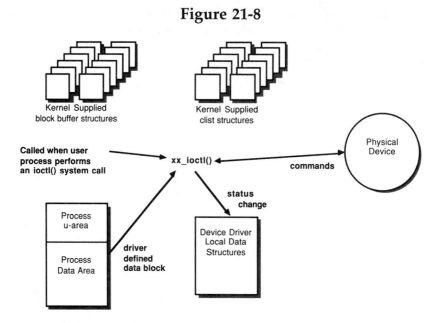

The Stack and Automatic Variables

When the device handler is executing the *xx_open()*, *xx_close()*, *xx_read()*, *xx_write()*, or *xx_ioctl()* entry points, it is essentially running as an extension to the process. However, the driver always executes in kernel, or "privileged" mode, and uses a stack set up for the process in the process' u-area. This stack is limited in size, so it is very inadvisable for any device driver routine to declare any stack or automatic variables that are not absolutely necessary. Particularly taboo are temporary buffers on the stack. For example:

```
xx_write(dev)
int dev;
{
char buf1[512], buf2[512];
```

will likely cause the system to panic.

During interrupt time, when *xx_intr()* has been entered, the system uses whatever kernel mode stack was set up at the time the system was interrupted. Care must be taken not to place too high of a demand on the stack in this case as well. Also note that no data structure within the user's u-area is available to *xx_intr()*. This means that the kernel support routine *sleep()* cannot be called at this time, although *wakeup()* can.

Interrupt routines can also be interrupted by routines of higher priority, and device drivers in general should be written so that they are reentrant.

The I/O Devices

The I/O device itself will be described by its *Programmer's Reference Manual* or *Technical Reference Manual*. However, the function of most I/O devices is very similar, and there are two categories of devices:

1. Programmed I/O device

2. DMA devices.

The sections describe these devices in a generic way, and provide a basis for our understanding of how a device driver must interact with a device.

Programmed I/O Devices

A lower speed device will usually be set up that it will transfer one byte or word to or from the device under the control of a CPU input or output instruction. This type of a device is called a "Programmed I/O device," because each byte is transferred under control of a CPU program. In the case of a terminal, when the user presses a key, a character is sent from the terminal to the controller, where the character appears in a register that can be read with a CPU INB instruction.

If the CPU does not read the byte, and the user presses another key, the previous byte will be lost. So in order to avoid losing any bytes on input the CPU must continually check to see whether the character is available, or allow itself to be interrupted when a new character comes in. For output, there is a similar problem. Most I/O devices that use programmed I/O can only accept characters at a certain rate, which is bound to be much slower than what the CPU can generate. If the CPU attempts to send data via an *OUT* instruction before the prior one is sent, data will be lost. In this case it will be necessary for the CPU to wait for each data byte to be sent, or allow itself to be interrupted when the device is ready to receive another character.

Because UNIX is a multi-user system, it is not feasible to require the CPU to be continually polling each device that requires this type of service. The overhead expenditure would be overwhelming. For this reason we set up each device we want to service to interrupt the CPU. The system gives a device work to do, then goes and does something else itself. Using this methodology, we have a sequence of events that appears in Figure 21-9.

Figure 21-9

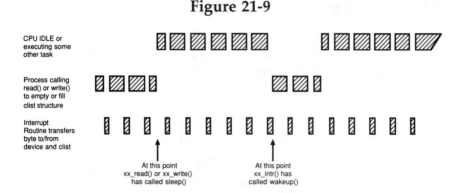

Note that in the chart that the CPU is interrupted for each character that is input or output. Although we attempt to make the interrupt routine as short as possible, this is the weakness of Programmed I/O devices. If we had four terminals, all updating a display at 9600 baud, the interrupt routine would be entered about 3840 times per second. This means that if the interrupt routine takes more than 0.00026 seconds to execute, there will be no CPU time left for other tasks until the output is complete.

DMA

A device that typically moves large amounts of data to and from RAM memory without any translation will usually be built to use DMA, or Direct Memory Access. From a device driver's point of view there is not much difference between a DMA device and a Programmed I/O device, except that the interrupt routine *xx_intr()* is only called once at the end of the transfer, and *xx_intr()* need not make any provision for executing I/O instructions for each byte/word transferred. This yields an event map as shown in Figure 21-10.

Figure 21-10

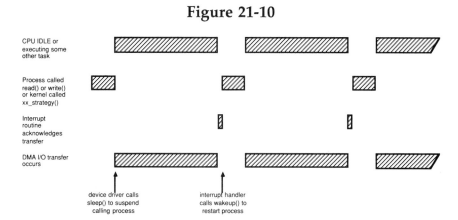

Essentially a DMA device accomplishes a device to RAM transfer with a RAM base address and a byte count without executing any CPU instructions beyond what it takes to set the operation up. During that time, the CPU is free to perform other tasks, and that is what makes the extra hardware necessary for DMA worth the expense.

Conclusion

We have briefly visited all the bits and pieces of a device driver. The only way to learn more is to actually examine or write one, which we will do in Chapter 23.

22
Kernel Support Routines for Device Drivers

As previously mentioned, each kernel provides a series of routines that allow the device driver to perform certain functions. These functions are documented in the *SCO XENIX Programmer's Guide Vol. II*, and the *Microport Runtime System Manual*, so we will not go into great detail here. They are grouped into the following categories:

1. Sleep and wakeup functions. These routines give the device handler the capability of suspending and resuming the execution of a process to synchronize I/O.

2. Change the interrupt level. When executing critical sections of code, these functions can disable and enable certain interrupts that might otherwise interfere with the device driver's logic.

3. Allocate or free kernel managed buffer space. Both the *clist* and the buf structures may be accessed this way.

4. Pass data to or from the process's buffer in its virtual address space.

5. Miscellaneous, such as print a message or crash the system.

A brief summary of some of these routines follows:

```
spl5()
spl6()
spl7()
splx(x)
int  x;             /* priority level to set */
```

These routines change the current allowed interrupts for the system. They all return the previous priority, which can be used as a parameter to the *splx()* function to reset the priority.

```
sleep(chn, pri)
char *chn;              /* event identifier */
int  pri;               /* priority after wakeup */
```

This routine will put to sleep the current process. The *chn* parameter is a unique number which is used to identify the sleeping process on the *wakeup()* call (see below). To keep these numbers unique, one method of assigning them is to use the address of some relevant object within the device driver, usually the structure which holds the status bits of the device. This routine must not be called either directly or indirectly by *xx_intr()* or *xx_strategy()*.

```
wakeup(chn)
char *chr;              /* event identifier */
```

This routine will wake up a sleeping process. The chn parameter must be the same number as was used in the corresponding *sleep()* call.

```
timeout(fnc, arg, tim)
int (*fnc)();           /* function to enter after timeout */
int  arg;               /* argument to function */
int  tim;               /* time in clock ticks */
```

This function will make sure a device driver will be entered at a specific time, regardless of other events. This is used in the case where it is possible that interrupts might be lost, or when the device driver is waiting for an event that might never happen.

```
copyin(uad, sad, num)
char *uad;              /* user address */
char *sad;              /* system address */
int  num;               /* number of bytes to copy */
```

This routine copies data from the user area to the system area.

```
copyout(sad, uad, num)
char *sad;              /* system address */
char *uad;              /* user address */
int  num;               /* number of bytes to copy */
```

This routine copies data from the system area to the user area.

Chapter 22 Kernel Support Routines for Device Drivers

```
putchar(c)
int   c;              /* character to display */

printf(fmt, p1, p2 ...)
char *fmt;            /* printf format */
```

Both these routines are similar in operation to their counterparts in the stdio.h routines. Their output will be displayed on the system console. These should be used for serious error conditions only, because the system will lock up for the duration of the output.

```
panic(str);
char *str;            /* panic message */
```

If the device driver attains a state where it is not possible to logically proceed, or senses corruption of its data, it should call this routine. The system will be halted with the panic message on the screen.

```
getc(cp)
struct clist *cp;     /* clist structure */
```

Returns a character from the end of a *clist* structure.

```
putc(chr, cp)
int   chr;            /* character to place in clist */
struct clist *cp;     /* clist structure */
```

Places a character at the beginning of a *clist* structure.

```
cpass()
```

Get a character from the current I/O buffer in the user's address space. Returns -1 if the buffer is empty.

```
passc(c)
int c;                /* character to send */
```

Transfer a character to the current I/O buffer in the user's address space. Returns -1 if the buffer was filled.

Other kernel support routines will be seen in the sample device driver in Chapter 23.

23
Sample Device Driver

In this chapter we present an actual device driver for a programmed I/O device. The device chosen is a terminal device which provides four modems on a single card, which all share a common interrupt vector.

I have attempted to make the comments in the code sufficient to explain what is going on, although the following additional notes should be taken into consideration:

1. This device handler was compiled and run on a Microport System V/386 system.

2. There are certain kernel support routines that are called, which are not documented in the *Microport Runtime System* manuals, but they are documented in the *SCO XENIX Programmer's Guide*.

3. The device driver may be changed to accommodate more modems by altering the define set aside for that purpose at the beginning of the program.

This device driver is available on the software diskette that is sold on this volume, in the directory *./quad*.

```
 1 0: /*title q1200.c - Device driver for Omnitel Q1200
 2 0*
 3 0*   Alan Deikman 3/88
 4 0*
 5 0*   This device driver is for the Omnitel Q1200 modem board.  The Q1200
 6 0*   provides 4 modems on a single full-sized IBM AT board, all of which
 7 0*   operate independently.
 8 0*
 9 0*   The programming protocol for the Q1200 is the same as for the IBM
10 0*   asynchronous communications adapter except that there are four
11 0*   devices, and four sets of I/O ports, serviced by a single interrupt
12 0*   line.  Any time any one of the four device interrupts, we can read
13 0*   the IRR (Interrupt Routing Register) to see which device(s) have
14 0*   interrupts pending.
15 0*
16 0*   This device driver is set up for IRQ4 and the base address for
17 0*   the first device is 0x280.  The second, third, and fourth modems
18 0*   have base addresses of 0x288, 0x290, and 0x298 respectively.
19 0*
20 0*   */
21 0:
22 0: /*foot Copyright (c) 1988 by Alan Deikman */
23 0:
24 0: #include <sys/types.h>
25 0: #include <sys/param.h>
26 0: #include <sys/tty.h>
27 0: #include <sys/termio.h>
28 0: #include <sys/conf.h>
29 0: #include <sys/dir.h>
30 0: #include <sys/signal.h>
31 0: #include <sys/user.h>
32 0: #include <sys/errno.h>
33 0:
34 0: /* Driver configuration constants */
35 0:
36 0: #define BASE    0x280   /* Base address of first modem */
37 0: #define IRQL    4       /* IRQ line */
38 0: #define NUNITS  4       /* Four units */
39 0:
40 0: /* I/O port offsets */
41 0:
42 0: #define TXB    0        /* Transmit buffer */
43 0: #define RXB    0        /* Receive buffer */
44 0: #define DLL    0        /* Divisor latch LSB */
45 0: #define DLM    1        /* Divisor latch MSB */
46 0: #define IER    1        /* Interrupt Enable Register */
47 0: #define IIR    2        /* Interrupt Identification Register */
48 0: #define LCR    3        /* Line Control Register */
49 0: #define MCR    4        /* Modem Control Register */
50 0: #define LSR    5        /* Line Status Register */
51 0: #define MSR    6        /* Modem Status Register */
```

Chapter 23 Sample Device Driver

```
 52 0: #define IRR     7       /* Interrupt Routing Register */
 53 0:
 54 0: /* Bits for the Interrupt Enable Register */
 55 0:
 56 0: #define IER_RI  0x01    /* Enable Receiver Interrupt */
 57 0: #define IER_TI  0x02    /* Enable Transmitter Interrupt */
 58 0: #define IER_RSI 0x04    /* Enable Receiver Status Interrupt */
 59 0: #define IER_MSI 0x08    /* Enable Modem Status Interrupt */
 60 0:
 61 0: /* Values for the Interrupt Identification Register */
 62 0:
 63 0: #define IIR_RCH 0x06    /* Receiver Line Status Changed */
 64 0: #define IIR_RR  0x04    /* Received Data Available */
 65 0: #define IIR_TR  0x02    /* Transmit Buffer Available */
 66 0: #define IIR_MCH 0x00    /* Modem Status Change */
 67 0:
 68 0: /* Bits for the Line Control Register */
 69 0:
 70 0: #define LCR_5   0x00    /* For 5 data bits */
 71 0: #define LCR_6   0x01    /* For 6 data bits */
 72 0: #define LCR_7   0x02    /* For 7 data bits */
 73 0: #define LCR_8   0x03    /* For 8 data bits */
 74 0: #define LCR_ST1 0x00    /* For 1 stop bit */
 75 0: #define LCR_ST2 0x04    /* For 2 stop bits */
 76 0: #define LCR_PAR 0x08    /* For parity */
 77 0: #define LCR_EVN 0x10    /* For even parity */
 78 0: #define LCR_MRK 0x20    /* For mark (parity always one) */
 79 0: #define LCR_BRK 0x40    /* Send break char */
 80 0: #define LCR_DLA 0x80    /* Divisor Latch Access (DLAB in IBM) */
 81 0:
 82 0: /* Bits for Modem Control Register */
 83 0:
 84 0: #define MCR_DTR 0x01    /* Data Terminal Ready */
 85 0: #define MCR_RTS 0x02    /* Request to Send */
 86 0: #define MCR_1   0x04    /* User defined #1 */
 87 0: #define MCR_2   0x08    /* User defined #2 */
 88 0: #define MCR_LOP 0x10    /* Loopback mode */
 89 0:
 90 0: /* Bits for Line Status Register */
 91 0:
 92 0: #define LSR_RCA 0x01    /* Receive Character is Available */
 93 0: #define LSR_OVR 0x02    /* Overrun */
 94 0: #define LSR_PAR 0x04    /* Parity Error */
 95 0: #define LSR_FRM 0x08    /* Framing Error */
 96 0: #define LSR_BRK 0x10    /* Break detected */
 97 0: #define LSR_TXB 0x20    /* Transmit Buffer ready */
 98 0: #define LSR_TSB 0x40    /* Transmit Shift register ready */
 99 0:
100 0: /* Bits for the Modem Status Register */
101 0:
102 0: #define MSR_DCS 0x01    /* Delta CS */
```

```
103 0: #define MSR_DDR 0x02    /* Delta DR */
104 0: #define MSR_DRI 0x04    /* Delta RI */
105 0: #define MSR_DCD 0x08    /* Delta CD */
106 0: #define MSR_CS  0x10    /* Clear to Send */
107 0: #define MSR_DR  0x20    /* Data set Ready */
108 0: #define MSR_RI  0x40    /* Ring Indicator */
109 0: #define MSR_CD  0x80    /* Carrier Detect */
110 0:
111 0: /* Since we are programming the QM1200 to work only at 1200
112 0*    baud, we have a constant value for the DLL and DLM latches */
113 0:
114 0: #define DLM_VAL 0x00
115 0: #define DLL_VAL 0xC0
116 0:
117 0: /* This external allows us access to the copyright message routine */
118 0:
119 0: extern int max_copyrights;       /* number of copyright slots available */
120 0: extern char *oem_copyrights[];   /* copyright message slots */
121 0:
122 0: /* This is the local data defined by the Q1200 driver */
123 0:
124 0: struct tty qm__tty[NUNITS];      /* One tty structure per modem */
125 0:
126 0: /*subtitle qm_init() - Initialize Q1200
127 0*
128 0*    This routine, called at system bootstrap time, will simply set up
129 0*    all the modem devices with interrupts off */
130 0:
131 0: qm_init() {
132 1:
133 1:    register int i, base, x;
134 1:    int qm_kick();
135 1:    char *cn = "\nQ1200 driver Copyright (c) 1988 by Alan Deikman";
136 1:
137 1:    /* place our copyright notice in the boot-up display */
138 1:
139 1:    for (i = 0; i < max_copyrights &&
140 1:                oem_copyrights[i] &&
141 1:                strcmp(oem_copyrights[i], cn); i++);
142 1:    if (i < max_copyrights && !oem_copyrights[i]) oem_copyrights[i] = cn;
143 1:
144 1:    /* loop for each device for initialization */
145 1:
146 1:    for (i = 0; i < NUNITS; i++) {
147 2:       base = BASE + (i * 8);
148 2:
149 2:       /* Disable interrupts, and set the baud rate divisor to 1200 baud */
150 2:
151 2:       x = spl7();
152 2:       outb(base + IER, 0);
153 2:       outb(base + LCR, LCR_DLA);
```

Chapter 23 Sample Device Driver

```
154 2:      outb(base + DLL, DLL_VAL);
155 2:      outb(base + DLM, DLM_VAL);
156 2:
157 2:      /* Set the default rate to 8 bits, 1 stop bit, no parity */
158 2:
159 2:      outb(base + LCR, LCR_8 | LCR_ST1);
160 2:      outb(base + MCR, 0);
161 2:
162 2:      /* clear all pending interrupts */
163 2:
164 2:      inb(base + RXB);
165 2:      inb(base + IIR);
166 2:      inb(base + LCR);
167 2:      inb(base + MCR);
168 2:      outb(base + IRR, 0x80);     /* enable board interrupts */
169 2:      qm_intr(i);
170 2:      splx(x); }
171 1:
172 1:   /* done with initialization */
173 1:
174 1:   timeout(qm_kick, 0, 3000);
175 1:   return; }
176 0:
177 0: /*subtitle qm_open() - Open device
178 0*
179 0*   This routine is called each time any process make an open()
180 0*   call to the qm driver.  The minor device number selects which
181 0*   modem on the q1200 to use.  This routine will
182 0*
183 0*       1. Enable Interrupts on that device
184 0*       2. Initialize the tty structure for the device
185 0*       3. Raise the TR and RTS signals on the line
186 0*
187 0* */
188 0:
189 0: extern int asy_vad[];
190 0:
191 0: qm_open(dev, flg)
192 0: int     dev;    /* Minor device number */
193 0: int     flg;    /* Flags from 3rd parameter of open() call */
194 0: {
195 1:   register struct tty *l;
196 1:   register int base;
197 1:   int qm_proc(), x;
198 1:
199 1:   /* error if we have been opened with a bad minor device */
200 1:
201 1:   dev &= 0xFF;
202 1:   if (dev >= NUNITS) {
203 2:     u.u_error = ENXIO;
204 2:     return; }
```

```
205 1:
206 1:     l = &qm__tty[dev];
207 1:     base = BASE + (dev * 8);
208 1:
209 1:     /* initialize if not already open */
210 1:
211 1:     if ((l->t_state & (ISOPEN | WOPEN)) == 0) {
212 2:         ttinit(l);
213 2:         l->t_proc  = qm_proc;
214 2:         l->t_oflag = OPOST  | ONLCR;
215 2:         l->t_iflag = ISTRIP | IXON;
216 2:         l->t_lflag = ECHO   | ICANON | ISIG | ECHOE | ECHOK;
217 2:         l->t_state |= CARR_ON;
218 2:         qm_control(base, l); }
219 1:
220 1:     /* call line discipline routine, then we're done */
221 1:
222 1:     x = spl7();
223 1:     (*linesw[l->t_line].l_open)(l);
224 1:     splx(x);
225 1:     return; }
226 0:
227 0: /*subtitle qm_close() - Close device
228 0*
229 0*   Here we will close off the device and drop DTR, which should cause
230 0*   the modem to hang up.  We also shut off interrupts.  */
231 0:
232 0: qm_close(dev)
233 0: int     dev;    /* Minor device number */
234 0: {
235 1:     register struct tty *l;
236 1:     register int base;
237 1:     int x;
238 1:
239 1:     /* error if we have been opened with a bad minor device */
240 1:
241 1:     dev &= 0xFF;
242 1:     if (dev >= NUNITS) {
243 2:         u.u_error = ENXIO;
244 2:         return; }
245 1:
246 1:     l = &qm__tty[dev];
247 1:     base = dev + (dev * 8);
248 1:
249 1:     /* call line discipline module */
250 1:
251 1:     (*linesw[l->t_line].l_close)(l);
252 1:
253 1:     /* disable interrupts and shut down modem */
254 1:
255 1:     outb(base + IER, 0);
```

Chapter 23 Sample Device Driver

```
256 1:    outb(base + MCR, 0);
257 1:
258 1:    /* done */
259 1:
260 1:    return; }
261 0:
262 0: /*subtitle qm_read(), qm_write() - Modem line I/O
263 0*
264 0*    These lines depend on the line discipline modules, and as such
265 0*    there is little else for them to do.  */
266 0:
267 0: qm_read(dev)
268 0: int      dev;    /* Minor device number */
269 0: {
270 1:    register struct tty *l = &qm__tty[dev & 0xFF];
271 1:
272 1:    /* error if called with bad device number */
273 1:
274 1:    l->t_state |= CARR_ON;
275 1:    dev &= 0xFF;
276 1:    if (dev >= NUNITS) {
277 2:       u.u_error = ENXIO;
278 2:       return; }
279 1:
280 1:    /* call line discipline module and return */
281 1:
282 1:    (*linesw[l->t_line].l_read)(l);
283 1:    return; }
284 0:
285 0: qm_write(dev)
286 0: int      dev;    /* Minor device number */
287 0: {
288 1:    register struct tty *l = &qm__tty[dev & 0xFF];
289 1:
290 1:    /* error if called with bad device number */
291 1:
292 1:    dev &= 0xFF;
293 1:    if (dev >= NUNITS) {
294 2:       u.u_error = ENXIO;
295 2:       return; }
296 1:
297 1:    /* call line discipline module and return */
298 1:
299 1:    (*linesw[l->t_line].l_write)(l);
300 1:    return; }
301 0:
302 0: /*subtitle qm_intr() - Process Interrupt
303 0*
304 0*    This routine must determine which device(s) had an interrupt
305 0*    pending, and take the appropriate action.
306 0*
```

```
307 0*   */
308 0:
309 0: qm_intr(dev)
310 0: int     dev;    /* interrupt vector */
311 0: {
312 1:   register int i;
313 1:   register int iir;
314 1:
315 1:   /* loop until no more interrupts pending (there might be more than
316 1*      one */
317 1:
318 1:   for (i = 0; i < NUNITS; i++)
319 1:      while ((iir = (inb(BASE + (i * 8) + IIR) & 0x6)) != 0) qm_intr1(i, iir);
320 1:
321 1:   /* cleared all interrupts.  we can go back */
322 1:
323 1:   outb(BASE + IRR, 0x80);
324 1:   return; }
325 0:
326 0: /* process interrupt on a specific line */
327 0:
328 0: qm_intr1(dev, iir)
329 0: int     dev;    /* Minor device number */
330 0: int     iir;    /* Interrupt identification register */
331 0: {
332 1:   int  base = BASE + (dev * 8);   /* base I/O port */
333 1:   struct tty *l = &qm__tty[dev & 0xFF]; /* tty structure for this device */
334 1:   int i, stat;
335 1:
336 1:   /* process receive data available interrupt */
337 1:
338 1:   i = inb(BASE + LSR);
339 1:   if (iir == IIR_RR) {
340 2:
341 2:      /* get input character and status, and translate status */
342 2:
343 2:      i = inb(base + RXB);
344 2:      stat = inb(base + LSR);
345 2:      stat = ((stat & LSR_OVR) ? OVERRUN : 0) |
346 2:             ((stat & LSR_PAR) ? PERROR  : 0) |
347 2:             ((stat & LSR_FRM) ? FRERROR : 0);
348 2:
349 2:      /* if no receive buffers have been set up, throw input character
350 2*         away */
351 2:
352 2:      if (l->t_rbuf.c_ptr == NULL) return;
353 2:
354 2:      /* process XON or XOFF if this terminal has enabled it */
355 2:
356 2:      if (l->t_iflag & IXON) {
357 3:
```

```
358 3:        /* if output is halted, and we have received an XON character,
359 3*           resume output and return   */
360 3:
361 3:        if (l->t_state & TTSTOP && (i == CSTOP || l->t_iflag & IXANY)) {
362 4:          qm_proc(l, T_RESUME);
363 4:          if (i == CSTOP) return; }
364 3:
365 3:        /* if output is running, and we have received an XOFF character,
366 3*           halt output and return */
367 3:
368 3:        else if (!(l->t_state & TTSTOP) && i == CSTOP) {
369 4:          qm_proc(l, T_SUSPEND);
370 4:          return; } }
371 2:
372 2:     /* If we have sensed a break key, ignore the input if the terminal
373 2*        is set to "ignore break" mode */
374 2:
375 2:     if (stat & (FRERROR | OVERRUN) == (FRERROR | OVERRUN)) {
376 3:       if (l->t_iflag & IGNBRK) return;
377 3:       (*linesw[l->t_line].l_input)(l, L_BREAK);
378 3:       return; }
379 2:
380 2:     /* if we have a parity error and the terminal is set to ignore
381 2*        parity errors, ignore input */
382 2:
383 2:     if (stat & PERROR && l->t_iflag & IGNPAR) return;
384 2:
385 2:     /* strip character and send it */
386 2:
387 2:     if (l->t_iflag & ISTRIP) i &= 0x7F;
388 2:     *l->t_rbuf.c_ptr = i;
389 2:     l->t_rbuf.c_count--;
390 2:     (*linesw[l->t_line].l_input)(l, L_BUF);
391 2:     return; }
392 1:
393 1:  /* process a transmit buffer available interrupt */
394 1:
395 1:  if (iir == IIR_TR) {
396 2:    l->t_state &= ~BUSY;
397 2:
398 2:    /* if we need an XON character sent, send it */
399 2:
400 2:    if (l->t_state & TTXON) {
401 3:      outb(base + TXB, CSTART);
402 3:      l->t_state &= ~TTXON; }
403 2:
404 2:    /* if we need an XOFF character, send it*/
405 2:
406 2:    else if (l->t_state & TTXOFF) {
407 3:      outb(base + TXB, CSTOP);
408 3:      l->t_state &= ~TTXOFF; }
```

```
409 2:
410 2:       /* otherwise, just send next character */
411 2:
412 2:           else qm_proc(l, T_OUTPUT);  }
413 1:
414 1:   /* process a modem status change */
415 1:
416 1:   if (iir == IIR_MCH) {
417 2:       i = inb(base + MSR); }
418 1:
419 1:   /* process a line status change */
420 1:
421 1:   if (iir == IIR_RCH) {
422 2:       i = inb(base + LSR); }
423 1:
424 1:   /* done with interrupts for this line */
425 1:
426 1:   return; }
427 0:
428 0: /*subtitle qm_ioctl() - Process ioctl call
429 0*
430 0*   This routine relies on the kernel supplied ttiocom()
431 0*   program, then acts on the result through qm_control()   */
432 0:
433 0: qm_ioctl(dev, cmd, arg, mod)
434 0: int      dev;     /* Minor device number */
435 0: int      cmd;     /* Command made by process */
436 0: char     *arg;    /* Command block */
437 0: int      mod;     /* Mode */
438 0: {
439 1:   register struct tty *l = &qm__tty[dev & 0xff];
440 1:   int base = BASE + ((dev & 0xff) * 8);
441 1:
442 1:   /* error if called with bad device number */
443 1:
444 1:   l->t_state |= CARR_ON;
445 1:   dev &= 0xFF;
446 1:   if (dev >= NUNITS) {
447 2:       u.u_error = ENXIO;
448 2:       return; }
449 1:
450 1:   if (ttiocom(l, cmd, arg, mod)) qm_control(base, l);
451 1:   return; }
452 0:
453 0: /*subtitle qm_control() - Control modem device
454 0*
455 0*   This routine will read the tty structure for a device and
456 0*   make sure the device is sending the actual signals.  This will
457 0*   also enable or disable interrupts
458 0*
459 0*   Since we are supporting this device for 1200 baud only, we will
```

Chapter 23 Sample Device Driver

```
460 0*   ignore baud rate changes.
461 0*
462 0*   */
463 0:
464 0: qm_control(base, l)
465 0: int      base;           /* base address of device */
466 0: struct tty *l;           /* tty structure for device*/
467 0: {
468 1:    register int x;
469 1:    register int i;
470 1:    register int cflag = l->t_cflag;
471 1:
472 1:    /* set up line control register and output */
473 1:
474 1:    switch (cflag & CSIZE) {
475 2:       case CS5:   i = LCR_5;  break;
476 2:       case CS6:   i = LCR_6;  break;
477 2:       case CS7:   i = LCR_7;  break;
478 2:       case CS8:   i = LCR_8;  break;  }
479 1:    if ( cflag & CSTOPB ) i |= LCR_ST2;
480 1:    if ( cflag & PARENB ) i |= LCR_PAR;
481 1:    if (!(cflag & PARODD)) i |= LCR_EVN;
482 1:    outb(base + LCR, i);
483 1:
484 1:    /* set up modem control register and make sure interrupts
485 1*       are enabled */
486 1:
487 1:    if (!(l->t_state & ISOPEN)) {
488 2:       x = spl7();
489 2:       outb(base + IER, 0);
490 2:       for (i = 0; i < 3; i++) inb(base + RXB);
491 2:       for (i = 0; i < 3; i++) inb(base + IIR);
492 2:       for (i = 0; i < 3; i++) inb(base + LSR);
493 2:       for (i = 0; i < 3; i++) inb(base + MSR);
494 2:       while (!(inb(base + LSR) & LSR_TXB)) {
495 3:          splx(x);
496 3:          for (i = 2000; i; i--);
497 3:          x = spl7(); }
498 2:       for (i = 0; i < 3; i++) inb(base + MSR);
499 2:       for (i = 0; i < 3; i++) inb(base + IIR);
500 2:       outb(base + MCR, MCR_DTR | MCR_RTS);
501 2:       outb(base + IER, IER_RI | IER_TI | IER_RSI | IER_MSI);
502 2:       outb(base + IRR, 0x80);
503 2:       i = inb(0x21);
504 2:       i &= ~(1 << IRQL);
505 2:       outb(0x21, i);
506 2:       splx(x); }
507 1:
508 1:    return; }
509 0:
510 0: /*title qm_proc() - Process driver commands
```

```
511 0*
512 0*   This routine is called by all the others to start some sort of
513 0*   output on the transmit device */
514 0:
515 0: qm_proc(l, cmd)
516 0: struct tty *l;           /* tty device structure for device */
517 0: int cmd;                 /* command to be performed */
518 0: {
519 1:    int qm_intr();
520 1:    register struct ccblock *t;   /* to reduce address callculations */
521 1:    int dev = 1 - qm__tty;        /* crock: a sloppy way to get dev   */
522 1:    int base;
523 1:    int ttrstrt();
524 1:    int i;
525 1:    base = BASE + (dev * 8);
526 1:
527 1:    if (i & LSR+TXB) l->t_state &= ~BUSY;
528 1:    switch (cmd) {
529 2:
530 2:       /* process an input request */
531 2:
532 2:       case T_INPUT:
533 2:       break;
534 2:
535 2:       /* process a timeout */
536 2:
537 2:       case T_TIME:
538 2:       l->t_state &= ~TIMEOUT;
539 2:       qm_control(base, l);
540 2:       goto start;
541 2:
542 2:       /* flush the output buffer */
543 2:
544 2:       case T_WFLUSH:
545 2:       l->t_tbuf.c_size -= l->t_tbuf.c_count;
546 2:       l->t_tbuf.c_count = 0;
547 2:
548 2:       /* resume output */
549 2:
550 2:       case T_RESUME:
551 2:       l->t_state &= ~TTSTOP;
552 2:
553 2:       /* start output */
554 2:
555 2:       case T_OUTPUT:
556 2:       start:
557 2:       if (l->t_state & (TIMEOUT | TTSTOP | BUSY)) break;
558 2:       t = &l->t_tbuf;
559 2:       if (t->c_ptr == NULL || t->c_count == 0) {
560 3:          if (t->c_ptr) t->c_ptr -= t->c_size - t->c_count;
561 3:          if (!(CPRES & (*linesw[l->t_line].l_output)(l))) break; }
```

Chapter 23 Sample Device Driver

```
562 2:          l->t_state |= BUSY;
563 2:          outb(base + TXB, *t->c_ptr++);
564 2:          t->c_count--;
565 2:          break;
566 2:
567 2:          /* suspend output */
568 2:
569 2:          case T_SUSPEND:
570 2:          l->t_state |= TTSTOP;
571 2:          break;
572 2:
573 2:          /* block input (by sending CSTOP character) */
574 2:
575 2:          case T_BLOCK:
576 2:          l->t_state &= ~TTXON;
577 2:          l->t_state |= TBLOCK;
578 2:          if (l->t_state & BUSY) l->t_state |= TTXOFF;
579 2:          else outb(base + TXB, CSTOP);
580 2:          break;
581 2:
582 2:          /* flush input queue */
583 2:
584 2:          case T_RFLUSH:
585 2:          if (!(l->t_state & TBLOCK)) break;
586 2:
587 2:          /* unblock input (by sending CSTART character) */
588 2:
589 2:          case T_UNBLOCK:
590 2:          l->t_state &= ~(TTXOFF | TBLOCK);
591 2:          if (l->t_state & BUSY) l->t_state |= TTXON;
592 2:          else outb(base + TXB, CSTART);
593 2:          break;
594 2:
595 2:          /* send a break character */
596 2:
597 2:          case T_BREAK:
598 2:          outb(base + LCR, LCR_BRK);
599 2:          l->t_state |= TIMEOUT;
600 2:          timeout(ttrstrt, l, HZ/4);
601 2:          break;
602 2:
603 2:          /* bad command */
604 2:
605 2:          default:
606 2:          printf("qm_proc(): bad command %d\n", cmd); }
607 1:
608 1:     /* done */
609 1:
610 1:     return; }
611 0:
612 0: qm_kick() {
```

```
613 1:     qm_intr(0);
614 1:     timeout(qm_kick, 0, 3000);
615 1:     return; }
```

Appendix A
UNIX Documentation

As we had mentioned previously, one the biggest weaknesses of UNIX as a commercial product is not the software, its performance or features, but the documentation that comes with it. That is the reason for this volume and the many others that have been published to supplement UNIX documentation.

The original UNIX documentation package, as published by AT&T, is organized into eight chapters, as shown in Figure A-1. Each chapter is a series of articles, with an "INTRO" article as the first and the rest organized alphabetically. Each of the articles are in a relatively fixed format, typeset with the *troff* text processing software, and that is they way the articles are maintained. The troff source files are maintained in a directory hierarchy underneath the directory */usr/man*.[1]

This structure allowed the easy maintenance and update of the UNIX documentation while it was at AT&T. Whenever a programmer altered, added, or (occasionally) deleted a program, the only thing affected was a single file or two in one of the */usr/man* subdirectories. Users could maintain and print their own hard-copy versions of the manuals by periodically checking the modification times on these files.

However, in the commercial environment where SCO XENIX and Microport UNIX are used, we generally do not have such routine modifications to the operating system in use. The printed manuals are what we use and stick with.

The problem is not so much the availability of information, but its organization and relevance. You cannot find an article you don't know is there. On top of that, almost every UNIX article will tell you "what," but almost never "why," in the form of examples or discussion of theory. One of the

---

[1] The */usr/man* directory is accessible on many UNIX systems as an on-line manual through the *man* command. However, for space economy reasons, neither SCO or Microport distribute the */usr/man* directory with their packaged products.

best examples of this problem I can think of is the articles describing the AWK programming language.

Figure A-1

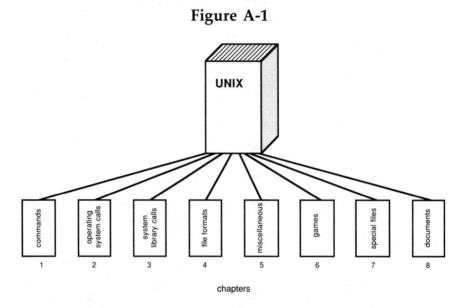

The Microport article on AWK is the AT&T version, which contains an estimated 400 or so words on just over two pages. The SCO XENIX version of the AWK article was rewritten and much improved, but contains no more information and uses six pages. This is an entire programming language, and one of the most useful report generating tools in UNIX. Yet the documentation is so obscure and dense that I had used UNIX for years before I found this treasure tucked away. And I did not find it in the documentation. Another programmer presented me with some programs. How many hours of programming did I waste simply because I did not know?

To their credit, the Santa Cruz Operation and, to a lesser extent, Microport, have made a sizeable investment in making the documentation more palatable to the UNIX user, both new and seasoned. Figures A-2 and A-3 show the migration of the original UNIX documentation into the manuals presently delivered. Even so, when confronted by the entire suite of SCO XENIX manuals, one feels like Hercules must have felt when confronted by the Augean stables. Just unwrapping the manuals, stuffing them, and getting all the labeled tabs in the right place takes a half hour of concentrated work.

Appendix A UNIX Documentation

Figure A-2
SCO Documentation

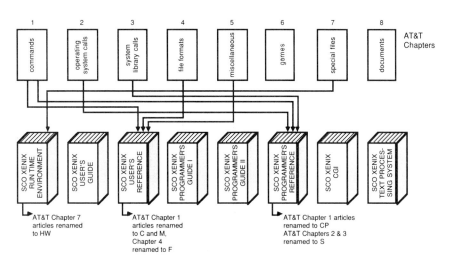

Figure A-3
Microport Documentation

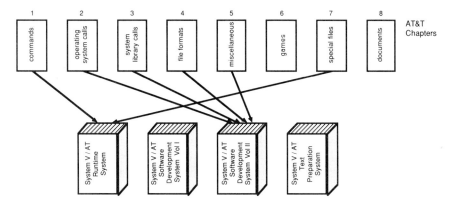

That is one of the reasons for this volume. Periodically, we have made references to the manufacturer's manuals. What is needed is a road map, or at least a mental model, to guide us where to find things. Hopefully, this volume serves a large part of that purpose. It helps, at least, that the articles in the standard documentation follow a standard format, as shown in Figure A-4.

Figure A-4

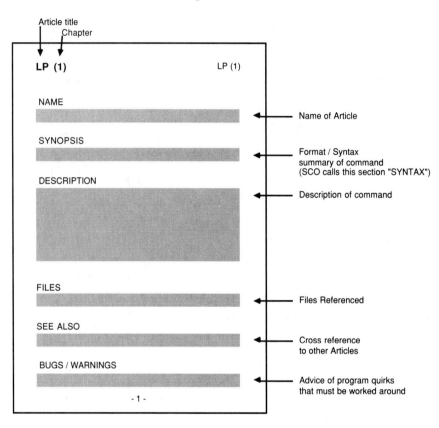

The format of manual articles is supported by the troff "man" macro package,[2] and may include other sections depending on the content and chapter of the article. Notably, in chapters 2 and 3, which describe C callable functions, there is always a section entitled "RETURN VALUE" which describes just that in relation to the functions being documented. Other sections to look for are:

DIAGNOSTICS—A summary of the possible error or advisory messages the program can generate.

---

[2] The *man* macro package source is stored in the file */usr/lib/tmac.an* and is invoked by the *-man* option on the *troff* command line.

EXIT CODE—When the program being documented is designed to be called by a shell script program, the return status is often significant. This section identifies the possible return values.

NOTES and **CAVEATS**—interesting commentary on the part of the program author.

AUTHOR—a perk for the person who wrote the program.

One note on the sections entitled "WARNINGS" and "BUGS." You do not normally see this sort of self-criticizing commentary in software product manuals, except in supplementary release notes. Part of the reason they appear here is because UNIX was originated in an atmosphere that encouraged academic candor, rather than commercial self-interest. However, don't expect the problems mentioned here to be fixed in a foreseeable time frame. The user is expected to work around the "bugs" which, for the most part, are not severe enough to justify a reprogramming effort on the part of the author.

Appendix B
Shell Script Examples

In Chapter 4 we learned about Bourne Shell programming and its usefulness as an everyday tool. In this appendix, we present a series of shell command scripts that demonstrate a number of the shell programming features. These programs are available on this volume's companion floppy disk.

We use the Bourne shell for these programs because it is not generally safe to assume that every system has the C shell available. Some of these scripts are very simple with one command, and are meant to save typing time more than anything else. Others are more complex, and are usable as components of larger programs.

Each of these programs has an associated manual file, appearing with the same name suffixed with a *.1*. A manual page may be printed with either *nroff* or *troff*.

The following briefly describe the programs, and the items to note.

convdate

Programs often require the user to type in a date, and often the input, although it makes sense to a human, makes no sense whatsoever to a program unless it is typed in a specific format. This script will take an almost arbitrarily formatted date input (just so long as the elements are Month, Day, and Year, in that order) and covert it to a specified format.

This script makes extensive use of case statements to accomplish this.

Listing

```
: date line parser
# Input date must be in mm dd yy order but may be in any form
OUT=C
 while test -n "$1"
 do
```

```
        case $1 in
        -l) OUT=L;shift; break;;
        -d) OUT=D;shift; break;;
        -s) OUT=S;shift; break;;
        -c) OUT=C;shift; break;;
        -*) echo   Unknown option 1>&2 ;exit ;;
         *) break;;
        esac
 done

DATE=$*

if [ -z "$DATE" ]
then
     read DATE
fi

echo $DATE | sed 's/,/ /'|tr "/" " " |tr "-" " "|
while read LINE
do
        set $LINE
        ANS=$1
        da=$2
        year=$3

case $ANS in
        1|01|jan*|Jan*) mon=January;  mo=01;m=1;;
        2|02|feb*|Feb*) mon=Febuary;  mo=02;m=2;;
        3|03|mar*|Mar*) mon=March   ; mo=03;m=3;;
        4|04|apr*|Apr*) mon=April   ; mo=04;m=4;;
        5|05|may|May)   mon=May     ; mo=05;m=5;;
        6|06|jun*|Jun*) mon=June    ; mo=06;m=6;;
        7|07|jul*|Jul*) mon=July    ; mo=07;m=7;;
        8|08|aug*|Aug*) mon=Augest  ; mo=08;m=8;;
        9|09|sep*|Sep*) mon=September;mo=09;m=9;;
       10|oct*|Oct*   ) mon=October; mo=10;m=10;;
       11|nov*|Nov*   ) mon=November;mo=11;m=11;;
       12|dec*|Dec*   ) mon=December;mo=12;m=12;;
        *) echo Invalid Month Entry 1>&2; exit;;
esac
case $da in
        1|01) day=01;Day=1;;
        2|02) day=02;Day=2;;
        3|03) day=03;Day=3;;
        4|04) day=04;Day=4;;
        5|05) day=05;Day=5;;
        6|06) day=06;Day=6;;
        7|07) day=07;Day=7;;
        8|08) day=08;Day=8;;
        9|09) day=09;Day=9;;
        [0-9]*) day=$da;Day=$da;;
```

Appendix B Shell Script Examples

```
                *) echo Invalid Day of Month Entry 1>&2 ; exit;;
esac
case $year in
        [0-9][0-9]) Year=${year};;
        19[0-9][0-9]) Year=`echo ${year}|sed 's/..//'`;;
        *) echo Invalid Year Entry 1>&2 ; exit;;
esac
case $OUT in
        L) echo $mon $Day, 19$Year;;
        C) echo ${Year}${mo}${day};;
        S) echo ${m}/${Day}/${Year};;
        D) echo ${m}-${Day}-${Year};;
esac
done
```

copier

Sometimes it is convenient to copy a selected list of files from one directory to another, but not all of them. This script uses the command *xargs* to optionally poll the user for each file in a directory and get a confirmation before actually doing the copy.

Listing

```
#- cmover - copies all files in one directory to another
echo "This command will copy all files from one directory to another.
Do you want to be asked about each file before it is copied ?\c "
read Ans
echo "What is the source directory? \c"
read Source
echo "What is the destination directory? \c"
read Dest

case $Ans in
  n|N)   ls $Source | xargs -i -t cp $Source/{} $Dest/{} ;;
  y|Y)   ls $Source |xargs -i -p cp $Source/{} $Dest/{} ;;
  *) echo "You must answer y or n to the first question!";;
esac
```

cpcommand

The *PATH* environment variable provides a list of directories which are searched when the shell receives a command. If you want to obtain a copy of a command file you can use this command without having to search for it manually through all of the directories in *PATH*.

Usually this is done when the command is a shell script, and you want to make a variation of the command.

Listing

```
#- cpcommand - copies a command in path to to another location
USAGE='usage: cpcommand commandname   location'
EOK=0
EUSAGE=1
ENOFIND=2
if test "$#" -lt 2
then
        echo $USAGE 1>&2
        exit $EUSAGE
fi
COMMAND=$1
LOCATION=$2
OLDIFS=$IFS
IFS=:
set $PATH
IFS=$OLDIFS
for DIR in $*
do
        if test -r $DIR/$COMMAND
        then
                cp $DIR/$COMMAND $LOCATION
                exit $EOK
        fi
done
echo Command  $COMMAND not found
exit $NOFIND
```

dater

When sorting a data file which contains a date, the United States date format has a problem in that the year is treated as the least significant component of the sort. For that reason, it is desirable to convert the date to "stardate" format, with the year first and the slashes removed. This script uses *sed* to do this.

Listing

```
#- dater - slash date format to stardate format
```

```
sed -e "s/\(..\)\/\(..\)\/\(..\)/\3\1\2/g"
```

findvi

This script is linked as both *findvi* and *pgfile*. It allows the user to either edit (with *vi* by invoking *findvi*) or peruse (with *pg* by invoking *pgfile*) a file which is called up by description, rather than by name. To do this, it accesses a data base file maintained by the *nufile* and *rmfile* scripts. Because more than one file can have a similar description, this script queries the user in a loop to isolate the correct document. Also maintained in the file is the original creation date of the file.

Listing

```
#- findvi - pgfile - look-up and open file that match string
# master lookup and edit of files in document tracking program(findvi mode)
# read files in document tracking program (pgfile mode)
PROG=`basename $0`
DATADIR=${HOME}/logs/doc.log
case $PROG in
findvi)
        MSG="-------------File will be opened for editing with vi editor. "
        ACTION=/usr/bin/vi
        ;;
pgfile)
        MSG="----------------------File may be read (Using program pg). "
        ACTION=/usr/bin/pg
        ;;
*) echo "$PROG: Error Name of the program must be findvi or pgfile"
        exit ;;
esac

NAME=$*


CLEAR=`tput clear`  # used if using terminfo
#   CLEAR=`termput cl`  # used if using termcap

                # save standin
        exec 4<&0
        grep -i ${NAME}   $DATADIR> /usr/tmp/dc.tmp
        IFS="   "
        exec 3</usr/tmp/dc.tmp
        exec 0<&3
        read LINE
        while [ -n "$LINE" ]
        do
```

```
        set $LINE
        echo "${CLEAR} File Name Is: $1
Located in      $2
Subject of file is: $4
Created on:     $3"
echo "Is this correct? \c"
                # go back to actual standin to read keyboard response
        exec 0<&4
        Ans=`getchar`
        echo $Ans
case "$Ans" in
        y|Y)
        echo "${MSG}"
        $ACTION ${2}/${1}
        exit ;;
        *)         ;;
esac
                # read next line of p.tmp
        exec 0<&3
        read LINE
        done
```

getit

This is the same as *findvi* except that the user is not queried.

Listing

```
#- getit - searches current directory for a string and opens all with vi
:
echo 'This program will find files in the present directory that contain
a string and open each of them for editing.

Enter the string to search for'
read String

vi `grep -l $String *`
```

humandate

This is the opposite of *convdate*, which will take a computer date format file and generate a "human readable" date of various formats.

Listing

```
: date line parser
```

Appendix B Shell Script Examples

```
# Input date must be in mm dd yy order but may be in any form
OUT=L
 while test -n "$1"
  do
          case $1 in
          -l) OUT=L;shift; break;;
          -d) OUT=D;shift; break;;
          -s) OUT=S;shift; break;;
          -c) OUT=C;shift; break;;
          -*) echo  Unknown option 1>&2 ;exit ;;
           *) break;;
          esac
  done

DATE=$*

if [ -z "$DATE" ]
then
     DATE=`todaysdate`
fi

echo $DATE | sed 's/../& /g'|
while read LINE
do
         set $LINE
         ANS=$2
         da=$3
         year=$1

case $ANS in
         1|01|jan*|Jan*) mon=January; mo=01;m=1;;
         2|02|feb*|Feb*) mon=Febuary; mo=02;m=2;;
         3|03|mar*|Mar*) mon=March   ; mo=03;m=3;;
         4|04|apr*|Apr*) mon=April   ; mo=04;m=4;;
         5|05|may|May)   mon=May     ; mo=05;m=5;;
         6|06|jun*|Jun*) mon=June    ; mo=06;m=6;;
         7|07|jul*|Jul*) mon=July    ; mo=07;m=7;;
         8|08|aug*|Aug*) mon=Auguest ; mo=08;m=8;;
         9|09|sep*|Sep*) mon=September;mo=09;m=9;;
         10|oct*|Oct*  ) mon=October; mo=10;m=10;;
         11|nov*|Nov*  ) mon=November;mo=11;m=11;;
         12|dec*|Dec*  ) mon=December;mo=12;m=12;;
         *) echo Invalid Month Entry 1>&2; exit;;
esac
case $da in
         1|01) day=01;Day=1;;
         2|02) day=02;Day=2;;
         3|03) day=03;Day=3;;
         4|04) day=04;Day=4;;
         5|05) day=05;Day=5;;
         6|06) day=06;Day=6;;
```

```
        7|07) day=07;Day=7;;
        8|08) day=08;Day=8;;
        9|09) day=09;Day=9;;
        [0-9]*) day=$da;Day=$da;;
        *) echo Invalid Day of Month Entry 1>&2 ; exit;;
esac
case $year in
        [0-9][0-9]) Year=${year};;
        19[0-9][0-9]) Year=`echo ${year}|sed 's/..//'`;;
        *) echo Invalid Year Entry 1>&2 ; exit;;
esac
case $OUT in
        L) echo $mon $Day, 19$Year;;
        C) echo ${Year}${mo}${day};;
        S) echo "${m}/${Day}/${Year}\c";;
        D) echo ${m}-${Day}-${Year};;
esac
done
```

mkfloppy

This script helps you keep from having to type *cpio* commands exactly right every time. This version is for Micrport but could easily be altered for XENIX.

Listing

```
#- mkfloppy - generates a cpio format floppy (needs list of files) -verify
echo "what is the name of the file that contains the list for output? \c"
        read FILE
        echo "the following files will be put on the floppy"
        cat $FILE|cpio -ov >/dev/rdsk/fd
banner DONE
echo "Do you want to see the contents of the floppy? \c "
        read Ans
        if test $Ans = y;
                then
                cpio -ivt </dev/rdsk/fd
                else
echo "No list will be printed"
        fi
```

Appendix B Shell Script Examples

nufile

This script will introduce a new document into the data base file that is accessed by *findvi* and *pgfile*. The data base has within it the name, the directory, the creation date, and the subject (as supplied by the user) of the file.

Listing

```
# nufile - master document tracking program.  this script will
# establish a new document in the log
DATADIR=$HOME/logns/doc.log
NAME=$*
CDIR=`pwd`
ORDATE=`date '+%y%m%d'`
echo "Subject of this document: \c"
read SUBJ
vi $NAME
echo "$NAME\t$CDIR\t$ORDATE\t$SUBJ" >> $DATADIR
```

rmfile

The script will remove a document from the data base file accessed by *findvi* and *pgfile*.

Listing

```
# rmfile - remove a file from the data base used by findvi
# and the file as well
DOR=`pwd`
DIR=`echo $DOR | tr / : | sed s/:/"\\\\\\\\\/"/g`
NAME=$*
sed /"$NAME $DIR"/d $HOME/logs/doc.log > $$tmp
mv $$tmp $HOME/logs/doc.log
/bin/rm $NAME
```

phone

This script allows you to quickly query a *phone* data base, and optionally dial the person you looked up.

Listing

```
# ----------Modify to the next dashed line as required for your system---------
# >>>> change the variables below inside the "" on the next 5 lines
```

409

```
DIR="/usr/a/ray/misc.d"  # location of your database
DATA="ph.d"              # name of your data base, phone data
MODEM="/dev/tty5"        # device name where your modem is connected
MC="ATDT"                # Modem control string (Hayes ATTENTION, Dial, Tone)
LOG="${HOME}/logs/phone.log"  # Location of phone log

CLEAR=`tput clear`       # used if using terminfo
#  CLEAR=`termput cl`    # used if using termcap

#-------------------------Do not modify below this line---------------
cd $DIR
        exec 4<&0
        grep -i $* ${DATA} >p.tmp
        IFS="   "
        exec 3<p.tmp
        exec 0<&3
        read LINE
        while [ -n "$LINE" ]
        do
        set $LINE
        echo "${CLEAR}$1 $2 
$4
$3"
echo "Is this correct? \c"
        exec 0<&4
        read Ans
case "$Ans" in
        y|Y)
        echo "Do you want that number dialed for you ? \c "
        read Dial
        case "$Dial" in
                        stty 1200 < ${MODEM} ; (echo "${MC}$3";sleep 10)
>${MODEM}
                        DATE=`date '+%y%m%d'`
                        TIME=`date '+%H:%M'`
                        ph_no=$3
                        Person="$1 $2 "
                        set `date '+%H   %M'`
                        Hs=$1
                        Ms=$2
                        echo "
The call to $Person at phone No. $ph_no has been placed"
                        echo "Was the call sucessful? \c"
                        read Ans
                        if test $Ans = y
                        then
                        set `date '+%H   %M'`
                        He=$1
                        Me=$2
                        Min=`echo "((($He}-${Hs})*60)+${Me})-${Ms}" |bc
                        echo "${DATE}   ${TIME} $ph_no  $Min     $Person" >>${LOG}
```

```
                    else
                    echo No call logged
                    fi
                    break   ;;
            *) exit;;
            esac ;;
    *)          ;;
esac
        exec 0<&3
        read LINE
        done
```

pmesg

This is a phone message mailer. When you receive a phone call at the office, this script will take the message, and use *mailx* to send it to the person you took a message for. The advantage of doing it this way is that an automatic log of these messages can be kept.

Listing

```
#   This program is for automatic mail messages concerning phone calls

echo "      login name of person this message is for? \c "
read Login
echo "      Message for (actual persons name)? \c "
read To
echo "      From? (person calling) \c "
read From
echo "      Company? (of person calling) \c "
read Comp
echo "      Phone Number? \c "
read PNum
echo "\n Write message below.  Hit ^D when done\n"
cat > /tmp/pmesg$$
(
echo "To ${To}              `date '+Date: %m/%d/%y Time: %H:%M:%S'`"
echo "From ${From}          Phone Number $PNum"
echo "Of ${Comp}"
cat /tmp/pmesg$$
) > /tmp/pmesg.1$$
cat /tmp/pmesg.1$$ >> /usr/mail/pmesg
mailx -s "Call From ${From}" $Login < /tmp/pmesg.1$$
/bin/rm /tmp/pmesg$$ /tmp/pmesg.1$$
```

sdater

This script uses *sed* to convert dates of the form *MM/DD/YY* to a written form of the date. This can be used as a pipe on a text file.

Listing

```
#- sdater- slash date format to Leter date format
# sed -e "s/\(..\)\/\(..\)\/\(..\)/\3\1\2/g"

sed -e "s/\(01\)\/\(..\)\/\(..\)/January \2, 19\3/" -e
"s/\(02\)\/\(..\)\/\(..\)/Febuary \2. 19\3/" -e
"s/\(03\)\/\(..\)\/\(..\)/March
\2. 19\3/" -e "s/\(04\)\/\(..\)\/\(..\)/April \2. 19\3/" -e
"s/\(05\)\/\(..\)\/\(..\)/May \2. 19\3/" -e "s/\(06\)\/\(..\
)\/\(..\)/June \2. 19\3/" -e "s/\(07\)\/\(..\)\/\(..\)/July \2. 19\3/" -e
"s/\(08\)\/\(..\)\/\(..\)/August \2. 19\3/" -e
"s/\(09\)\/\(..\)\/\(..\)/September \2. 19\3/" -e
"s/\(10\)\/\(..\)\/\(..\)/October \2. 19\3/" -e
"s/\(11\)\/\(..\)\/\(..\)/November \
2. 19\3/" -e "s/\(12\)\/\(..\)\/\(..\)/December \2. 19\3/g"
```

talk

One problem with the *write* command is that the receiving user is interrupted before a multi-line message is available. The *write* script gathers input, and sends it all at once to get around this problem.

Listing

```
#- talk writes to user on system, message and notice at same time.
echo "Writing to $1.  Enter message and end with a Control D\n"
cat > /tmp/$$talk
write $1 < /tmp/$$talk
rm /tmp/$$talk
```

timein

This program allows you to keep a data base of cities and their respective time zones, and get the current time of a city with the *timein* command. The time zone data base is assumed to be in the local file *timezone*.

Appendix B Shell Script Examples

Listing

```
set `grep -i $* timezone`

echo "In $3 $4 it is: \c"
TZ=${2} ;export TZ


set `date '+%a %h %d %H %M'`
day=$1
mon=$2
date=$3
hour=$4
min=$5
if [ $hour -gt 12 ]; then
    hour=`expr $hour - 12`
    mm=PM
else
    mm=AM
fi
all="$day $mon $date $hour:$min $mm"
echo "$all"
```

whatday

The *cal* program provided with UNIX displays a current month calender. This script takes the output of *cal*, and modifies it with *sed*, so that today's date on the calendar is highlighted.

Listing

```
#- whatday formatted and highlighted calendar for current month
b=`tput smso`
e=`tput rmso`
set `date '+ %m 19%y %d`
tmp=$3
if test $3 -lt 10
then
tmp=" `echo $3 | cut -c2`"
fi
cal $1 $2 |sed -e "s/^$tmp /${b}${tmp} ${e}/" -e "s/ $tmp$/ ${b}${tmp}${e}/" -e
"s/ $tmp / ${b}${tmp}${e} /"
```

All these scripts were constructed to help provide desktop convenience features. If you are like most people, you will probably be interested in building your own scripts. Hopefully, these will give you some ideas to start you out.

The foregoing shell programs are part of a software package called the *Personal Assistant* and were contributed by Ray A. Jones of Onager Systems.

Appendix C
List of Curses Functions

The following are the available curses functions. Many of these functions are #*define* macros to other versions of a similarly named function.

Initialization
initscr()	Initialize screen
endwin()	Terminate windows package
newterm()	Set up output to an additional terminal
set_term()	Direct output to a different terminal
longname()	Provide a long name of the terminal being used

Mode setting
clearok()	OK to clear window on *wrefresh()*
idlok()	OK to use insert/delete feature
keypad()	OK to use keypad
leaveok()	OK to leave the cursor in obscure position
meta()	Return 8 bits on *getch()*
nodelay()	Cause *getch()* to return even if no input is available
intrflush()	Flush input on interrupt
typeahead()	Enable type-ahead check
scrollok()	Enables scrolling
setscrreg()	Set scrolling region on screen
wsetscrreg()	Set scrolling region on window

Terminal mode setting
cbreak()	Input on every character
nocbreak()	Input on buffer terminated
echo()	Echo characters
noecho()	Do not echo characters
nl()	Map newline to newline, carrige return (on *output_*)
nonl()	Do not map newline
raw()	Raw mode (see below)
noraw()	Cooked mode (see below)
resetty()	Reset terminal to saved state
savetty()	Save state of terminal

Window manipulation
    newwin()   Create a new window
    newpad()   Create a pad data structure
    subwin()   Create a sub-window
    delwin()   Delete a window
    mvwin()   Move a window
    touchwin()   Circumvent cursor optimization on window
    overlay()   Overlay one window on another
    overwrite()   Overwrite one window with another

Output functions
    refresh()   Refresh screen
    wrefresh()   Refresh window
    doupdate()   Update mode on screen
    wnoutrefresh() Screen output
    prefresh()   Pad refresh
    pnoutrefresh() Output to pad

Window writing
    move()   Move cursor to given location on screen
    wmove()   Move cursor to given location on window

Writing Characters
    addch()   Output character
    waddch()   Add character to window
    mvaddch()   Move cursor and add character to screen
    mvwaddch()   Move cursor and add to window

Writing strings
    addstr()   Add string to screen
    waddstr()   Add string to window
    mvaddstr()   Move cursor and add string to screen
    mvwaddstr() Move cursor and add string to window

Clearing areas of the screen
    erase()   Erase screen
    werase()   Erase window
    clear()   Clear screen
    wclear()   Clear window
    clrtobot()   Clear from cursor to end of screen
    wclrtobot()   Clear from cursor to end of window
    delch()   Delete character

Appendix C List of Curses Functions

wdelch()   Delete character in window
mvdelch()   Move cursor and delete character
mvwdelch()   Move cursor and delete character in window
deleteln()   Delete line in screen
wdeleteln() Delete line in window
insch()   Insert character
winsch()   Insert character in window
mvinsch()   Move cursor and insert character
mvwinsch()   Move cursor and insert character in window

Formatted output
printw()   Perform *printf()*
wprintw()   Perform *printf()* on a window
mvprintw()   Move cursor and perform *printf()*
mvwprintw() Move cursor and perform *printf()* on a window

Other output routines
box()   Draw box around a window
scroll()   Scroll a window
beep()   Ring bell on terminal
flash()   Flash screen

Input from a window (from WINDOW structure)
getyx()   Return the x, y cursor position of a window
inch()   Input a character from the standard screen
winch()   Input a character from a window
mvinch()   Move cursor and get character
mvwinch()   Move cursor in a window and get character

Input from the terminal
getch()   Get a character
wgetch()   Get character from a window
mvgetch()   Move cursor and get character
mvwgetch()   Move cursor and get character from a window
getstr()   Get a string
wgetstr()   Get a string from window
mvgetstr()   Move cursor and get a string
mvwgetstr()   Move cursor and get a string from window

Formatted input from the terminal
scanw()	Perform *scanf()*
wscanw()	Perform *scanf()* within a window
mvscanw()	Move cursor and perform *scanf()*
mvwscanw()	Move cursor and perform *scanf()* within a window

Video attributes
attroff()	Turn off specified attributes
wattroff()	Turn off specified attributes in window
attron()	Turn on attributes
wattron()	Turn on attributes in window
attrset()	Set attributes
wattrset()	Set attributes in window
standout()	Set attributes to make text stand out
standend()	Set attributes to stop making text stand out
wstandout()	Same as *standout()* for a window
wstandend()	Same as *standend()* for a window

Miscellaneous
baudrate()	Return baud rate of terminal
erasechar()	Return user selected erase character
killchar()	Return user selected line kill character
flushinp()	Dump type-ahead input
draino()	Pause until output has completed
napms()	Pause for specified number of milliseconds

Appendix D
Programming Style Notes

In my general consulting practice, I have had to answer the following questions several times: What is the difference between C and COBOL? Which is better to use? It so happened that I was talking to some business managers who were just starting their first MIS projects. They all were getting conflicting reports out of other programmer/consultants about what the "best" language would be for the project at hand. C and COBOL came up more often than other languages, although other contenders included BASIC, FORTH, and Pascal.

Starting with the second question, my experience has led me to conclude that determining the "best" language is a very subjective affair. There are many variables that affect the choice of language for a project, I will argue with anyone that it makes no difference what the virtues or faults of a language are if that language is not what the programmer actually doing the project wants to use. If the programmer or team of programmers dislike the environment they are working in, they can lose their motivation. It is dangerous to underestimate the power of this effect.

A friend of mine who works in an IBM mainframe based data processing shop at the UC Berkeley campus tells a story about programmer prejudice. She was at a party and was asked by a Computer Science graduate student, who worked exclusively on UNIX systems, what she did.

"I program the University's payroll system," she replied. "Oh, really? What language do you use?" "COBOL." "Oh," the inquirer replied. "Well, I guess someone has to do it." His tone was so dry, so disdainful, that my friend could think of no other response than: "Well, gee! It's not like cleaning toilets!"

But to the UNIX guru it was. It is immaterial to him that many multi-user and multi-process data base and transaction processing functions can be accomplished easily with COBOL and its library of support software, and that no such infra-structure exists for C. Also, there are a lot more programmers working in COBOL than in C. I cannot believe that this would be true if programming in COBOL is a universally negative experience. It's probably just as well that that particular person does not work on the University payroll system.

So much for the "best" language. As for the difference between C and COBOL, my own summary is as follows: "C is easy to write but hard to read, and COBOL is hard to write but easy to read." No doubt this kind of statement will offend many parties in both camps. However, if you look at any well written COBOL program, or even one not so well written, it is rarely difficult to make sense out of it. At the same time, no one can deny that COBOL programming can be laborious with it's dogmatic, narrow rules and strict formats. As far as C is concerned, the sky's the limit when a programmer's innovation is involved. Try interpreting the statement:

```
char *p, *q;
for (p=q;*p;*(p++)++);
```

or for that matter, the following statement right out of the *stdio.h* file:

```
#define getc(f) (--(f)->_cnt >= 0 ? 0xff & *(f)->_ptr++ : _filbuf(f))
```

It's easy to write such things if you're used to it, but try to decipher a page full of such statements written by somebody else, particularly when they don't leave any comments in the code. It would take much longer than the equivalent amount of COBOL code.

I do not contend that it is impossible to write a hard-to-read COBOL program (all you need to do is scramble the symbols in the data dictionary) or that all C programs are easy to write. The tendency of what occurs in practice tends to support my position.

It is also very possible to write very readable C programs, and that is the subject I am addressing here. C allows a great deal of freedom in how a program is formatted because the syntax allows white space and line breaks anywhere but within a symbol, keyword, or within string constants. Along these lines, the C program I write follow a loosely defined set of formatting rules which, it is to be hoped, make the programs more pleasant to read. In addition, I have written a listing program that paginates the program with headers, footers, line and bracket counts. The listing program interprets command disguised as C comments in the source file. The program, called *clist*, is provided on this volume's companion software disk.

Appendix D Programming Style Notes

The formatting rules are:

1. Any rule can be broken if it makes the program more readable.

2. White space surrounds all binary operators, including =, except where doing so will cause a troublesome line break.

3. At least one space after each semi-colon, right brace, and comma.

4. Repetitive constructs are aligned in columns, inserting extra white space (including new-line characters to) do so. For example:

    ```
    mss->ptr    = qual;
    mss->value  = last_val;
    mss->functx = x;
    ```

    or

    ```
    if  (mss->ptr   !=   (char *) 0)   &&
         mss->value  >=   4              &&
         count       ==   1 ) {
    ```

5. A left brace appears on the last line of the statement that started the structure, except for the first left brace in a function. For example:

    ```
    if (a == b) { for (b = a; b < c; b++) { while (x) {
    ```

    On the other hand, a function might be declared:

    ```
    putstr(str)
    char *str;            /* string to output */
    {
    ```

6. A right brace appears at the end of the last line that terminates a structure, except for the *do* statement, where a right brace starts the line on which the *while* keyword appears. For example:

    ```
    while (icnt > 0) {
      if (*p == ' ') {
        strcpy(p, p + 1);
        icnt--; }
      else {
    ```

421

```
        jcnt++;
    printf("%s\n", p); }}
```

7. The first character of every statement, except where required to align multiple occurrences of a statement element (see Rule 4), is indented a fixed number of spaces (I usually use two) times the number of unclosed left braces preceding it in the function.

8. Comments appear block-indented at the same level as do the statements they comment, and are surrounded by one blank light before and after. Mixing of comments and code is avoided, except for declarations.

There are other rules I follow regarding the handling of small structures and long statements, which we need not go into here.

The rule that causes the most people problems is the one regarding the positioning of braces. Many people vehemently disagree with this methodology, but for myself I will always stick to this. The reasons:

1. Excessive white space is eliminated, allowing more of a program to be shown within a given set of lines. For programs composed on a 24 line CRT, this becomes a real time saver.

2. Structure nesting bugs are easier to trace, because more loops will fit on a single screen, and the intended nesting depth of a particular statement can always be deduced.

Consider the following code segment, which appears in the *capp.c* program which is used as an example in this volume. The traditional method of coding, which originated with Kernighan & Ritchie, might be:

```
    if (isprint(c))
        {
        dat[i] = c;
        addch(c);
        refresh(c);
        if (++i >= len)
            {
            i = len - 1;
            move(row, icl+i);
            }
```

Appendix D Programming Style Notes

```
        }
```

Admittedly, this is not necessarily hard to read. Also, the other advantage is that it is easier to add a line to either of the structures, should the need arise. After applying the previously stated formatting rules, the result is:

```
    if (isprint(c)) {
        dat[i] = c;
        addch(c);
        refresh(c);
        if (++i >= len) {
            i = len - 1;
            move(row, icl + i);  } }
```

The convention regarding the placement of braces is what has the most effect. There are seven lines instead of eleven. This does not seem like much but the big advantage to this comes when we are composing programs directly on the CRT. If you have a four or more deep structure, or a long loop, it makes all the difference in the world if you can see the whole thing at once.

Most of us using UNIX on the 286/386 will not have the advantage of one of the elegant, 19-inch CRT screens with multiple windows that come with the higher end workstation systems now being produced. Composing programs on one of those is a treat compared to the standard 25 line editor, and the braces convention I use would not be so important. For the C and script programs provided with this book, I decided to use these conventions to reduce the page count and help the example functions fit on a page.

All of this might not be your cup of tea. If not, it is to be hoped that my programming style does not get in the way of your enjoyment of this book. I hope you find the sample programs contained herein easy to read and instructive. In any event I would like to hear your input.

To further make C programs more readable on printout, I provided a simple listing utility that will paginate C listings, with a line number and bracket count on the right-hand side of every line. It will also "expand" include files. Using this program to list itself, the result is:

```
       cl.c - C listing program        Mar 20 06:49:30 1989 Page 1
                                       clist.c

 1 0: /*title cl.c - C listing program
 2 0*
 3 0*   Alan Deikman 4/86
 4 0*
 5 0*   This program creates a paginated listing for C programs.  Include files
 6 0*   are optionally expanded.  Certain control words in the source file are
 7 0*   recognized, disguised as comment lines.  These are:
 8 0*
 9 0*      title <title>         Place <title> at top of each page (performs
10 0*                            page eject unless we are at line 1)
11 0*      subtitle <subtitle>   Place <subtitle> on second line of each page,
12 0*                            and perform page eject.
13 0*      foot <footer>         Footer line at bottom of each page, starting
14 0*                            with current page
15 0*      eject                 Eject a page
16 0*      listall               List all include files from now on
17 0*      listuser              List all user include files from now on (only
18 0*                            those with " marks delimitating name
19 0*      listmain              List only the main stream: no include files
20 0*
21 0*   The program is invoked as follows:
22 0*
23 0*      clist [-o17] [-o10] [-27] [-tN] fn ...
24 0*
25 0*   where fn are the names of the C source files, which may be - to
26 0*   list the standard input, and
27 0*
28 0*         -o17          to print in Okidata 17CPI format
29 0*         -o10          to print in Okidata 10CPI format
30 0*         -27           to insert control codes for portrait mode
31 0*                       printing on a Xerox 2700 laser printer
32 0*         -tN           will set the tabs to every N spaces
33 0*
34 0*   options and files may be intermixed in any order on the line, but
35 0*   all parameters are processed from left to right.
36 0*
37 0*   */
38 0:
39 0: /*foot Copyright (c) 1986, 1987, 1988 M&T Publishing */
40 0:
41 0: #include <stdio.h>
42 0: #include <malloc.h>
43 0:

   Copyright (c) 1986, 1987, 1988 M&T Publishing
```

Appendix D Programming Style Notes

```
cl.c - C listing program              Mar 20 06:49:30 1989 Page 2
  data definitions                      clist.c


 44 0: /*subtitle data definitions */
 45 0:
 46 0: /* current page and line status variables */
 47 0:
 48 0: char          line[110];     /* current line */
 49 0: unsigned      page = 0;      /* page number */
 50 0: unsigned      brak = 0;      /* bracket level */
 51 0: unsigned      l_brak = 0;    /* last line bracket level */
 52 0: unsigned      comm = 0;      /* comment flag */
 53 0: unsigned      l_comm = 0;    /* last line comment flag */
 54 0: unsigned      squo = 0;      /* single quotes flag */
 55 0: unsigned      dquo = 0;      /* double quotes flag */
 56 0: unsigned      escape = 0;    /* backslash flag */
 57 0: unsigned      prtl = 999;    /* current print line counter */
 58 0: unsigned      tabs = 8;      /* tabstop interpretation */
 59 0: char          titl[50];      /* current title line */
 60 0: char          subt[50];      /* subtitle line */
 61 0: char          foot[80];      /* footer line */
 62 0: unsigned      mode = 0;      /* 0 = listmain, 1 = listuser, 2 = listall */
 63 0: unsigned      xmod = 0;      /* true for cross reference */
 64 0:
 65 0: /* file stack */
 66 0:
 67 0: unsigned      file = 0;      /* file stack pointer */
 68 0: FILE          *fstk[_NFILE]; /* file stack */
 69 0: char          *fnam[_NFILE]; /* file name stack */
 70 0: unsigned      flct[_NFILE];  /* line count for each file */
 71 0:
```

Copyright (c) 1986, 1987, 1988 M&T Publishing


```
cl.c - C listing program              Mar 20 06:49:30 1989 Page 3
  main routine                          clist.c


 72 0: /*subtitle main routine
 73 0*
 74 0*    The main program processes the options and calls the cl() function
 75 0*    for each main file.  To add new options to the command line (for other
 76 0*    types of printers), add an else if structure in this function
 77 0*
 78 0*    */
 79 0:
```

```
 80 0: main(argc, argv)
 81 0: int argc;
 82 0: char *argv[];
 83 0: {
 84 1:   int i;
 85 1:
 86 1:   /* initialize titles */
 87 1:
 88 1:   strload(titl, " ", 49);
 89 1:   strload(subt, " ", 49);
 90 1:   strload(foot, " ", 79);
 91 1:
 92 1:   /* if no parameters just process standard input */
 93 1:
 94 1:   if (argc == 1) {
 95 2:     fstk[file] = stdin;
 96 2:     fnam[file] = " ";
 97 2:     flct[file] = 0;
 98 2:     cl(); }
 99 1:
100 1:   /* process parameters */
101 1:
102 1:   else {
103 2:     for (i = 1; i < argc; i++) {
104 3:
105 3:       /* okidata font changes */
106 3:
107 3:       if (strcmp(argv[i], "-o17") == 0) putchar(29);
108 3:       else if (strcmp(argv[i], "-o10") == 0) putchar(30);
109 3:
110 3:       /* xerox 2700 job header */
111 3:
112 3:       else if (strcmp(argv[i], "-27") == 0) {
113 4:         printf("%cUDK=\033\n", '=');
114 4:         printf("\033+1Titan10iso-P\n");
115 4:         printf("\0331\n");
116 4:         printf("\033m660,0,0,0,510\n");
117 4:         printf("\033w\n");
118 4:         printf("\033k\n"); }
119 3:
120 3:       /* set tab stops */
121 3:
```

Copyright (c) 1986, 1987, 1988 M&T Publishing

Appendix D Programming Style Notes

```
cl.c - C listing program              Mar 20 06:49:31 1989 Page 4
  main routine                          clist.c

122 3:        else if (strncmp(argv[i], "-t", 2) == 0) tabs = atoi(argv[i] + 2);
123 3:
124 3:        /* process files */
125 3:
126 3:        else {
127 4:          file = 0;
128 4:          if (strcmp(argv[i], "-")) fstk[file] = fopen(argv[i], "r");
129 4:          else                      fstk[file] = stdin;
130 4:          if (fstk[file] == NULL)
131 4:            fprintf(stderr, "Cannot open %s\n", argv[i]);
132 4:          else {
133 5:            fnam[file] = argv[i];
134 5:            flct[file] = 0;
135 5:            cl(); } } } }
136 1:
137 1:   exit(); }
138 0:
```

Copyright (c) 1986, 1987, 1988 M&T Publishing

```
cl.c - C listing program              Mar 20 06:49:31 1989 Page 5
  cl() - process current file           clist.c

139 0: /*subtitle cl() - process current file
140 0*
141 0*   This function is called to list a file currently opened by the main
142 0*   routine.  It loops on the cline() function until EOF, then examines
143 0*   the line to see if it is a clist command.  If not, it is printed through
144 0*   the p_std() routine, otherwise the appropriate command function is called.
145 0*
146 0*   */
147 0:
148 0: cl() {
149 1:
150 1:   /* loop until out of lines for this file */
151 1:
152 1:   while (cline() != EOF) {
153 2:
154 2:     /* print line if it does not start with a slash asterix
155 2*        and is not an #include statement */
156 2:
157 2:     if (strncmp(line, "/*", 2) != 0) {
158 3:       if (strncmp(line, "#include", 8) == 0) p_include();
159 3:       else p_std(); }
160 2:
```

```
161 2:      /* scan for recognized command */
162 2:
163 2:      else if (strncmp(line, "/*title",    7) == 0) p_title();
164 2:      else if (strncmp(line, "/*subtitle", 10) == 0) p_subtit();
165 2:      else if (strncmp(line, "/*foot",     6) == 0) p_foot();
166 2:      else if (strncmp(line, "/*eject",    7) == 0) p_eject();
167 2:      else if (strncmp(line, "/*listall",  9) == 0) p_setmode(2);
168 2:      else if (strncmp(line, "/*listuser", 10) == 0) p_setmode(1);
169 2:      else if (strncmp(line, "/*listmain", 10) == 0) p_setmode(0);
170 2:
171 2:      /* just print line if it is not recognized */
172 2:
173 2:      else p_std(); }
174 1:
175 1:    p_end();
176 1:    return; }
177 0:
```

Copyright (c) 1986, 1987, 1988 M&T Publishing

cl.c - C listing program   Mar 20 06:49:31 1989 Page 6
cline() - Get a C line and scan   clist.c

```
178 0: /*subtitle cline() - Get a C line and scan
179 0*
180 0*   A line is collected in the line char array and a rudimentary parsing
181 0*   action takes place.  If the EOF is reached, the currently open file
182 0*   is closed and we go down one on the stack of files currently open.
183 0*
184 0*   The parsing is not exhaustive, and it can be fooled under certain
185 0*   conditions.  We are making assumptions that it only has to work with
186 0*   "clean" source code.
187 0*
188 0*   Note that the code that counts the parentheses level as part of the
189 0*   bracket level is commented out.  Remove the comments if you want
190 0*   that feature.
191 0*
192 0*   The reason the variables single and quote are automatic variables instead
193 0*   of #define constants is that I ran into a C compiler that had a bug in
194 0*   it that would not let it compile any other way.
195 0*
196 0* */
197 0:
198 0: cline() {
199 1:
200 1:    int c;
201 1:    char single, quote;
202 1:    int j = 0;
```

Appendix D Programming Style Notes

```
203 1:      static int last_c;
204 1:
205 1:      single = '\'';
206 1:      quote  = '"';
207 1:      l_comm = comm;
208 1:      l_brak = brak;
209 1:
210 1:      /* get characters from current file until EOF */
211 1:
212 1:      while ((c = getc(fstk[file])) != EOF) {
213 2:
214 2:        /* on a newline, null terminate and return a zero */
215 2:
216 2:        if (c == '\n') {
217 3:          line[i] = 0;
218 3:          flct[file]++;
219 3:          if (!escape) squo = dquo = 0;
220 3:          escape = 0;
221 3:          return 0; }
222 2:
223 2:        /* pad out tab chars */
224 2:
225 2:        else if (c == '\t') {
226 3:          line[i++] = ' ';
227 3:          while (i % tabs != 0) line[i++] = ' '; }
```

Copyright (c) 1986, 1987, 1988 M&T Publishing

cl.c - C listing program   Mar 20 06:49:31 1989 Page 7
cline() - Get a C line and scan   clist.c

```
228 2:
229 2:      /* interpret backslash, quotes, and brackets */
230 2:
231 2:      else if (c == '\\') escape = !escape;
232 2:      else if (c == quote  && !escape && !squo && !comm) dquo = !dquo;
233 2:      else if (c == single && !escape && !dquo && !comm) squo = !squo;
234 2:      else if (c == '{' && comm + dquo + squo == 0) brak++;
235 2:      else if (c == '}' && comm + dquo + squo == 0) brak--;
236 2:      /*
237 2*      else if (c == '(' && comm + dquo + squo == 0) brak++;
238 2*      else if (c == ')' && comm + dquo + squo == 0) brak--;
239 2*      */
240 2:
241 2:      /* detect comments (not nestable) */
242 2:
243 2:      else if (c == '*' && last_c == '/' && !dquo && !comm) comm = !comm;
244 2:      else if (c == '/' && last_c == '*' && !dquo && comm ) comm = !comm;
```

```
245 2:
246 2:     /* put character in buffer */
247 2:
248 2:     if (escape  && c != '\\') escape = !escape;
249 2:     if (c != 13 && c != '\t') line[i++] = last_c = c;
250 2:
251 2:     /* if line overflowed, just return it */
252 2:
253 2:     if (i >= 99) {
254 3:       line[99] = 0;
255 3:       return; } }
256 1:
257 1:   /* if we have an EOF, return any partial line.  if there is
258 1*      an file prior to this one on the stack pop the stack */
259 1:
260 1:   if (i > 0) return 0;
261 1:   if (file <= 0) return EOF;
262 1:   free(fnam[file--]);
263 1:   return cline(); }
264 0:
```

Copyright (c) 1986, 1987, 1988 M&T Publishing

cl.c - C listing program   Mar 20 06:49:31 1989 Page 8
p_include() - Process #include lines   clist.c

```
265 0: /*subtitle p_include() - Process #include lines
266 0*
267 0*  If the mode permits, open an include file, push it on the file
268 0*  descriptor stack, and start listing that new file.
269 0*
270 0* */
271 0:
272 0: p_include() {
273 1:
274 1:   char *p = line, *q;
275 1:   int   i = file + 1;
276 1:   int   len = 0;
277 1:   char  path[40];
278 1:
279 1:   /* print line */
280 1:
281 1:   p_std();
282 1:
283 1:   /* if we are expanding includes, can for the first " or <
284 1*      character */
285 1:
286 1:   if (mode > 0) {
```

Appendix D Programming Style Notes

```
287 2:      while (*p && *p != '"' && *p != '<') p++;
288 2:
289 2:      /* if the include did started with a < and we are in listuser mode
290 2*         don't list it */
291 2:
292 2:      if (*p == '"' || mode > 1) {
293 3:        if (*p == '<') strcpy(path, "/usr/include/");
294 3:        else           path[0] = 0;
295 3:        q = ++p;
296 3:        while (*p && *p != '"' && *p != '>') { len++; p++; }
297 3:
298 3:        /* includes too deep */
299 3:
300 3:        if (i >= _NFILE) {
301 4:          printf("        ERROR: too many files open\n");
302 4:          prtl++;
303 4:          return; }
304 3:
305 3:        /* build a path name and try to open it */
306 3:
307 3:        if (len > 0) {
308 4:          strncat(path, q, len);
309 4:
310 4:          /* can't find a place to store file name */
311 4:
312 4:          if ((p = malloc(strlen(path) + 1)) == NULL) {
313 5:            printf("        ERROR: Out of memory!\n");
314 5:            exit(1); }
```

Copyright (c) 1986, 1987, 1988 M&T Publishing

cl.c - C listing program   Mar 20 06:49:31 1989 Page 9
p_include() - Process #include lines   clist.c

```
315 4:
316 4:          /* error if file can't be opened */
317 4:
318 4:          strcpy(p, path);
319 4:          if ((fstk[i] = fopen(p, "r")) == NULL) {
320 5:            printf("        ERROR: Cannot open INCLUDE file: %s\n", p);
321 5:            prtl++;
322 5:            return;  }
323 4:
324 4:          /* set stack variables and return */
325 4:
326 4:          file = i;
327 4:          fnam[file] = p;
328 4:          flct[file] = 0; } } }
```

431

```
329 1:
330 1:   return; }
331 0:
```

Copyright (c) 1986, 1987, 1988 M&T Publishing

```
  cl.c - C listing program              Mar 20 06:49:31 1989 Page 10
  p_std                                  clist.c

332 0: /*subtitle p_std
333 0*
334 0*   Print a line of source code, ejecting a page if necessary.
335 0*
336 0*   */
337 0:
338 0: p_std() {
339 1:
340 1:   char f = ':';
341 1:   char *date, *ctime();
342 1:   long time(), t;
343 1:
344 1:   t = time((long *) 0);
345 1:   date = ctime(&t);
346 1:   date[24] = 0;
347 1:
348 1:   /* reached end of page */
349 1:
350 1:   if (prtl > 50) {
351 2:
352 2:     /* print footer if this is not the first page */
353 2:
354 2:     if (prtl != 999) {
355 3:       for ( ; prtl < 51; prtl++) printf("\n");
356 3:       printf("\n\n  %s\n\014", foot); }
357 2:
358 2:     /* reset pointers and print header */
359 2:
360 2:     prtl = 1;
361 2:     printf("\n  %-50s %s Page %d\n", titl, date + 4, ++page);
362 2:     printf("  %-50s %s\n\n\n", subt, fnam[file]); }
363 1:
364 1:   /* print line */
365 1:
366 1:   if (l_comm > 0) f = '*';
367 1:   printf(" %4d%2d%c %s\n", flct[file], l_brak, f, line);
368 1:   prtl++;
369 1:   return; }
370 0:
```

Appendix D Programming Style Notes

Copyright (c) 1986, 1987, 1988 M&T Publishing

cl.c - C listing program   Mar 20 06:49:31 1989 Page 11
titles subroutines   clist.c

```
371 0: /*subtitle titles subroutines
372 0*
373 0*   These routines grab header and footer text from the current line,
374 0*   to be printed on the next page eject
375 0*
376 0*   */
377 0:
378 0: /* main title */
379 0:
380 0: p_title() {
381 1:
382 1:    strload(titl, &line[8], 49);
383 1:    if (prtl != 999) prtl = 100;
384 1:    p_std();
385 1:    return; }
386 0:
387 0: /* subtitle */
388 0:
389 0: p_subtit() {
390 1:
391 1:    strload(subt, &line[11], 49);
392 1:    if (prtl != 999) prtl = 100;
393 1:    p_std();
394 1:    return; }
395 0:
396 0: /* page footer */
397 0:
398 0: p_foot() {
399 1:
400 1:    strload(foot, &line[7], 79);
401 1:    p_std();
402 1:    return; }
403 0:
404 0: p_eject() {
405 1:
406 1:    prtl = 100;
407 1:    p_std(); }
408 0:
409 0: p_end() {
410 1:
411 1:    for ( ; prtl < 56; prtl++)
412 1:       printf("\n");
```

```
413 1:    printf("\n\n%s\n", foot);
414 1:    printf("\014"); }
415 0:
```

Copyright (c) 1986, 1987, 1988 M&T Publishing

```
cl.c - C listing program              Mar 20 06:49:31 1989 Page 12
misc subroutines                      clist.c

416 0: /*subtitle misc subroutines */
417 0:
418 0: /* set listing mode (listall, listuser, listmain) */
419 0:
420 0: p_setmode(val)
421 0: int val;
422 0: {
423 1:    mode = val;
424 1:    p_std(); }
425 0:
426 0: /* string load subroutine - copy input line to destination,
427 0*    and remove any trailing comment delimiter */
428 0:
429 0: strload(dst, src, num)
430 0: char *dst;
431 0: char *src;
432 0: int num;
433 0: {
434 1:    int i = 0;
435 1:
436 1:    strncpy(dst, src, num);
437 1:    for (i = strlen(dst); i >= 0 && dst[i] <= ' '; i--);
438 1:    if (i > 1 && dst[i] == '/' && dst[i - 1] == '*') dst[i - 1] = 0;
439 1:    return; }
440 0:
```

Copyright (c) 1986, 1987, 1988 M&T Publishing

The above listing also gives an example of how to situtate *clist* directives such as /*title* and /*foot*. Properly used, this can help give a C program a polished, professional look, and make it easier for another reader to learn the program.

Appendix E
Directory of Software Companion Disk

Some of the software that appears in this volume, plus other programs that do not appear, are available on a companion disk. If you wish to obtain the disk, use the order form at the beginning of this book.

The files are stored in *cpio* format on a 48TPI, 9 sector disk. To read this volume, place the floppy disk in the drive and enter the following commands:

```
mkdir book
cd book
cpio -ivd < /dev/rfd048
```

for SCO XENIX. For Microport, we suggest:

```
mkdir book
cd book
cpio -ivd < /dev/rdsk/fd048
```

This will create the subdirectory book, and copy the following files into it. These are briefly described below:

```
./awk/checkreg.awk        Check register report program
./awk/checks              Sample checks data
./awk/cword.awk           Sample awk program
./awk/glossary            Shell script for generating glossary
./awk/quicksum.awk        Sample awk program
./awk/stripjunk.c         Filter to process text files
./clist/clist.c           Program to list C programs
./curses/capp.c           Sample C program demostrating curses
./curses/capp.dat         Sample data file
./curses/cappmain.0       Help screen data
./curses/cappmain.1       Help screen data
```

./curses/cappmain.2	Help screen data
./curses/cappmain.3	Help screen data
./curses/capprec.0	Help screen data
./curses/capprec.1	Help screen data
./filesys/dirlist.c	C program to list directories
./filesys/dumpinode.c	C program to list inodes
./filesys/dumpsb.c	C program to dump the superblock
./filesys/findlink.c	C program to find links
./ipc/chatter.c	Chatter-board program
./ipc/daylog.c	System daylog subroutine
./ipc/log.c	System daylog shell command
./ipc/syslog.c	System daylog daemon
./quad/config	Config file for Q1200 driver
./quad/q1200.c	Sample device driver for Q1200
./quad/space.c	Sample space file for Q1200
./shell/convdate	Shell script example
./shell/copier	Shell script example
./shell/cpcommand	Shell script example
./shell/dater	Shell script example
./shell/diftotable	Shell script example
./shell/findvi	Shell script example
./shell/getit	Shell script example
./shell/humandate	Shell script example
./shell/input	Shell script example
./shell/man/convdate.1	Manual page for shell script example
./shell/man/copier.1	Manual page for shell script example
./shell/man/cpcommand.1	Manual page for shell script example
./shell/man/dater.1	Manual page for shell script example
./shell/man/diftotable.1	Manual page for shell script example
./shell/man/findvi.1	Manual page for shell script example
./shell/man/getit.1	Manual page for shell script example
./shell/man/humandate.1	Manual page for shell script example
./shell/man/input.1	Manual page for shell script example
./shell/man/megs.1	Manual page for shell script example
./shell/man/messenger.1	Manual page for shell script example
./shell/man/mkfloppy.1	Manual page for shell script example
./shell/man/multifm.1	Manual page for shell script example
./shell/man/notes.1	Manual page for shell script example
./shell/man/output.1	Manual page for shell script example
./shell/man/pgfile.1	Manual page for shell script example
./shell/man/phone.1	Manual page for shell script example
./shell/man/pmesg.1	Manual page for shell script example

Appendix E Directory of Software Companion Disk

./shell/man/rmfile.1	Manual page for shell script example
./shell/man/sdater.1	Manual page for shell script example
./shell/man/tabletodif.1	Manual page for shell script example
./shell/man/talk.1	Manual page for shell script example
./shell/man/timein.1	Manual page for shell script example
./shell/man/whatday.1	Manual page for shell script example
./shell/megs	Shell script example
./shell/messenger	Shell script example
./shell/mkfloppy	Shell script example
./shell/multifm	Shell script example
./shell/notes	Shell script example
./shell/output	Shell script example
./shell/pgfile	Shell script example
./shell/phone	Shell script example
./shell/pmesg	Shell script example
./shell/rmfile	Shell script example
./shell/sdater	Shell script example
./shell/tabletodif	Shell script example
./shell/talk	Shell script example
./shell/timein	Shell script example
./shell/whatday	Shell script example
./spool/basiclp.c	Spooler filter for basic lp
./spool/lpinterf	Sample interface program
./spool/ptable.c	Sample C program

Bibliography

Design of the UNIX Operating System, The. Maurice J. Bach. Prentice-Hall, 1986.

Writing A UNIX Device Driver. Janet I. Ega and Thomas J. Teixeria. John Wiley & Sons, Inc. 1988.

80386 Programmer's Refrence Manual. Intel, 1986.

IBM AT Technical Reference Manual. IBM, 1984.

80386/387 Architecture, The. Stephen P. Morse, Eric J. Isaacson and Douglas J. Albert. John Wiley & Sons, Inc. 1987.

About the Author

Alan Deikman resides in Fremont, California. He is the Director of Software R&D for Mylex Corporation. Deikman has written for *Dr. Dobb's Journal* and is the author of several technical computer manuals.

Index

/bin, 164
/etc/partitions, 75
/etc/passwd, 341, 347
/usr/bin, 164
/usr/include/signal.h, 52
/usr/include/sys/filsys.h, 80
/usr/spool/lp, 203

32 bit Pointers, 308-309
80386 Processor, 293-297

a.out file, 63, 224-225
alias, 172
Apple, 15
Archive Program, 223-225
Assembly Language, 29
at Command, 166
awk, 106, 157-158, 177-199

Background Processes, 118
Bad Block Table, 75
Bourne Shell, 17, 93-128
brk(), 46-47

C Shell, 17, 129-145
C Shell, History Substitutions, 130-134
C Shell, I/O Redirection, 143-145
cat, 167
cc Command, 215-223
close(), 41
COBOL, 13
Command Parameters, 103-105
Command Substitutions, 114-116
Command, pr, 103-104
Commands, @, 140-143
Commands, accept, 210
Commands, Alias, 136-137
Commands, ar, 223-225
Commands, at, 166
Commands, cancel, 208

Commands, case, 123-124
Commands, cat, 96, 109, 167
Commands, cc, 215-223
Commands, cp, 167-168, 259
Commands, cpio, 260, 264-268
Commands, dd, 260, 268-269
Commands, disable, 208
Commands, du, 169-170, 350
Commands, egrep, 170-171
Commands, enable, 208
Commands, export, 164
Commands, expr, 112
Commands, fdisk, 74
Commands, fgrep, 170-171
Commands, file, 169
Commands, find, 169-170
Commands, for, 121-122
Commands, foreach, 135
Commands, fsck, 90-91
Commands, grep, 158, 170-171, 234, 235
Commands, if, 125-127
Commands, kill, 171
Commands, ld, 223
Commands, ln, 69, 167-168
Commands, lp, 204-207
Commands, lpadmin, 209-210
Commands, lpsched, 210
Commands, lpshut, 210
Commands, lpstat, 208-209
Commands, ls, 96, 171-172, 266
Commands, mkdir, 172-173
Commands, mkfs, 343
Commands, mknod, 72, 236, 358-359
Commands, more, 173
Commands, mv, 167-168
Commands, od, 173-174
Commands, pack, 174
Commands, pcat, 174
Commands, pr, 147
Commands, prof, 218

Commands, read, 150
Commands, reject, 210
Commands, rm, 174
Commands, setenv, 164
Commands, sort, 108
Commands, sort, 197
Commands, tar, 260
Commands, tar, 263-264
Commands, tput, 108-110
Commands, unpack, 174
Commands, while, 127-128
Commands, who, 96
core file, 53
cpio Command, 260, 264-268
cron process, 29
curses Library, 253, 324-326

Daemons, 202-203
Damaged File Systems, 91
dd Command, 260, 268-269
Device Drivers, 355-375
Device Files, 69-71
Device Handlers, 17
Device Numbers, 358-359
Directories, Conventional, 65
Disk Partitions, 73
Disk Space Allocation, 350
DMA, 374-375
DOS, 18-19, 55
DOS Support, 271-276
du Command, 169-170
Dual, 15
dup(), 39-40, 42

errno, 43
errno variable, 30-31
exec(), 48-50
Execution Profiling, 218
exit(), 50-51

far Keyword, 309-310
FIFO, 37-38
File Descriptors, 32
File Systems, 78
file Command, 169
File, Model, 35-36

File, Pointer, 35
Filters, 101, 166
find Command, 169-170
Floating Point, 299-302
Floppy Disks, 72
fork(), 41-42, 50-51, 98
Free list, 90

getpid(), 47, 48
grep, 170
Group ID, 346-347
GUARDIAN, 13

Hardware Error, 26

i-node table, 83
IBM AT Console, 320
init process, 29
Instruction Set, 286-290
Intel, 15, 277-278
Intel, Processor Family, 278-279
Interactive Systems, 15, 19
Interactive Utilities, 164
ioctl(), 45-46

ld Command, 223
libc.a library, 31
Link Editor, 223
Links, 69, 88
lpadmin Command, 209-210
lpsched Program, 202-203
ls Command, 171-172
lseek(), 44-45

make Utility, 226-228
malloc(), 24
Memory Models, 304-306
Memory System, 282-283, 295-296
Message Queues, 17
Microport, 15
mkdir Command, 172-173
mkfs Command, 343
Motorola 68000, 15
Mountable File Systems, 77

Named Pipe, 37-38, 72, 233-245

Index

near Keyword, 309

O_APPEND, 38
O_CREAT, 38
O_EXCL, 38
O_NDELAY, 38, 244
O_RDONLY, 37
O_RDWR, 37
O_TRUNC, 38
O_WRONLY, 37
open(), 36-40
Optional Software, 344-345
OS/2, 21-22

Passwords, 346-347
Path names, 56-62
Path names, Conventions, 61-62
Path names, Rules, 60-61
Pathname Substitutions, 116-117
Patterns, 182-185
PDP-8, 23
pipe(), 41-42
Pipelines, 100-103, 147
Pipes, 17
Printer Classes, 207
Printer Interface, 210-213
Privileged Programs, 348
Process Management, 46-52
Process, ID, 27
Process, Model, 28-29
Process, Organization, 25
Process, Priority, 26
Process, Table, 26-27
Processes, Background, 118
prof Command, 218
Programmed I/O, 373-374
Programming Tools, 165-166

Race Conditions, 249-250
read(), 42-43
Register Set, 280-282, 294-295
Ritchie, Dennis, 14
Root File System, 75
RS-232, 319
RSTS/E, 14
RSX-11, 73

SCCS Utility, 228-231
SCO, 15
Security, 20
Segment Register Programming, 303-315
Segment Registers, 278, 284, 295-297
Shared Memory, 17, 247-269
Shared Memory, Identifier, 251
Shared Memory, Key, 251
Shell, Comment Lines, 119
Shell, Environment, 114
Shell, Exit status, 120-121
Shell, Meta-characters, 99-100
Shell, Pipelines, 100-103
Shell, Prompt, 99
Shell, Variables, 111-114
SIGALARM, 53
SIGCLD, 53
SIGHUP, 52
SIGKILL, 52, 53
signal(), 53-54
Signals, 52-55
SIGPIPE, 53
SIGUSR1, 53
SIGUSR2, 53
Spooler, 18, 201-214
Stack, 290-291, 306-308
Standard Error, 33
Standard I/O, 101-102
Standard Input, 32
Standard Output, 32
Sun Microsystems, 15
Super Block, 78
Swap Area, 76
System Administration, 341-353
System Calls, 30
System Calls, brk(), 46-47, 312-315
System Calls, brkctl(), 312-315
System Calls, close(), 41
System Calls, dup(), 39-40, 42
System Calls, exec(), 48-50
System Calls, exit(), 50-51
System Calls, File System, 32
System Calls, fork(), 41-42, 50-51, 98

445

System Calls, getpid(), 47-48, 250
System Calls, getuid(), 48
System Calls, ioctl(), 45-46
System Calls, Low level I/O, 32
System Calls, lseek(), 44-45
System Calls, open(), 36-40
System Calls, pipe(), 41-42
System Calls, read(), 42-43
System Calls, sbrk(), 312-315
System Calls, shmat(), 252
System Calls, shmctl(), 252
System Calls, shmget(), 252
System Calls, signal(), 53-54
System Calls, sleep(), 250
System Calls, sync(), 83
System Calls, write(), 43-44
System Library, closedir(), 63
System Library, malloc(), 24
System Library, opendir(), 63
System Library, readder(), 63

tar Command, 260, 263-264
termcap Data Base, 320-323
Terminal Programming, 317-340
terminfo Data Base, 323-324
Thompson, Ken, 14

UC Berkeley, 14
User File System, 76
User ID, 27, 346-347
uucp, 18

Variable Substitutions, 137
VAX/VMS, 13
VP/IX, 19, 275

Wicat, 15
write(), 43-44

More Programming Tools from M&T Books

DESQview: A Guide to Programming the DESQview Multitasking Environment

by Stephen R. Davis

DESQview is currently the most sophisticated and versatile multitasking software integrator. This new book provides users with the information needed to get the most out of DESQview. Discussed are the object-oriented DESQview 2.0 API (Application Program Interface) and the multitasking concepts necessary to program the DESQview environment. These concepts are applied by creating example programs that control and interact with DESQview's API. These sample programs demonstrate such concepts as windowing, intertask communication, memory management (including EMS-type "expanded memory"), software objects, and subtask control. *DESQview: A Guide to Programming the DESQview Multitasking Environment* is fully endorsed by Quarterdeck Office Systems, publisher of DESQview.

Book & Disk (MS-DOS)   Item #006-0 $39.95
Book only   Item # 028-1 $24.95

Programmer's Essential OS/2 Handbook

by David E. Cortesi

For writers of OS/2 programs, *The Programmer's Essential OS/2 Handbook* will provide the OS/2 technical information that will enable you to write efficient, reliable applications in C, Pascal, or assembler. Two indexes and a web of cross-referencing provide easy access to all OS/2 topic areas. There's even detailed technical information that is not included in the official OS/2 documentation. Equal support for Pascal and C programmers is provided.

Inside you'll find an overview of OS/2 architecture and vocabulary, including references to where the book handles each topic in depth: a look at the 80286 and a description of how the CPU processes data in real and protected mode; an overview of linking, multiprogramming, file access, and device drivers; and an in-depth discussion of important OS/2 topics, including dynamic linking, message facility, the screen group, inputs, outputs, the queue, the semaphore, and more.

The Programmer's Essential OS/2 Handbook is written in precise language and is a resource no programmer developing in the OS/2 environment can afford to be without.

Book & Disk (5-1/4" & 3-1/2" OS/2)   Item #89-5 $39.95
Book only   Item #82-8 $24.95

More Programming Tools ...

/Util: A UNIX-Like Utility Package for MS-DOS

by Allen Holub

When used with the Shell, this collection of utility programs and subroutines provides you with a fully funcitonal subset of the UNIX environment. Many of the utilities may also be used independently. You'll find executable versions of cat, c, date, du, echo, grep, ls, mkdir, mv, p, pause, printevn, rm, rmdir, sub, and chmod.

The /Util package includes complete source code on disk. All programs and most of the utility subroutines are fully documented in a UNIX-style manual. For IBM PCs and direct compatibles.

Manual & Disk (MS-DOS)   Item #12-7 $29.95

NR: An Impelementation of the UNIX NROFF Word Processor

by Allen Holub

NR is a text formatter that is written in C and is compatible with UNIX's NROFF. Complete source code is included in the *NR* package so that it can be easily customized to fit your needs. *NR* also includes an implementation of how -ms works. NR does hyphenation and simple proportional spacing. It supports automatic table of contents and index generation, automatic footnotes and endnotes, italics, boldface, overstriking, underlining, and left and right margin adjustment. The *NR* package also contains: extensive macro and string capability, number registers in various formats, diversions and diversion traps, and input and output line traps. NR is easily configurable for most printers. Both the ready-to-use program and full source code are included. For PC compatibles.

Manual & Disk (MS-DOS)   Item #33-X-1 $29.95

More Programming Tools ...

On Command: Writing a UNIX-LIke Shell for MS-DOS

by Allen Holub

On Command and its ready-to-use program demonstrate how to write a UNIX-like shell for MS-DOS, with techniques applicable to most other programming languages as well. The book and disk include a detailed description and working version of the Shell, complete C source code, a thorough discussion of low-level MS-DOS interfacing, and significant examples of C programming at the system level.
   Supported features include: read, aliases history, redirection and pipes, UNIX-like command syntax, MS-DOS compatible prompt support, C-like control-flow statements, and a Shell variable that expands to the contents of a file so that a program can prduce text that is use by Shell scripts.

The ready-to-use program and all C source code are included on disk. For IBM PC and direct compatibles.

Book & Disk (MS-DOS)   *Item #29-1*   *$39.95*

To Order: Return this form with your payment to **M&T Books**, 501 Galveston Drive, Redwood City, CA 94063 or **CALL TOLL-FREE 1-800-533-4372** Mon-Fri 8AM-5PM Pacific Standard Time (in California, call 1-800-356-2002).

❏ **YES!** Please send me the following: ❏ Check enclosed, payable to **M&T Books**.

Item#	Description	Disk	Price

Charge my ❏ Visa ❏ MC ❏ AmEx
Card No. _____ Exp. Date _____
Signature _____

Name _____
Address _____
City _____
State _____ Zip _____

                       Subtotal _____   7025
     CA residents add sales tax __ % _____
     Add $2.99 per item for shipping
                    and handling _____
                       TOTAL _____